1 MONTH
FREE
READING

at

www.ForgottenBooks.com

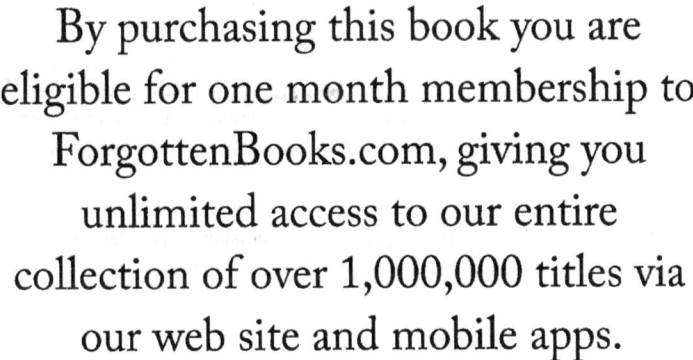

By purchasing this book you are eligible for one month membership to ForgottenBooks.com, giving you unlimited access to our entire collection of over 1,000,000 titles via our web site and mobile apps.

To claim your free month visit:
www.forgottenbooks.com/free524020

* Offer is valid for 45 days from date of purchase. Terms and conditions apply.

ISBN 978-0-483-29975-7
PIBN 10524020

This book is a reproduction of an important historical work. Forgotten Books uses state-of-the-art technology to digitally reconstruct the work, preserving the original format whilst repairing imperfections present in the aged copy. In rare cases, an imperfection in the original, such as a blemish or missing page, may be replicated in our edition. We do, however, repair the vast majority of imperfections successfully; any imperfections that remain are intentionally left to preserve the state of such historical works.

Forgotten Books is a registered trademark of FB &c Ltd.
Copyright © 2018 FB &c Ltd.
FB &c Ltd, Dalton House, 60 Windsor Avenue, London, SW19 2RR.
Company number 08720141. Registered in England and Wales.

For support please visit www.forgottenbooks.com

Moore Anderson & Co Publishers

LIFE

OF

THOMAS CHALMERS D.D., LL.D.:

EDITED BY

REV. JAMES C. MOFFAT, M.A.,

PROFESSOR OF LATIN AND LECTURER ON HISTORY, IN THE
COLLEGE OF NEW JERSEY, PRINCETON.

SECOND EDITION.

CINCINNATI:
MOORE, ANDERSON, WILSTACH & KEYS.
28 WEST FOURTH STREET.
NEW YORK;—NEWMAN & IVISON.
1853.

Entered, according to act of Congress, in the year 1853, by
MOORE, ANDERSON & COMPANY,
In the Clerk's Office of the District Court for the District of Ohio.

CINCINNATI:
C. A. MORGAN & CO., STEREOTYPERS
HAMMOND ST.

MORGAN & OVEREND
PRINTERS.

PREFACE.

The present volume lays claim to nothing above the fidelity of an abstract, designed for the use of those who wish to know the outline of Dr. Chalmers's career; but who either cannot afford to purchase, or have not the leisure nor the taste to peruse, many volumes on the subject. In preparing it, care has been taken to present the principal facts contained in the Memoirs by Dr. Hanna, briefly and consecutively, retaining his own words in all cases, where consistent with the desired brevity: elsewhere, his narrative has been abridged, and only so much extracted from the letters, journals and speeches as seemed necessary to exhibit the character and spiritual growth of the man. Many readers will always prefer the whole work, and find therein nothing which they would willingly spare; a large number, however, are practically excluded by its voluminousness from the benefit of the noble lesson it contains.

The circumstances of our country, and the age in which we live, are such as urgently to demand that spirit of aggressive activity, which the influence of Dr. Chalmers's converted life is calculated to promote. Among the youth preparing for the gospel ministry a most valuable qualification is the virtue of prudent enterprise. The church needs men of energy to go forth into the mass of the irreligious, and build up new outworks of the Kingdom of God. Nor is such effort to be confined to the professional servants of the church alone. When infidelity, both openly and under many disguises, is so active, and the system of Romish idolatry is straining every nerve, the call is imperative on all who love the Lord to be also progressive. In this light it seems desirable that the example of a life devoted to the work of elevating the degraded, of instructing the ignorant, of animating the indifferent, and awakening in all the fire of christian enterprise, should be submitted to the public in an easily-accessible form.

March 23, 1853.

CONTENTS.

CHAPTER I.
BIRTH—Childhood—College Life—License—Residence at Edinburgh—Assistantship at Cavers—Mathematical Assistantship at St. Andrew's. Page 11

CHAPTER II.
Ordination at Kilmany—Winter at St. Andrew's—Chemical Lectures Repeated at St. Andrew's—Presbyterial Interference—Candidate for the Natural Philosophy Chair at St. Andrew's—And for the Mathematical Chair at Edinburgh—First Publication—Chemical Lectures at Kilmany and Cupar—Double Commission in the Volunteers—Incident at Kirkaldy; His Brother George's Death—First Visit to London—Publication of his Work on Stability of National Resources—Death of his Sister Barbara—Engaged to Contribute to the Edinburgh Encyclopædia — First Speech in General Assembly—Death of Mr. Ballardie—Severe Illness and its Effects . . . . Page 25

CHAPTER III.
Efforts after a Pure and Heavenly Morality—Intention of abandoning Mathematics—Preparation of the Article Christianity—Contributes to the Christian Instructor—Hospitality—James Anderson . Page 37

CHAPTER IV.
Study of the Bible—Bible Society—Extracts from Journal—His Marriage—Missions—Visit of Andrew Fuller—Extempore Preaching . Page 47

CHAPTER V.
Publication of the Evidences and Authority of the Christian Religion—Origin of his Views on Pauperism—On the Moravians as Missionaries—Appearance in Ecclesiastical Courts . . . . Page 58

CHAPTER VI.
Ministry at Kilmany—First Seven Years—The Change—Visiting and Examining—Class for the Young—The Pulpit—The Result—Funeral Sermon at Bendochy—Deputation from Glasgow—Election to the Tron Church of Glasgow—Farewell Sermon at Kilmany . . Page 66

CHAPTER VII.
First Sermon in Glasgow—Attachment to Mr. Thomas Smith—Degree of Doctor of Divinity Conferred—Speech on Pluralities in General Assembly—Sermon before Lord High Commissioner . . Page 84

CHAPTER VIII.
Plans for Pastoral Work—Secularization of the Clergy—Denunciation of that Evil—Sabbath School Society—Excursion in Fifeshire—First Appearance before a London Audience—Visit to Mr. Montgomery—Sermons in London—Letter from Robert Hall—Appointment at Stirling—Article on Pauperism—Highest Exhibition of his Power as a Preacher—His own estimate of Popularity—His Father's declining Health and Death. . Page 99

CHAPTER IX.
Publication of a Volume of Sermons — Translation to the parish of St. John's—Educational Efforts—Pauper Management—Rev. Ed. Irving—

(ix)

Radical Riots—Parochial Lodgings—Christian and Civic Economy of Large Towns—Chapel of Ease—Professorship at St. Andrew's—Appearance in Church Courts—Dr. Chalmers in his Family, and in Society—Farewell Discourses at St. John's—Results of his Labors in Glasgow—Installment at St. Andrew's . . . . . Page 137

CHAPTER X.

First Winter at St. Andrew's—Appearance in General Assembly—Overture on Theological Course of Study—Gaelic Chapel—Dr. Chalmers and Sir Walter Scott—Glasgow Revisited—Preaching at Stockport . Page 177

CHAPTER XI.

Session of 1824-5—Manner of Instruction—General Assembly of 1825—Extracts from Journal—Difficulties at St. Andrew's—Endeavors to Excite a more Profound Religious Feeling—Death of his Mother and Sister Isabel—Professorship at London—Treatise on the Use and Abuse of Literary and Ecclesiastical Endowments—Standard of Scholarship in Scottish Universities—Dr. Chalmers elected to the Chair of Theology in Edinburgh—Valedictory at St. Andrew's—General Assembly of 1828—Dr. Chalmers's Inauguration, and first Session at Edinburgh—Speech on Catholic Emancipation—Death of his Brother Alexander—Errors of Mr. Irving and Others—Examination in relation to the Irish Poor—Bible in Education—Meeting with Coleridge—Conversations reported by Mr. Gurney—Dr. Chalmers one of the Deputation to William IV—Last Meeting with Mr. Irving—Death of Dr. Thomson . . . Page 188

CHAPTER XII.

Publication of his Work on Political Economy—Bridgewater Treatise—Cholera—System of Popular Instruction for Scotland—Dr. Chalmers Moderator of the General Assembly of 1832—Patronage—Moderate and Evangelical Parties—Veto Law . . . Page 249

CHAPTER XIII.

Excursion through England . . Page 277

CHAPTER XIV.

Annuity Tax—Sudden Illness—Missionary Operations—"Water of Leith" Village—Church Extension . . Page 294

CHAPTER XV.

Literary Distinctions—Endowment of Theological Chair in Edinburgh—Lectures on Endowments—Visit to France—Efforts in behalf of Church Extension—Results . . . Page 303

CHAPTER XVI.

Non-Intrusion Controversy . . Page 314

CHAPTER XVII.

Final Conflict between the Church and State—Disruption . Page 369

CHAPTER XVIII.

Progress of the Free Church—Westport—Dr. Chalmers's Professorial Career—German Philosophy—The Famine . . Page 395

CHAPTER XIX.

Domestic Habits—Times and Modes of Composition—Success of the Free Church—Visit to London—Last Sabbath—Death . **Page 417**

LIFE

OF

THOMAS CHALMERS, D.D.. LL.D.

CHAPTER I.

THOMAS CHALMERS was born on the 17th of March, 1780, at Anstruther, a small town in Fifeshire, Scotland. His parents, John and Elizabeth Chalmers, were both persons of more than common force of character and of exemplary piety; and their standing in society was that which belongs to the household of a respectable merchant, who has risen to be provost of his native town.

Thomas was the sixth, in their large family, of fourteen children. His earlier years were marked by no precocity of attainment, nor were the means of instruction furnished by his native place of a kind to inspire love of knowledge or to mould him to habits of industry. Committed at the age of three years to the hands of a superannuated school tyrant, who retained little but the cruelty of his better days, it is not wonderful that the pupil, with his warm and noble impulses just budding into life, should have been distinguished only as "one of the idlest, strongest, merriest, and most generous-hearted boys in Anstruther school." An assistant teacher introduced more lenient measures, but added nothing to the course of instruction. The impulse of genius, untrained by adequate education, found exercise and enjoyment for itself. The ability to read, very early acquired, furnished him a means of independent self-instruction. Among the books which earliest enlisted his attention are mentioned Gaudentia di Lucca and the Pilgrim's Progress. But chiefly the beautifully simple narratives of Scripture had even then begun to shape his habits of thinking for those pursuits which occupied his maturer powers. As illustrative of their hold upon his imagination even in childhood, it is told of him that when not quite three years old, having heard his father read the story of Absalom's rebellion and death, and the subsequent lament of David, he was afterward found alone in the nursery, walking backward and forward, excited and absorbed, repeating to himself the words "Oh my son, Absalom, oh Absalom, my son, my son!"

Though not distinguished by any religious impressions, he very early declared his intention to be a minister. The call of genius preceded that of divine grace. The purpose to which the Creator had designed him was demonstrated even in his childish amusements. It is mentioned by a sister of one of his playmates, that one time breaking in upon them, she found the future orator mounted upon a chair and discoursing with great zeal to his single auditor.

Having mounted from class to class, until he had reached the highest in the school, in process of time, rather than of preparation, he was sent to college. He was entered as a student of the United College of St. Andrews while yet only in his twelfth year, and so ignorant of the elements of education as not to be able to write his native tongue with ordinary correctness. And from his defective knowledge of Latin, he was utterly disqualified to appreciate or profit by the prelections of "that distinguished philosophical grammarian, Dr. John Hunter, who was then the chief ornament of St. Andrew's University." As might have been expected from his age, these deficiencies were not compensated for by any unusual application to study. Too young to be left so much to the disposal of his own time, as college life permits, or to understand the value of its advantages, he spent the greater part of his first two sessions in boyish amusements, without making any respectable advance in his education. At the same time, all those who then knew him best testify to the rectitude and purity of his character; and even in those days of boyish idleness he gave evidence of his native strength of mind by enthusiastically persevering in everything that he undertook. He would often pursue some favorite idea in the midst of his noisy companions, unembarrassed by their laughter and efforts to interrupt him, and then, when he had followed to the end of his cogitation, join in the merriment with the most hearty good-humor. The survivors of that then youthful band fondly recall evidences of the warmth and kindliness of his affections.

Such was Chalmers's life until his fourteenth year, when a new era dawned upon his intellect. In his third session at college he took up the study of mathematics under the instruction of Dr. James Brown, assistant professor in that department, a teacher of more than ordinary success in awakening the interest of pupils in his favorite science, and one to whom Dr. Chalmers, in after days, declared that he was more indebted than to all his other instructors together. The subject, in itself, was one to interest a mind like his, naturally prone to consecutive thinking, and firm and decided in its grasp of truth, and with the additional charm lent it by the illustrations of his eminent teacher, it is not wonderful that it succeeded in entirely absorbing his attention. "Pure geometry had especial attractions for him. With the higher powers of the modern analysis he became afterward familiarly acquainted, but he never lost his relish for the demonstrations of geometry, nor did he ever cease to think that from the closeness and consecutiveness of its successive steps, geometry furnished one of the very best instruments of mental training."

To the same excellent instructor was due his introduction to various other subjects which afterward employed his matured powers. Being admitted to the friendship of Dr. Brown, he derived much instruction as well as healthy intellectual stimulus from his rich and eloquent conversation. In his company he frequently met with Sir John Leslie and Mr. James Mylne, the one afterward professor of Natural History in the University of Edinburgh, and the other professor of Moral Philosophy in Glasgow, then both young men; but so much older than

Chalmers, as, together with the real maturity of their thoughts, to give a predominant weight to their opinions in his mind; and those opinions were most frequently connected with the subjects of ethics and politics. In his father's household he had heard nothing but the staunchest conservatism; from whose narrow and uncompromising bounds his young intellect was easily tempted by the charm with which young men of such talent adorned their free and more suggestive range of thought. The rigid Calvinism of his father's faith also became, in his estimation, under the same influences, " a religion of confinement and intolerance unworthy of entertainment by a mind enlightened and enlarged by liberal studies." Godwin's Political Justice became the object of his profound admiration, and the cold, religious formalism which then prevailed in the university, tended to check anything like the growth of piety in his soul. He himself testifies, that " St. Andrew's was, at this time, overrun with Moderatism, under the chilling influences of which, we inhaled not a distaste only, but a positive contempt, for all that is properly and peculiarly gospel, insomuch that our confidence was nearly as entire in the sufficiency of natural theology, as in the sufficiency of natural science." His own clear intellect soon delivered him from the political errors "into which ne was thus temporarily seduced; from the religious it needed many years, and other than human influences, to recall him."

To the same period of his academical career belong also his first attempt in English composition. " Here he had to begin at the very beginning. Letters, written by him even after his second year at college, exhibit a glaring deficiency in the first and simplest elements of correct writing; and he had to become very much his own instructor; guiding himself by such models as the prelections of Dr. Hunter and Dr. Brown, and the writings of Godwin or other favorite authors, presented. A few of his first efforts in this way have been preserved. They exhibit little that is remarkable in style. The earliest compositions of those who have afterward become distinguished as poets, or orators, or eloquent writers have generally displayed a profuse excess of the rhetorical or the imaginative, which it took time and labor to reduce to becoming proportions. In the college exercises of Dr. Chalmers this order is reversed. The earliest of them are the simplest and plainest, with scarce a gleam of fancy or sentiment ever rising to play over the page. They give token of a very vigorous youthful intellect disciplining itself at once in exact thinking and correct perspicuous expression, never allowing itself to travel beyond the bounds of the analysis or argument which it is engaged in prosecuting, never wandering away to pluck a single flower out of the garden of the imagination, by which illustration or adornment might be supplied. Those who, as the result of their analysis, have concluded that in Dr. Chalmers's mental constitution the purely intellectual largely predominated; that fancy was comparatively feeble, and that imagination, potent as she was, was but a minister of other and higher powers, might find historic verification of their analysis in the earliest of his college compositions. But his progress here was marvelously rapid. Habit of accurate and easy composition, which, in many instances, it costs half a lifetime to acquire to the same degree, were acquired by him within two years; and the ordinary difficulties of expression once mastered, that burning fervor, which glowed with such constant intensity within, got free and natural opportunity to outflow, and shaping spontaneously the language that was employed for the utterance of thought or sentiment, moulded it into forms of beauty and power.

In the work of cultivating his talent for literary composition he derived great advantage from his connection with the Political Society, an association of students for the purpose of literary improvement.

In November, 1795, while not yet sixteen years of age, "he was enrolled as a student of Divinity. Theology, however, occupied but little of his thoughts." Mathematics still retained the principal place in his esteem, and having now acquired enough knowledge of the French language to enable him to read easily mathematical works, therein new stores of delight were laid open to him in the beautiful and far-reaching analyses which had then found no adequate interpreter in the English tongue. Even the able theological lectures of Dr. Hill were unable to win him from his favorite science, and the most of the year was spent by him without making "entry upon the theological field." It is a striking proof of the light in which religion was regarded both by himself and the university, that, while thus professedly preparing for the work of the gospel ministry and utterly neglecting the necessary studies, and without any distinguishing marks of piety, he could yet compose prayers for oratorical effect and an audience would crowd to enjoy the literary treat. It was then the practice at St. Andrew's for the daily prayers in the public hall to be conducted by the theological students in rotation, and when it came to Chalmers's turn, the truly pious heart must have trembled for the boy of fifteen, yet ignorant of the power of the spirit of God, whose prayer is made an object of public admiration.

Though the greater part of that year was suffered to pass without much profit to the objects of the course, ere it came to a close a second era had opened in the intellectual life of the young student, induced by the celebrated treatise of Edwards on Free Will. The enthusiastic devotion which had previously been expended on mathematics was now addressed in still higher degree to the contemplation of the sovereignty of God, the grandeur of the Almighty government, and the beauty of that order according to which God has foreordained whatsoever comes to pass. Speaking of this period, Prof. Duncan says: "He studied Edwards on Free-Will with such ardor, that he seemed to regard nothing else, could scarcely talk of anything else, and one was almost afraid of his mind losing its balance;" and he himself remarked of it, at a later time, "that not a single hour elapsed in which the overpoweringly impressive imagination did not stand out bright before the inward eye; and that his custom was to wander early in the morning into the country, that amid the quiet scenes of nature he might luxuriate in the glorious conception." For nearly twelve months this magnificent vision of the Godhead, and subordination of all things to the one sovereign will, continued. Yet it does not seem to have interfered materially with the practicality of his views of inferior things; for during a visit, in the summer of 1796, to his brother James, then residing near Liverpool, he recorded in his journal the particulars of his observations, with as much care and precision as if he had never entertained an idea above them — a true illustration of the manner in which the largest and most engrossing of his ideas ruled without obliterating the minute.

From the transactions of a debating society, sustained by the theological students, it appears that the influence of the great thoughts of Jonathan Edwards upon his mind, was far from being of a superficial or ephemeral character; for, the next session (1796-7), he delivered, in the society, "a systematic discourse on predestination;" and Prof. Duncan adds, that the subject of that discourse "occupied him intensely during that session." Again, in the session of 1798-9, he took out for the subject of debate, "Is man a free agent?" and chose the negative side. In the theological society he was associated with Lord Campbell, John Leyden, Prof. Duncan, and several others, afterward well known in the world of letters.

It is a striking proof of the rapidity with which the mind and style of Chalmers came to maturity, after a stimulus worthy of his powers had roused him to activity, that part of an exercise written while he was a theological student, was, forty years afterward, adopted by him, word for word, before a convocation of the evangelical ministers of the Church of Scotland, and of which Dr. Hanna says, that "no passage he ever wrote was uttered with more fervid energy, or a more overwhelming effect."

In the last year of his college course, as it was not required of him to attend lectures more than three months, he resolved to employ the intervening time in teaching, with a view to opening up some field of independent effort, as well as to avoid imposing the additional burden of supporting him upon his father. Accordingly, he soon succeeded in engaging himself as a private tutor, and entered upon his duties as such in May,

1798. The disposition of the family was such as to render his situation anything but pleasant. A haughty, supercilious manner on the part of the parents toward the tutor, was not likely to leave high esteem for him in the minds of his pupils, unless counteracted by some inherent dignity in his own character. Chalmers felt that, and correctly and manfully sustained himself against overbearing aristocratic pretension. But the contest was exceedingly disagreeable, and was relinquished at the end of about six months. Soon afterward, he applied to the presbytery of St. Andrew's for license to preach the Gospel. Though some difficulty was raised on account of his youth, yet, in consideration of the extraordinary promise of the latter years of his residence at college, the presbytery consented to his licensure, which took place on the 31st of July, 1799; four months after he had completed his nineteenth year.

Immediately afterward, he made a second journey into England, and preached his first sermon in the Scotch Church, at Wigan. At the house of his brother James, who was now settled in business in Liverpool, he met two other brothers, George, three years older, and David, about as much younger than himself, both of whom, as well as William had been for some time at sea, and had agreed upon this occasion of meeting. The last-mentioned was prevented from joining them, and within a year afterward perished in the destruction of the ship to whose crew he belonged. It had been the intention of Thomas to avail himself of that opportunity to instruct his younger brother, David, in navigation; he had even made some progress therein, when a summons, requiring his immediate presence in Edinburgh, broke up the lessons, which were never to be renewed. A situation had become vacant, which, if on the spot, he might procure. He obeyed, but was disappointed. He remained, however, in Edinburgh, during the whole of the ensuing winter, prosecuting his mathematical studies under Prof. Playfair. At the beginning of the session, he had hoped that, by taking pupils, he might keep himself from pressing upon his father's resources. In this particular, owing to the lateness of his appearance in Edinburgh, where arrangements for the session had already been made, he did not succeed to his expectation. During two months subsequent to his return to Scotland, he preached only once, and in January, 1800, expressed himself as so fully occupied with his mathematical studies, that he should regret anything occurring as an interruption to them. That whole winter was devoted to mathematics, under the instruction of one of the ablest professors in Europe. In the succeeding summer, nothing occurred to prevent his continuation of his favorite pursuit in the retirement of his native place.

The next winter he returned to Edinburgh, with a view to attend the classes in natural science and in moral philosophy. His attention to chemistry, especially, was indefatigable. The lectures of Professor Stewart he attended regularly; but the subject seems to have had fewer attractions for him at that time, and with the methods of the lecturer he expressed himself somewhat dissatisfied. There seemed, to his close mathematical turn of mind, a want of firmness and convergency in the arguments, and a careful avoiding of points involving difficult or lengthened disquisition, and a desultoriness in the instructions of that celebrated philosopher. "The Edinburgh professor, of whom he at once entertained the profoundest admiration, and to whom he was most largely indebted, was Dr. Robison."

Mr. Chalmers had now been licensed about two years, and yet had given no particular attention to his profession, and seems never once to have thought of his duty to immortal souls. Ambition to excel in mathematical science burned within him, to the exclusion of those higher motives which ought to have dictated his choice of the gospel ministry. It is clear, however, that such motives were yet entire strangers to his heart. For some years he had even been more or less under the cloud of a secret infidelity. In addition to the erroneous notions contracted while in college, and which were afterward, to some extent, counteracted by Edwards on the Will, in 1798, a work by Baron Holbach, entitled the System of Nature, and published under the assumed name of Mirabaud, came into his hands, and for a time unsettled his faith in the "stability of the foundations on which all truth, moral and religious," rests. After suffering much distress from his accumulating doubts, upon leaving the family in which he had been residing as private tutor, he went to live at St. Andrew's with Mr. Miller, who states of him that, "His mind was at that time in a most interesting, but unhappy condition. He was earnestly searching for the truth, saw some things very clearly and satisfactorily, but could not find his way to the understanding and belief of some of the most obvious doctrines of natural and revealed religion. Those who were not particularly acquainted with him, thought him fast going into a state of derangement. One very common expression in his public prayers, and which showed the state of his mind at that time— 'Oh, give us some steady object for our mind to rest upon,' was uttered with all his characteristic earnestness and emphasis. I knew that he was exceedingly earnest in seeking the light of truth at that time in his private devotion, and was often on his knees at my bedside after I had gone to bed."

To a mind like his, enthusiastically fond of the study of nature, and incapable of repose in vague notions, the book of Holbach was the most ingenious machine of torture, converting his daily pursuits into instruments of continual irritation, and meeting him at the very foundations of all belief with a regularly constructed system of doubt. The infidel labored to prove that what we call intellect, is only the result of organization; that organization and every other phenomenon, having the appearance of design, was only the multifarious effects which flow from the natural development of the essential properties of matter; that truth is only the accidental relation thus arising between the character of the thinker and the subject of his thoughts, and that it is quite possible that to minds differently constituted, our truth may become falsehood, and falsehood truth. It is possible that the terrors of this philosophical skepticism drove Mr. Chalmers to labor with the greater zeal in the field of natural science, conscious that he could obtain rest only by thoroughly investigating and settling his opinions. Here the instructions of Dr. Robison were of incalculable value to him, setting over against the views of the skeptic, the harmonious and spontaneous belief of all mankind, in which the native faith of all minds is confirmed by the evidence of sense and the hourly experience of all living beings; demonstrating that both human minds and material things are real and of independent existence, and consequently, their adaptation, the one to the other, must be the work of express design to that effect. Chalmers's own struggles with this artifice of unbelief, led him frequently, in his published writings, to recur to the argument by which it was dissipated from his own mind.

In the summer of 1801, he made another visit to England, and upon his return, through the kindness of his friend, Mr. Shaw, he was selected to fill the place of assistant to the Rev. Mr. Elliot, of Cavers, a "parish in Roxburghshire, lying along the southern banks of the Teviot, a few miles below Hawick." Mr. Shaw had himself occupied that situation, but was now removed to the neighboring parish of Roberton. His residence was about seven miles from the church of Cavers, and it was soon arranged that they should live together in the manse of Roberton, which meeting no opposition from Mr. Chalmers's principal, enabled the young pastor to enjoy the counsel and society of a valuable and congenial friend.

While this arrangement was yet maturing, the professor of Church History in St. Andrew's, died, and it seems that Mr. Cook, of Kilmany, was immediately thought of as his successor. In that case, the church of Kilmany, one of those in the gift of the united college of St. Andrew's, would become vacant. It was a matter of no great difficulty to obtain, among the faculty of the college, a majority of votes in favor of Mr. Chalmers; but as some time might elapse before that could be settled, he continued his services in Cavers.

In the course of the winter, another prospect opened up before him, still more accordant to his then predominant likings. Professor Vilant, who held the mathematical chair in St. Andrew's, had long been an invalid, and conducted his classes by the intervention of assistants. Dr. Brown, the assistant during

Mr. Chalmers's undergraduate course, had been removed to the professorship of Natural Philosophy, in Glasgow. The assistantship had since passed into other hands, and was again vacant. Had Mr. Chalmers's "aims been purely professional, the certainty of the appointment to Kilmany might have satisfied him. Nay, if anything like the same feeling of ministerial responsibility which he afterward entertained, had been then experienced, he would never have thought of undertaking an office requiring such very laborious preparations, and that on the eve of his entrance on the christian ministry. But, as yet, unvisited with those profounder sentiments, as to the objects and responsibilities of that ministry, science still swayed it over theology. His thirst for literary distinction was intense. To fill the mathematical chair in one of our universities, was the high object of his ambition. To this, the assistantship at St Andrew's, might prove a stepping-stone. It would give him, at least, the opportunity so ardently longed for, of proving and exhibiting his capabilities for such an office. In spite, therefore, of the peculiar circumstances in which he was placed, he resolved to make a vigorous effort to obtain the appointment. Informed that his presence at St. Andrew's was desirable, he left Roberton in the end of April, to return in a few weeks, not only with the assurance reiterated and confirmed of his receiving the presentation to Kilmany, but with the mathematical assistantship secured. It might not be until Whitsuntide, of the following year, that he would be ordained as a minister; in November he would enter upon the duties of the mathematical class. Inflamed by the literary ardor which the prospect now before him had kindled, he returned to Teviotdale, resolved to devote the summer months to strenuous study;" and so faithfully did he carry out his resolution, that when November arrived, his preparations were nearly complete.

As early as the beginning of September, he left his country congregation, in order to pursue his studies more favorably at St. Andrew's. "Early in October, Mr. Cook resigned the living of Kilmany; and on the 2d of November, the principal and professors cordially and unanimously agreed to elect Mr. Chalmers his successor."

His ordination was not to take place until next spring, and in the meanwhile he devoted himself with the most ardent enthusiasm to the business of his classes. Instead of contenting himself, as mathematical teachers commonly do, with the bald abstractions constituting the science, he labored to exhibit them in all the interesting associations with which they were connected in his own mind. The connections of mathematics with the various fields of natural science and the arts, were habitually presented before his pupils, rendering the study, as one of his pupils writes, "hardly less a play of the fancy than a labor of the intellect; the lessons of the day being continually interspersed with applications and illustrations of the most lively nature: so that he secured, in a singular manner, the confidence and attachment of his pupils." From the fragments of his lectures delivered this session, it is clear that, with all his passion for science and remarkable success in its pursuit, the orator in his intellectual character overruled the mathematician. The old professor was astonished and alarmed at the reports which reached him of the eloquence and enthusiasm which, under the influence of his new assistant, were lighting up the subject over which he had so long presided in dignified apathy. His disapprobation was expressed, and attempts were made to interfere and to dictate to the assistant a method more consistent with the dull routine of other days. It was granted that the classes were more thoroughly instructed, and interested in the study to an unprecedented degree; but because they had not gone over the same extent of ground as in former years, occasion was taken to malign the professional character of the instructor. It was not to be expected that one of Mr. Chalmers's ardent temperament, and "so keenly alive to everything which he considered ungenerous and unjust," should endure in silence. In closing the session, he expressed his opinion of the conduct of his superior both before his class and before the professors assembled at examination. On the latter occasion, he was so sarcastic and vehement in his remarks on the conduct of professor Vilant, that the chairman of the board found it necessary to call him to order.

"Mr. Chalmers had already intimated to his father that he meant to devote to a visit to Edinburgh the short interval which would occur between the breaking up of the classes at St. Andrew's and his settlement at Kilmany. His father disliked the proposition. He knew how engrossed his son had been throughout the winter with mathematics. He looked forward with anxiety to the commencement of his ministry. He feared that science had the hold which he wished so much that the gospel of God's redeeming grace should have; and thinking that the short season, which now remained ere the sacred duties of an ambassador of Christ were entered on, might be more fitly and profitably employed, he ventured to remonstrate with his son, suggesting that, as they had seen so little of him during the winter, he might give this interval to Anstruther, where he could find seclusion and repose." The reply was more in the spirit of self-righteousness and assumed superiority than any other of its author that has yet been published. It took for granted that he was fully prepared for the work of the ministry and stood in no need of any special season of preparation, and that regarding his literary motives they were of a kind above the reach of his father's comprehension. It would be most painful to read but for the consideration that the time came when no one would have condemned it more than its author.

CHAPTER II.

Mr. Chalmers was ordained to the work of the gospel ministry in the parish of Kilmany, on the 12th of May, 1803. Notwithstanding the low estimate he had formed of his profession, he proved by no means neglectful of the external duties belonging to it. His preparations for the pulpit were made with care, and the work of pastoral visiting and catechizing was performed with all fidelity to established form, while the zeal and warmth of his character won the esteem and affections of his parishioners. Still he did not resign his hopes of distinction and had counted upon retaining his place at St. Andrew's. In consequence, however, of the assault made by him upon his principal, professor Vilant, at the close of the term, and perhaps of the professor's dissatisfaction with his manner of teaching, he had received information that his services would not be required there any further. This step, on the part of his principal, he considered as an attempt to blast his reputation and to put him down as incompetent, without affording him an opportunity to vindicate himself from misrepresentation: an indignity and injustice to which he was determined not to submit. The setting up of a private class, in opposition to those in college, was somewhat new in Scotland, and would excite much hostility as well as astonishment; but conceiving such a step necessary to his reputation as a teacher, he resolved to adopt it. Accordingly he declared his intention to open mathematical classes of his own in St. Andrew's, under the very eyes of the man who had attempted to dishonor him. The attendance, notwithstanding the opposition of the college faculty, was such as to encourage the young adventurer to further enterprise, and toward the end of December he commenced a course of lectures on chemistry, which were still more fully attended. He had now three classes of students in mathematics and one in chemistry, as well as his pulpit in Kilmany, to supply any one of which, to most young men of three-and-twenty, would have been work of abundant toil. Yet he writes of it as "just the life for which he was formed — a life of constant and unremitting activity." He spent most of the week in St. Andrew's, going out to Kilmany every Saturday and returning early on Monday. Such was the excellence of his instructions, and perhaps, more than all, the eloquence with which they were enforced, that his popularity as an instructor rapidly increased, and the opposition which bitterly encountered him at first, gradually yielded to the course of the tide. The youth who, unfriended and single-handed, had entered the lists with the university, not out of wanton bravado, not from selfish obtrusion, but in order to remove a stain unjustly cast upon his reputation, had completely triumphed.

A journal kept during that winter goes to prove how thoroughly scientific ambition then engrossed all the warmest feelings of his soul. His church and the cause of God in the soul of man, certainly occupied the inferior place in his esteem; and it only sets the matter in a more unfavorable light, if his congregation perceived in his conduct no particular reason to be dissatisfied. Some of the ministers of his presbytery, however, saw the impropriety of it, and determined to use their influence to impose a check upon it. If they had previously indulged other ministers in a similar course, they were to be pitied for that, rather than blamed for the juster views which they now maintained. His defense was ably written; but presents no argument higher than his literary reputation, and indeed assumes that in vindication thereof, he was fully justified in neglecting, to such a degree, the high responsibilities he had assumed to the souls of men. The case was not brought before presbytery so soon as he expected, and next winter he determined to repeat his chemical lectures in St. Andrew's, deeming it sufficient concession to the objections of his brethren to have relinquished the intention of re-opening mathematical classes. In view of this determination, " at a meeting of the presbytery of Cupar, held on the 4th of September, 1804,

Dr. Martin begged the presbytery to insert in their minutes that, in his opinion, Mr. Chalmers's giving lectures in chemistry is improper, and ought to be discontinued. To this request the presbytery acceded. On which Mr. Chalmers begged it to be inserted in the minutes, that after the punctual discharge of his professional duties, his time was his own ; and he conceived that no man or no court had a right to control him in the distribution of it." In his defense there was no better spirit manifested than that of a high-minded man of the world. He challenges comparison with other clergymen — maintains that he had fully satisfied all the demands of his profession, and defies his opponent to " find a single individual " of his parishioners who would say that he had been outstripped by any of his predecessors in the regularity of his ministerial attentions, or that anything had been discovered in his conduct betokening a contempt for religion, or indifference for its sacred interests ; and closes with an expression of hightoned resentment of the interference with what he deemed his rights. He " spurns the attempt as he would the petty insolence of a tyrant," and declares that to the last sigh of his heart he "would struggle for independence, and eye with proud disdain the man who presumes to invade it," with other expressions characteristic of the impetuous youth of noble feelings and lofty ambition ; but not one trace of the Christian. Accordingly, in utter contempt of this remonstrance, he resumed his chemical lectures at St. Andrew's in the succeeding November, spending two days every week in that way—spare time, which he says, in a letter of that day, would otherwise have been fretted "away in indolence and disgust." In the meanwhile, upon the death of Dr. Rotheram, professor of Natural Philosophy in St. Andrew's, Mr. Chalmers presented himself as a candidate for the vacant chair, but without success. Again, in the following January, when Dr. Robison, Professor of Natural Philosophy in the University of Edinburgh died, and Professor Playfair was removed to that department, he entered the lists as a competitor for the professorship of mathematics ; but there also failed to obtain the favorable notice of the electors, who were divided between Mr. Leslie and Mr. Macnight, one of the ministers of Edinburgh. Though the former was the successful candidate, the design of the latter to retain his pastoral charge, in case of his election to the professorship, gave rise to a discussion, in which Mr. Chalmers, as might have been expected, took a prominent part. Professors Playfair and Stewart had each addressed letters to the lord provost, in which they remonstrated against ministers, in possession of a pastoral charge, holding also a professorship; and Mr. Playfair had also urged that not only were few clergymen in the church of Scotland competent to the duties of a mathematical professorship, but that the successful pursuit of science was "incompatible with clerical duties and habits." Mr. Chalmers resented this as a "cruel and illiberal insinuation" against "the whole order of churchmen," and responded at length in a pamphlet published under the title, "Observations on a Passage in Mr. Playfair's Letter to the Lord Provost of Edinburgh, relative to the Mathematical pretensions of the Scottish Clergy," in which, by his zeal to vindicate the science of his brother ministers, he presents a lamentable view of their professional fidelity. "The author of this pamphlet," he said, "can assert, from what to him is the highest of all authority, the authority of his own experience, that after the satisfactory discharge of his parish duties, a minister may enjoy five days' uninterrupted leisure for the prosecution of any science in which his taste may dispose him to engage;" and his estimate of the dignity of his profession may be inferred from the fact that he speaks of one confined to it and excluded from literary and scientific distinction, as "a being who must bid adieu to every flattering anticipation, and drivel out the remainder of his days in insignificance." His ambition was also apparent in the zeal with which he urged the sale of his pamphlet, and the obvious desire to earn a little literary reputation from it.

The succeeding winter (1805), he delivered a course of chemical lectures to his parishioners at Kilmany, and also at the neighboring town of Cupar. His intensely energetic mind, yet unenlightened as to the resources and full demands of his sacred calling, craved occupation from other fields of effort, and labored from the mere love of activity. Nor were these intellectual enterprises enough to exhaust his exuberant energy; the great public events of that stirring time occupied their full share of his attention. The career of Bonaparte, from the first, had been to him an object of profound interest; and when the threat of invasion impended over the country, he did not content himself with lifting up his voice in the pulpit against the national enemy, but also enrolled himself in the St. Andrew's corps of volunteers, " holding a double commission as chaplain and lieutenant." While on service in that body in 1805, an incident occurred which goes, together with many other things, to prove the impulsive generosity of his nature, even before it was actuated by the holier motive of pious benevolence. In the outskirts of the town of Kirkaldy, " where his corps was then on permanent duty, he recognized an old acquaintance, a member of the secession church, whose family was sunk in poverty, and visited with fever. Anxious to contribute to their relief, Mr. Chalmers requested Mr. Fleming, the minister of Kirkaldy, to give him the use of his pulpit, that he might preach a sermon, and make a collection on behalf of the sufferers. Knowing the applicant only as the author of the recently published pamphlet, and as one addicted more to lectures on chemistry than to purely professional effort, Mr. Fleming refused. The will, however, was too strong not to find for itself a way. Although Mr. Chalmers could not get a pulpit to preach, he could find a room to lecture in. A suitable apartment was forthwith engaged; a course of lectures on chemistry was announced. Though the admission ticket was somewhat high in price, goodly audiences crowded nightly around the lecturer; and at the close, he had the exquisite satisfaction of handing over to a respectable, but unfortunate family, what not only relieved them from present distress, but supported them for some time afterward in comfort." The same feature of his character appeared also in his intercourse with the people of his pastoral charge, and his kindness to the poor old man who had been the imperfect teacher of his boyhood. His house had generally as many of his younger brothers and sisters in it, as it could conveniently accommodate, and of the education of some of them, he assumed the principal care as well as expense. Though he had ceased to lecture at St. Andrew's, he still continued to spend most of his time during the winter in that place, superintending the education of his younger brother, Charles.

In the spring of 1806, his brother George, who had been at sea for several years, returned with a constitution already undermined by the progress of consumption. For some time he resided at Kilmany, but in October, removed to his father's house, at Anstruther, where Thomas followed him, and never left him until he died. The calm resignation and elevated piety of that favorite brother, seems to have had a most salutary effect upon Mr. Chalmers's mind. Although in the end of October he wrote of him as having "all the manly indifference of his profession," and as being "perfectly resigned under the confident idea that his death is inevitable," he must have felt compelled, ere the earthly career of that pious brother was closed, to refer his composure to something higher than manly indifference or blind resignation to inevitable destiny. "Every evening, at George's own request, one of Newton's sermons was read at his bedside, by some member of the family in rotation. It was one of the very books which, a short time previously, Thomas had named, and denounced from the pulpit. Bending over the pulpit, and putting on the books named the strong emphasis of dislike, he had said, "Many books are favorites with you, which, I am sorry to say, are no favorites of mine. When you are reading Newton's Sermons, and Baxter's Saint's Rest, and Doddridge's Rise and Progress, where do Matthew, Mark, Luke and John go to?" As he now read one of these books to his dying brother, and witnessed the support and consolation which its truths conveyed, strange misgivings must have visited him. He was in the room, when those pale and trembling lips were heard to say, "I thank thee, O Father, Lord of Heaven and Earth, that thou hast hid these things from the wise and prudent, and revealed them unto babes." Perhaps, as the words were uttered, the thought arose, that in his own case, as compared with that of his brother, the words might be verified. In company with a weeping household, he bent over the parting scene, and heard the closing testimony given, "Lord, now lettest thou thy servant depart in peace, for mine eyes have seen thy salvation." George died on the 16th December, 1806. It was the first death of a near relative which Thomas had witnessed, and the deep impression which it made, was the first step toward his own true and thorough conversion unto God."

A few weeks after this event, Mr. Chalmers paid a visit to his brother James, who had now taken up his residence in London. The journal kept during that trip, bears evidence to the range and minuteness of his observations, and the practical turn of his mind. It discusses the characters met in traveling, descriptions of scenery, of mechanical operations and inventions, of chemical apparatus and lectures, of works of art, of plants, of natural scenery, of landscape gardening, manufactories, antiquities, objects of historical interest, life and manners, preachers, political speakers and speeches, the palaces, the royal family, the theater, and actors. In short, no class of objects seems to have escaped his attention, except those, which a few years later, absorbed the whole enthusiasm of his nature. He also visited the great universities of England, but was most interested in Cambridge, from its association with the name of Sir Isaac Newton, who was the object of his highest admiration. On his way home, he delayed at Alnwick, to look upon the ancient halls of the Percies, and the ruins on Holy Isle; after which, making his way on foot along the banks of the Tweed and the Teviot, in about a week he reached the house of his friend, Mr. Shaw, of Roberton. In that hospitable family he was detained longer than he had intended. Mr. Shaw's account of this part of his journey admits us to an interesting view of some features of his character: " I proposed when he left, to accompany him to Dr. Hardie's (about six miles distant), whence he intended to get to Pennycook next day. We set out accordingly on a Monday after breakfast.

The next morning, I expressed a wish that we should go as far as Galashiel's, and call on Dr. Douglass, to which he consented, on condition that it must be only a short call. There, however, we were induced to spend the day. Next morning, we took our departure on the way to Peebles; but in passing the hospitable residence of a family, with whom I was intimately connected, I prevailed on him to call, and being much delighted with our kind reception, we remained till next morning, when we took our leave, after breakfast. On our way up the Tweed, I suggested the propriety of our calling on my friend, Nicol, of Traquair, whose manse was situated only about half a mile off the road; 'Well, sir,' was the reply, 'but it must be only for a minute or two, as I must get to Pennycook this night.' There, however, we spent the day most comfortably, and in the evening, were so delighted with the music of the piano, that we could not refrain dancing a few merry reels. At last, Chalmers took hold of my arm, and exclaimed, 'It's out of the question, my getting home this week. You have a good horse, so you must just proceed to-morrow morning to Kilmany, and I will go back to Roberton.' To this proposal I readily agreed. Nicol was amazed, and seemed to think we were both getting deranged. On awakening next morning, and perceiving that it rained, I began to groan a little, when my friend pulled me out of bed, and ordered me to set off with all convenient speed. Off, I accordingly rode, and reached Kilmany about eight o'clock at night. Chalmers went from Nicol's to Hardie's on Friday—we parted at Traquair—and on Saturday, to Roberton parish, where he wrote a poetical farewell to Teviotdale, and preached a brilliant sermon on 'Look not on the wine when it is red.' (Prov. xxiii, 31). Afterward, on his way home, he called at Abbotshall, and gave me a minute and amusing account of all his proceedings, concluding with high glee and emphasis, 'This famous exploit will immortalize us, sir.' I regret that I cannot find his Farewell to Teviotdale, which I must have somehow mislaid."

From this time forward, his conduct is marked by more steady residence in his parish, and attention to his pastoral duties, but without any apparent change in the state of his affections toward God. Lectures on chemistry were discarded for discussions on political economy. The new subject could be treated without wandering from the bounds of his own study, and naturally awakened a warmer interest in men and their temporal well-being in his mind—a mind that never suffered any of its ideas to slumber in the abstract. He was now employed during the latter part of the year 1807, in preparing his work on the "Stability of National Resources," called forth by the then existing circumstances of the British nation. Napoleon, by means of his continental system, had excluded British commerce from all the ports to which his influence extended, cutting off, as it seemed, the principal resources of his enemy, at a time when she was involved in a most expensive war. The fears excited on this occasion, Mr. Chalmers considered entirely groundless, and endeavored to prove that if his country were without commerce, she would only be deprived of some expensive luxuries, but not of the wealth whereby they are bought, and therefore, really stronger in internal resources, and better able to sustain the government in keeping up the war, than before. The topics treated were of great and immediate importance, and at that time, occupied much of public attention, and were treated by the ablest political writers of that day, yet the work of the young minister of Kilmany is distinguished among them all for largeness of view, and the practicalness of its suggestions. Some of its propositions, though undervalued at the time, as the offspring of an unknown author, have since become operative principles of the British government. He was impeded in the completion of this work by a protracted illness, so that it was not brought out until the spring of 1808. A small edition was printed in Edinburgh, and the sale being very fair, suggested the idea of a new edition from the London press. On this point, he manifested considerable anxiety, and interested both his brother and Mr. Wilkie in its behalf; but their negotiations with booksellers were not successful. He concluded to go up to London, and attend to the management of the business himself, but Providence ordered it otherwise, and he was detained in a place more conducive to the growth of religion in his soul—the sick, dark room of a dying sister. The same disease which had removed his brother George, had now laid its inexorable hand upon his sister Barbara, and another beautiful proof was set before the ambitious man, of the value of that heavenly hope, which is as an anchor of the soul, sure and steadfast, of the reality of the believer's possession amid the imperfect and fleeting objects of temporal desire. His sister died on the 19th of August, 1808, and next day, in a letter to his brother James, he declared that he had no decided intentions regarding his book.

Some months previous to his sister's death he had been requested by Dr. Brewster to become a contributor to the Edinburgh Encyclopedia, and had chosen the article Trigonometry. But after his sister's death he wrote again to Dr. Brewster, requesting that the article Christianity might be committed to him, and Dr. Andrew Thomson, to whom it had been already assigned, consented to give it up upon learning Mr. Chalmers's desire to undertake it. He expressed extreme desire to do the subject justice and resolved to take up his abode for three or four months at St. Andrew's for the purpose of having access to the necessary authorities. On the 8th of February, 1809, he preached his sermon on the occasion of the battle of Corunna, to a small body of his parishioners, collected through the storm in his own dining-room at Kilmany. On the 25th of May succeeding, he made his first speech before the General Assembly of the Church of Scotland, in support of an overture from the Presbytery of Cupar relative to the act regulating the augmentation of clergymen's salaries. Through neglect of the necessary formalities the motion was lost; but the power of the address had awakened the attention of the Assembly to the fact, that a master-mind was rising up among them. "Do you know anything of this man?" said Dr. Campbell, a minister who sat near him, "he is surely a most extraordinary person." The question was on many lips beside Dr. Campbell's as the speaker sat down. He was beset with solicitations to publish his address, and when these were urged by such men as Dr. Brewster and Dr. Andrew Thomson, it would have been the falsest delicacy to decline. The speech was accordingly committed to the press.

On his return from Edinburgh he was met by the tidings of the death of an uncle who had long been a "kind of second father to his nephews and nieces." "Mr. Ballardie's wife had been dead for many years, and his house had been kept by her sister." One evening he retired to his room after tea. He remained longer than usual and his sister-in-law, entering his room, found him kneeling by a chair. His spirit had passed away in the very act of prayer. He left his nephew, Thomas, the heir of his house, and, along with his father, constituted him his trustee. But Mr. Chalmers had contracted a severe illness on his way home from the Assembly, which prevented his leaving Kilmany till the beginning of August. He visited Anstruther in the close of September, but some exposure, on his return, threw him into a long sickness, in which, for four months, he never left his room; for half a year he was unable to appear in his pulpit, and twelve months elapsed before he could again discharge all the duties of his office. At the time he was residing at the farm-house of Fincrags while the manse of Kilmany was undergoing repairs. His illness, which was a disease of the liver, requiring the application of the strongest medicines, reduced him to the last degree of bodily debility; "but the mind was left in untouched vigor, and into it, now left to its own profound and solitary musings, there sunk the deepest and most overpowering impression of human mortality." The repeated deaths of those whom he loved, and now the belief that his own end was near bore forcibly in upon him the truth of the shortness of mortal existence and the conviction that all of it is needed for the accomplishment of all its duties. In February of the next year, he thus wrote to his friend, the Rev. Mr. Carstairs, of Anstruther: "My confinement has fixed on my heart a very strong impression of the insignificance of time; an impression which, I trust, will not abandon me though I again reach the heyday of health and vigor. This should be the first step to another impression still more salutary, the magnitude of eternity. Strip human life of its connection with a higher scene of existence, and it is the illusion of an instant, an unmeaning farce, a series of visions and projects, and convulsive efforts, which terminate in nothing. I have been reading Paschal's thoughts on religion: you know his history; a man of the richest endowments, and whose youth was signalized by his profound and original speculations in mathematical science, but who could stop short in the brilliant career of discovery, who could resign all the splendors of literary reputation, who could renounce, without a sigh, all the distinctions which are conferred upon genius, and resolve to devote every talent and every hour to the defense and illustration of the Gospel. This, my dear sir, is superior to all Greek and to all Roman fame."

CHAPTER III.

Mr. Chalmers had now entered upon a new era of existence. Those long months of sickness and hourly contemplation of impending death, deepening the solemn impression already made by the last hours of his brother and sister, and bringing up before him in strong contrast the littleness of time, and grandeur of eternity, caused him to look back upon his past life with profound regret and condemnation. He perceived that, while holding the place of a minister of Christ, he had been pre-eminently attached to the pursuits and honors of the world; that he had not labored for eternity; that although his views of God had been sublime, and in many respects scriptural; though he had enjoyed large adoring thoughts of the Creator and sovereign ruler of all, he had never known that humble, childlike faith and love by which the renewed soul reposes upon God in Christ as the gratuitous giver of a complete salvation to which the sinner can add nothing of his own. He felt that he had been proud and self-righteous, and that he had not given himself to the work of the Lord with singleness of purpose. Now recognizing his Almighty Master's right to the service of all the powers of his being, he resolved, if life should be prolonged, henceforth to live for God, and to devote himself more assiduously to all the duties of his sacred calling.

With this change of feeling a corresponding change took place in his speculative belief. Views of the depravity of human nature, which previously he would have rejected with disdain, grew up before him, and enlarged, though still imperfect conceptions of the atonement occupied his mind. For some time longer he relied upon his own determination to conform to the principles of divine law. It cost the struggle of another year before he could assign the whole credit and work of salvation to the Saviour, and that only after humiliation had been induced by frequent and conscious failure of his efforts to conform to the requisitions of the law. In the journal kept during a part of that time, there appears the proof of a continuous endeavor to subdue the impetuous and haughty spirit of former years, wherein self-reliance, most prominent at the beginning, gives place afterward to earnest and increasing supplication for divine aid, and aspirations after honors yields to the desire to "secure a quiet and virtuous passage through this the country of his pilgrimage," and that his chief ambition may be to please God and maintain the life which is hid with him in Christ.

Mathematical studies still occupied a part of his time. In March, 1810, he suspended them, in order to prepare a review of Dr. Charters's sermons. On the sixth of May, 1810, he preached for the first time in thirty-one weeks. A few days later he made a visit to his father's house, and found his sister lying dangerously ill. His brother Alexander had also been sick for some time. These sources of sorrow increased the solemnity of his feelings; and writing from St. Andrews, not long afterward, he records a growing indifference to university preferments. In mentioning his own quiet country residence as a better theater of moral discipline than Anstruther, his own journal recognizes that period as the infancy of his religious course. Under the date of August 21st, he mentions his intention of abandoning severe mathematics, and of expending his strength upon theological studies. He confesses the painfulness of the sacrifice, but resolves to "leave himself entire for all those discussions which are connected with the defense of Christianity, the exposition of its views, and the maintenance of its interests, as affected by the politics or philosophy of the times." Still, he did not yet entirely lay aside mathematical reading, but confined it to a very subordinate place. Prayers like these frequently occur in his journal: "Let me never forget the pre-eminence of religion;" "Let me give my strength to the grand business of being useful in my profession," and "O God, give me the spirit of prayer and the spirit of watching."

His sister Lucy died on the 23d of December, 1810, upon which he returned to Anster to comfort his father who was now sinking under repeated affliction and increasing blindness. At the same time he took up Wilberforce's "Practical View of religion," a book destined to mark an era in his spiritual history. So far, under deeply solemnized feelings, and the purpose of a holier life, he had been struggling to his purpose by means of virtuous principle. The result was, a restless dissatisfaction with all his efforts. He had failed in attaining that heavenly excellence and calmness of spirit at which he aimed. Wilberforce showed him that, correct as was the end he had in view, the path he was pursuing would never lead him there. That he must abandon the hope of recommending himself by his own good deeds, and submit to trust the whole work of his salvation and acceptance with God to the Lord Jesus Christ. Fully prepared to confirm the position of the author, that repose was not to be found in attempts to secure a legal righteousness, he felt as he never had felt before the force of that fundamental injunction, "Believe in the Lord Jesus Christ and thou shalt be saved." "For upward of a year he had striven with all his might to meet the high requirements of the divine law; but that law rose in its demands as he rose in his endeavors." In his own words; "It still kept ahead of him, with a kind of overmatching superiority to all his efforts. His attempts to scale the heights of perfection, to quell the remonstrances of a challenging and not yet appeased commandment, were like the laborious ascent of him, who, having so wasted his strength that he can do no more, finds that some precipice still remains to be overcome, some mountain brow that scorns his enterprise and threatens to overwhelm him. "He repaired to the atonement to eke out his deficiencies, and as the ground of assurance that God would look upon him with a propitious eye; but notwithstanding an unappeasable disquietude hung heavy upon his heart, and "he walked among the elements of uncertainty and distrust," till at last he came to see that the Saviour had already and completely done for him what, with so much strenuousness, but with so little success, he had been striving to do for himself. He felt the insecurities of his position he had been in vain endeavoring to strengthen, by mixing up the merits of Christ with the sincerity of his repentance and the painstaking of his obedience, to form together the ingredients of his hope and security before God. But the conviction was now wrought in him that he had been attempting an impossibility, that he had been trying to compound elements that would not amalgamate; that it must be either on his own merits wholly, or on Christ's merits wholly that he must lean; and that by introducing, to any extent, his own righteousness into the ground of his meritorious acceptance with God, " he had been inserting a flaw, he had been importing a falsehood into the very principle of his justification."

It was through the spring of 1811, that this revolution in his spiritual character was silently progressing, in the course of which he obtained valuable assistance from Scott's "Force of Truth," and Hannah More's Essay on Practical Piety, which were followed in the summer by Baxter's "Body of Divinity," and the whole year was a laborious and solid progress in the most valuable religious knowledge. The simplicity of a complete salvation, offered entire as a free gift, did not break upon his mind suddenly, but rose before him slowly, as the summer morning in his native clime, after a long dawn of progressive light.

His growth in grace was sensibly impeded by remaining habits of conformity with fashionable indifference to the peculiar doctrines of Christianity. This appeared in other things as well as in the fact that although now feeling the love of God in Christ to be dearer to him than all the honors and approbation of earth, he experienced a struggle with his convictions, when any of his worldly friends spent the night with him, in view of conducting family worship in their presence.

The article upon the evidences of Christianity, commenced before his sickness, was not laid aside; but in the midst of mental anxiety and bodily debility, was slowly progressing toward completion. For many months the work of composition had to be suspended; but still some part of the day was generally allotted to reading or to hearing others read on the subject. The work enlisted his most ardent enthusiasm, and as the cogency and number of the evidences of Christianity accumulated before him, his admiration and delight in the subject were beyond bounds. "I have seen him," says a friend, writing of the summer months of 1810, while he was still so feeble as to be debarred from composition, "almost in an ecstasy when he was speaking of the grandeur and excellency of Christianity, and of the clearness and force of the evidence by which it is supported. His mind was almost overwhelmed by it. One day he called on me and said: 'Tell me all that ever you heard against Christianity from its enemies; I am more than able to refute them all. The evidences of our religion are overwhelming.' It is utterly impossible for me to convey, in language, an idea of the manner in which he uttered these and similar expressions. His whole soul was completely absorbed, and he gave vent to his feelings in language peculiarly his own."

Dr. Andrew Thomson had recently been called to the New Gray-friars' church, Edinburgh, and coming into the midst of fashionable indifference and aristocratic self-satisfaction, sustained by high literary talents and attainments, found himself called upon to employ the utmost available power of the press, as well as of the pulpit, and accordingly commenced the publication of the Christian Instructor, a periodical devoted to the interests of practical Christianity, the first number of which appeared in August, 1810. In January of the following year, he wrote to Mr. Chalmers requesting him to become a contributor, and suggesting, as a subject of criticism, a work, recently issued in London, on Toleration. Mr. Chalmers fell in with the proposal, and having still lying by him his review of Dr. Charters's sermons, composed in the previous spring and intended for the Edinburgh Review, though never sent to it, he now forwarded it as a beginning of his work in the review department of the new periodical. Some doctrinal points were objected to by the editor, and a correspondence took place in regard to it, frank, manly, and amiable, in the course of which Mr. Chalmers wrote in his journal his determination of acquiescence in the decision of Dr. Thomson, for the time, inasmuch as he felt himself to be on the eve of some great revolution in his own religious views. In the spring of 1811 his review of the "Hints on Toleration" appeared in the Christian Instructor, and in July of the same year his review of Dr. Charters's sermons, accompanied by an explanatory note from the pen of the editor, the justice of which was recognized by Mr. Chalmers, at the time, and many years afterward was by himself transferred together with the review into the series of his works.

His mathematical studies were now finally abandoned, from a conviction that they seriously interfered with the faithful discharge of his pastoral duties. Contrary to the position which he had so warmly defended seven years before in his pamphlet, in reply to Prof. Playfair, he now declared, in a letter to his brother James, dated June 15th, 1811, "That a minister, if he gives his whole heart to his business, finds employment for every moment of his existence; and I am, every day, getting more in love with my professional duties and more penetrated with a sense of their importance;" and in a letter to his mother, of September 5th, he writes: "You may tell my father that I have at length come into his opinion, that the peculiar business of his profession demands all the time, all the talents, and all the energy that any minister is possessed of." His reading was now almost entirely confined to works connected more or less with practical religion. To dry theoretical works he now attached much less importance than to those presenting the gospel plan of salvation and the righteousness which is by faith in a simple scriptural manner. His doctrinal views, in the course of that year, were advancing toward what is called Calvinism; but he rejected the hard one-sidedness of any of the doctrinal systems of the Church, declaring his preference for the broad, "free, and spontaneous manner" of the New Testament. The point of his attainment toward the end of the year, appears in one of his letters to Mr. Anderson, dated Dec. 18th, in which, having quoted the text "He that believeth in me, though he were dead, yet shall he live," he goes on: "This is my firm hold, and I will not let it go. I sicken at all my own imperfect preparations. I take one decisive and immediate step and resign my all to the sufficiency of my Saviour. I feel my disease, and I feel that my want of alarm and lively affecting conviction forms its most obstinate ingredient. I try to stir up the emotion, and feel myself harassed and distressed at the impotency of my own meditations. But why linger without the threshold in the face of a warm and urgent invitation? 'Come unto me.' Do not think that it is your office to heal one part of the disease and Christ's to heal up the remainder." "I come to him with my heart *such as it is;* and I pray that the operation of His Spirit and the power of His sanctifying faith would make it *such as it should be.* That abhorrence of sin which I now feel to be in a manner dead, I hope, through Him strengthening me, will be made to quicken and revive. Repentance is the gift of God, and I look to him for the fulfillment of His gracious promise, that he who 'hath given us His own son, will also with Him freely give us all things. I see that this son is exalted on high, to give repentance and the remission of sins,' and I trust that that being who has said, 'Without me ye can do nothing,' will enable me to 'do all things in the name of Jesus.'"

In the neighboring parish of Balmenius, a new church was erecting, and in the meanwhile, that congregation attended services in the church of Kilmany. Their minister, Mr. Thomson, thus preached to the united congregations, during all the time of Mr. Chalmers's sickness, and for more than a year afterward, while he was slowly regaining his strength, divided the labor with him, their arrangement for the Sabbath being, that Mr. Chalmers should preach in the morning, and Mr. Thomson in the afternoon. This connection came to an end in the beginning of November, when Mr. Chalmers entered again upon the whole of his parochial duties, after an interval of about two years, for four months of which he could not leave his room, for more than half a year he could not appear in his pulpit at all, and the most of the remainder was spent in the debility of very slow convalescence. But he emerged from that illness with the principles of a new life kindled within him, with new views of the world and of his duty to it, and with a consecration of all his energies to the service of that Master, whom he had only coldly served before. The haughty, domineering and self-sufficient spirit of earlier years had all disappeared and given place to the humility and amiableness of the child of God. The old impetuosity of temper still was there, the restless activity and enthusiasm, but they were now subjected to the control of a new principle, and directed toward the attainment of a higher end. The sole object to which his remaining life was now to be devoted, was the work of winning souls to God. And yet this change was not wrought in him through the operation of the fear of death, upon a gloomy and severe temperament. All the time, even when lying, with the probability of early dissolution before his eyes, his natural cheerfulness was never extinguished, and during the long period of his recovery, while the most solemn change was passing upon his soul, his conduct was entirely free from anything like austerity or sanctimonious assumption. The pleasures of his society were attested by the number and character of those who courted it, consisting not only of neighboring clergymen, but of persons of various occupations and of no occupation, from St. Andrew's, from Dundee and other cities around, and including such men us Prof. Duncan, Mr. James Anderson, Mr. Mudie, Prof. Leslie, and others of most diverse tastes and pursuits. His hospitality was profuse, and scarcely limited by his means. Though living in a country parish his house was almost daily the residence of guests. In his journal, the fact that he spent an evening alone, is now and then recorded as an unusual occurrence. Sometimes that generosity of his character was abused, as in the case of a Frenchman, named Bataille, who, through means of the workmen engaged about the manse, obtained an introduction to him, and who, though evidently a hollow and essentially gross creature, succeeded, for some two months, in imposing upon his kindhearted indulgence. Finding the minister an agreeable person, and his table well supplied, Mr. Bataille took the liberty of bringing another of his countrymen to enjoy his good fortune with him. Mr. Chalmers did not fail to perceive that his French guests drank too freely, and recorded his disapprobation of that grossness, yet such was his natural disposition to look upon all things in the most charitable light, that in view of Bataille's poverty, he had contemplated giving him money to purchase clothes. The two Frenchmen were, in fact, proceeding to make the agreeable parson's house a place of jovial resort, when one evening, Bataille put an end to the whole play by getting grievously drunk. As soon as they could comprehend reason, they were fully enlightened as to their host's opinion of their conduct, and, if they could not understand the nature of his principles, were left without any doubts on the subject of what measures it behooved them instantly to take.

During all this time, Mr. Chalmers's studies, beside what were immediately addressed to preparation for the pulpit, were concerned with his article on Christianity. For more than five months, indeed, he had not been able to pen a line; but he had all along been making progress in reading for it. Some of his published sermons were also written at this time, as that on Psalm, xi, 1, that on Rom. iii, 10, and the lecture on Psalm cxxxvii, 1–6. His weekly allowance of careful composition was then about one sheet closely written.

In the latter part of the year 1811, a correspondence arose between him and Mr. James Anderson, a young man of uncommon intellectual promise, which, for the light it throws upon the spiritual state of Mr. Chalmers as well as of his correspondent, is highly interesting. Mr. Anderson, the son of a wealthy merchant in Dundee, had sought his acquaintance on account of his mathematical reputation, and becoming attached to him personally, was gradually led by his kindly conversation to the examination of that greatest of all subjects, then engrossing the best of Mr. Chalmers's thoughts. Upon Mr. Anderson's return to Dundee, the letters which passed between them were chiefly on the subject of practical religion. In endeavoring to lead his young friend to the happiness of faith in Christ, Mr. Chalmers is led to statements of his own experience, fuller and more satisfactory than perhaps it would otherwise have occurred to him to make.

The liberality of his views was manifested by his sympathy with all those movements then new in the church, which were calculated to extend the interests of true religion and human happiness, whatever denomination of Christians might have the honor of originating them. The Bible Society received his most hearty co-operation, and the Baptist Missions not only enlisted his interest, but in his own words, "deeply impressed him with the worth and utility of those Christians." This would not be worth remarking, but for its variance from the spirit of intolerance which then prevailed in the Establishment toward all dissenting bodies. The most marked external change in his character, was activity in instructing and catechizing his congregation, in visiting and administering to the wants of the sick and the destitute, in talking with all on the subject of their salvation, and in the fervor and unction of piety which characterized his pulpit ministrations; in short, a predominant and burning zeal for the glory of God in the salvation of men.

CHAPTER IV.

In the course of the great change which had passed upon his own spirit, Mr. Chalmers had perceived the importance of deriving his religious views directly from the Bible, his regular and earnest study of which, was one of the most notable effects of his conversion. A near neighbor and frequent visitor, John Bouthron, who, on account of his age, was admitted to an easy and privileged familiarity, had once, in former years, remarked to him, "I find you aye busy, sir, with one thing or another; but come when I may, I never find you at your studies for the Sabbath," and had received the reply, "Oh, an hour or two on the Saturday evening is quite enough for that," latterly observed, with similar freedom, "I never come in now, sir, but I find you aye at your Bible." "All too little, John, all too little," was the answer, whose sincerity was demonstrated by the consistent labor of all his remaining years.

On the 29th of September, 1812, he made the following entry in his journal: "I finished, this day, my perusal of the New Testament by daily chapters, in which my object was to commit striking passages to memory. I mean to begin its perusal anew, in which this object shall be revised, and the object of fixing upon one sentiment of the chapter for habitual and recurring contemplation, through the day, shall be added to the former." He also recommenced the study of the Greek and Hebrew languages.

At the same time, the claims of the British and Foreign Bible Society, which had been instituted only a few years before, were enlisting the enthusiastic co-operation of the ablest minds in the various denominations of protestant churches in the United Kingdom. The feelings of Mr. Chalmers induced him to enter very heartily into its vast measures of benevolence. He spoke in its favor, wherever he had opportunity; he wrote in its behalf, he got up a branch society in his own parish, and actively co-operated with his presbytery in the effort to establish parochial branches throughout the country. It was the first great christian enterprise which won his sympathies and engaged his public advocacy. It " rose, in his estimation, as the most magnificent scheme that ever was instituted for bettering the moral condition of the species." The system of penny-a-week subscriptions to the cause, recommended itself to him as one calculated to bring in every class of community as contributors. And " when the Kilmany Bible Association was formed, the subscriptions were strictly limited to a penny a week; those who desired to give more, doing it either in the way of donations, or by entering the names of different members of their family as contributors." This method he advocated on the principle that it is more blessed to give than to receive, and that the poor Christian should not be discouraged from giving by the larger subscriptions of his richer neighbors, and thereby deprived of his share of that higher blessedness; and also on the ground that it was the way in which most funds could actually be raised, as well as that it furnishd a truly universal expression of christian sympathy for the heathen.

On the 15th of January, 1812, his sister Jane, who had been his housekeeper, was married, and immediately removed to the residence of her husband, Mr. Morton, who although a native of the neighboring parish, was then settled in England, near Dulverton, in Somersetshire. This change seriously affected the constitution of Mr. Chalmers's household. Although entertaining no humble opinion of his own talents as a housekeeper, it seems to have been ill sustained by facts. A story is told of his being left, a few months previously, during a visit which his sister made to Anstruther, to a similar test: and how Mr. Duncan and Mr. Mudie came in upon him from Dundee, and he, retiring soon after their arrival, to consult regarding the means of dining, found, to his dismay, that there was nothing whatever in the house but two parcels of fish, and how after leading his friends a good long healthy walk, in view of a spirited hunting scene, he set them down to a table on which two promising dishes flourished, and as the covers were removed, invited them to make choice from the abundant variety of "hard fish from St. Andrews and hard fish from Dundee." The experiment, which had been productive of such results, was now to be repeated, and, to all appearance, for more than a few weeks. Moreover, the absence of one to whom he was so warmly attached, made his home seem desolate. He accompanied the married party as far as Carlisle, and spent about a week, in the middle of February, with Dr. Charters. He now found that the Doctor and he no longer held their former similarity of religious views. Mr. Chalmers preached before him a sermon, in which he advanced the incompetency of reason to decide upon the subject of revelation from previous and independent material of its own. Dr. Charters, by expressing his disapprobation of the doctrine, both then, and afterward by letter, testified how far he had been left behind by his younger brother.

Some time previously he had been expecting from the court of session a considerable addition to his stipends. Immediately after his sister's marriage, he learned that a decision had been given of sixty pounds in his favor. This was only half of what he had been given to expect as his right, and, at the advice of his agent, he presented a reclaiming petition, which, however, was ineffectual. This result he learned upon his return from England in the latter part of February. He re-entered his solitary home with a resolution to be contented with his very moderate income, and devote himself, without any further concern for these things, entirely to the work of his calling. In closing up, on the 16th of March, the second year of his journal, he writes as follows :

"Have carried my journal to the termination of a second year, and, from its varying complexion, it appears that there lies a vast and indefinite field before me—much to aspire after in love to God, in the steadiness of my faith, in the clearness of my views, in the christian purity of my conduct: O God, may I build a right superstructure, on a right foundation. May I make mention of that name, than which there is none other given under heaven whereby men can be saved. Work in me that which is well pleasing in Thy sight and make me altogether a new creature in Christ Jesus my Lord. Recall me from my habitual estrangement; correct the miserable wanderings of my heart; form Christ in me, and may he be to me the anchor of hope, and the steady unfailing principle of sanctification. O Lord, give me to be cleansed more and more. Seal me as one of thine own, and naming the name of Jesus, may I depart from iniquity. My health, last year, was variable. But I fall miserably short of what I might do and ought to do. The following is a list of my performances:

Read Lardiner's Jewish and Heathen Testimonies; Prideaux's Connection; Macknight's Credibility of the Gospel; Baxter's Call to the Unconverted; Scott's Marmion; Hannah More's Practical Piety; Life of Mathew Henry: Buchanan's Researches; Buchanan's Sermons; Doddridge's Life, by Orton; and Paley's Horæ Paulinæ.

In addition to my ordinary supplies for the pulpit, wrote last part of my review of Hints upon Toleration, the last part of my performance on Christianity, a speech for Dr. Playfair, part of which I delivered at the Synod, a sermon on Hebrews vi, 19; another on Luke x, 26; another on Romans xv, 1; and about two sheets of devotional composition. In all about seventeen sheets, a very small proportion indeed.

Read more than the New Testament in English, and the Greek to the end of the Acts, as also a Greek Grammar. At family worship read Isaiah, Psalms, Job, and Proverbs.

Let me set more value on my time, and let my future Journal be more directed to the particular record of my way of spending it. O God, give me a more decided bent of heart to the service of Thee in Christ Jesus."

In the record of the next day we find the following account of the renewal of his self dedication to God:

"Begin with taking a view of my state previous to entering into the covenant. Find it an unsheltered and condemned state. Was convinced, but was not lively in my apprehension of it, and was far short of transport or vivacity in any part of this service. Prayed that faith might be wrought in me. Thought of faith in Christ, and had some joyful moments, when I thought of the promise annexed to it. Found that it was not by looking to myself but to Jesus that I obtained light and direction. I then thought of being sanctified by faith. This turned me to myself. I read with delight the promise of the spirit to those who believe; but when turning to myself and to my sanctification, I felt a dullness and insipidity, and when I prayed I did it with languor. O that I could fix a full and unqualified look upon Christ—there lies efficacy, and comfort, and sanctification. After this I made my dedication. I counted the cost of it and perhaps underrated the difficulties of the Christian warfare. I concluded with a solemn dedication of myself to God as my sovereign, to Christ as my Saviour, and to the Holy Ghost as my sanctifier, and prayed for strength, and direction, and support from on high, that I may be enabled to keep my vows to the Lord. Rose in comfort and peace. Let me bear up, hold fast Christ, even though He should be clouded from me; confess Him with the mouth to be the only Saviour, feel Him to be my anchor, and never, never let Him go."

About this time it was his practice to spend the first Monday in every month, chiefly in devotional exercises. The following is a record of one of these occasions, April 6th, 1812:

"Begun at twelve. Was fatigued and feverish, but my emotions pleasurable, and I did obtain a nearness to God. Prayed for my sanctification in general terms. Read the Bible and Clarke's 'Promises,' and descended in my next prayer to the particular duties. Mr. C. interrupted me, and I felt that my mind was wholly in business while he was present. When he left me, I felt the infirmity, and recurred as my next topic of pious and aspiring meditation, to my peculiar business as a minister. Have not that lively repentance for my past misconduct and negligence that I would like; but let me press on to the things that are before. Prayed to God that he would make me an able minister of the New Testament. My physical sensations partook of the pleasurable delirium of an incipient fever, but I trust that my confidence is building upon

God in Christ, and that my dependence is upon the spirit, as the revealed instrument by which I am made to apply the remedy, and to go on in the sanctification of the gospel. Let me not be highminded, but fear. Let him that thinketh he standeth take heed lest he fall. At two o'clock I went out and visited people in the village. Returned, and offered my intercessions for parish, friends, enemies, relations, and the church of Christ; and I pray that God would not suffer me to be deluded by the formality of an external service; but, oh, settle in my heart the faith of Christ working by love. O God, give me to rejoice in thee, and lift my affections from earth to heaven. May thy law be my delight, and may I never shrink from the cross of discipline and duty. Purify my heart, and may the following passages be my direction and my joy: Phil. iv, 6 ; Luke vi, 35."

On the 14th of April, a meeting of clergymen to the number of forty was held at Kirkaldy for the purpose of instituting a Fifeshire Bible Society. Here Mr. Chalmers's views on that subject were first published beyond the bounds of his own neighborhood, and met with general approbation. Measures were taken to promote the formation of associations in all the parishes, on the plan of penny-a-week subscriptions; and the readiness with which they were responded to by the people was most encouraging to the projectors.

On the last Sabbath of April, he preached in Dundee, and in the early part of May visited Aberdeen and vicinity, returning about the middle of the month. The attention which his preaching was now attracting, both at home and abroad, constituted a subject of deep concern to himself lest it might beget in him a feeling of self importance. In his journals we find frequently such entries as these : " My frequent cogitations about the Dundee exhibition argue, I am afraid, a devotion to the praise of men. Force me wholly into Thyself, O God." " *Sunday, May* 3.—Is it right to fatigue myself thus, or to soar so selfishly and ostentatiously above the capacities of my people ? O God, may I make a principle of this, and preach not myself but Christ Jesus my Lord." The same point is also brought forward in the following record of another of his days with God.

"Invocation for God's blessing and direction upon the exercise. Feel the force of God's entreaty and his command to believe in Christ, and am elevated by a joyful confidence. Read the promises to prayer, and prayed for acceptance through Christ and general sanctification. Not rapturously near, but feel serene and confident. Prayed for knowledge, for the understanding and impression and remembrance of God's word; for growth in grace, for personal holiness, for that sanctification which the redeemed undergo. Thought of the sins that most easily beset me; confessed them and prayed for correction and deliverance. They are anxiety about worldly matters, when any suspicion or uncertainty attaches to them; a disposition to brood over provocations; impatience at the irksome peculiarities of others; an industriousness, from a mere principle of animal activity, without the glory of God and the service of mankind lying at the bottom of it; and, above all, a taste and an appetite for human applause. My conscience smote me on the subject of pulpit exhibitions. I pray that God may make usefulness the grand principle of my appearances there. Read the promises annexed to faithful ministers; and prayed for zeal and diligence, and ability in the discharge of my ministerial office. Prayed for the people; individually for some, and generally for all descriptions of them. Prayed for friends individually and relations. Read the promises relative to the progress of the gospel, and conversion of the Jews. Prayed for those objects. Through the whole of this exercise felt calm, and I hope, confident. I have not felt much rapture, nor have I that near sense of the presence and glory of God which I aspire after. Let my maxim be, 'Faint, yet pursuing,' and let me look up in Christ for all those spiritual blessings which can only be enjoyed in perfection on the other side of time, and of the grave. Concluded the whole with a prayer for God's blessing upon the exercise."

It had formerly been his custom to do much of his preparation for the pulpit on the Sabbath morning. One of the marks of his spiritual growth, was the recognition of the propriety of having that work so completed, that the whole Lord's day could be given to devotion.

His plans of independent housekeeping, of which his friends were not quite so sanguine as himself, came to an end in the course of this summer, in an event, which, for many other and higher reasons, is to be set down as one of the most important contributions to his usefulness. On the 4th of August, he was married to Miss Grace Pratt, the second daughter of Captain Pratt, of the 1st Royal Veteran Battalion, who had been residing for some time with her uncle at Starbank, in the parish of Kilmany. As the situations he was afterward called upon to occupy, were very different from that of a country minister, " he always recognized it as Heaven's greatest providential gift, that he was united to one whose presence graced the society in which he moved, upon whose judgment, in the details of life, he placed implicit confidence, and whose wisely compliant and affectionate disposition made his home one, from which he always went out revived and re-invigorated, and to which he always returned to find peaceful and pleasurable repose after toil, or soothing sympathy amid trials."

The succeeding months of the year were spent in the faithful discharge of his professional duties, in systematic study, and in the enjoyment of domestic happiness; a visit to Dr. Brewster at Edinburgh, to his friends in Anstruther, and to his sister's relations, the Mortons at Flisk, and to Dundee, where he preached the annual Missionary sermon, diversifying the regularity of his occupations.

That missionary sermon, the first delivered upon any public occasion after his conversion, was preached on the 26th of October, 1812. The collection then taken up, was, in accordance with his own previous design, appropriated to repairing the loss which the Serampore missionaries had recently met, in the destruction of their printing office by fire. At the request of the Society, the sermon was published at Dundee, in January, 1813. "Its sale was so rapid that a month or two afterward it was republished by Mr. Whyte of Edinburgh; and before the end of the following year, four editions of it had been circulated. This, with another sermon, and a review of Foster's 'Essays,' which appeared in the May number of the 'Christian Instructor,' comprised all that he published during 1813, a year almost exclusively dedicated to his private and parochial duties."

In his journal of this year the topics of most frequent occurrence, are his own growth in grace, his duties to the world as a minister of Christ, and frequent prayers to be delivered from the sins of an impetuous temperament, and the love of human approbation. His own summaries, drawn up at the end of each year of his journal, constitute valuable contributions to his biography: that for the year closing on the 16th of March, 1813, is as follows:

"On the review of last year, I look back upon a life checkered with frailty and sin, but I trust, aspiring after righteousness, and feeling restless and uneasy under relapses. If in anything I have made sensible improvement, it is in feeling the more immediate connection which subsists between the practical virtues and the faith of Christ, leading me to cultivate union with Him, and dependence upon that spirit which is at his giving. O my God, give me to redeem the time given me to make an entire business of my sanctification; and in all the duties of the redeemed Christian may I abound more and more. But, above all, establish me thoroughly on Christ, that I may believe on Him to the saving of my soul, that I may be grafted in Him as my vine, that I may rest on Him as my foundation, that I may partake in Him as my righteousness. Believing, may I love; loving, may I obey.

"In addition to my ordinary supplies for the pulpit, wrote a speech for the Bible Society, since published; a sermon on Gal. iii, 23; do. on John iv, 10; do. on Rom., x, 17, since published; do. on 2 Tim., i., 10; do. on 2 Thess. iii., 1; a review of Foster's 'Essays;' and a speech on the Catholic question; in all, about eighteen sheets."

In August of this year, the Rev. Andrew Fuller made a visit to the north, during which he formed the acquaintance of Mr. Chalmers, and spent a short time in his house. The great powers and deepening piety of his entertainer, were quickly discerned by that large minded man; and upon leaving Kilmany, he expressed himself strongly of his expectations in regard to both. His friendly opinions seem to have been frankly offered and most kindly received ; and there were few whose opinions were so highly esteemed by Mr. Chalmers. In one respect, however, the attempt to follow his advice, was made without success. "Under the very strong conviction that his use of manuscript in the pulpit impaired the power of his Sabbath addresses, Mr. Fuller strenuously urged upon his friend the practice of extempore preaching, or preaching from notes. 'If that man,' said he to his companion, Mr. Anderson, after they had taken leave of Kilmany manse, 'if that man would but throw away his papers in the pulpit, he might be king of Scotland.' Mr. Chalmers was perfectly willing to make the experiment, and he gave full time and all diligence to the attempt; but it failed. He read, reflected, jotted down the outlines of a discourse, and then went to the pulpit, trusting to suggestion of the moment for the phraseology he should employ ; but he found that the ampler his materials were, the more difficult was the utterance. His experience in this respect, he used to compare to the familiar phenomenon of a bottle with water in it, turned suddenly upside down : the nearly empty bottle discharges itself fluently, and at once ; the nearly full one, labors in the effort, and lets out its contents with jerks, and large explosions, and suddenly stops, as if choked by its own fullness. So it was with Mr. Chalmers in his first efforts at extempore preaching. A twofold impediment lay in the way of his success. It was not easy to light at once upon words or phrases which could give anything like adequate conveyance to convictions so intense as his were ; and he could not be satisfied, and with no comfort could he proceed, while an interval so wide remained between the truth as it was felt, and the truth as his words had represented it. Over and over again was the effort made to find powerful enough and expressive enough phraseology. But even had this difficulty not existed — even though he had been content with the first suggested words, he never could be satisfied till he had exhausted every possible way of setting forth the truth, so as to force or win for it an entrance into the minds of his hearers. So very eager was he at this period of his ministry, to communicate the impressions which glowed so fervidly within his own heart, that even when he had written a sermon to deliver, he often, as if dissatisfied with all that he had said, would try at the close to put the matter in simpler words, or present it in other lights, or urge it in more direct and affectionate address. But when the restraints of a written composition were thrown away, when not at the close only, but from the very beginning of his address, this powerful impulse operated, he often found that instead of getting over the ground marked down in his study to be traversed, the whole allotted time was consumed while he was laboring away with the first or second preliminary idea. After a succession of efforts, the attempt at extempore preaching was relinquished; but he carried into the study that insatiable desire to effect a secure and effective lodgment of the truth in the minds of others, which had so much to do with the origin of all that amplification and reiteration with which his writings abound. In preparing for the pulpit, he scarcely ever sat down to write without the idea of other minds, whom it was his object to impress, being either more distinctly or more latently present to his thoughts; and he seldom rose from writing without the feeling that still other modes of influential representation remained untried."

CHAPTER V

During the succeeding years of Mr. Chalmers's residence at Kilmany, the one grand, all-pervading thought of salvation trough Christ Jesus runs through all the productions of his pen; imbues his correspondence, it was the only cause for which he published and spoke, and it fills the pages of his journal. Regularly recur his monthly dedications, those days of solemn renewal of his self-consecration to the service of God. And more frequently were portions of days set apart for meditation, prayer, and self-examination.

Those years were also the germinating time of all those ideas whose maturity constituted the greatness of his after life.

"The volume of the Edinburgh Encyclopedia, which contained the article 'Christianity,' was published early in 1813." Although with so general a title, the article was restricted to external evidences of Christianity. Its merits as an argument, on that point, were readily recognized; but the manner in which the author had set aside the consideration of internal evidence, created dissatisfaction among many of his warmest friends; and when, afterward, the proprietors of the Encyclopedia issued it in a separate volume, the reviews, generally favorable in other respects, united in condemnation of that feature. A volume was also published by Professor Mearns, of Aberdeen, to prove that Mr. Chalmers had made common cause with Atheism, giving rise to some farther bickerings, wherein Mr. Chalmers declined to participate. He was unwilling to barricade his mind, by means of controversial excitement, against any future accession of enlarging views. To the criticisms he never replied; but went to work more thoroughly to examine the ground of their objections; nor was it until sixteen years afterward that he gave the public any indication of the fruits which those attacks upon his treatise had assisted in maturing, and still seven years later we find him adding to the extent and value of the same work.

The treatment of miracles had been designedly omitted in the article Christianity, as belonging more properly to the head of 'Testimony,' which had also been assigned to Mr. Chalmers. An article in the Edinburgh Review, indorsing the doctrine of Hume, stimulated his endeavor to have that treatise published also; but no such zeal, co-operating with the solicitations of friends, could prevail upon him to issue anything immature on so important a point. It was not until many years afterward, that he found leisure enough to do justice to it. "And when at last, in his preparations for the Theological Chair in Edinburgh, he entered upon the investigation, the result—precious in proportion to the time taken in maturing it—was a new and triumphant answer to Hume, an original and most valuable contribution to the evidences of Christianity."

"About the time at which the article 'Christianity,' was presented in a separate form to the public, Mr. Chalmers issued his pamphlet entitled 'the Influence of Bible Societies upon the Temporal Necessities of the Poor.' When he went to reside in Hawick, a legal assessment for the relief of the poor, had for many years existed in that parish. The mode and results of its operation were to him a matter of new and most interesting investigation. After his own settlement at Kilmany, where there were no poor-rates, he instituted a comparison between the two parishes. As Hawick embraced a considerable manufacturing population, it was natural to expect that its pauperism should be relatively greater than that of a purely agricultural parish; but the rapid rate at which the amount of the assessment had increased, so much beyond the rate of increase of the population, was incapable of being accounted for by the occupations in which the people were engaged. Taking again the same number of paupers in each parish, the expenditure in Hawick greatly exceeded that in Kilmany; and yet, when the houses, the food, the clothing, the comforts of each were inspected, the condition of the latter, instead of being much worse, was found to be much better than that of the former. Further inquiry satisfied Mr. Chalmers, that where there were no poor-rates, where the parish bounty was spontaneous, consisting of the offerings at the church doors, and distributed by members of the kirk session, who knew the position and habits of those to whose wants they ministered, the sum contributed, by public charity, constituted but a small portion of those supplies by which the existing poverty was relieved ; the remaining, and larger portion, coming from relatives and neighbors. A public fund, raised not by voluntary subscription, but by legal enforcement, and which ostensibly charged itself with the full and adequate relief of all the poverty of a neighborhood, had the direct effect of cutting off that second and more copious current of supply. It was in this way that the Hawick pauper, on the whole, lost more by the operation of an assessment, than he gained by the increase of his allowance. At Kilmany, the receiving of parochial aid was felt to be almost a reproach, and it was frequently refused. But Mr. Chalmers noticed, and was much struck with the fact, that when those who, if they had remained in his parish, never would have suffered their names to appear in the poor roll, removed to Dundee, and there became claimants upon the legally-enforced liberality of the public, on their return to Kilmany, exhibited a tone of feeling and line of practice altogether changed. It was common enough for those who received aid from a kirk session administering the free alms of the people, when their circumstances improved, voluntarily to relinquish what had thus been allowed ; but such conduct was never exemplified by those who had become paupers at Dundee. Pursuing his inquiries into the condition of the poor, and into their moral feelings and habits, as affected by the way in which their wants were relieved, Mr. Chalmers was prepared, so early as the year 1808, publicly to affirm : ' It is in the power of charity to corrupt its object : it may tempt him to indolence ; it may lead him to renounce all dependence upon himself ; it may nourish the meanness and depravity of his character ; it may lead him to hate exertion, and resign, without a sigh, the dignity of independence. It could easily be proved, that if charity were carried to its utmost extent, it would unhinge the constitution of society. It would expel from the land the blessings of industry. Every man would repose on the beneficence of another; every incitement to diligence would be destroyed. The evils of poverty would multiply to such an extent as to be beyond the power of the most unbounded charity to redress them; and instead of an elysium of love and of plenty, the country would present the nauseating spectacle of sloth, and beggary, and corruption.'"

The observations of his brother-in-law, Mr. Morton, upon the working of the poor-rates in England, went to confirm him in the correctness of his views. Settling in a purely agricultural district in Somersetshire, and in a parish whose population was just four above that of Kilmany, Mr. Morton was astonished to find that the poor-rates amounted to £1260, while the poor of Kilmany were supported on from £20 to £30. " There could not have been a fairer comparison, or a more instructive contrast: nor was it very long till public and effective use was made of it."

About the same time, another mine was opened which he afterward wrought with eminent success, in the application of science to the service of religion. The above mentioned pamphlet " was still in the hands of the printer, when Mr. Chalmers was requested, by Mr. Andrew Thomson, to prepare a notice of Cuvier's recently translated work. Werner was but beginning to be known, Hutton's speculations had only recently appeared in the ' Transactions of the Royal Society of Edinburgh,' and Playfair was as yet gathering the materials for his ' Illustrations of the Huttonian Theory,' when the attention of Mr. Chalmers was first turned to the subject of geology. This infant science was imagined by theologians generally (even in the confused and conflicting babbling of its childhood), to speak in a tone decidedly infidel, and with a haste and an injustice equal to that which they charged upon their fancied adversary, they would have stifled a voice which appeared to conflict with that of the divine oracles. The merit, I believe, belongs to Mr. Chalmers of having been the first clergyman in the country, who, yielding to the evidence in favor of a much higher antiquity being assigned to the earth than had previously been conceived, suggested the manner in which such a scientific faith could be harmonized with the Mosaic narrative, and who, even in the dreaded investigations of the geologist, discerned and indicated fresh 'footprints of the Creator.'"

Another step was also taken in the service of the Missionary cause, by an article contributed to the Eclectic Review, and written in the autumn of 1814. The subject was suggested by one which had recently appeared in the "Edinburgh Review," referring the success of the Moravians, as missionaries, to the assumed fact, that they began by instructing the heathen in the art of civilization, and asserting that it is by such a method alone that "those in a certain state of ignorance and barbarism are to be gained over to the truth." "Mr. Chalmers undertook to manifest the reviewer's total ignorance of the means which had been actually pursued by the Moravians, whose labors were so applauded, and out of those very labors to construct the most convincing of all arguments against the theory which at that period, was such a favorite with the opponents of missionary efforts, namely, that you must civilize before you can christianize a barbarous community." Indeed, one of the most instructive lessons on this subject, is derived from the experience of the Moravians. For many years their "missionaries in Greenland, had labored to train the natives to habits of industry, and to instruct them in the first and simplest truths of religion, studiously withholding from them the deeper mysteries of the christian faith; but no sensible effect followed. One day, however, while one of their number was engaged in making a fair copy of a translation of one of the gospels, a crowd of natives gathered round him, curious to know the contents of the book. He read to them the history of our Saviour's sufferings and death. 'How was that?' said one of the savages, stepping up to the table at which the missionary was sitting, his voice trembling with emotion as he spoke, 'How was that?' Tell me that once more, for I, too, would fain be saved!' 'These words,' writes the missionary, 'the like of which I had never heard from any Greenlander, pierced my very soul, and affected me so much, that with tears in my eyes, I related to them the whole history of the sufferings of Christ, and the counsel of God for our salvation. The Greenlander who put the question was the first convert to the truth; and the mode of his conversion was so instructive, that ever afterward the first office of the Moravian missionaries was to proclaim the death of Jesus as the great expiation for human guilt, and only ground of the sinner's hope for eternity."

In the business of Church Courts, in which he was afterward so prominent an actor, Mr. Chalmers had hitherto taken little interest. The records of the presbytery of Cupar, of which he was a member for more than twelve years, exhibit but a solitary instance, in which his name stands connected with any presbyterial act. "But within the bounds of his own synod a question had now arisen, in which his interest was too great to suffer him to remain inactive. The junction of a professorship in a university with the charge of a country parish had been rarely known, and had frequently been disallowed in the practice of the Church of Scotland; and although the General Assembly of 1800 had decided in favor of the junction of the two offices in the instance of Dr. Arnot's settlement in Kingsbarns, the conviction gained ground that it was a union which violated the constitution of the Scottish Establishment, which had always required constant residence in their parishes on the part of all its ministers. That conviction was very unequivocally expressed when, in the year 1813, the Rev. William Ferrie, Professor of Civil History in the University of St. Andrews, was presented to the living of Kilconquhar. At first, the presbytery of St. Andrew's refused to admit him to the pastoral charge, unless he gave them the assurance, which he refused to do, that before, or at the time of his ordination, he would resign his professorship. Upon appeal to the General Assembly, held at Edinburgh, in May, 1813, by the narrow, and, at that time, unusually small majority of five, the decision of the Presbytery of St. Andrew's was reversed, and they were appointed to proceed with Mr. Ferrie's settlement as minister of Kilconquhar, 'with all convenient speed, according to the rules of the Church.' In compliance with this decision of the Supreme Court, a committee of Presbytery met at Kilconquhar for the purpose of moderating in a call, and reported to a subsequent meeting that no signatures whatever had been attached to it. At the same time, however, a letter was laid before the Presbytery, in which all the principal landholders of Kilconquhar, three out of four of the elders, and many heads of families, apologized for not having signed the call at the proper time, and expressed their concurrence in Mr. Ferrie's settlement. At this stage the matter was referred to the Synod, for the meeting of which, on the 12th October, Mr. Chalmers, made the most anxious and careful preparation. It had been his impression that the want of a call would oppose an effectual barrier against Mr. Ferrie's ordination, or that an opportunity would, at least, present itself for discussing the general question of the propriety of such pluralities. But he was disappointed. Mr. Ferrie's friends yielded the question as to the sustaining of the letter as equivalent to a call, and the Synod, appointing the Presbytery to moderate in a new call, left the decision of the General Assembly to be carried into effect. It was to Mr. Chalmers a 'day of mortification,' from which he returned home 'jaded, mortified, useless.' But, although they were obliged to yield to the decision of their supreme judiciary, upon this particular case, the opponents of such pluralities had become too numerous and too zealous throughout the church to abandon the question in despair." The question was brought "in its general form before the Assembly of 1814, and the 'day of mortification' in the Synod, more than compensated by a day of triumph in the Assembly." Mr. Chalmers took a prominent and most successful part in the debate, which terminated in declaratory enactment, "prohibiting, in future, such pluralities as had been permitted in the cases of Dr. Arnot and Mr. Ferrie. A succeeding Assembly was persuaded to cancel this enactment, on the alleged ground that it was incompetent and unconstitutional to pass such an act without the advice of the presbyteries of the Church. An overture, embodying its terms, was sent down to the presbyteries by the General Assembly of 1816; and a majority of the returns having been in its favor, it passed into a standing law of the Church of Scotland in 1817, that a chair in a university cannot be held in conjunction with a country parochial charge."

CHAPTER VI.

"Parochial duty pressed lightly upon Mr. Chalmers during the first seven years of his ministry at Kilmany. If he 'expended as much effort upon the religious improvement of his people as any minister within the bounds of his presbytery,' if he could triumphantly challenge his brethren to prove that he had been 'outstripped by any of his predecessors in the regularity of his ministerial attentions,' the standards to which he thus appealed must have been miserably low. The sick and the dying among his parishioners had not, indeed, been neglected during those earlier years. Kindly inquiries were made, tender sympathy was shown, and needful aid was tendered; but no solicitude was manifested as to their religious condition, no references occurred in visiting them to their state and prospects for eternity, and it was only when specially requested to do so that he engaged in prayer. Two or three weeks were annually devoted to a visitation of his parish, so rapidly conducted that he scarcely did more than hurriedly enter many a dwelling, to summon its inmates to a short address, given in some neighboring apartment, and confined generally to one or other of the more ordinary moralities of domestic life. With the general body of his parishioners he had little intercourse. They might meet him occasionally on the road, and receive the kindliest notice, but the smile of friendly recognition broke over a countenance of dreamy abstraction: and when the quickly-made but cordial salutation was over, and he was gone, his wondering parishioners would gaze after him as upon a man wholly addicted to very strange, and, in the eyes of many of them, very questionable pursuits. Comparatively little time or care was bestowed upon his pulpit preparations. 'I have known him,' says Mr. Smith, 'not to begin them till Sabbath morning. He told me that he wrote in short-hand, and when once he began he kept the pen going till he had finished the discourse. His sermons were in general very short,' but they were written in a fervid strain, and delivered with energetic animation. The first effect, indeed, of the great spiritual change, was to chasten rather than to stimulate the vehemence of his delivery in the pulpit. In those earlier days, whether from choice or from necessity, he frequently preached without any written notes. The obstructions afterward complained of, and felt to be invincible, do not then appear to have stood much in his way, for he never used so ardent and so significant an elocution, as in those fervid extempore expostulations upon stealing, or lying, or backbiting, explained, according to popular belief, by the circumstance, that the minister had come home late on the Saturday evening, and that the indefatigable newsmonger, John Bonthron, had been seen entering the manse shortly after his arrival. When the impulse moved, or the occasion invited, Mr. Chalmers could write as eloquently then as he ever did afterward. The two fast-day sermons of this period have been compared with that splendid discourse which the occasion of the first of them elicited from Robert Hall. Without pressing that comparison to an issue, it may be taken as a very signal proof of the native genius of their author, that two discourses written off-hand, written, in all likelihood, each at a single sitting, prepared for thin audiences of unsympathizing rustics, and thrown aside as soon as delivered, should be capable of bearing a comparison with an effort which was made, in the first instance, before a crowded and intelligent audience, and upon which all the care and skill of one of the greatest masters in the art of composition had afterward been lavished. Upon the whole, however, and till the period of his illness at Fincraigs, Mr. Chalmers's ministry was unpopular and ineffective, his church but poorly attended, and his private ministrations followed with but trifling effects. But the great change came, and with it a total alteration in the discharge of all parochial duty. From a place of visible subordination, the spiritual care and cultivation of his parish was elevated to the place of clear and recognized supremacy. To break up the peace of the indifferent and secure by exposing at once the guilt of their ungodliness, and its fearful issue in a ruined eternity; to spread out an invitation wide as heaven's own all-embracing love, to every awakened sinner to accept of eternal life in Jesus Christ; to plead with all, that instantly and heartily, with all good-will, and with full and unreserved submission, they should give themselves up in absolute and entire dedication to the Redeemer; these were the objects for which he was now seen to strive, with such a 'severity of conviction' as implied that he had *one thing to do*, and 'with such a concentration of his forces as to idle spectators looked like insanity.'

"The first use he made of that returning strength which, after so many months' confinement, enabled him to cross again the threshold of Fincraigs, was to visit all the sick, the dying, and the bereaved in his parish; and when all trace and feeling of his own infirmity had departed, he still delighted to mingle his sympathies with the weak and the sorrowful. There was, indeed, such a restless activity about his manner, such a physical incapacity for very soft or gentle movements, that the sick-room seemed an uncongenial place; yet there was such exquisite tenderness of feeling, such rapid appreciation of the condition of the patient, and such capacity in a few short and weighty sentences to minister to his spiritual sorrows or perplexity, that a brief visit from him was often sufficient to shed a flood of light upon the understanding, or to pour a full tide of comfort into the heart. Extreme delicacy of feeling and his own great reserve threw obstacles in his way, which were often very painfully felt by him. But if he could not at once overcome the barriers which lay in the way of an immediate, free, and confidential spiritual intercourse, he could speak of Him whose love to sinners had no limits, and lay under no restraints. 'No one ever preached the gospel to the dying with greater simplicity or fullness, and yet with characteristic simplicity, he would often say, 'Oh! that I could preach to the sick and dying as Mr. Tait, of Tealing, does.'" His interest in this, as in every other part of his ministerial labors, grew with his own advancing light and love. During the years 1813, 1814, the only two years of full ministerial labor at Kilmany, he made a few short hand memoranda, entitled, 'Records of spiritual intercourse with my people,' from which our limits permit us to make only one or two extracts:

"*February 21st.*—Visited at Dalyell Lodge. They are in great affliction for the death of a child. I prayed with them. O God, make me wise and faithful, and withal affectionate in my management of these cases. I fear that something of the sternness of systematic orthodoxy adheres to me. Let me give up all sternness; but let me never give up the only name by which men can be saved, or the necessity of forsaking all to follow Him, whether as a Saviour or a Prince.

"*June 2d.*—Mr. ―――― sent for me in prospect of death; a man of profligate and profane habits, who resents my calling him an unworthy sinner, and who spoke in loud and confident strains of his faith in Christ, and that it would save him. O God, give me wisdom in these matters to declare the whole of thy counsel for the salvation of men. I represented to him the necessity of being born again, of being humbled under a sense of his sins, of repenting and turning from them. O may I turn it to my own case. If faith in Christ is so unsuitable from his mouth because he still loves sin, and is unhumbled because of it, should not the conviction be forced upon me that I labor myself under the same unsuitableness? O my God, give me a walk suitable to my profession, and may the power of Christ rest upon me.

"*August 9th.*—Miss ―――― under religious concern. O my God, send her help from Thy sanctuary. Give me wisdom for these cases. Let me not heal the wound slightly; and, oh, while I administer comfort in Christ, may it be a comfort according to godliness. She complains of the prevalence of sin. Let me not abate her sense of its sinfulness. Let me preach Christ in all his entireness as one that came to atone for the guilt of sin, and to redeem from its power.

"Prosecuting his earlier practice of visiting and examining

in alternate years, he commenced a visitation of his parish in 1813, which, instead of being finished in a fortnight, was spread over a whole year. As many families as could conveniently be assembled in one apartment were in the first instance visited in their own dwellings, where, without any religious exercise, a free and cordial conversation, longer or shorter as the case required, informed him as to the condition of the different households. When they afterward met together, he read the Scriptures, prayed, and exhorted, making at times the most familiar remarks, using very simple yet memorable illustrations. 'I have a very lively recollection,' says Mr. Robert Edie, ' of the intense earnestness of his addresses on occasions of visitation in my father's house, when he would unconsciously move forward on his chair to the very margin of it, in his anxiety to impart to the family and servants the impression of eternal things that so filled his own soul.' ' It would take a great book,' said he, beginning his address to one of these household congregations, ' to contain the names of all the individuals that have ever lived, from the days of Adam down to the present hour, but there is one name that takes in the whole of them—that name is *sinner*, and here is a message from God to every one that bears that name, 'The blood of Jesus Christ, His Son, cleanseth us from all sin.' '' Wishing to tell them what kind of faith God would have them to cherish, and what kind of fear, and how it was that instead of hindering each other, the right fear and the right faith worked into each other's hands, he said, 'It is just as if you threw out a rope to a drowning man. Faith is the hold he takes of it. It is fear which makes him grasp it with all his might, and the greater his fear, the firmer his hold.' Again, to illustrate what the Spirit did with the Word : ' This book, the Bible, is like a wide and beautiful landscape, seen afar off, dim and confused ; but a good telescope will bring it near, and spread out all its rocks, and trees, and flowers, and verdant fields, and winding rivers at one's very feet. That telescope is the Spirit's teaching.'

" In the autumn of 1813, Mr. Chalmers opened a class in

his own house upon the Saturdays, for the religious instruction of the young. At first he intended that it should meet monthly: the numbers, however, who presented themselves for instruction, and the ardor with which they entered upon the tasks prescribed, induced a change of purpose. After the first meeting or two, he announced his intention to hold the class each fortnight, and erelong it met weekly at the manse. He drew out a series of simple propositions, which embraced a full system of Christian doctrine; appending to each a reference to those passages of the Bible in which the truth declared in the proposition was most clearly or fully revealed. These propositions, with their proofs, were printed at Dundee; and the little volume which they formed has already been circulated in thousands among those who have interested themselves in the religious education of the young. Beside his exercises upon Scripture doctrine, Mr. Chalmers read and explained portions of the Bible, and prescribed select passages for committal to memory. He was highly gratified by the whole youth of the parish, even from its remoter districts, coming forward with such willingness; and he repaid their readiness to receive instruction by making diligent preparation for communicating to them the knowledge of the truth, and fixing religious impressions on their hearts. In no department of his ministerial labors did he take a deeper interest, and upon none, in proportion to the space which it covered, did he bestow more pains. It was only during a year and half that the class continued, and yet three years after his removal from Kilmany he could say: 'I met with a more satisfying evidence of good done by a school which I taught when at Kilmany, than by all I ever did there beside. A good encouragement this for the efforts of private Christians in this way.'

Of the change in the manner of his pulpit preparations no person is entitled to speak with so much authority as his son-in-law, Dr. Hanna, as having access to all the manuscripts and acquaintance with many of the eye and ear-witnesses of those earlier efforts. I shall, therefore, permit the narrative of that time to continue in his words.

"Much, however, as may have been accomplished by the class, the pulpit was, after all, the chief instrument of power; and from the time when profound religious convictions penetrated his spirit, Mr. Chalmers labored to wield that instrument with effect. There must have been something particularly pathetic in his Sabbath ministrations during the summer months of 1810. The muffled invalid, who had been seen to make his first round of visits to all the houses of mourning in the parish, and of whose altered bearing and impressive prayers village rumor had already begun to speak, appeared once more in the pulpit. His sunk and sallow countenance told of the ravages of disease. He looked like one who had drawn very near to death, and whom a few steps backward would carry again to the very edge of the grave; and his most frequent topic was human mortality, the shortness of time, the nearness and awfulness of eternity. 'Where are the men,' he asked, his own voice sounding over the congregation like an echo from the tomb, 'who a few years ago gave motion and activity to this busy theater? where those husbandmen who lived on the ground that you now occupy? where those laboring poor who dwelt in your houses and villages? where those ministers who preached the lessons of piety, and talked of the vanity of this world? where those people who, on the Sabbaths of other times, assembled at the sound of the church-bell, and filled the house in which you are now sitting? Their habitation is the cold grave, the land of forgetfulness. . . . . . And we are the children of these fathers, and heirs to the same awful and stupendous destiny. Ours is one of the many generations who pass in rapid succession through this region of life and of sensibility. The time in which I live is but a small moment of this world's history. When we rise in contemplation to the roll of ages that are past, the momentary being of an individual shrinks into nothing. It is the flight of a shadow; it is a dream of vanity; it is the rapid glance of a meteor; it is a flower which every breath of heaven can wither into decay; it is a tale which as a remembrance vanisheth; it is a day which the silence of a long night will darken

turned into a fixed, intelligent, and devout attention. It was not easy for the dullest to remain uninformed; for, if the preacher sometimes soared too high for the best trained of his people to follow him, at other times, and much oftener, he put the matter of his message so as to force for it an entrance into the most sluggish understanding. Nor was it easy for the most indifferent to remain unmoved, as the first fervors of a new-born faith and love found such thrilling strains in which to vent themselves. The church became crowded. The feeling grew with the numbers who shared in it. The fame of those wonderful discourses which were now emanating from the burning lips of this new evangelist, spread throughout the neighborhood, till, at last, there was not an adjacent parish which did not send its weekly contribution to his ministry. Persons from extreme distances in the county, found themselves side by side in the same crowded pew. Looking over the congregation, the inhabitant of Dundee could generally count a dozen or two of his fellow-townsmen around him, while ministers from Edinburgh or Glasgow were occasionally detected among the crowd.

" All this told distinctly enough of the popularity of the preacher; but within the parish, and as the effect of such a ministry as has now been described, what were the spiritual results? Too delicate a question this for any full or satisfactory reply; but of one Sabbath's service we shall tell the fruits. It was in the spring of 1812, and the preacher's text was John, iii, 16: ' God so loved the world that he gave his only begotten Son, that whosoever believeth in Him should not perish, but have everlasting life.' Two young men heard this sermon, the one the son of a farmer in the parish, the other the son of one of the villagers. They met as the congregation dispersed. ' Did you feel anything particularly in church to-day?' Alexander Patterson said to his acquaintance, Robert Edie, as they found themselves alone on the road. ' I never,' he continued, 'felt myself to be a lost sinner till to-day, when I was listening to that sermon.' ' It is very strange,' said his companion; ' it was just the same with me.' They were near a plantation, into which they wandered, as the conversation proceeded. Hidden at last from all human sight, it was proposed that they should join in prayer. Screened by the opening foliage, they knelt on the fresh green sod, and poured out, in turn, their earnest petitions to the hearer and answerer of prayer. Both dated their conversion from that day. Alexander Patterson went shortly afterward to reside in the neighboring parish of Dairsie, but attended regularly on the Sabbath at Kilmany church. His friend, Robert Edie, generally conveyed him part of the way home. About one hundred yards from the road along which they traveled, in the thickly-screened seclusion of a close plantation, and under the shade of a branching fir-tree, the two friends found a quiet retreat, where, each returning Sabbath evening, the eye that seeth in secret, looked down upon these two youthful disciples of the Saviour on their knees, and for an hour their ardent prayers alternately ascended to the throne of grace. The practice was continued for years, till a private footpath of their own had been opened to the trysting-tree; and when, a few years ago, after long absence on the part of both, they met at Kilmany, at Mr. Edie's suggestion, they revisited the spot, and, renewing the sacred exercise, offered up their joint thanksgivings to that God who had kept them by his grace, and in their separate spheres had honored each of them with usefulness in the church. Mr. Patterson has now labored for twenty-two years as a missionary in the Canongate of Edinburgh, not without many pleasing evidences that his labors have been blessed; and I have reason to believe that by his efforts in behalf of Bible and Missionary Societies, through means of Sabbath Schools and prayer meetings, and by the light of a guiding and consistent example, Mr. Edie's life, while one of active industry, has also been one of devoted christian usefulness.

Other individual instances of spiritual benefit derived from Mr. Chalmers's ministrations, it would have been a pleasant task to record; and had he not been so soon removed from Kilmany, the hopeful appearances which were presenting themselves, especially among the young who attended his Saturday classes, might have ripened into a goodly spiritual fruitage. One general testimony, however, as valuable, perhaps, as ever minister left behind him, and given by Mr. Chalmers himself, as to the separate effects of his ministry during the two periods into which, spiritually contemplated, it divided itself, must not be withheld.

"And here, I cannot but record the effect of an actual, though undesigned experiment, which I prosecuted for upward of twelve years among you. For the greater part of that time, I could expatiate on the meanness of dishonesty, on the villainy of falsehood, on the despicable arts of calumny; in a word, upon all those deformities of character which awaken the natural indignation of the human heart against the pests and the disturbers of human society. Now, could I, upon the strength of these warm expostulations, have got the thief to give up his stealing, and the evil speaker his censoriousness, and the liar his deviations from truth, I should have felt all the repose of one who had gotten his ultimate object. It never occurred to me that all this might have been done, and yet the soul of every hearer have remained in full alienation from God; and that even could I have established in the bosom of one who stole, such a principle of abhorrence at the meanness of dishonesty, that he was prevailed upon to steal no more, he might still have retained a heart as completely unturned to God, and as totally unpossessed by a principle of love to him as before. In a word, though I might have made him a more upright and honorable man, I might have left him as destitute of the essence of religious principle as ever. But the interesting fact is, that during the whole of that period, in which I made no attempt against the natural enmity of the mind to God, while I was inattentive to the way in which this enmity is dissolved, even by the free offer on the one hand, and the believing acceptance on the other, of the gospel salvation, while Christ, through whose blood the sinner, who by nature stands afar off, is brought near to the heavenly Lawgiver whom he has offended, was scarcely ever spoken of, or spoken of in such a way as stripped Him of all the importance of his character and his offices, even at this time I certainly did press the reformations of honor, and truth, and integrity among my people; but I never once heard of any such reformations having been effected among them. If there was anything at all brought about in this way, it was more than ever I got any account of. I am not sensible that all the vehemence with which I urged the virtues and the proprieties of social life, had the weight of a feather on the moral habits of my parishioners. And it was not till I got impressed by the utter alienation of the heart in all its desires and affections from God; it was not till reconciliation to Him became the distinct and the prominent object of my ministerial exertions; it was not till I took the scriptural way of laying the method of reconciliation before them; it was not till the free offer of forgiveness through the blood of Christ was urged upon their acceptance, and the Holy Spirit given through the channel of Christ's mediatorship to all who ask Him, was set before them as the unceasing object of their dependence and their prayers; in one word, it was not till the contemplations of my people were turned to these great and essential elements in the business of a soul providing for its interests with God and the concerns of its eternity, that I ever heard of any of those subordinate reformations which I aforetime made the earnest and the zealous, but I am afraid at the same time, the ultimate object of my earlier ministrations. Ye servants, whose scrupulous fidelity has now attracted the notice, and drawn forth in my hearing a delightful testimony from your masters, what mischief you would have done had your zeal for doctrines and sacraments been accompanied by the sloth and the remissness, and what, in the prevailing tone of moral relaxation, is accounted the allowable purloining of your earlier days! But a sense of your Heavenly Master's eye has brought another influence to bear upon you; and while you are thus striving to adorn the doctrine of God your Saviour in all things, you may, poor as you are, reclaim the great ones of the land to the acknowledgment of the faith. You have at least taught me, that to preach Christ is the only effective way of preaching morality in all its branches; and out of your humble cottages have I gathered a lesson, which I pray God I may be enabled to carry, with all its simplicity, into a wider theater, and to bring with all the power of its subduing efficacy upon the vices of a more crowded population.'"

In the midst of these labors, one day, while he was preaching at Bendochy, in Perthshire, the funeral sermon of a much valued friend, the pastor of that parish, a group of auditors attended as members of the town council of Glasgow to hear him, as one who had been named among them for the Tron Church of that city, then vacant. Unawares to the preacher, he was made the subject of a criticism destined to have no little influence upon many of the best years of his life. Such was the crowd that it was found expedient, as the day was calm and beautiful, to take out one of the windows and erect a platform against the sill, from which the preacher could be heard by the congregation without, as well as within the building. The scene is thus described on the authority of one who was an eye-witness of it. "A hum in the crowd, and a melancholy tolling of the bell, announced the approach of the preacher, who seated himself for a minute or two in an old elbow-chair, took the psalm-book from a little table before him, turned hastily over a few of the leaves, and then rose in the most awkward and even helpless manner. Before he read the lines which were to be sung, his large and apparently leaden eyes were turned toward the recent grave, with a look wildly pathetic, fraught with intense and indescribable passion. The psalm was read with no very promising elocution; and while the whole mass of the people were singing it, he sunk into the chair, turned seemingly into a monumental statue of the coldest stone, so deadly pale was his large broad face and forehead. The text was read: Deut., xxxii, 29, 'O that they were wise; that they understood this; that they would consider their latter end!' The doctrinal truth which he meant to inculcate being established on a basis of reasoning so firm that doubt could not move or sophistry shake it, he bounded at once upon the structure which he had reared; and by that inborn and unteachable power of the spirit, which nature has reserved for the chosen of her sons, and which shakes off all the disadvantages and incumbrances of figure, and voice, and language as easily as the steed shakes the thistle-down from his side, carried the hearts and passions of all who heard him with irresistible and even tremendous sway. 'It strikes me,' said the preacher, and as the words were spoken there was a silence among the living almost as deep as that which reigned among the dead who lay beneath, 'It strikes me as the most impressive of all sentiments, that it will be all the same a hundred years after this. It is often uttered in the form of a proverb, and with the levity of a mind that is not aware of its importance. A hundred years after this! Good heavens! with what speed and with what certainty will those hundred years come to their termination. This day will draw to a close, and a number of days make up one revolution of the seasons. Year follows year, and a number of years makes up a century. These little intervals of time accumulate and fill up that mighty space which appears to the fancy so big and so immeasurable. The hundred years will come, and they will see out the wreck of whole generations. Every living thing that now moves on the face of the earth will disappear from it. The infant that now hangs on his mother's bosom will only live in the remembrance of his grandchildren. The scene of life and of intelligence that is now before me will be changed into the dark and loathsome forms of corruption. The people who now hear me will cease to be spoken of; their memory will perish from the face of the country; their flesh will be devoured with worms; the dark and creeping things that live in the holes of the earth will feed upon their bodies; their coffins will have mouldered away, and their bones be thrown up in the new-made grave; and is this the consummation of all things? Is this the final end and issue of man? Is this the upshot of his busy history? Is there nothing beyond time and the grave to alleviate the gloomy picture, to chase away these dismal images? Must we sleep forever in the dust, and bid an eternal adieu to the light of heaven?'

"'I have seen,' adds our informant, 'many scenes, and I have heard many eloquent men, but this I have never seen equaled, or even imitated. It was not learning, it was not art; it was the untaught and the unencumbered incantation of genius, the mightiest engine of which the world can boast.'"

After various unobserved observations and representations, by word and letter, on the subject, in the course of which it was suggested to him to visit the city and give the council a chance to judge of his abilities, which of course, he decisively declined to do, Mr. Chalmers was elected minister of the Tron Church of Glasgow on the 25th of November, 1814.

The chief obstacles which presented themselves to his removal, were his fears as to the amount of unprofessional labor exacted of the clergymen of Glasgow, and his tender attachment to the neighborhood and people of Kilmany. The former, long courageous effort removed; the latter, never entirely passed away. "Looking to the hills which bounded his peaceful valley, and waving his staff to them as if in mournful farewell, he said to a friend, who was walking by his side, 'Ah, my dear sir, my heart is wedded to these hills.' Coming back to his old parish, more than twenty years after he had left it, he exclaimed, 'Oh, there was more tearing of the heart-strings at leaving the valley of Kilmany than at leaving all my great parish at Glasgow.'"

On the 10th of December he intimated his acceptance of the appointment; but did not remove to Glasgow until July of the following year.

"For some Sabbaths previous to the departure from Kilmany, the attendance at church was so numerous, that one of the large windows beside the pulpit was taken out, that Mr. Chalmers might address at once the in-door and out-door congregation. The great crowd of strangers which had assembled deprived, to some extent, his closing Sabbath (July 9, 1815) of the character which he would have liked it so much to wear, a parting of affectionate friends. There were few, even among the strangers, who did not share in the of the occasion, and the hearts of his own people were dissolved in tenderness, as these farewell words fell upon their ear:

"'Choose Christ, then, my brethren, choose Him as the Captain of your salvation. Let Him enter into your hearts by faith, and let Him dwell continually there. Cultivate a daily intercourse and a growing acquaintance with Him. Oh, you are in safe company, indeed, when your fellowship is with Him! The shield of His protecting mediatorship is ever between you and the justice of God; and out of His fullness there goeth a constant stream, to nourish, and to animate, and to strengthen every believer. Why should the shifting of human instruments so oppress and so discourage you, when He is your willing friend; when He is ever present, and is at all times in readiness; when He, the same yesterday, to-day, and forever, is to be met with in every place; and while His disciples here, giving way to the power of sight, are sorrowful, and in great heaviness, because they are to move at a distance from one another, He, my brethren, He has His eye upon all neighborhoods and all countries, and will at length gather His disciples into one eternal family! With such a Master, let us quit ourselves like men. With the magnificence of eternity before us, let time, with all its fluctuations, dwindle into its own littleness. If God is pleased to spare me, I trust I shall often meet with you in person, even on this side of the grave; but if not, let us often meet in prayer at the mercy-seat of God. While we occupy different places on earth, let our mutual intercessions for each other go to one place in Heaven. Let the Saviour put our supplications into one censer; and be assured, my brethren, that after the dear and the much-loved scenery of this peaceful vale has disappeared from my eye, the people who live in it shall retain a warm and ever-during place in my memory; and this mortal body must be stretched on the bed of death, ere the heart which now animates it can resign its exercise of longing after you, and praying for you.

that you may so receive Christ Jesus, and so walk in Him, and so hold fast the things you have gotten, and so prove that the labor I have had among you has not been in vain, that when the sound of the last trumpet awakens us, these eyes, which are now bathed in tears, may open upon a scene of eternal blessedness, and we, my brethren, whom the Providence of God has withdrawn for a little while from one another, may on that day be found side by side at the right hand of the everlasting throne.'"

CHAPTER VII.

On the 13th of July, 1815, Mr. Chalmers finally left Kilmany, and on the 21st of the same month was regularly admitted to his new charge. His first sermon in Glasgow had been preached some months previously before the society of the sons of the Clergy, on Thursday, the 30th day of March. Among the vast crowd, which had congregated on the occasion, a young student from Oxford was present, whose graphic pen, at a somewhat later time, delineating various prominent characters of Scotland, drew the following picture of the preacher:

"I was a good deal surprised and perplexed with the first glimpse I obtained of his countenance, for the light, that streamed faintly upon it for the moment, did not reveal anything like that general outline of feature and visage for which my fancy had, by some strange working of presentiment, prepared me. By-and-by, however, the light became stronger, and I was enabled to study the minutiæ of his face pretty leisurely, while he leaned forward and read aloud the words of the Psalm, for that is always done in Scotland, not by the clerk, but the clergyman himself. At first sight, no doubt, his face is a coarse one, but a mysterious kind of meaning breathes from every part of it, that such as have eyes to see, cannot be long without discovering. It is very pale, and the large, half-closed eyelids have a certain drooping melancholy weight about them, which interested me very much, I understood not why. The lips, too, are singularly pensive in their mode of falling down at the sides, although there is no want of richness and vigor in their central fullness of curve. The upper lip, from the nose downward, is separated by a very deep line, which gives a sort of leonine firmness of expression to all the lower part of the face. The cheeks are square and strong, in texture like pieces of marble, with the cheek-bones very broad and prominent. The eyes themselves are light in color, and have a strange, dreamy heaviness, that conveys any idea rather than that of dullness, but which contrasts in a wonderful manner with the dazzling, watery glare they exhibit when expanded in their sockets, and illuminated into all their flame and fervor in some moment of high entranced enthusiasm. But the shape of the forehead, is, perhaps, the most singular part of the whole visage; and, indeed, it presents a mixture so very singular, of forms commonly exhibited only in the widest separation, that it is no wonder I should have required some little time to comprehend the meaning of it. In the first place, it is, without exception, the most marked mathematical forehead I ever met with — being far wider across the eyebrows than either Mr. Playfair's or Mr. Leslie's — and having the eyebrows themselves lifted up at their exterior ends quite out of the usual line, a peculiarity which Spurzheim had remarked in the countenances of almost all the great mathematical or calculating geniuses—such, for example, if I rightly remember, as Sir Isaac Newton himself, Kaestener, Euler, and many others. Immediately above the extraordinary breadth of this region, which, in the heads of most mathematical persons, is surmounted by no fine points of organization whatever, immediately above this, in the forehead, there is an arch of imagination, carrying out the summit boldly and roundly, in a style to which the heads of very few poets present anything comparable, while over this again, there is a grand apex of high and solemn veneration and love, such as might have graced the bust of Plato himself, and such as in living men I have never beheld equaled in any but the majestic head of Canova. The whole is edged with a few crisp dark locks, which stand forth boldly, and afford a fine relief to the deathlike paleness of those massive temples........ Of all human compositions there is none surely which loses so much as a sermon does when it is made to address itself to the eye of a solitary student in his closet, and not to the thrilling ears of a mighty mingled congregation, through the very voice which nature has enriched with notes more expressive than words can ever be of the meanings and feelings of its author. Neither, perhaps, did the world ever possess any orator whose minutest peculiarities of gesture and voice have more power in increasing the effect of what he says — whose delivery, in other words, is the first, and the second, and the third excellence of his oratory — more truly than is that of Dr. Chalmers. And yet were the spirit of the man less gifted than it is, there is no question these, his lesser peculiarities, would never have been numbered among his points of excellence. His voice is neither strong nor melodious, his gestures are neither easy nor graceful; but, on the contrary, extremely rude and awkward; his pronunciation is not only broadly national, but broadly provincial, distorting almost every word he utters into some barbarous novelty, which, had his hearer leisure to think of such things, might be productive of an effect at once ludicrous and offensive in a singular degree. But, of a truth, these are things which no listener can attend to while this great preacher stands before him, armed with all the weapons of the most commanding eloquence, and swaying all around him with its imperial rule. At first, indeed, there is nothing to make one suspect what riches are in store. He commences in a low, drawling key, which has not even the merit of being solemn, and advances from sentence to sentence, and from paragraph to paragraph, while you seek in vain to catch a single echo that gives promise of that which is to come. There is, on the contrary, an appearance of constraint about him that affects and distresses you. You are afraid that his breast is weak, and that even the slight exertion he makes may be too much for it. But then, with what tenfold richness does this dim preliminary curtain make the glories of his eloquence to shine forth, when the heated spirit at length shakes from it its chill confining fetters, and bursts out elate and rejoicing in the full splendor of its disimprisoned wings. .... I have heard many men deliver sermons far better arranged in regard to argument, and have heard very many deliver sermons far more uniform in elegance both of conception and of style ; but, most unquestionably, I have never heard, either in England or Scotland, or in any other country, any preacher whose eloquence is capable of producing an effect so strong and irresistible as his.

"Mr. Chalmers's first sermon at Glasgow was chiefly occupied with the enforcement and illustration of principles applicable alike to all forms and varieties of christian charity. It contained, in embryo, his whole theory as to the proper treatment of pauperism, and is remarkable thus as indicating how firmly established in his mind that theory had become, even before his labors as a city clergyman had commenced."

Leaving his family for the summer in Anstruther, he entered upon his residence in Glasgow as a solitary lodger, and that among new scenes, strange faces, and a field of labor whose bounds he had yet to ascertain, and which, for the present, seemed to be boundless, occasioned him no very pleasant first impressions of the city. But the state of his spirits was not permitted to interfere with the discharge of his duty, which he entered upon with the utmost zeal and singleness of purpose to the glory of God. Week after week sustained and heightened the effect of his first appearance, and he soon won the hearts as well as the admiration of his people.

On the 16th of September, having removed his family to Glasgow, the solitary lodgings were exchanged for the fireside of home. But his warmly affectionate nature had not so long mingled with his new congregation without finding objects of its attachment. Ere the first month of his residence in Glasgow had gone by, he had become attached to one young man "by ties of such peculiar strength and tenderness, as threw over their brief earthly intercourse all the air of a spiritual romance. Mr. Thomas Smith, the son of a well known Glasgow publisher, was qualifying himself for the profession of a writer or attorney. His family having interested themselves in Mr. Chalmers's appointment, he was early introduced to the notice of his new minister, and occasionally invited to accompany him in his daily walk or ride. His intellectual accomplishments, his refined taste, his gentle bearing, his pure and aspiring aims, soon won Mr. Chalmers's heart. But what gave him a still stronger hold upon that heart than any personal endowment, was his being, so far as was known to Mr. Chalmers, the first-fruits spiritually of his ministry in Glasgow. As if all those affections, which, wrenched from their old objects, were in search of new ones, had suddenly concentrated on him, he became the object of an attachment which, in the brief entries of a private journal, now reduced to the ordinary measure of a single line for each succeeding day, vents itself in such expressions as the following: ' Called on Mr. Thomas Smith ; O God, purify, and christianize, and give salutary effect to my regard for him.' ' Had long walks and conversations with T. S. O my God, save me from all that is idolatrous in my regard for him !' The occasional soon turned into daily intercourse, a trysting-place being appointed on the banks of the Monkland Canal, where each day, at a set hour, they met. And the general conversation of ordinary friendship soon flowed in that new channel into which it was directed by a heart yearning for the spiritual and eternal welfare of its object. Erelong, close and affectionate as it was, the outdoor intercourse was not enough. There were meetings beside, for reading the Holy Scriptures and for prayer ; and great as were the efforts and fatigues of the Tron Church pulpit, an hour each Sabbath evening was set apart for conjoined devotion."

When Mr. Chalmers was in the city, nothing was suffered to interfere with those daily meetings. If the weather was unfavorable for walking, they met at one or other of their houses : and when a week at Blochairn or Kilmardinny broke in upon the accustomed fellowship, an almost daily interchange of letters took place, occasioning a correspondence in which the questions of election and vows, and the propriety of attending public assemblies for dancing, were discussed. "Step by step the christian minister leads along the youthful and beloved disciple — thrown once or twice into anxiety which breaks at last into exulting joy as he discerns the clear and unmistakable tokens of a true and firm and advancing faith in the Redeemer." If sickness prevented one or the other from leaving his room, that sick-room became the place of meeting; and if business intervened the intervals of business were seized to keep up their intercourse by the pen. The tone of those thoughts which led them to take so much pleasure in each other's society may be judged of by a few extracts. The first is from a letter written by Mr. Chalmers from Kilmardinny, Jan. 6th, 1816.

"You complain of the turmoil of business. In as far as it takes you away from the more congenial exercise of study or prayer or religious contemplation, I can conceive, my dear sir, that it might be a matter of violent dislike to you. But remember that this is not of your own voluntary adoption. In your present circumstances, business is laid upon you by another, and you are acquitting yourself of your duty to Him when you are giving your time and your attention to it. I can conceive a man who felt more happiness in the duties of the closet than in those of society, to be making a sacrifice of principle to inclination in the very midst of religious exercises. Do feel that you are religiously employed when you are giving your faithful attention to the matters of the office; and instead of thinking that religion is a kind of secret indulgence, to be snatched by a kind of stealth from the ordinary affairs of life, do make a study of spreading religion over all your daily path, and then will you realize the habit of walking before God *all the day long*, of doing all things to His glory."

Mr. Smith's health was delicate, and toward the close of January an illness which did not for some weeks stop the forenoon interviews, occasionally prevented him from going to Mr. Chalmers's residence on the Sabbath evenings. On one of those occasions he received from his friend a letter presenting some opinions as to what should be the subject of their Sabbath conversations, advancing that it should not treat of religion in an argumentative way; but as an affair of the heart and conscience, continuing thus :

"Agreeably to this I shall not take up the remainder of time with any topic of observation whatever, but reco-

that Dr. Samuel Johnson often wrote his prayers, and found this a more powerfully devotional exercise than if he had said them, I entreat my dear friend's indulgence if I do the same at present; and as a blessing on that tender intimacy to which God, who turneth the heart of man whithersoever He will, has turned our hearts, is the great burden of my present aspiration to heaven, I send it to you, that you may, if you approve, join in it, and that the promise may be realized in us, that if two shall agree touching anything they shall ask it shall be done unto them.

"O God, do Thou look propitiously on our friendship. Do Thou purify it from all that is base, and sordid, and earthly. May it be altogether subordinated to the love of Thee. May it be the instrument of great good to each of our souls. May it sweeten the path of our worldly pilgrimage; and after death has divided us for a season, may it find its final blessedness and consummation at the right hand of Thine everlasting throne.

"We place ourselves before Thee as the children of error. O grant that in Thy light we may clearly see light; for this purpose let our eye be single. Let our intention to please Thee in all things be honest. With the childlike purpose of being altogether what Thou wouldst have us to be, may we place ourselves before Thy Bible, that we may draw our every lesson, and our every comfort out of it. O that Thy Spirit may preside over our daily reading of Thy word, and that the word of our blessed Saviour may dwell in us richly in all wisdom.

"O Save us from the deceitfulness of this world. Forbid that any one of its pleasures should sway us aside from the path of entire devotedness to Thee. Give us to be vigilant, and cautious, and fearful. May we think of Thine eye at all times upon us; and may the thought make us to tremble at the slightest departure from that narrow way of sanctification which leads to the house of our Father who is in heaven.

"We desire to honor the Son even as we honor the Father. We act in the presumption of our hearts when we think of placing ourselves before Thee in our own righteousness. Draw us to Christ. Make Him all our desire and all our salvation. Give remission of sins out of His blood. Give strength out of His fullness; and crowned with all might, may we not only be fellow-helpers to each other, but may the work of turning sons and daughters unto righteousness prosper in our hands. All we ask is for the sake of Thy Son and our Saviour, Jesus Christ. Amen.

"By the end of February Mr. Smith's illness had assumed a more alarming aspect—not yet confining him entirely to the house, but exciting the darkest apprehensions that consumption had begun its fatal work."

Anxiety now fanned affection; and not content with visits almost daily, frequent letters reminded the invalid of the strong attachment of his friend in Christ. Thus Mr. Chalmers writes on the 22d of February: "It is remarkable, that when all taste for other employment has abandoned me, I still find relief in the work of unbosoming myself to you. I can assure you that frequent and friendly conversation with you, ever rising to higher degrees of Christian faith and purity and elevation, is a mighty ingredient with me of this world's happiness. May God turn this taste to such an account as that a happiness so mingled, and so imperfect, and lying so open to interruption from the fearfulness of each of the parties in this dark scene of existence, may, after death has suspended it, reappear in a brighter and more enduring scene, and be fed with its immediate supplies from the throne of that God who will stand revealed to the pure in heart, and will dispense a blessedness which knows no alloy and shall experience no termination. I have not yet had heart either for my chapter or my prayer, but I trust that God will be present with me now that I am going to them. I shall pray for you, I trust, with a Christian tenderness."

In a letter of the next day he writes: "My heart is greatly enlarged toward you, and there is not a more congenial exercise for it at this moment than to pour it out before my high and my heavenly Witness in the fervency of prayer, that He will cause you to abound more and more—that He will keep up and increase the supplies of that purifying influence by which you have hitherto been preserved from falling—that He will bless the common tenderness which fills each of our hearts and knits us together in a friendship far more endearing than any I ever before experienced—that He will Christianize the whole of this friendship, and direct it to the love of himself, and make it the instrument of a growing knowledge of, and attachment to, His sacred word, and render us wise unto salvation, reducing us to the lowliness of little children, and making us to derive all our hopes of acceptance from the merits of His Son, and all our progress in sanctification from that kind and free Spirit, which will never be refused to our humble, earnest, and persevering prayers."

Again on Feb. 26th: "Will you forgive me, my excellent and aspiring fellow-Christian, if I venture to state one point in which we both are deficient, and have much before us. We are not yet sufficiently humbled into the attitude of dependence on the Spirit of God. We do not yet bow with enough of veneration at the name of Christ for sanctification. There is still a very strong mixture of self-sufficiency and self-dependence in our attempts at the service of God. I speak my own intimate experience when I say that, as the result of all this presumption, I feel as if I had yet done nothing. I can talk, and be impressed, and hold sweet counsel with you; but in the scene of trial I am humbled by my forgetfulness of God, by my want of delight in the doing of His commandments, by the barrenness of all my affections, by my enslavement to the influences of earth and of time, by my love to the creature, by my darkness, and hardness, and insensibility as to the great matters of the city that hath foundations, of the new heavens and the new earth wherein dwelleth righteousness.

"In these circumstances, let us flee for refuge to the hope set before us in the gospel. Let us keep closer by Christ than we have ever yet done. Let us live a life of faith on the Son of God. Let us crucify all our earthly affections, and by the Spirit mortify the deeds of the body, that we may live."

"March opened with brightening prospects of recovery, but closed amid greater darkness and uncertainty than ever. On Sabbath the 24th, Mr. Chalmers was to preach before the magistrates of the city. Excited groups of expectant auditors were already hurrying along the Trongate, hastening to secure their places in the church; and it was within half-an-hour of the time when the bell was to summon the preacher into the crowded sanctuary, that he sat down and penned the following lines:

"I cannot resist the opportunity of Mrs. C., who goes to inquire about you. May this be a precious Sabbath to you. If languid and weak, and unable to put forth much strength in the work of drawing near to God, may He put forth the strength of His resistless arm, and draw near unto you. May He benignantly reveal Himself to you as your gracious God and reconciled Father in Jesus Christ our Lord. Oh! may the consoling truths of the gospel be felt by you, and rejoiced in; and may you know what it is to have great peace and great joy in believing on Him who poured out His whole soul unto the death for you. Let Christ be on the foreground of all your religious contemplations. Feel that you are safely shielded from the wrath of God in the better righteousness of Him who yielded for you a pure and spotless obedience; and never, never let go your mild, and pleasing, and tender, and confiding impressions of all that love which the kind and willing Saviour bears to you. You may have much pain and weakness: look on it all as coming from God. Feel yourself in His hand, my dearest friend, and this feeling will temper all your sufferings, and sweeten them all. I do God great injustice, for I feel that I do not rise to an adequate conception of His loving-kindness and tender mercy. O may this sweet assurance of God be more quietly and firmly established in your heart every day, and on this day may there be much of the comfort and tranquillity of Heaven's best influences to make you tranquil and happy."

After morning service Mr. Chalmers visited the sick-room of his friend. In the afternoon he delivered before a vast assembly the brilliant discourse on the restlessness of human ambition; but neither excitement nor fatigue could shut out from his heart the predominant anxiety, as appears from this note dispatched on the same evening :

"*Six*, P. M.—Tell me by the servant *verbally* how you are. May the everlasting arms be round about and underneath you. May you have much peace and joy in the Holy Ghost. May you, throughout all the varieties of your condition, be enabled to display the triumphs of faith; and however you are, may the blessed assurance of your reconciled God ever be present in your heart to strengthen and to sustain you. My very dear sir, yours, with much regard, "THOMAS CHALMERS."

"Not unfrequently Mr. Chalmers took his manuscript over with him to Stockwell, and carried on the composition of his sermon in the sick-room. A friend who one day found him so employed, expressed his wonder that he could compose in such a situation. 'Ah! my dear sir,' said Mr. Chalmers, casting a look of profound and inexpressible sympathy toward the sufferer, 'there is much in mere juxtaposition with so interesting an object.'

"The sacrament was now close at hand, and those evening hours which Mr. Chalmers had been accustomed to spend with his friend, now so weak and apparently dying, had to be devoted to the examination of intending communicants; but snatching intervals which few ministers either would or could so use, he sustained the intercourse."

In the month of April, Mr. Smith's health appeared to be recovering, and Mr. Chalmers sought relief from the fatigue of his excessive labors, in an excursion into his native county, during which, journal letters were addressed to his friend for his amusement and instruction. Our limits preclude all but a single specimen:

"*April 22d*, 1816.—Let Mrs. Chalmers know that I was delighted to see the first man from Kilmany parish I had seen for nine months, that is, Mr. Anderson, of Star—that old Mr

C—— of Rathillet, is dying—that I walked from Kirkaldy to Duniface, about eight miles, on Saturday afternoon—that I there got a horse, which carried me forward to Pilmuir—that I have been enjoying myself on the verge of a most beautiful landscape, and, what is still more exquisite, that in Mr. Fortune's family here I have revived an early friendship, and am delighted with all that heart and kindness, and aspiring piety, in the bosom of which I have been reposing—that I did not go to the church at Largo, but that I did what I am not sorry for having done, gave a service in the house to about twenty-five people : and she will be much interested to know that Miss Robina Coutts, who is on a visit to her grandfather, was among my auditors.....

"I did not carry with me here the book I brought from Glasgow, but trusted my reading to such as I could find when I came, and the one I fell upon was the English Prayer Book, with which I was greatly refreshed and edified all yesterday. It will determine me, I think, when I get a church so cool that I can afford to prolong the service a little, to have a great deal more reading of the Bible introduced into my public ministrations. The Prayers and—with the exception of two flaws, one in the Burial and the other in the Baptismal service—all the other devout compositions are very admirable, and I do regard the whole composition as an interesting monument of the piety and sound intelligent Christianity of better days.

"The weather was milder yesterday, and I never felt a more delicious calm than when I walked a little at the front of the house, and my eye rested on the beauteous perspective before me, and the whole amplitude of the Forth stretched majestically in front and on each side of me, and the intervening country which lay between the rising ground on which my hospitable lodging stands and the shore, spread itself around me in all the garniture of fields, and spires, and woods, and farms, and villages, and the sun threw its unbounded splendors over the whole of this charming panorama, and the quietness of the Sabbath lent an association of inexpressible delight to these scenes of my nativity and youthful remembrance. If there be so much beauty on the face of this dark and disordered world, how much may we look for in that earth and those heavens wherein dwelleth righteousness!"

During Mr. Chalmers's absence, his friend died, and he returned in time only to preach his funeral sermon. He received, as a last memento, a ring, with some of Mr. Smith's hair, which was fondly treasured down to old age. It was even resumed, after being laid aside for years, and worn by him for a month, "during the year which preceded his own death."

The degree of Doctor of Divinity was conferred on Mr. Chalmers by the University of Glasgow, on the 21st of February, 1816, and soon afterward he was elected, by the presbytery of Glasgow, one of its representatives to the ensuing General Assembly, in which capacity he willingly served, on account of an impending discussion, in which he particularly desired to take a part.

In view of a fundamental law of the Scottish Establishment, requiring every minister to reside within his parish, the General Assembly of 1814, prohibited the holding of a country living in conjunction with a professor's chair. The act was simply declaratory; whereby a definite application was made of an old law. The friends of pluralities endeavored to convince the church that it was a new act of legislation, and therefore of no force, as the rule had not been complied with, which requires that, in such cases, the presbyteries must be consulted and the consent of a majority of them obtained; and so successful were their efforts, that no less than thirty overtures were transmitted from presbyteries praying that for the reason assigned, the resolution of 1814 should be set aside. Dr. Chalmers, on the other hand, from his experience in Glasgow, deeply impressed with a sense of the onerousness of a city charge, was prepared to combat not only one, but all kinds of pluralities. "The General Assembly met in Edinburgh, on Friday, 17th May, 1816. On the forenoon of that day, Dr. Chalmers preached in St. Andrew's church, before the society of the Sons of the Clergy, the same sermon which he had delivered before a similar institution in Glasgow. 'Probably no congregation, since the days of Massillon,' such was the testimony of an auditor, 'ever had their attention more completely fixed, their understandings more enlightened, their passions more agitated, and hearts more improved. When, at the conclusion of his discourse, Dr. Chalmers drew the picture of a clergyman's family leaving the place of their nativity and long residence, we observed many an eye suffused with tears.'"

The question of pluralities came up on the 22d. Intense interest was manifested in the debate, which, though maintained by both parties with great spirit and ability, for more than twelve hours, gave occasion to not one unpleasant personality or unseemly word. The substance of Dr. Chalmers's speech was thus reported in a publication of that time:

"The Reverend Doctor then contended, that if it was necessary to prevent a country minister from holding a professorship on account of his having enough to do in discharging the duties of his office without it, *a fortiori*, was it proper to prevent such union in the case of a town minister. This topic was illustrated by the speaker in a torrent of eloquence which seemed to astonish the house, and which has, in the opinion of the best critics and judges, perhaps never been exceeded. He contended that there was no other way of preventing the danger arising to the good order of society from the hostile attacks of an illiterate rabble, who were seen in such crowds at certain hours to issue from their workshops and manufactories, than by the kindly and unwearied attentions of their pastors among them. This would reclaim them when the gibbet, with all its terrors, would have no effect. Who could view, without alarm, that neglected population who scowled upon you as you passed, with an outlandish stare, who had never spoken to a clergyman in their life, and who were perfectly amazed when he began to put a few plain questions to them in the way of his official duty? There could be no more fitting object than these people for the attention of all who wished well both to religion and to the civil Government. Give not, therefore, a town clergyman anything else to do beyond his clerical duties. They will be enough—more than enough in most cases. He wished that a petition should be presented to an enlightened and paternal Government (who, he had no doubt, would listen to it when once they knew the fact, which at present they did not), to employ some other persons than clergymen to give certificates for the receiving of prize money and of money granted to soldiers' wives, and numberless things of this sort, which harassed a clergyman, and cut up his time intolerably; which totally secularized him, and converted him from a dispenser of the bread of life into a mere dispenser of human benefits."

"'I know not what it is,' said the greatest critic of our age,* after hearing Dr. Chalmers upon this occasion, 'but there is something altogether remarkable about that man. It reminds me more of what one reads of as the effect of the eloquence of Demosthenes than anything I ever heard.'"

When the vote was taken, the majority was found to be in favor of consulting the presbyteries. The Assembly of next year, however, found that a majority of the presbyteries had decided against the kind of plurality in question, which accordingly was abolished.

On the Sabbath succeeding, Dr. Chalmers preached before the Lord High Commissioner, on which occasion the accounts of the sermon and of the crowds that pressed to hear, and of the effects produced upon them, though giving no tangible conception of the peculiar charm of his oratory, as what description could embody an element consisting to so great a degree in the flashes of emotion attendant on the present creations of genius, testify very abundantly to a degree of oratorical power which it has fallen to the lot of few generations of mankind to witness.

---

* The late Lord Jeffrey.

CHAPTER VIII

Dr. Chalmers had now pretty well defined the extent of his duties in his parish, and made up his mind as to the amount which was to be deducted from the multifarious tasks presenting themselves with claims upon his time. He could not rest satisfied with merely addressing those who chose to come within the reach of his voice on the Sabbath. One of his favorite plans was that of carrying christian instruction into every family of his parish, to which end he determined to visit, and, in his own person, learn the actual condition of all. Pastoral visitation and instruction, from house to house, is the acknowledged duty of every clergyman of the Scottish Establishment, and in the country parishes it is, in general, faithfully observed; but in the cities, a burdensome round of secular duties had been suffered to interfere therewith, until it had become almost entirely neglected. Dr. Chalmers was convinced that the degraded condition of so much of the city population was due to this neglect, and also, that neither the neglect nor degradation were irremediable evils. He could perceive no reason why a city minister's services should be less efficacious than those of his brethren in the country, and full of hope, he resolved, with the help of God, to put his opinion to the test of experience, and to visit every family of his charge within a year. The population of the Tron church was then estimated at from eleven to twelve thousand. His visits, consequently, were, of necessity, very short. A few kindly remarks, a few questions as to education and church attendance, and an invitation to attend a discourse in some neighboring school-room, or other convenient place on an approaching week day evening, was all that his time permitted. Through close and filthy alleys, up steep and narrow stairs to many a house of wretched poverty, he made his way, often to the exhaustion of the elder who attended him, but with unflagging energy, pursuing his work to its completion. "Well," said he, looking kindly over his shoulder upon his elder, who, scarcely able to keep pace with him, was toiling up a long and weary stair, 'Well, what do you think of this kind of visiting?' Engrossed with the toils of the ascent, the elder announced that he had not been thinking much about it. 'Oh! I know quite well,' said Dr. Chalmers, "that if you were to speak your mind, you would say that we are putting the butter very thinly upon the bread." Those brief visits were not without the most valuable results. They brought him face to face with all his people, and revealed to him their actual condition, both physical and moral. "Writing to Mr. Edie early in February, 1816, he says, 'I have commenced a very stupendous work lately—the visitation of my parish. A very great proportion of the people have no seats in any place of worship whatever, and a very deep and universal ignorance on the high matters of faith and eternity obtains over the whole extent of a mighty population."

With the cares of the Tron church pulpit and of the pastoral instruction of such a population upon his mind, it is not wonderful that he should have been impatient of the many interruptions to which he felt himself exposed. It had been the custom in Glasgow, as perhaps in some other great cities, to impose a large amount of unministerial labor upon the ministers. The personal attendance upon public occasions, demanded of them, is thus pleasantly described by himself in a letter of the 27th October, 1815, to his old friend and neighbor, the Rev. Mr. Watson, of Leuchars:

"They must have four to every funeral, or they do not think that it has been genteelly gone through. They must have one or more to all the committees of all the societies. They must fall in at every procession. They must attend examinations innumerable, and eat of the dinners consequent upon these examinations. They have a niche assigned them in almost every public doing, and that niche must be filled up by them, or the doing loses all its solemnity in the eyes of the public. There seems to be a superstitious charm in the very sight of them, and such is the manifold officiality with which they are covered, that they must be paraded among all the meetings and all the institutions. I gave in to all this at first, but I am beginning to keep a suspicious eye upon these repeated demands ever since I sat nearly an hour in grave deliberation with a number of others upon a subject connected with the property of a corporation, and that subject was a *gutter*, and the question was whether it should be bought and covered up, or let alone and left to lie open. I am gradually separating myself from all this trash, and long to establish it as a doctrine that the life of a town minister should be what the life of a country minister might be, that is, a life of intellectual leisure, with the *otium* of literary pursuits, and his entire time disposable to the purposes to which the Apostles gave themselves wholly, that is, the ministry of the word and prayer."

Those customs, which had encumbered the operations of his predecessors, and rendered them, notwithstanding the zeal and energy of many of them, utterly unable to stem the torrent of worldly-mindedness pervading all classes, Dr. Chalmers soon found that it would be necessary to break through. He perceived that if such a course of secular and profitless toil were pursued, neither time nor strength would be left him to carry out the higher objects of the christian ministry. Indeed, not a few of his fellow laborers, finding hardly any leisure for either study or the decent discharge of their proper duties, in utter weariness of spirit, had, to a great extent, neglected both. But not only was their time thus abused, they were called upon to assume tasks calculated to pervert the nature of their influence with the people. The administration of public charities, having been thrown upon them, the consequence was, that the poor looked upon the minister as only the distributor of money, and his visit, when he could afford time to make one, was valued only by the amount of the donation. For some months, however, Dr. Chalmers silently submitted to prevailing custom, and, perhaps, wisely, until his personal character and motives should be generally understood, and until he should distinctly comprehend the breadth and entire bearing of the evil. He began his reformation by declining all share in the management of the pauperism of his parish, giving his people to understand that he "dealt in only one article, that of christian instruction." He also withheld attendance upon all public meetings of a merely secular nature; but the calls upon him in his study, he could not so easily dispose of.

"Harassed at every point of his progress, and exposed to ignorant and ill-applied reproach, he resolved, at last, in some more public and effectual manner, to assert the proper and spiritual functions of the christian ministry, to vindicate his injured prerogatives, and, if the voice of remonstrance and rebuke could do it, to effect a deliverance for himself and for his brethren." On the 13th of October, 1816, he gave out for his text, in the morning, Acts vi, 2: '' Then the twelve called the multitude of the disciples unto them, and said, It is not reason that we should leave the word of God and serve tables.' Then followed a singular detail of the manifold exactions that were made upon the time of the ministers of Glasgow, whereby they had been withdrawn from prayer and the ministry of the word.

"'I have already said much,' he continued, 'of the interruption and the labor which the public charities of the place bring along with them; and yet I have not told you one-half the amount of it. I have only insisted on that part of it which takes a minister from his house, and from which the minister, at the expense of a little odium, can at all times protect himself, by the determined habit of sitting immovable under every call and every application. All that arrangement which takes a minister away from his house, may be evaded — but how shall he be able to extricate himself from the besetting inconveniences of such an arrangement as gives to the whole population of a neighborhood a constant and ever-moving tendency toward the house of the minister? The patronage with which I think it is his heavy misfortune to be encumbered, gives him a share in the disposal of innumerable vacancies, and each vacancy gives rise to innumerable candidates, and each candidate is sure to strengthen his chance for success by stirring up a whole round of acquaintances, who, in the various forms of written and of personal entreaty, discharge their wishes on the minister, in the shape of innumerable applications. It is fair to observe, however, that the turmoil of all this electioneering has its times and its seasons. It does not keep by one in the form of a steady monsoon. It comes upon him more in the resemblance of a hurricane; and, like the hurricanes of the atmosphere, it has its months of violence and its intervals of periodical cessation. I shall only say that when it does come, the power of contemplation takes to herself wings and flees away. She cannot live and flourish in the whirlwind of all that noise and confusion by which her retreat is so boisterously agitated. She sickens and grows pale at every quivering of the household bell, and at every volley from the household door, by which the loud notes of impatience march along the passages, and force an impetuous announcement into every chamber of the dwelling-place. She finds all this to be too much for her. These rude and incessant visitations fatigue and exhaust her, and at length banish her entirely; nor will she suffer either force or flattery to detain her in a mansion invaded by the din of such turbulent and uncongenial elements."

The subject thus treated in the morning, was further pursued in the afternoon, in a spirit of mingled irony and pathos. He dwelt especially upon the loss which the literature of theology and the learning of its ministers had thereby sustained. That day's work effected its purpose. Henceforward Mr. Chalmers received no more invitations to preside at public festivities or sit in scavenger committees. He had other work laid out for himself, and not only for himself, but also for many others under his direction, which he was burning to execute as soon as that rubbish should be cleared away—work more consistent with the spirit of his sacred calling.

The population of the city of Glasgow had increased so much beyond the means of christian instruction, that many of the parishes had become quite unmanageable, and with the pastoral visitation all attempts at religious instruction, except from the pulpit, had been discontinued. The consequence was that coldness and formality prevailed among the higher classes, and the great mass of the poor were left in worse than heathen ignorance. "Till Dr. Chalmers came to Glasgow," so says a most competent authority,* "parochial christian influence was a mere name — it was not systematic, it was not understood—there was not the machinery for the moral elevation of a town population. The people were let alone. Some of the elders of the Tron church were excellent men, but their chief duty was to stand at the plate, receive the free-will offerings of the congregation as they entered, and distribute them to the poor by a monthly allowance. Their spiritual duties and exertions were but small and almost exclusively confined to a few of the sick." Their old habits would have presented many an obstacle to new efforts; and Dr. Chalmers, with a wisdom equal to his energy, had a few younger men, who, less prejudiced, might be more active coadjutors, ordained to the eldership. "His strong hand not only never tried to put new wine into old bottles, but it was with a very gentle motion that even into the new bottles the new wine was poured."

The first step in reformation was that of increasing the number and efficiency of the Sabbath schools. A few zealous members of his congregation were induced to form themselves into a society for the purpose of opening such schools in various districts of the parish, and of visiting the various families to obtain the regular attendance of the children; and such was the energy and judgment with which they proceeded, that in two years that society had not less than twelve hundred pupils under its instruction. Communication and harmonious co-operation was maintained among the teachers by means of monthly meetings, at which they consulted concerning the best method of teaching and governing, and the wisest measures for extending the operation of the enterprise. "Our meetings," says Mr. Thomson, one of the members of the society, "were very delightful. I never saw any set of men, who were so animated by one spirit, and whose zeal was so steadily sustained. The Doctor was the life of the whole. There was no assuming of superiority—no

---
* David Stow, Esq.

appearance of the minister directing everything; every one was free to make remarks or suggestions, Dr. Chalmers ever the most ready to receive a hint or a suggestion from the youngest or least experienced member; and if any useful hint came from such a one he was careful to give him the full merit of it—calling it, indeed, generally by his name. Although we had no set forms of teaching, yet we conversed over all the modes that we might find out the best. On one point we had much discussion, namely, whether or not punishment should be resorted to in a Sabbath school. Mr. Stow was very strenuous in condemning its introduction. I was rather inclined the other way. Among other strong cases, Mr. Stow told us of a boy who had been so restless, idle, and mischievous, that he was afraid he would have to put him away, when the thought occurred to him to give the boy an office. He put, accordingly, all the candles of the school under his care. From that hour he was an altered boy, and became a diligent scholar. An opportunity soon occurred of trying my way of it also. A school, composed of twenty or thirty boys, situated in the east end of the parish, had become so unruly and unmanageable, that it had beaten off every teacher who had gone to it. The society did not know what to do with it, and the doctor asked me if I would go out and try to reduce it to order. I was not very fond of the task, but consented. I went out the next Sabbath, and told the boys, whom I found all assembled, that I had heard a very bad account of them, that I had come out for the purpose of doing them good, that I must have peace and attention, that I would submit to no disturbance, and that, in the first place, we must begin with prayer. They all stood up, and I commenced, and certainly did not forget the injunction, Watch and pray. I had not proceeded two sentences, when one little fellow gave his neighbor a tremendous dig in the side; I instantly stepped forward and gave him a sound cuff on the side of his head. I never spoke a word, but stepped back, concluded the prayer, taught for a month, and never had a more orderly school.

The case was reported at one of our own meetings. The doctor enjoyed it exceedingly, and taking up my instances, and comparing it with Mr. Stow's, he concluded that the question of punishment or non-punishment stood just where it was, inasmuch as it had been found that the judicious appointment of a candle-snuffer-general and a good cuff on the *lug* had been about equally efficacious."

One of the improvements early adopted by the society was that of confining each of its schools to a very small locality and charging the teacher with the supervision, as far as that kind of instruction was concerned, of its families. Each teacher thus became well acquainted with the condition and spiritual wants of his district and became a valuable auxiliary to the minister. In Dr. Chalmers's own language the system became "an effectual preaching of the gospel from door to door." From this Sabbath school society, others soon afterward branched off and multiplied until no less than eight existed in different parts of the city and suburbs. One of these is mentioned, which in six months from its formation counted twenty-six schools and seven hundred and thirty-two children in attendance. "I consider," writes Mr. Stow, one of those engaged in the work, "had Dr. Chalmers done nothing more than promote the principle of this local system of Sabbath-schools, he would not have lived in vain. You can easily conceive the labor and fatigue he must have undergone, first to convince his agents of the propriety of his plan, and then to keep them from breaking the rules. You also know the difficulty of retaining Sabbath-school teachers for any lengthened period under any system of management, untrained as they are to the art, and over sanguine of *immediate* results. The doctor's Christian simplicity, however operated, powerfully in retaining nearly all."

Many were opposed to these methods of instruction; it was objected that they interfered with the proper domestic training of the young; that they engaged laymen in work which was proper to clergymen alone, and that they would be the means of promoting fanaticism. In one of his sermons, delivered in his own pulpit about the end of the year 1816, Dr. Chalmers "entered upon a vigorous and animated defense of Sabbath-schools, the very tone and manner of which sufficiently testifies as to the state of public feeling at that time in Glasgow. 'It is not easy for me,' he said in closing this defense, ' to describe my general feeling in reference to the population with which I have more immediately to do. I feel as if it were a mighty and impenetrable mass, truly beyond the strength of one individual arm, and before which, after a few furtive and unavailing exertions, nothing remains but to sit down in the idleness of despair. It is a number, it is a magnitude, it is an endless succession of houses and families, it is an extent of field which puts at a distance all hope of a deep or universal impression— it is an utter impossibility, even with the most active process of visitation, to meet the ever-pressing demands of the sick and the desolate and the dying, it is all this, I confess, which tempts me to seek for relief in some wise and efficient system of deputation.' In these circumstances I do feel greatly obliged by every contribution to the great cause of instructing and of moralizing. I do rejoice particularly in the multiplication of those humble and often despised seminaries. I think I am certain that they are well suited to the present needs and circumstances of our population, that they may be made to open up a way through a mass that would be otherwise impenetrable, and to circulate a right and a healthy influence through all the untraveled obscurities which abound in it—that an unction of blessedness may emanate abroad upon every neighborhood in which they are situated—that they occupy a high point of command over the moral destinies of our city, for the susceptibilities of childhood and of youth are what they have to deal with. It is a tender and inflexible plant to which they aim at giving a direction. It is conscience at the most impressible stage of its history which they attempt to touch, and on which they labor to engrave the lessons of conduct and of principle. And I doubt not that when we are mouldering in our coffins, when the present race of men have disappeared and made room for another succession of the species, when parents of every cast and of every character have sunk into oblivion, and sleep together in quietness, the teachers of these institutions will leave behind them a surviving memorial of their labor, in a large portion of that worth and piety which shall adorn the citizens of a future generation.'"

About midsummer of 1816, Dr. Chalmers escaped from the incessant labor and confinement of his parish, to enjoy a few weeks of recreation in the country, and the neighborhood of his relations and old acquaintances. In the course of that tour he visited Kirkaldy, Anstruther, and Kilmany. During his stay, in the latter place, the zeal of his former parishioners to see him was such, that he was surrounded by a perpetual crowd. And when it was known that he was to preach on Sabbath, numbers came in also from the neighboring parishes, and one minister, the Rev. Mr. Melvil, announcing no sermon in his own church, transferred himself and congregation, bodily, to Kilmany. The assembly was so great that the preacher took his station at an open window, so as to be heard also by those who could find no accommodation within.

After similar visits to friends of earlier days in Cupar, Dundee, and elsewhere, occupying about a fortnight more, he returned to Glasgow. His absence had not been all holiday, as we learn that "scarcely a single day was suffered to elapse in which an hour or two was not redeemed from its busiest periods, and consecrated to composition. Between Glasgow and Kirkaldy the full preparations for a Sabbath's services were completed. At Kirkaldy, on the Saturday, 'Dr. Jones's Sermons,' with a copy of a letter from Mr. Josiah Condor, then editor of the Eclectic, accepting his offer to review the volume, were put into his hands; and though he 'never preached with greater fatigue or discomfort' than on the succeeding Sabbath, the Monday's Journal has the following entry: 'I yoked to the review of "Jones," have read three of his sermons, and thrown off a tolerable modicum of observations on sermons in general. I trust I shall be able to finish my review of him this week.' He carried the volume in his pocket, reading it often as he walked, and snatching the readiest hours in the houses of his acquaintances to carry forward his review. 'I have this forenoon,' is his entry on Wednesday at Pilmuir, 'thrown off a full modicum of additional review of "Jones's Sermons." I have also written to Dr. Ireland, and offered him a sight of the manuscript on its way to London, lest the friends should be resting too high an expectation on my account of the volume.'—'After breakfast,' such is the note of progress at Elie. 'I retired to my bedroom, where I read "Jones." His sermons at Glasgow and Kilmany are in the volume, but they look sadly reduced and enfeebled in print. Anstruther, Saturday, half past one—I have now finished the review of "Dr. Jones's Sermons." I am heartily tired of this kind of work, and should like henceforward to decline it altogether.'

"Tired, however, as he felt on the Saturday of the work of reviewing, another work was taken up on the Monday, and one, we should have thought, as little likely to be undertaken amidst such a life of varied and perpetual motion as he now was living. 'I began,' he says, 'my fourth astronomical sermon to-day.' And in a small pocket-book, with borrowed pen and ink, in strange apartments, where he was liable every moment to interruption, that sermon was taken up and carried on to completion. At the manse of Balmerino; disappointed at not finding Mr. Thomson at home, and having a couple of hours to spare—at the manse of Kilmany, in the drawing-room, with all the excitement before him of meeting, for the first time, after a year's absence, many of his former friends and parishioners—at the manse of Logie, into which he turned at random by the way and found a vacant hour—paragraph after paragraph was penned of a composition which bears upon it as much of the aspect of high and continuous elaboration, as almost any piece of writing in our language.

"I believe that literary history presents few parallel instances of such power of immediate and entire concentration of thought, under such ready command of the will, exercised at such broken intervals, amid such unpropitious circumstances, and yet yielding a product in which not a single trace either of rupture in argument or variation in style appears. Those ingenious critics, who, on their first appearance of the 'Astronomical Sermons,' in print, spoke of the midnight oil which must have been consumed, and the vast elaboration which must have been bestowed, how much would they have been surprised had they but known the times and modes, and places in which one, at least, of these discourses had been prepared!

"But higher even than the literary interest which attaches to the record of this visit to Fifeshire, are those brief notices given to us of the spiritual condition of the writer. 'I am not attempting,' he in one place says, 'any more at present than a sheet of severe composition in the week; and as I had nearly completed this, I resolved to abandon myself to the stream of events throughout this day (Saturday), and upon the whole, I hope that the uncomplying severity of system is now giving way with me, under a milder and more attractive principle of forbearance with others. I speak, however, with great humility, and am sure that nothing but Divine grace will uphold me in that which is good and acceptable unto the Lord. I trust, amid all my imperfections, that I may be getting on in earnest, humble, and spiritual Christianity. I feel, however, my barrenness, my forgetfulness of God, my miserable distance from the temper and elevation of the New Testament, my proneness to self and its willful and headlong gratifications, and, above all, a kind of delusive orthodox satisfaction with the mere confession of all this, without a vigorous putting forth of any one revealed expedient for getting the better of it.'".... "I have much to learn in the way of observing all the kindnesses and all the facilities of social intercourse; and I can not withhold it, as a testimony to the power and importance of gospel faith, that the more I feel of peace with God, the more largely and the more freely I take in of those promises which are yea and amen in Christ Jesus, the more I have my eye open to the sufficiency of His atonement, and the subduing efficacy of His Spirit—in a word, the more I am exercised with all that is direct and peculiar in piety, the more do I feel my heart attuned to the cordialities, and the patience, and the facilities of benevolence and good-will. Oh! that I was making more steady and decided progress than I have ever yet done—that all the asperities of temper were softening within me—that I was becoming better as the member of a company and the member of a family, and growing every day in conformity to the image of my all-pure and all-perfect Saviour.'"

"At the time of Dr. Chalmers's settlement in Glasgow it was the custom that the clergymen of the city should preach in rotation on Thursday, in the Tron church, a duty which, as their number was then but eight, returned to each within an interval of two months. On Thursday, the 23d of November, 1815, this week-day service devolved on Dr. Chalmers. The entire novelty of the discourse delivered upon this occasion, and the promise held out by the preacher that a series of similar discourses was to follow, excited the liveliest interest, not in his own congregation alone, but throughout the whole community. He had presented to his hearers a sketch of the recent discoveries of astronomy—distinct in outline, and drawn with all the ease of one who was himself a master in the science, yet gorgeously magnificent in many of its details, displaying amid 'the brilliant glow of a blazing eloquence;' the sublime poetry of the heavens. In his subsequent discourses, Dr. Chalmers proposed to discuss the argument, or rather, prejudice, against the Christian Revelation which grounds itself on the vastness and variety of those unnumbered worlds which lie scattered over the immeasurable fields of space. This discussion occupied all the Thursday services allotted to him during the year 1816. The spectacle which presented itself in the Trongate upon the day of the delivery of each new astronomical discourse, was a most singular one. Long ere the bell began to toll, a stream of people might be seen pouring through the passage which led into the Tron church. Across the street, and immediately opposite to this passage, was the old reading-room, where all the Glasgow merchants met. So soon, however, as the gathering quickening stream upon the opposite side of the street gave the accustomed warning, out flowed the occupants of the coffee-room; the pages of the Herald or the Courier were for a while forsaken, and during two of the best business hours of the day, the old reading-room wore a strange aspect of desolation. The busiest merchants of the city were wont, indeed, upon those memorable days to leave their desks, and kind masters allowed their clerks and apprentices to follow their example. Out of the very heart of the great tumult an hour or two stood redeemed for the highest exercises of the spirit; and the low traffic of earth forgotten, heaven, and its high economy, and its human sympathies, and eternal interests, engrossed the minds, at least, and the fancy of congregated thousands.

"In January, 1817, this series of discourses was announced as ready for publication. It had generally been a matter of so much commercial risk to issue a volume of sermons from the press, that recourse had been often had, in such cases, to publication by subscription. Dr. Chalmers's publisher, Mr. Smith, had hinted that perhaps this method ought, in this instance, also to be tried. 'It is far more agreeable to my feelings,' Dr. Chalmers wrote to him a few days before the day of publication, 'that the book should be introduced to the general market, and sell on the public estimation of it, than that the neighborhood here should be plied in all the shops with subscription papers, and as much as possible wrung out of their partialities for the author.' Neither author nor publisher had at this time the least idea of the extraordinary success which was awaiting their forthcoming volume. It was published on the 28th of January, 1817. In ten weeks, 6000 copies had been disposed of, the demand showing no symptom of decline. Nine editions were called for within a year, and nearly 20,000 copies were in circulation. Never previously, nor ever since, has any volume of sermons met with such immediate and general acceptance. The 'Tales of my Landlord,' had a month's start in the date of publication, and even with such a competitor, it ran an almost equal race. Not a few curious observers were struck with the novel competition, and watched, with lively curiosity, how the great Scottish preacher and the great Scottish novelist kept for a whole year so nearly abreast of one another. It was, beside, the first volume of sermons which fairly broke the lines which had separated too long the literary from the religious public. Its secondary merits won audience for it in quarters where evangelical Christianity was nauseated and despised. It disarmed even the keen hostility of Hazlitt, and kept him for a whole forenoon spell-bound beneath its power. 'These sermons," he says, 'ran like wild-fire through the country, were the darlings of watering-places, were laid in the windows of inns, and were to be met with in all places of public resort...... We remember finding the volume in the orchard of the inn at Burford Bridge, near Boxhill, and passing a whole, and very delightful morning in reading it without quitting the shade of an apple-tree."

The reviews, as usual, found many faults to blame, more or less radical, and Chalmers himself was persuaded into the notion that some were correct in blaming; but the public continued faithful to the favorite volume, notwithstanding, and to this day it "commands a larger sale than any other portion" of its author's writings.

"It was amidst the full burst of that applause which his volume of sermons had elicited, that Dr. Chalmers appeared for the first time in a London pulpit. Mrs. Chalmers and he, accompanied by Mr. Smith, his publisher, left Glasgow for London, on the morning of Monday, the 14th of April, 1817. Their progress was slow and circuitous. Crossing from Cumberland to Yorkshire, visiting the scenery of Rokeby, and pausing to inspect the Moravian establishment of Fulneck, they did not reach Birmingham till the evening of Friday, the 23d."

At Sheffield they waited upon Mr. Montgomery, the poet, who has furnished the following interesting details of his first interview with Dr. Chalmers:

"On a dark evening, about the end of April (I have forgotten the year), two strangers called at my house in Sheffield, where I then resided, one of whom introduced himself as Mr.

Smith, bookseller of Glasgow, and his companion as the Rev. Dr. Chalmers, of the same city, who, being on a journey to London, where he was engaged to preach the annual sermon for the Missionary Society, desired to have a short interview with me. Of course I was glad to have the opportunity of becoming personally acquainted with so great and good a man, and we soon were earnestly engaged in conversation on subjects endeared to us both ; for, though at first I found it difficult to take in and decipher his peculiar utterance, yet the thoughts that spoke themselves through the seemingly uncouth words came so quick and thick upon me from his lips, that I could not help understanding them ; till, being myself roused into unwonted volubility of speech, I responded as promptly as they were made to his numerous and searching inquiries concerning the United Brethren (commonly called Moravians), among whom I was born, but especially respecting their scriptural method of evangelizing and civilizing barbarian tribes of the rudest classes of heathen. In the outset he told me that he had come directly from Fulneck, near Leeds, one of our principal establishments in England, and where there is an academy open for the education of children of parents of all Christian denominations, in which I had been myself a pupil about ten years in the last century. At the time of which I am writing, and for several years in connection, there were many scholars from the North, as well as Irish and English boarders, there. My visitor said that he had invited all the Scotch lads to meet him at the inn there, and 'how many, think you, there were of them?' he asked me. 'Indeed, I can not tell,' I replied. He answered, 'there were *saxtain* or *savantain ;'*—(I can not pretend to spell the numbers as he pronounced them to my unpracticed ear ;)—and I was so taken by surprise, that I exclaimed abruptly, ' It is enough to corrupt the English language in the seminary !' In that moment I felt I had uttered an impertinence, though without the slightest consciousness of such an application to my hearer ; and, as instantly recovering my presence of mind, I added, ' When I was at Fulneck school, I was the only Scotch lad there.' Whether this slip was noticed or passed off as mere waste of breath in the heat of conversation, I know not; but on we went together in another vein, on a theme which deeply interested my illustrious visitor, and to the discussion of which I was principally indebted for the honor of this sudden and hasty call upon me, as he was to set off for town early the next morning. 'An angel visit, short and bright,' it was to me, and I do not remember that I ever spent half an hour of more animated and delightful intercommunion with a kindred spirit in my life. As I have noticed already, our discourse turned principally on the subject of the Moravian Missions in pagan lands, and the lamentable inability of our few and small congregations in Christendom to raise among themselves the pecuniary expenses of maintaining their numerous and comparatively large establishments in Greenland, Labrador, North and South America, the West Indies, and South Africa, but that, providentially, they received liberal help from the friends of the gospel of other evangelical denominations; hereupon Dr. Chalmers said—evidently not from sudden impulse, but a cherished purpose in his heart—' I mean to raise five hundred pounds for the Brethren's Missions this year!' 'Five hundred pounds for our poor missions!' I cried;—' I never heard of such a thing before!' He rejoined, 'I will do it.' But while I heartily thanked him, and implicitly believed in the integrity of his intention, I could only hope that he might be able to fulfill it, and within myself I said, 'I will watch you, doctor.' I did so, and traced him through sermons, subscriptions collections, and donations, till these had realized, to the best of my recollection, a sum nearer to six than five hundred pounds. Now, considering in how many comprehensive concerns he was at that very time putting forth all his strength—originating, promoting, and accomplishing economical, local, patriotic, and Christian plans for the well-being of populous communities—in comparison with which this effort in aid of the brethren was like the putting forth of his little finger only—yet, I confess, that 'small thing,' not to be despised, gave me a most magnificent idea of the intellectual, moral, and sanctified power for good with which the human being who stood before me was endowed from on high. And surely, if ever ten talents were committed by Him who is Lord of all in his kingdom of heaven on earth, Dr. Chalmers was so invested; and judging by the labors which he did in his day, and the works *which remain, as well as have followed* him to his account, we may fervently believe that the treasure lent to him was doubled by his faithful occupation of the same, and that his 'joy of the Lord,' which was his ' strength ' in life, is now his portion for ever."

On this journey, Dr. Chalmers also made the acquaintance of the Rev. Robert Hall, at Leicester, between whom and himself there existed a mutual reverential regard. The traveling party separated at Warwick, and while Mr. Smith proceeded to Paris, Dr. and Mrs. Chalmers went into Gloucestershire, to spend a fortnight with Mr. and Mrs. Morton.

" The three travelers met again in London on the evening of Tuesday, the 13th May. On the following day, Dr. Chalmers preached, in Surrey Chapel, the anniversary sermon for the London Missionary Society. Although the service did not commence till eleven o'clock, ' at seven in the morning the chapel was crowded to excess, and many thousands went off for want of room.' The two front seats in the gallery were reserved for ministers and students of theology to the number of between two and three hundred. An occupant of one of those seats informs us, that ' on the termination of the church service, and after an extempore prayer by Dr. Kollock, from America, Dr. Chalmers entered the pulpit in his usual simple and unpretending manner, and sat down, while all eyes were fixed upon him. He rose and gave out his text from 1 Cor. xiv, 22-25. The singularity of the text, and the originality of the exordium awakened a breathless attention, which was increased by the northern accent of the preacher, and the apparent weakness or unmanageableness of his voice. The late Dr. Styles, of Brighton, and Dr. Henry Burder, of London, who were sitting directly before me, looked at each other with anxiety and regret, as if doomed to disappointment; but he had not proceeded many minutes till his voice gradually expanded in strength and compass, reaching every part of the house, and commanding universal attention. At the close of many of his long periods there was a sensible rustling throughout the audience, as if stopping to take breath. Toward the middle of the discourse, the preacher became quite exhausted by the violence of his action, and sat down, while two verses of a hymn were singing, accompanied as usual by the organ. He then rose and recommenced his sermon, which occupied about an hour and a half in the delivery. Old Rowland Hill stood the whole time at the foot of the pulpit, gazing on the preacher with great earnestness, and whenever any sentiment was uttered which met his approval, signifying his assent by a gentle nod of the head, and an expressive smile."

Of the same occasion, his fellow-traveler, Mr. Smith, remarked in a letter to his friends in Glasgow, "The carrying forward of minds never was so visible to me; a constant assent of the head from the whole people accompanied all his paragraphs, and the breathlessness of expectation permitted not the beating of a heart to agitate the stillness."

"On Thursday, the 22d, Dr. Chalmers preached again in Surrey Chapel, on behalf of the Scottish Hospital for the relief of aged and destitute natives of Scotland, who never having acquired a settlement in England, had no claim for parochial aid. In announcing this discourse in the newspapers, the Committee of the Hospital had thought it desirable to make the following intimation: 'Divine service begins at eleven o'clock, but the Committee have issued tickets to a part of the church, for the better securing of accommodation to the friends of the charity, it is requested that those holding tickets may be at the chapel at the opening of the doors, at half-past nine o'clock, to prevent disappointment.' The sermon preached for this Hospital was the same which Dr. Chalmers had delivered before the Society of the Sons of the Clergy in Glasgow and Edinburgh. The growing evils of the poor-laws, as then administered in England, were attracting much of the attention of public men; and while they were only planning methods for mitigating these evils, it must have surprised a London audience not a little, to hear from the pulpit a bold and uncompromising attack on the principle and expediency of all forms of legalized charity."

"On the forenoon of Sabbath, the 25th, Dr. Chalmers preached in the Scotch church, London Wall, for the benefit of the Hibernian Society. 'The desire,' says the Rev. Dr. Manuel, who, at the time, was the minister of this church, 'felt by all classes, but particularly by the higher classes of society, to hear him, upon this occasion, was extreme, exceeding almost all precedent. Among his auditors were a number of the most distinguished clergy of the Church of England, several peers, many members of Parliament, the lord mayor of the city, and literary characters of all classes and denominations. Anticipating the pressure, a large chapel in the neighborhood was engaged to receive the overflow. Not only the Scotch Church, but this chapel also was crammed to suffocation, hundreds seeking admission, but going away without getting into either place of worship. .... At the close of the sermon, the lord mayor went up into the pulpit, and importuned Dr. Chalmers to preach on behalf of some city object, which he was obliged to decline.' 'All the world,' writes Mr. Wilberforce, in his diary, 'wild about Dr. Chalmers. He seems truly pious, simple and unassuming. *Sunday 25th.*—Off early with Canning, Huskisson, and Lord Binning, to the Scotch Church, London Wall, to hear Dr. Chalmers. Vast crowds. Bobus Smith, Lords Elgin, Harrowby, etc. I was surprised to see how greatly Canning was affected; at times, he was quite melted into tears.' The passage which most affected him was at the close of the discourse. He is reported to have said, that although at first he felt uneasy in consequence of Dr. Chalmers's manner and accent, yet that he had never been so arrested by any oratory. 'The tartan,' so runs the speech attributed to him, 'beats us all.'

"On the afternoon of the same Sabbath, Dr. Chalmers

preached for the Rev. Dr. Nicol, minister of the Scotch Church, Swallow-street. The crowd here had nearly lost its object by the very vehemence of its pursuit. On approaching the church, Dr. Chalmers and a friend found so dense a mass within and before the building, as to give no hope of effecting an entrance by the mere force of ordinary pressure. Lifting his cane and gently tapping the heads of those who were in advance, Dr. Chalmers's friend exclaimed, 'Make way there—make way for Dr. Chalmers.' Heads indeed were turned at the summons, and looks were given, but with not a few significant tokens of incredulity, and some broad hints that they were not to be taken in by any such device, the sturdy Londoners refused to move. Forced to retire, Dr. Chalmers retreated from the outskirts of the crowd, crossed the street, stood for a few moments, gazing on the growing tumult, and had almost resolved altogether to withdraw. Matters were not much better when Mr. Wilberforce and his party approached. Access by any of the ordinary entrances was impossible. In this emergency, and as there was still some unoccupied space around the pulpit, which the crowd had not been able to appropriate, a plank was projected from one of the windows till it rested on an iron palisade. By this privileged passage Mr. Wilberforce and the ladies who were with him, were invited to enter, Lord Elgin waving encouragement and offering aid from within. 'I was surveying the breach,' says Mr. Wilberforce, 'with a cautious and inquiring eye, when Lady D., no shrimp you must observe, entered boldly before me, and proved that it was practicable.' The impression produced by the service which followed, when all had at last settled down into stillness, was deeper than that made by any of those which preceded it, and we may hope it was also more salutary; as the preacher dealt throughout with truths bearing directly on the individual salvation of his hearers."

"With Mr. Smith once more as their traveling companion," Dr. and Mrs. Chalmers left London on Monday, the 26th of May. Upon their journey northward, they visited the west of England

and Wales, and among other celebrated persons, had the pleasure of seeing Mrs. Hannah More and Mr. Foster. After his return to Scotland, Dr. Chalmers did not immediately proceed to Glasgow, but took up his abode, for the purpose of study, among the mountains, at a place called Douglas Mill. In a letter to his sister, Mrs. Morton, from that place, recapitulating some of the impressions of his London trip, he declared his acquaintance with Wilberforce by far the most valuable acquisition he had made thereby, although he could reckon the names of Lord Grenville and Canning, and Sir Thomas Ackland among the number.

"Some time after his return to Glasgow, Dr. Chalmers received a communication from the Rev. Robert Hall, in which he says: 'It would be difficult not to congratulate you on the unrivaled and unbounded popularity which attended you in the metropolis, but I am convinced, from the extreme modesty of your nature, such an overwhelming tide of distinction and applause would be quite distressing to you. When you consider, however, the thousands who have probably benefited by the unparalleled energy of your public ministrations, you will be the more easily reconciled to the inconvenience inseparable from high celebrity. The attention which your sermons have excited is probably unequaled in modern literature, and it must be a delightful reflection that you are advancing the cause of religion in innumerable multitudes of your fellow creatures, whose faces you will never behold till the last day. My ardent prayer is, that talents so rich in splendor, and piety so fervent, may long be continued to be faithfully and assiduously devoted to the service of God and of your generation."

In the spring of 1817, Dr. Chalmers was elected to the first church in Sterling, in which his fatigue would have been less and his emoluments greater than in Glasgow, but declined, on the ground that the field he already occupied was the larger and the more necessitous. The offer, however, contributed to induce his friends in Glasgow to relieve him of those difficulties which had hitherto been suffered to embarrass his operations. They also proposed to raise his stipends, to rent or buy him a house in any place of his own choosing, and to procure him a regular assistant to do half the work on the Sabbath, and also to relieve him of some of the out-door work during the week. He did not, however, " allow things to be carried to the proposed length. The offer of a manse and of an increase of income, were respectfully declined; but he gratefully accepted the offer of an assistant. Additional labor would be thereby bestowed upon parochial cultivation, while, at the same time, additional leisure would be secured to himself for literary engagements. His first article on Pauperism appeared in the March number of the Edinburgh Review, and he had engaged to follow it up by a comparison of the English and Scottish systems of parochial relief. His visit to England, and the large arrears of ministerial labor awaiting his return, filled up the summer months; and there was so little hope of finding time enough in Glasgow, that he resolved on a short excursion to Anstruther, during which his second article was to be drawn up." With this view, he had got as far as Kilmany, on Saturday, the 15th of November, where he preached next day. On his way to church, a letter was put into his hands which effectually broke up his plan. It was a request that he should preach in his own pulpit on the succeeding Wednesday, a discourse appropriate to the public calamity of the death of the Princess of Wales, whose funeral services the magistrates of Glasgow had resolved to celebrate on that day. On Monday, accordingly, he returned with the utmost expedition to Glasgow, where he arrived early on Tuesday morning, and on Wednesday forenoon preached one of his most celebrated discourses, " composed during the intervals, and after the exhaustion of this rapid and fatiguing journey."

Some misrepresentations of it having appeared in the public prints, the sermon was published in self vindication, which its appearance completely effected.

With the intention of finishing his article on Pauperism, Dr. Chalmers again, in the month of December, betook himself to his contemplated retreat in Fifeshire, and this time succeeded in accomplishing his purpose. His present reason for treating of that subject was a conviction that the English method of assessment was positively injurious, and that a valuable service would be rendered his own country by repressing the growing inclination to the adoption of such a method there. When he compared the independent spirit of the Scottish poor, with the degradation of the same class under a system of poor-rates; contemplated the people in their kindly sympathies, their mutual and unforced contributions to each other's necessities, he naturally dreaded any touch that could profane that spontaneous benevolence which aids without impairing the noble feeling of self reliance, and which interferes with none of the humanizing duties of the filial relation; and thus strongly did he express himself in view of that relation. "We want no such ignominy to come near our Scottish population as that of farming our poor. We want no other asylum for our aged parents than that of their pious and affectionate families. We can neither suffer them, nor do we like the prospect for ourselves, of pining out the cheerless evening of our days away from the endearments of a home. We wish to do as long as we can without the apparatus of English laws and English workhouses; and should like to ward forever from our doors the system that would bring an everlasting interdict on the worth, and independence, and genuine enjoyments of our peasantry. We wish to see their venerable sires surrounded, as heretofore, by the company and playfulness of their own grandchildren; nor can we bear to think that our high-minded people should sink down and be satisfied with the dreary imprisonment of an almshouse as the closing object in the vista of their earthly anticipations. Yet such is the goodly upshot of a system which has its friends and advocates in our own country — men who could witness, without a sigh, the departure of all those peculiarities which have both alimented and adorned the character of our beloved Scotland — men who can gild over with the semblance of humanity, a poisoned opiate of deepest injury both to its happiness and to its morals—and who, in the very act of flattering the poor, are only forging for them such chains as, soft in feeling as silk, but strong in proof as adamant, will bind them down to a state of permanent degradation."

" Dr. Chalmers returned to Glasgow on Saturday, the 27th of December, and on the following day found a prodigious crowd awaiting his appearance in the Tron church pulpit. His popularity, as a preacher, was now at its very highest summit, and, judging merely by the amount of physical energy displayed by the preacher, and by the palpable and visible effects produced upon his hearers, we conclude that it was about this period, and within the walls of the Tron church, that by far the most wonderful exhibitions of his power, as a pulpit orator, were witnessed. 'The Tron church contains, if I mistake not,' says the Rev. Dr. Wardlaw, who, as frequently as he could, was a hearer in it, 'about 1400 hearers, according to the ordinary allowance of seat-room; when crowded, of course, proportionally more. And though I cannot attempt any pictorial sketch of the place, I may, in a sentence or two, present you with a few touches of the scene which I have, more than once or twice, witnessed within its walls; not that it was at all peculiar, for it resembled every other scene where the doctor in those days, when his eloquence was in the prime of its vehemence and splendor, was called to preach. There was one particular, indeed, which rendered such a scene in a city like Glasgow, peculiarly striking. I refer to the time of it. To see a place of worship, of the size mentioned, crammed above and below, on a Thursday forenoon, during the busiest hours of the day, with fifteen or sixteen hundred hearers, and these of all descriptions of persons, in all descriptions of professional occupation, the busiest as well as those who had most leisure on their hands, those who had least to spare, taking care so to arrange their business engagements previously as to make time for the purpose, all pouring in through the wide entrance at the side of the Tron steeple, half an hour before the time of service, to secure a seat, or content, if too late for this, to occupy, as many did, standing room — this was, indeed, a novel and strange sight. Nor was it once, merely, or twice, but month after month the day was calculated when his turn to preach again was to come round, and anticipated, with even impatient longing, by multitudes."

"Suppose the congregation thus assembled — pews filled with sitters, and aisles, to a great extent, with standers, They wait in eager expectation. The preacher appears. The devotional exercises of praise and prayer having been gone through with unaffected simplicity and earnestness, the entire assembly set themselves for the treat, with feelings very diverse in kind, but all eager, and intent. There is a hush of dead silence. The text is announced, and he begins. Every countenance is up — every eye bent, with fixed intentness on the speaker. As he kindles, the interest grows. Every breath is held — every cough is suppressed — every fidgety movement is settled — every one riveted himself by the spell of the impassioned and entrancing eloquence, knows how sensitively his neighbor will resent the very slightest disturbance. Then, by-and-by, there is a pause. The speaker stops—to gather breath—to wipe his forehead — to adjust his gown, and purposely, too, and wisely, to give the audience, as well as himself, a moment or two of relaxation. The moment is embraced — there is a free breathing — suppressed coughs get vent—postures are changed — there is a universal stir, as of persons who could not have endured the constraint much longer—the preacher bends forward — his hand is raised — all is again hushed. The same stillness and strain of unrelaxed attention is repeated, more intent still, it may be, than before, as the interest of the subject and the speaker advance, and so, for perhaps four or five times in the course of a sermon, there is the relaxation, and the '.at it again,' till the final winding up.

"And then, the moment the last word was uttered, and followed by the—'let us pray,' there was a scene for which no excuse or palliation can be pleaded but the fact of its having been to many a matter of difficulty, in the morning of a week-day, to accomplish the abstraction of even so much of their time from business — the closing prayer completely drowned by the hurried rush of large numbers from the aisles and pews to the door ; an unseemly scene, without doubt, as if so many had come to the house of God not to worship, but simply to enjoy the fascination of human eloquence. Even this much it was a great thing for eloquence to accomplish. And how diversified soever the motives which drew so many together, and the emotions awakened and impressions produced by what was heard — though, in the terms of the text, of one of his most overpoweringly stirring and faithful appeals, he was to not a few ' as one that had a pleasant voice and could play well on an instrument,' yet there is abundant proof that, in the highest sense, ' his labor was not in vain in the Lord ;' that the truths which, with so much fearless fidelity and impassioned earnestness, he delivered, went in many instances farther than the ear, or even the intellect — that they reached the heart, and, by the power of the Spirit, turned it to God."

" On Thursday, the 12th of February, 1818," I now quote from a manuscript of the Rev. Mr. Fraser, minister of Kilchrennan, 'Dr. Chalmers preached in the Tron church before the Directors of the Magdalene Asylum. The sermon delivered on this occasion was that ' On the Dissipation of Large Cities.' Long before the service commenced every seat and passage was crowded to excess, with the exception of the front pew of the gallery, which was reserved for the magistrates. A vast number of students deserted their classes at the university and were present. This was very particularly the case in regard to the moral philosophy class, which I attended that session, as appeared on the following day when the list of absentees was given in by the person who had called the catalogue, and at the same time a petition from several of themselves was handed in to the professor, praying for a remission of the fine for non-attendance, on the ground that they had been hearing Dr. Chalmers. The doctor's manner during the whole delivery of that magnificent discourse was strikingly animated, while the enthusiasm and energy which he threw into some of its bursts rendered them quite overpowering. One expression which he used, together with his action, his look, and the very tones of his voice when it came forth, made a most vivid and indelible impression upon my memory: 'We, at the same time,' he said, 'have our eye perfectly open to that great external improvement which has taken place, of late years, in the manners of society. There is not the same grossness of conversation. There is not the same impatience for the withdrawment of him who, asked to grace the outset of an assembled party, is compelled, at a certain step in the process of conviviality, by the obligations of professional decency, to retire from it. There is not so frequent an exaction of this as one of the established proprieties of social or of fashionable life. And if such an exaction was ever laid by the omnipotence of custom on a minister of Christianity, it is such an exaction as ought never, never to be complied with. It is not for him to lend the sanction of his presence to a meeting with which he could not sit to its final termination. It is not for him to stand associated, for a single hour, with an assemblage of men who begin with hypocrisy, and end with downright blackguardism. It is not for him to watch the progress of the coming ribaldry, and to hit the well-selected moment when talk and turbulence and boisterous merriment are on the eve of bursting forth upon the company, and carrying them forward to the full acme and uproar of their enjoyment. It is quite in vain to say, that he has only sanctioned one part of such an entertainment. He has as good as given his connivance to the whole of it, and left behind him a discharge in full of all its abominations; and, therefore, be they who they may, whether they rank among the proudest aristocracy of our land, or are charioted in splendor along, as the wealthiest of our citizens, *or flounce in the robes of magistracy*, it is his part to keep as purely and indignantly aloof from such society as this, as he would from the vilest and most debasing associations of profligacy.'

"The words which I have underlined do not appear in the sermon as printed. While uttering them, which he did with peculiar emphasis, accompanying them with a flash from his eye and a stamp of his foot, he threw his right arm with clenched hand right across the book-board, and brandished it full in the face of the Town Council, sitting in array and in state before him. Many eyes were in a moment directed toward the magistrates. The words evidently fell upon them like a thunderbolt, and seemed to startle like an electric shock the whole audience.

"Another interesting memorial of this sermon is supplied by Dr. Wardlaw, who was present at its delivery. 'The eloquence of that discourse was absolutely overpowering. The subject was one eminently fitted to awaken and summon to their utmost energy all his extraordinary powers; especially when, after having cleared his ground by a luminously scriptural exhibition of that supreme authority by which the evils he was about to portray were interdicted, in contradistinction to the prevailing maxims and practices of a worldly morality, he came forward to the announcement and illustration of his main subject—'*the origin, the progress, and the effects of a life of dissipation.*' His moral portraitures were so graphically and vividly delineated — his warnings and entreaties, especially to youth, so impassioned and earnest — his admonitions so faithful, and his denunciations so fearless and so fearful—and his exhortations to preventive and remedial appliances so pointed and so urgent to all among his auditors who had either the charge of youth, or the supervision of dependents! It was thrilling, overwhelming. His whole soul seemed in every utterance. Although saying to myself all the while, 'Oh! that this were in the hands of every father, and master, and guardian, and young-man in the land!' I yet could not spare an eye from the preacher to mark how his appeal was telling upon others. The breathless, the appalling silence told me of that. Any person who reads that discourse, and who had the privilege of listening to Dr. Chalmers during the prime and freshness of his public eloquence, will readily imagine the effect of some passages in it, when delivered with even more than the preacher's characteristic vehemence.

"The wish that haunted my mind during the discourse went home with me; and in bed that night the thought came across me, that I might write to him, and respectfully but earnestly suggest the desirableness of having such an appeal put into circulation. I did so, and while I expressed strongly my delight and my wishes, I ventured at the same time, with all due diffidence, to hint the desirableness, were the discourse to appear thus by itself, of his introducing at the close, in his own style, a statement of that gospel — that scheme and message of divine mercy—by which 'the wrath of God which cometh on the children of disobedience,' of which his text had led him to speak, was to be escaped, and His favor and forgiveness to be obtained; a statement which would perfect the fitness of the appeal for the ends to be answered by its circulation."

To the note written in pursuance of this purpose Dr. Chalmers answered by kindly but firmly declining the suggestion for publication.

"In the afternoon of Sabbath the 22d March, 1818," we now resume Mr. Fraser's memoranda, "Dr. Chalmers preached in the college chapel. It being publicly known a few days previously that he was to do so, the college courts became crowded with students and others not connected with the university about an hour before the commencement of the service. So soon as the doors were opened, the rush toward them was tremendous. I was in the stream that was flowing in by the main entrance, and made good progress until I got within the door, when, in consequence of the great pressure behind, I was suddenly thrown out of the current as I had almost reached the foot of the hanging spiral staircase leading to the chapel, and so compact was the mass that was pouring on, that all my efforts to wedge myself into it were vain. Under these circumstances, I made up my mind to do what might have led to very serious consequences. I ascended sideway on the outside of the rails, holding on with a death-grasp of them at every step, and upon reaching the top, had no little difficulty, even with the assistance I received, in getting over them, so dense was the crowd. The sermon preached by Dr. Chalmers was the one entitled 'The judgment of men compared with the judgment of God.' I had a complete view of the professors' bench directly opposite to the pulpit. It was quite full, and had a very imposing appearance. Every eye in it was intently fixed upon the preacher. But there was one individual who formed a very prominent object in the group — Mr. Young, professor of Greek. The magic of the doctor's eloquence told most powerfully on him. He was evidently fascinated and enraptured. The expression of his fine countenance more than once indicated intense emotion. During the delivery of the peroration he was overpowered and in tears.

"On Sabbath evening in the Tron church Dr. Chalmers preached from Proverbs i, 29. The power of the oratory, and the force of the delivery were at times extraordinary. At length, when near the close of the sermon, all on a sudden his eloquence gathered triple force, and came down in one mighty whirlwind, sweeping all before it. Never can I forget my feelings at the time, neither can I describe them. 'And what,' he said, warning us against all hope in a death-bed repentance, ' what, we would ask, is the scene in which you are now purposing to contest it with all this mighty force of opposition you are now so busy in raising up against you? What is the field of combat to which you are now looking forward as the place where you are to accomplish a victory over all those formidable enemies whom you are at present arming with such a weight of hostility as, we say, within a single hair-breadth of certainty, you will find to be irresistible? Oh the folly of such a misleading infatuation! The proposed scene in which this battle for eternity is to be fought, and this victory for the crown of glory is to be won, is a death-bed. It is when the last messenger stands by the couch of the dying man, and shakes at him the terrors of his grisly countenance, that the poor child of infatuation thinks he is to struggle and prevail against all his enemies—against the unrelenting tyranny of habit—against the obstinacy of his own heart, which he is now doing so much to harden—against the Spirit of God, who perhaps long ere now has pronounced the doom upon him. 'He will take his own way, and walk in his own counsel; I shall cease from striving, and let him alone'—against Satan, to whom every day of his life he has given some fresh advantage over him, and who will not be willing to lose the victim on whom he has practiced so many wiles, and plied with success so many delusions. And such are the enemies whom you who wretchedly calculate on the repentance of the eleventh hour are every day mustering up in greater force and formidableness against you; and how can we think of letting you go with any other repentance than the repentance of the precious moment that is now passing over you, when we look forward to the horrors of that impressive scene on which you propose to win the prize of immortality, and to contest it single-handed and alone, with all the weight of opposition which you have accumulated against yourselves—a deathbed—a languid, breathless, tossing, and agitated deathbed; that scene of feebleness, when the poor man cannot help himself to a single mouthful—when he must have attendants to sit around him, and watch his every wish, and interpret his every signal, and turn him to every posture where he may find a moment's ease, and wipe away the cold sweat that is running over him, and ply him with cordials for thirst, and sickness, and insufferable languor. And this is the time, when occupied with such feelings and beset with such agonies as these, you propose to crowd within the compass of a few wretched days the work of winding up the concerns of a neglected eternity!"

"It was a transcendently grand—a glorious burst. The energy of the doctor's action corresponded. Intense emotion beamed from his countenance. I cannot describe the appearance of his face better than by saying, as Foster said of Hall's, it was 'lighted up almost into a glare.' The congregation, in so far as the spell under which I was, allowed me to observe them, were intensely excited, leaning forward in the pews like a forest bending under the power of the hurricane—looking steadfastly at the preacher, and listening in breathless wonderment. One young man, apparently by his dress a sailor, who sat in a pew before me, started to his feet, and stood till it was over. So soon as it was concluded, there was (as invariably was the case at the close of the doctor's bursts) a deep sigh, or rather gasp for breath, accompanied by a movement through the whole audience.

"On another Sabbath evening a scene occurred which I shall never forget. About an hour before the service commenced all the seats were occupied. A broad passage runs through the area of the church from the main inner door to the pulpit. This passage it was intended should be kept vacant upon the present occasion for the better ventilation of the house. So soon, therefore, as the pews which entered from it (in one of which I sat) were filled, the door, consisting of two leaves, was bolted from within. Very soon all the other passages above and below were crowded to overflowing. A dense mass was by this time congregated in the lobby, many of whom observed through the windows of a partition wall which ran between the lobby and the interior of the church that the middle passage was empty. Those in the background, who could not themselves observe this, were made immediately aware of it. They all became very clamorous for admission, and many a good thump did the door receive. Those in charge of it, however, having got, as was said, positive orders to keep the passage clear, were inexorable. Matters went on in this manner until the bell commenced, which seemed to be the signal for increased clamor and importunity on the part of the crowd without. At length the door began to creak. The bell ceased. The beadle entered the pulpit with the bible. All was still for a few moments. Every eye within sight of the vestry-door was anxiously fixed upon it to see who would appear, lest it might *not* be the doctor, as he had on more occasions than one sadly disappointed the congregation. No sooner, however, was he observed entering the church, than an expression of intense delight rustled very perceptibly through the house. There was actually (I do not exaggerate) a movement of the whole congregation. At this moment a crash at the passage-door was heard; crash after crash followed in rapid succession, intermingled with screams from the outer porch, chiefly from terrified females. Two of the door-keepers who were standing in the passage rushed to the door, which was evidently yielding, to prevent, if possible, its being forced in. They quickly retreated, seeing, as they did at once, that neither door nor door-keepers could withstand the pressure. The door immediately gave way with a thundering noise, one of the leaves torn from its hinges and trampled under foot. The rush was tremendous. In one instant the whole vacant space in front of the pulpit was crammed, and the torrent flowed on, flowing into and filling to its very end at the vestry-door the passage through which the doctor had just entered. The occurrence grieved, and for a little while discomposed him, and upon rising to begin the service, he administered a sharp and impassioned rebuke to the parties involved in it."

"Dr. Wardlaw, who was present on this occasion, also informs us, 'I stepped into the vestry at the dismission of the congregation, and walked home with him, our dwellings lying in the same direction. On the way home we talked, *inter alia*, of this occurrence. He expressed, in his pithy manner, his great annoyance at such crowds. 'I preached the same sermon,' said he, 'in the morning; and for the very purpose of preventing the oppressive annoyance of such a densely crowded place, I intimated that I should preach it again in the evening;' and with the most ingenuous guilelessness, he added, 'Have *you* ever tried that plan?' I did not smile—I laughed outright. 'No, no,' I replied, 'my good friend, there are but very few of us that are under the necessity of having recourse to the use of means for getting thin audiences.' He enjoyed the joke, and he felt, though he modestly disowned the compliment.'"

In the beginning of this period of unbounded popularity his journal presents evidence of a deep feeling of unworthiness, and of imperfect service of his master; and the same is manifested in an incident related of him about two years after his removal to Glasgow. "At the time I allude to," says J. Wright, Esq., "Dr. Chalmers had been preaching in the Barony church for the venerable Dr. Burns, on the Monday after the communion, which was in the suburban districts, about two months after the time of its celebration in the town churches. As was customary on such occasions, Dr. Burns invited the ministers who had assisted him, and some of his elders and friends, to dinner on the Monday. I was on that day one of the party, and I was exceedingly disappointed to see that Dr. Chalmers, who, in ordinary times, poured a fascinating influence over every company where he was, seemed extremely dull, nay, I may say, dejected. When he arose, about nine o'clock, to go away, as our tract homeward lay for some distance in the same direction, I left the company along with him. When we had got together, I said to the doctor, 'Are you well enough to-day, doctor? For I have noticed you have not to-day been in your usual trim.' 'Oh, yes,' he said, 'I am quite in good health, but I am not comfortable. I am grieved in my mind.' Seeing that he so frankly communicated to me the general cause of his unusual appearance, I used the freedom to say, 'Well, doctor, is this a matter that I may be made acquainted with? if it is not, I have no wish to pry into anything of a private nature.' 'Oh, yes,' he replied, 'you may perfectly know it, for it is a matter that presses very grievously upon me. In short, the truth is,' said he in his own emphatic manner, 'I have mistaken the way of my duty to God in at all coming to your city. I am doing no good. God has not blessed, and is not blessing, my ministry here.' On hearing this, I replied, 'Well, doctor, it is a very remarkable circumstance that, in the providence of God, you should have been sent with your complaint to me on this point, because I have it in my power at any rate to mention one instance in which your ministry has been made instrumental in bringing a soul from darkness to the marvelous light of the gospel of salvation.' 'Can you?' said he, 'then you will give me the best news I have heard since I came among you.' I then narrated to him the following particulars:

"At the time this took place I was an elder under the late venerated Dr. Balfour, minister of the Outer High Church, whose practice it was, when he read over the names of those who were applying for admission to the ordinance of the Lord's supper, to give us so much of their history and experience as he had been in conversation with them able to discover, and to request that some of the elders might, as far as possible, scrutinize further, and communicate to him the result. I well remember, at the sacrament, which in the town churches is always solemnized in the month of April, he mentioned the name of a young man who had applied to be a communicant. After he had read over his name 'By-the-by,' said the good servant of the Lord, 'I must tell you something about this young man, for his history is somewhat interesting and singular. He sat,' said Dr. Balfour, 'for nearly twenty years under my ministry, but did not appear to derive any good from it; but when my worthy friend, Dr. Chalmers (for that was the almost uniform designation he gave him when he had occasion to speak of him), 'came to Glasgow, he was attracted to him by his splendid talents, and sat under his ministry for about two years, and then it pleased the Lord to come to him in the day of his power; and I have every reason to think him a truly converted young man. And now that he wishes to become a member of the church he wishes to return to us. But,' added Dr. Balfour, with a truly sublime humility, 'it was not under my ministry that he was turned to the Lord, though he sat for the greater part of his lifetime in the Outer Church; but it was under the preaching of Dr. Chalmers.'

"You know what was Dr. Chalmers's ardent manner when anything that related to the glory of Christ's kingdom, or to the spiritual good of his fellow-creatures, was made known to him; but you may easily conceive with what exuberant joy he heard this simple annal of the good done through his pastoral superintendence. 'Ah!' said he, 'Mr. Wright, what blessed, what comforting news you give me; I knew it not; but it strengthens me; for really I was beginning to fail, from an apprehension that I had not been acting according to the will of God in coming to your city.'

"At a still later period of his Glasgow ministry, and after knowing, by a painful experience, how many bitter ingredients are often mixed in the cup of human applause, urging his agencies to increased activity in that home-walk of private benevolence, in which 'they could earn, if not a proud, at least a peaceful popularity—the popularity of the heart—the only popularity that is worth the aspiring after — the popularity that is won in the bosom of families and at the side of death-beds—he could not help pouring out his own later experience in these words : ' There is another, a high and a far-sounding popularity, which is indeed a most worthless article, felt by all who have it most to be greatly more oppressive than gratifying—a popularity of stare, and pressure, and animal heat, and a whole tribe of other annoyances which it brings around the person of its unfortunate victim, a popularity which rifles home of its sweets, and by elevating man above his fellows, places him in a region of desolation, where the intimacies of human fellowship are unfelt, and where he stands a conspicuous mark for the shafts of malice; and envy, and detraction—a popularity which, with its head among storms and its feet on the treacherous quicksands, has nothing to lull the agonies of its tottering existence but the hosannas of a driveling generation.'"

Intelligence of his father's declining health induced Dr. Chalmers to take his family to Anstruther, to spend the summer months of 1818 ; and leaving them there, he returned to the scene of his labors. Daily correspondence was kept up with them by means of those journal-letters which he constantly wrote to Mrs. Chalmers, whenever separated from her for more than a few days. On Friday, the 17th July, his father had an attack of paralysis. Intelligence was immediately dispatched to Dr. Chalmers, who arrived in time to watch over the last hours of his father's life. On the morning of the 26th of July, he wrote to Mrs. Morton :

"My dearest Jane:—The life of our revered father was

just lengthened out to half-past two this morning. He was permitted just to touch, as it were, one Sabbath more on earth ere he was transported to that everlasting Sabbath, among the worshipers of which he is now sitting in blessedness and in glory.......

"There was not much of the suffering of death, save the weariness and languor of dying. He ceased, we thought, to take an interest in what we said for about thirty hours before his death. We all sat up two nights in hourly expectation of the event, but it was postponed, and the transition made gentler in consequence. He calmly breathed his last, and his departing spirit has left a most saintly expression behind it."

During the same day, he also wrote to his brothers, Patrick and James, endeavoring to impress upon their minds the spiritual lesson of their pious father's life and death. For about two weeks after this event, he remained with his mother and family, and "was then obliged to plunge once more into the vortex at Glasgow."

CHAPTER IX.

During the winter of 1818-19, Dr. Chalmers added to his other labors the preparation of a volume of congregational sermons, of which a large edition was published in February, 1819. On the 24th of April of that year, he wrote thus: "I never kept so close by Glasgow, nor worked so hard in it as during this last winter. I have now preached twenty-nine Sabbaths, without intermission, in the Tron church, and that without a stated assistant, though I have occasionally got assistance for half a day."

He was anxious to complete the execution of his projects there, inasmuch as he already entertained others of greater variety in behalf of a more destitute population. A new city parish had been recently erected in a quarter inhabited chiefly by operatives, and embracing about ten thousand souls. There was a propriety in calling the great advocate of church extension and of religious instruction of the poor to this charge; and the very fact that it embraced a large number of the poorest families in Glasgow was a strong motive with Dr. Chalmers for accepting it; but another conspiring therewith was the freedom which was guaranteed to him in carrying out all those schemes of reformation in which he had been hitherto so much thwarted by established customs.

Accordingly on the 5th of June, 1818, Dr. Chalmers was elected, by the magistrates and town council, to the pastoral charge of the new parish of St. John's. The actual transfer, however, was not made until the following year, owing to unexpected delay in finishing the church edifice. In the month of June, 1819, he writes to his friend, Mr. Erskine, of Linlathen, "Sabbath first being the 30th, is the last of my connection with the Tron church, and as the church of St. John's is not yet ready for me, I am counting upon the interval of a good many weeks, during which I propose to expatiate among my friends in the country. My arrangements are going on most prosperously. I have now got thirty-five gentlemen and three lady teachers. I have also completed the survey of my parish, and have still 150 Sabbath-scholars to provide with teachers, beside an indefinite number of female teachers to look out for. Amid great physical distress and many difficulties among our population, it gives me comfort to think of an operation which I am sure alleviates, even at present, the burden which is upon their spirits, and will, I trust and pray, have fruit in eternity.

"I can not tell you how truly grateful I am for all you write and all you say on theological subjects. You have given most useful direction to my own mind, and I have endeavored in some of my later pulpit demonstrations to press home the lesson of salvation and spiritual health, being synonymous with each other. It is truly excellent what you say of not waiting at the pool. Be assured that many render the method of setting out on the business of Christianity so mystical and so separate from human agency, and so scrupulously remote from all that man can will or do in the matter, as absolutely to discourage him even from going to the pool, even from opening his Bible, even from directing his thoughts to the subject of it, even from hearing what Christ has got to say to him, and turning to its obvious application and purpose the plainest and most palpable of His requirements. Believe me, my dear sir, yours very truly,

"THOMAS CHALMERS."

In order to recruit his strength, exhausted by the unremitting labor of the preceding winter and spring, he went to spend a few days near the mineral waters of Dunblane. We are presented with a very precious fragment of a letter written by him, while there, to Mr. Erskine....... "I feel my want of capacity for the direct exercises of godliness—am in a state of longing and general earnestness, but want sadly a habitual frame of heavenly-mindedness. I read with mortification, and I had almost said envy, of the devotional feelings and delights of other men; and just feel myself, as it were, at the place of breaking forth, and on the margin only of that spiritual territory within which all is life, and light, and enlargement, and holy affection. It is easy to talk of a simple faith in the testimony: but there must be the issuing of a certain sound on the part of the trumpet to him who lingers at the threshold, and who, when told just to believe, and just to perform the bare act of faith, is still encompassed with helplessness, and impressed with the suspicions and the straightening of a mind not yet loosed from its bondage. Yet come the enlargement when it will, it must, I admit, come after all through the channel of a simple credence given to the sayings of God, accounted as true and faithful sayings. And never does light and peace so fill my heart as when, like a little child, I take up the lesson, that God hath laid on his own Son the iniquities of us all. Do believe me, my dear sir, yours, very truly,

"THOMAS CHALMERS."

" Thomas Erskine, Esq.

On the 27th, he was again in Glasgow, and fairly entered upon the negotiations regarding his plans for St. John's. He had already received an expression of good-will from the city authorities, but felt the necessity of something more in the shape of definite authoritative enactments to proceed upon. His system of parochial schools, and of pauper management needed to be legally delivered from all embarrassing connection with any others. Ten days were spent in preliminary efforts, and having placed his views fully before the Lord Provost and town council, and pending their answer, he paid a hasty visit to Anstruther. In the meanwhile an application had been made to him to permit his name to be presented as a candidate for the Chair of Natural Philosophy in the University of Edinburgh, then vacant by the death of Prof. Playfair. A report that he had complied therewith reached Glasgow, and created much anxiety among those who were just then so much depending upon his services.

In opening the first number of The Christian and Civic Economy of large Towns, issued on the 24th of September, he took occasion to explain away the misunderstanding, but what was more satisfactory to his Glasgow friends, was his own reappearance among them. And just two days after the publication of the pamphlet containing that explanation, on the Sabbath, the 26th of September, the church of St. Johns was opened for public worship, as appears from the following account in the Glasgow Herald of next day: "Dr. Andrew Thomson, of Edinburgh, and Dr. Chalmers, the minister of the parish, preached in presence of the magistrates and a most crowded congregation. The first gentleman commenced the service of the day, and took for his text Hebrews, iii, 12; Dr. Chalmers, preached in the afternoon from Isaiah, xxix, 9—12. In the evening, the parochial sitters took their places, when Dr. Thomson again preached. From the intimations previously given, it was understood that the last of these services was meant for the exclusive benefit of the inhabitants of the parish, who are enabled, by a wise and liberal arrangement on the part of the magistrates and council, to obtain as good a right of occupation to the evening seats as is held by any other sitters among the day congregations of our city......The decidedly parochial aspect of the evening congregation was scarcely, if at all, impaired by any great admixture of hearers from the general and indiscriminate public; and it was felt as a novel and affecting singularity to witness such a multitude of the laboring classes of our city so respectably provided with Sabbath accommodation in one of the churches of the Establishment. The impression was much heightened upon observing that the great body of the population, on retiring from church, when they had reached the bottom of McFarlane-street, turned in nearly an unbroken stream to the east along the Gallowgate, or in the direction which leads to the main bulk of the parish and its inhabitants......It gives us pleasure to observe that the hour of meeting for the evening sitters is so early as four in the afternoon, thereby giving to this parochial diet the character and convenience of a day service, and enabling the hearers to spend an unbroken Sabbath evening in the bosom of their own families."

The parish of St. John's, in 1819, contained a population of more than ten thousand, a large proportion of whom had never attended religious instruction anywhere. It was one of the largest, and, at the same time, the very poorest parish in the city. " Nevertheless, suffered now to manage it in his own way, Dr. Chalmers entered upon the task with all the hopeful confidence of one emancipated from bondage, and all the hopeful confidence of one whose faith in the power of moral and spiritual influences, both human and divine, over the very worst of our species, was perhaps larger and stronger than that of any other man of his generation. The four years of his ministry in St. John's, were among the busiest in a life overcrowded in every portion with activities; and if we include the after and the indirect, as well as the immediate results accomplished by them, they formed four of the most productive of his years."

In this parish, as in that of the Tron church, his first efforts were addressed to the education of the young. At the commencement of his operations, he had a band of forty-one Sabbath School teachers formed; but that number was doubled before, according to his method of subdivision, the whole ground was covered.

Provision had also to be made for the elements of secular instruction, as very many children were growing up without that amount of education necessary to enable them to reap the true profits of Sabbath School effort. The existing schools were inadequate to the wants of the population. The plan by which Dr. Chalmers proposed to meet this want was that already adopted by the founders of the parochial schools of Scotland, according to which a school-house was to be built by a public fund, and a partial endowment provided for the teacher, not sufficient for his support but to enable him to admit scholars for very small fees. Thus education should be put within the reach of the poor, and yet not undervalued by being gratuitous. Accordingly, he got a few of the members of his church organized into an Education Committee, for the purpose of carrying out the plan in behalf of their own parish. The means were to be obtained by subscription, and Dr. Chalmers immediately put down his name for £100. Five others did likewise, and in a week or two the requisite amount was raised. The site fixed upon as most convenient, being one which belonged to the college, " Dr. Chalmers went to Principal Taylor to negotiate a purchase. In the hope of obtaining it on reasonable terms, he urged at once the novelty and the importance of the undertaking. The Principal acknowledged the importance, but demurred as to the novelty. "We have been talking for twenty years," he said, " of establishing parochial schools in Glasgow." "Yes; but how many years more did you intend to talk about it? Now, we are going to do the thing, not to talk about it, and so," said Dr. Chalmers, putting the Principal into good humor by some kindly saying, " you must even let the price be as moderate as possible, seeing we are going to take the labor of talking and projecting entirely off your hands." The application was successful — the ground was purchased — the building was commenced, and early in July, 1820, was ready for occupation." Care was taken to procure two of the most competent teachers, and such was the success of the scheme, that in one month it was found that the two schools, thus opened, were not enough to meet the educational demands of the parish. Another building was erected on the same plan, and went into equally successful operation. Thus, within two years from the beginning of his connection with St. John's, four efficient teachers, each endowed to the extent of £25 a year, were educating four hundred and nineteen scholars; and when he left Glasgow, in 1823, other school buildings were in the process of erection, capable of accommodating three hundred and seventy-four additional pupils; so that the fruits of four years' labor was the leaving behind him the means and facilities for giving, at a very moderate rate, a superior education to no less than seven hundred and ninety-three children, out of a population of *ten thousand souls.*

It has been stated that one great inducement with Dr.

Chalmers to the acceptance of the pastorate of St. John's was the hope of obtaining therein a separate and independent management of the poor, from which he was debarred in the Tron church parish by the manner in which it was connected with other bodies.

The prevailing system was somewhat complicated, two separate funds existed, one consisting of the results of the legal assessments, the other of the voluntary contributions received at the church-doors. These were kept apart, the latter being placed at the disposal of the general session, a body composed of all the ministers and elders of the city, and the former controlled by "the committee of the town hospital, an institution which had both in-door and out-door pensioners. The first application for public relief was made to the elder of the district in which the applicant resided. The case was then reported by this elder to the kirk-session of his own parish. But that kirk-session, not permitted to retain the collection made at its own church-door, and having no definite income with which to square its annual expenditure, had only to insert the name on the roll, fix the allowance, and report to the general session, from whose funds a monthly distribution was made among the separate kirk-sessions, according to the number and necessities of the cases on the roll of each. When these cases had multiplied beyond the power of the voluntary fund to meet them, or when the largest sum granted by the session, which rarely exceeded five shillings a month, was deemed insufficient, from the pauper becoming older or more necessitous, there occurred a transference to the town hospital, whose ampler fund admitted of larger allowances. 'So that each session,' says Dr. Chalmers, describing this cumbrous apparatus, 'might have been regarded as having two doors, one of them a door of admittance for the population who stand at the margin of pauperism, and another of them a door of egress to the town hospital, through which the occupiers of the outer court made their way into the inner temple. It will be seen at once how much this economy of things tended to relax still more all the sessional administration of the city, and with what facility the stream of pauperism would be admitted at the one end when so ready and abundant a discharge was provided for it at the other. We know not how it was possible to devise a more likely arrangement for lulling the vigilance of those who stood at the outposts of pauperism, and that too at a point where their firm and strenuous guardianship was of greatest consequence—even at the point where the first demonstrations toward public charity were made on the part of the people, and where their incipient tendencies to this new state, if judiciously while tenderly dealt with, might have been so easily repressed. To station one body of men at the entrance of pauperism, and burden them only with the lighter expenses of its outset, from which they have a sure prospect of being relieved by another body of men, who stand charged with the trouble and expense of its finished maturity—there could scarcely have been set a-going a more mischievous process of acceleration toward all the miseries and corruptions which are attendant on the overgrown charity of England."

The population of St. John's, the cost of whose pauperism had hitherto averaged £1400 yearly, he proposed to manage in the manner of an unassessed country parish, and to provide for all its indigence out of the fund raised by voluntary contributions at the church-door. In accordance with that proposal the magistrates of the city had consented that the entire control of that fund should be vested in the church-session of that parish. The design contemplated by Dr. Chalmers was not so much that of providing for pauperism as of preventing it, which he was convinced might be done to great extent by stimulating to industry, by using means to procure employment for the destitute, by eliciting the kindly sympathies of relations and neighbors, and by maintaining, through all available means, the invaluable feelings of independence and self-reliance among the poor. In this work much depended upon the careful scrutiny of individual cases; inasmuch as the least deserving of aid are generally the most forward in applying for it. The deacons of St. John's, accordingly, received distinct instructions for their guidance in relation to that matter. "When one applies for admittance through his deacon upon our funds, the first thing to be inquired into is, if there be any kind of work that he can yet do, so as either to keep him altogether off, or as to make a partial allowance serve for his necessities; the second, what his relatives and friends are willing to do for him; the third, whether he is a hearer in any dissenting place of worship, and whether its session will contribute to his relief. And if, after these previous inquiries, it be found that further relief is necessary, then there must be a strict ascertainment of his term of residence in Glasgow, and whether he be yet on the funds of the town hospital, or is obtaining relief from any other parish. If upon all these points being ascertained, the deacon of the proportion where he resides, still conceives him an object for our assistance, he will inquire whether a small temporary aid will meet the occasion, and state this to the first ordinary meeting. But if, instead of this, he conceives him a fit subject for a regular allowance, he will receive the assistance of another deacon to complete and confirm his inquiries by the next ordinary meeting thereafter, at which time the applicant, if they still think him a fit object, is brought before us, and received upon the fund at such a rate of allowance, as upon all the circumstances of the case, the meeting of deacons shall judge proper. Of course, pending these examinations, the deacon is empowered to grant the same sort of discretionary aid that is customary in other parishes."

The town hospital was to retain all its old pensioners of St. John's parish, the kirk session to take up and provide for new cases, and bear the charge of all the existing cases of sessional poor; and henceforth neither from the one class nor the other should a single pauper be sent to the town hospital, or be chargeable upon the general assessment for the city.

The collections made at the church-door amounted to about £480 a year; but Dr. Chalmers limited his expenditures to much less. For during the whole time, nearly four years, in which he presided over the operation of the scheme, the whole number admitted on his list of paupers was twenty, at the annual expense of only £66. The number of sessional poor thrown upon his hands at the beginning, as having belonged to the parishes out of which St. John's was composed, was ninety-eight, of whom thirteen were, after investigation, displaced, and twenty-eight, in the course of the four years, died. The whole number was, then, seventy-seven, whose yearly maintenance amounted to £190. Their large surplus encouraged the session to take the whole of the town hospital paupers connected with their parish, off that institution, involving themselves in an additional expense of £90 a year. So that all the old pauperism which had not originated under their management—and which they had every reason to estimate as much larger than under that management it should have been—and all the new pauperism which had arisen, was now managed at a yearly cost of £280. From one-tenth of the city, and that part composed of the poorest of its population, the whole flow of pauperism into the town hospital had been intercepted, and an expenditure which had amounted to £1400 was reduced to £280.

Thus, at the close of Dr. Chalmers's ministry, the session of St. John's had from their own church-door collections a surplus of £900, of which £500 had been appropriated for the endowment of one of their parochial schools. The success of the scheme was complete; but those who had predicted its failure now changed their plea and urged that however triumphant under Dr. Chalmers's management, it would always need a Chalmers to maintain its successful operation. The justice of this was also tested upon his removal, in 1823, when instead of failing, as its enemies expected, the scheme continued to prosper many years; and when, in 1837, it was relinquished, and the parish suffered to fall back into the general system of the city, it was only on account of the discouragements and embarrassments thrown in its way by the civic authorities.

It was impossible for the hand of one man to execute singly so many measures of public utility. But few have ever been endowed with a greater power of interesting others in his schemes and of enlisting their voluntary services than he who originated these reforms. The secret of his success lay in that attractive faculty whereby he gathered around him and stimulated to deeds of noble christian philanthropy so large a number of the intelligent and influential laity.

His parish was divided into twenty-five districts, called proportions, containing from sixty to one hundred families each. Over each of these Dr. Chalmers appointed an elder and a deacon, the spiritual interests being intrusted to the former and the temporal interests to the latter, the whole management of the pauperism being committed to the hands of the deacons. " In each district one or more Sabbath schools were instituted, male and female teachers, to the number of between forty and fifty, being engaged in this work, while a few classes were opened for the adult population."

This body of lay assistants Dr. Chalmers called his agency. But though making use of their labors, he never suffered the supervision of any part of the work to escape from his own hand. There were the regular times of reporting all proceedings, " the ordinary meetings of the kirk session, the monthly meetings of the deacons, monthly meetings of the Sabbath school teachers, monthly meetings in the church for missionary purposes, and frequent meetings of the educational association; all of which Dr. Chalmers regularly and punctually attended;" and even in the daily discharge of duty his vigilant eye attended every one of his agents. " Regular reports from all quarters were constantly coming in, and messages and requests and suggestions were as constantly being issued. Had his agents but preserved all the brief notes of a line or two which they received from Dr. Chalmers, it would be seen what an incessant shower of these little billets, not one of which was dispatched on a fruitless errand, he was constantly discharging. Intercourse at meetings or by letter was not enough; something closer and more familiar was required to bind all lovingly together. Every Monday morning in his own house there was agency breakfast, to which a general invitation was issued, and at which from six to eight of his elders, deacons, or Sabbath-school teachers, were generally present. More special invitations to tea were also given, and that with such frequency, that there was scarcely an agent who was not asked once to the house within each six weeks."

"His parochial arrangements were now complete, and with almost superhuman energy Dr. Chalmers guided and impelled every movement of the complicated apparatus. At the commencement of his ministry in St. John's he had secured the services of the Rev. Edward Irving, then a licentiate of the church. There were peculiarities both of thought and utterance which made Mr. Irving unpopular as a preacher. He had given up the prospect of a settlement at home and had resolved to leave his native land, full of the chivalrous romance of Christianity. His intention was, relying simply upon such resources as he could open up for himself by the way, to go as a missionary to Persia, after a preliminary wandering over Europe. To qualify himself for the self-imposed office, he applied himself to the study of the modern languages, and buried himself among his books. 'Rejected by the living,' as he told a friend, 'I was conversing with the dead.'" In the midst of his studies he was interrupted by a note from Dr. Andrew Thomson, asking him to preach in St. George's, and telling him that he would have Dr. Chalmers, who was looking out for an assistant, as an auditor. He complied with the request, and preached as he had been desired, without, however, having seen or conversed with Dr. Chalmers. Days and weeks elapsed without any indication of his preaching having made any favorable impression. His books were all packed up and dispatched to Annan, while he himself set off on a farewell tour round the west coast of Ayrshire to see some friends ere his departure for the east. Loitering on the quay at Greenock, he stepped into a steamboat which was to carry him, as he thought, to Stranraer. It was only after her paddles had commenced to move that he discovered that she was bound for the Highlands. He leaped ashore, and treading, in no pleasant frame of mind, the Greenock quay once more, he resolved that, carry him where she might, he would embark in the next boat that sailed. It so happened that the vessel was bound for Belfast, and having just time to write his father, saying, that if any letter came for him it should be addressed to Coleraine, he crossed the channel and wandered for two or three weeks over the north of Ireland, sleeping in the houses of the peasantry, and in all its lights and shadows seeing Irish life. In due time he reached Coleraine, where there awaited him a letter from Annan, containing an inclosure, which his father told him he would have copied if he could, but he could not decipher a single word. It was a letter from Dr. Chalmers, requesting his immediate presence in Glasgow. He hurried there, arriving on a Saturday, when he found that Dr. Chalmers had gone to Fifeshire. As there was nothing definite in the letter, and as weeks had passed since it was written, Mr. Irving was about to give up the matter altogether, when told by a friend that Dr. Chalmers had just returned. He saw him, and was told that it was his desire that he should be his assistant. 'Well, sir,' said Mr. Irving, after the unexpected tidings had been communicated to him, 'I am most grateful to you, but I must be also somewhat acceptable to your people. I will preach to them if you think fit, and if they bear with my preaching, they will be the first people that have borne with it.' "He did preach, proved acceptable, and for the two years which followed—the busiest, perhaps, in all his busy life—Dr. Chalmers was refreshed and sustained by the congenial fellowship and effective co-operation of a like-minded and noble-hearted associate. There were three public services every Sabbath in St. John's church, and one in a school-house situated in the eastern end of the parish, which commenced at the same time with the forenoon service in the church. These four services were shared equally between Dr. Chalmers and his assistant, the forenoon and evening service in the church on each alternate Sabbath, devolving upon the one, the service in the school-house and the afternoon service in the church, devolving upon the other. Dr. Chalmers commenced a series of lectures upon the Epistle to the Romans, and his assistant a series of lectures upon the Gospel of St. Luke. The same lecture which was delivered by each in the forenoon in the church, was re-delivered, but not on the same day, to the evening congregation, the series as preached in the forenoon being generally two or three lectures in advance of the series as delivered in the evening. It was particularly desired that the evening congregation should only consist of parishioners and those of the poorer classes whom the high seat-rents charged upon the general or forenoon congregation, served to exclude. The labors of household visitation were also shared between Dr. Chalmers and his assistant. In this department Mr. Irving was pre-eminently effective. In many a rude encounter, the infidel radicalism of the parish bent and bowed before him. His commanding presence, his manly bearing, his ingenuous honesty, his vigorous intellect, and above all, his tender and most generous sympathies melted the hearts of the people under him, and second only to that which his more illustrious colleague possessed was the parochial influence which, after a few months' visitation, he gained and most fruitfully exercised.* His own round among the families of the parish, Dr. Chalmers completed within two years. The general manner of these visits has already been described. Much greater pains, however, were now taken both by himself and the other parochial agents, to secure a large attendance at the evening addresses, by which these forenoon visitations were followed up. The success justified the effort. Multitudes, who otherwise would never have had the overtures of Divine mercy addressed to them, were brought within the sound of the preacher's voice. These local week-day, undress congregations assembled in a cotton-mill, or the workshop of a mechanic, or the kitchen of some kindly accommodating neighbor, with their picturesque exhibition of greasy jackets and unwashed countenances, and hands all soiled and fresh from labor turning up the pages of unused Bibles, had a special charm for Dr. Chalmers; and all

---

* "Mr. Irving remained for two years in Glasgow as Dr. Chalmers's assistant, after which he was called to the metropolis, where a speedy and unbounded popularity raised him to an elevation such as no presbyterian minister, before or since, has ever reached in London."

alive to the peculiar interest and urgency of such opportunities, he stirred up every faculty that was in him, while he urged upon the consciences and the hearts of such auditors the high claims of the christian salvation. His chosen and beloved friend, Mr. Collins—who, after such a life of honorable service in the cause of Christ as few laymen among us have ever lived, in that retirement into which feeble health has forced him, still cherishes with unabated zeal those interests which in by-gone years he toiled so much to further—often accompanied Dr. Chalmers to these evening meetings; and we have his reiterated and emphatic testimony, that no bursts of that oratory which rolled over admiring thousands in the Tron church or in St. John's, ever equaled, in all the highest qualities of eloquence, many of these premeditated but unwritten addresses, in which, free from all restraint, and intent upon the one object of winning souls to the Saviour, that heart which glowed with such intense desires for the present and eternal welfare of the working classes, unbosomed in the midst of them all the fullness of its christian sympathies."

Owing to various causes, of which the principal was overtrading, whereby continental markets were glutted with British goods, to which may be added the deficient crops of 1816, the years from 1817 to 1820 were times of great distress among the working classes of Great Britain, and especially among the operatives of the manufacturing towns. The pressure, consequently fell heavily upon a large body of the population of Glasgow. And in the spring of 1820, discontent, in some of the cities of both England and Scotland, had proceeded the length of open revolt, professing to have for its object a radical change in the government. The movement, however, was not sustained by the sympathy of the rest of the nation, and was consequently put down in a few days. It was a subject which deeply interested the mind of Dr. Chalmers, and his views in relation to it were variously expressed: first, in an article for the Edinburgh Review, written in January, 1820, in a series of letters addressed to Mr. Wilberforce, during that winter and succeeding spring, as well as in two sermons preached on the 30th of April and 7th of May, the design of which was to show the salutary effect of the religious element in government. These latter were afterward united into one discourse, and published on the 16th of May, under the title of "A Sermon on the Importance of Civil Government to Society." Two editions, amounting to 6000 copies, were sold off, and a third issued in twenty-four days. They were afterward included in the series of his works.

The Moral Philosophy chair in the University of Edinburgh had become vacant by the death of Dr. Thomas Brown, and Dr. Chalmers was requested to become a candidate, with the assurance that if he did so, he would obtain the appointment. Agreeable as that situation would have been to his feelings and habits of mind, he could not think of relinquishing his plans for the improvement of the condition of his parish while yet immature, and, accordingly, replied that he was too much interested in his present work to be willing to leave it at that stage of its progress, and could not offer himself as a candidate, nor encourage any of his friends to move in the matter. At the same time he privately recorded his intention to devote a larger proportion of the rest of his life to intellectual labor. In the meanwhile, he multiplied his efforts for the parish of St. John's, as if under a premonition that the period assigned to them could not be long.

"That he might prosecute his parochial labors with greater facility and less distraction, he rented a small apartment within the bounds of the parish," and thus, devoting himself entirely to his work, accomplished an amount of it which has seldom been paralleled. Spending four days a week in visiting the people, in company with his agents for the various districts into which he had divided his parish, he sometimes saw from 700 to 800 persons in a week. He had the company of his agency to tea almost every evening, when their past efforts were reviewed and future plans devised. At nine o'clock, he went out to family worship in some house belonging to the district of his lodging, where he collected the people of the vicinity. Fridays and Saturdays were his days of study. Every Friday evening he delivered an address before the people of the neighborhood, in the Calton Lancasterian school room, and a weekly address to those of the respective districts, as he went over them in regular visitation. Beside all this, he attended to such additional calls, as meetings of Sabbath school society, meetings of Presbytery, his Thursday sermon, meetings of session, and various other incidental business involved.

It has been stated that about the time of entering upon his ministry in St. John's, he issued a pamphlet on the " Christian and Civic Economy of Large Towns ;" the same subject was further pursued in a series of such pamphlets published quarterly, and continued for several years. In November, 1820, he published a volume of sermons, " On the Application of Christianity to the Commercial and ordinary Affairs of Life." Perceiving the very extensive field of usefulness now within the reach of his pen, in order to secure more time for writing and preaching, he delegated a large portion of the work of visitation and the cares attendant thereupon to his agency, still holding himself ready to go to any sick person, who might, through one of the elders, require his services, and also to go through all the houses in his parish once in two years, and invite each proportion to a week-day evening address ; and declaring himself desirous of making " attendance upon the parish funeral take precedence of all other duties and engagements whatever."

In the course of his quarterly publications, he came, in the spring of 1822, upon the great question of pauperism, and having discussed it in its Scottish aspects and bearings, meant to deal with it also in relation to England; but feeling distrust of his knowledge on that part of the subject, he resolved upon a tour of minute inquiry before attempting the treatment of it. In the course of that tour he made personal inspection of the working of the English poor-laws, of the workhouses, and of the plans pursued in particular parishes in respect to their poor. He also consulted on the subject many of the most eminent men of England, as Mr. Malthus, Mr. Wilberforce, Lord Calthorpe, Dr. Pye Smith, Messrs. Leigh Richmond, Zachary

Macauley, Babington, Buxton, Clarkson, and many others, eminent as statesmen and philanthropists.

He returned to Glasgow on the 19th of October. The effect of his observations evidently was to confirm him in adherence to the views he had already adopted. He had seen the English poor-laws everywhere operating to break down the feeling of self-reliance among the poor, to stop up the fountains of spontaneous benevolence, injuring thereby both the giver and receiver, and actually increasing the evil they were designed to remove. His periodical treatises were consequently continued on the same principles on which they had been commenced.

After all the assistance employed to carry the gospel into every family under his care, it was found that the enormous magnitude of the parish overmatched his efforts, and his favorite purpose, that of reaching frequently those who paid no attendance on the outward ordinances of religion, nor presented themselves to the preacher's voice, was still unattained. He therefore conceived the design of dividing his parish into two, and of planting another minister with a corresponding body of assistants in it. In vain, however, did he urge the magistrates and council to execute that work; they could not be made to feel its importance, and, as the only method open to him, he issued proposals to build a chapel of ease within the bounds of St. John's, the funds to be raised by shares of £100 each, on which the ordinary rate of interest should be paid. Having subscribed five shares himself, and eleven other persons one each, a constitution was obtained, according to which, the collections taken up in the new chapel, were to be at the disposal of the session of St. John's, for the relief of the poor in the chapel district. The enterprise was, at this stage, sustained by the liberality of Mr. Douglas of Cavers, who placed £500 at the disposal of Dr. Chalmers for that object, and before the building was complete, it received another donation from the same hand to the same amount. The chapel was opened for public worship in May, 1823, and in June, a minister was ordained to the charge of the district for which it was erected. Dr. Chalmers, however, did not thereupon resign all concern in it, but labored for its success to the utmost of his power, even after his removal from Glasgow, making a yearly visit to the city to preach for five or six successive Sabbaths in that chapel and visit among the parishioners.

Yet the project failed. Many causes conspired to this result, among which, was the fact that the minister's salary had to be paid from the pew rents, and these had been set so unreasonably high, that the attraction of the preaching, it seems, had not been sufficient to overcome the repulsion of the price demanded, and consequently the chapel sunk under a load of debt; being utterly unable to pay the interest of the money expended in its erection. Another cause was the want of tact and energy in the clergyman appointed to the charge. Though an excellent and pious man, he was deficient in many qualities necessary for so peculiar a sphere of duty. Some years later he wrote to Dr. Chalmers, requesting his interest in procuring for him a church elsewhere. The reply bore testimony to the greatness of Dr. Chalmers's disappointment and his conviction that inefficiency of the minister was the primary cause. That gentleman himself, under a sense of his unfitness for the place, soon afterward, voluntarily, "relinquished more than half of the limited salary, which the proprietors of the chapel had agreed to advance, in order that an assistant and successor might be appointed."

In the midst of these multifarious occupations, Dr. Chalmers received from the University of St. Andrew's a proposition tendering him, on the most kindly and liberal terms, the professorship of Moral Philosophy in that institution. "If your mind," wrote Principal Nicoll, "be at once decidedly against the plan, you will require no time for deliberation, but if you judge it deserving of consideration, then I think your best way would be to meet me in Edinburgh — where I am to be at a county meeting on Tuesday next — when we can have a conversation on the subject. Be assured, however, that I have no wish to converse with you on anything like jobbing politics.

"If you come among us you shall come free as the air you breathe. No favor will be considered as done to you, and consequently you will be under no obligation to any individual. My support will be given to your character — to your varied acquirements and splendid talents — to your integrity as a man — to your gentlemanlike and mild manners as a member of society; and if my colleagues give their support, I know that it will be given on the same grounds. The living, I am sorry to say, cannot be reckoned higher than £300 a year, but I think it will increase."

The interview in Edinburgh, proposed by Dr. Nicoll, took place; and on the 18th of January, 1823, Dr. Chalmers was unanimously elected to the chair of Moral Philosophy in St. Andrew's. Although he had previously declined many propositions from both vacant churches and chairs, this was so entirely congenial to his feelings, and coincided so well with his now fixed purpose of devoting much of his time to the work of authorship, and came to him also at a period when his various plans for his parish were all fairly in operation, that, without any further consultation, he frankly intimated his acceptance, with the understanding that he should not enter upon the duties of the office until November of the same year. This decision was forthwith made known to the gentlemen of his agency. The announcement was to them a most painful surprise. They found it difficult to comprehend the motive which could actuate a man to withdraw from a place of such publicity, popularity and success; to the obscurity of a professor's lecture-room, and they doubtless experienced a sinking of heart in view of their own future labors, when he who had been the mainspring of all should be withdrawn. But there was such a firm tone of decision in the language of his letter to them, that they perceived remonstrance to be in vain. The general public of Glasgow regretted that decision, and as the public frequently treats her favorites, when they cross her wishes, threw out here and there some very ungenerous imputations upon the motives leading thereto. Unmoved from his purpose by any such considerations, Dr. Chalmers proceeded with increased assiduity in all the duties of his parish until the last day of his connection therewith. Especially did his new chapel occupy his attention, being the only one of his parochial measures still immature. In the course of the spring and summer all the arrangements necessary to its operation being complete, he felt himself acquitted of his obligations to his church, and ready to leave it in prosperous condition to his successor.

The principal occasions on which Dr. Chalmers took any part in Ecclesiastical Court matters, in those days, were in the General Assemblies of 1821 and 1822, on the question of theological education, and in the Synod of Glasgow and Ayr, in 1823, in a case of plurality. The former was a matter which, indeed, seems to have urgently demanded reformation, for as they then stood, the requisitions of candidates for the gospel ministry may be said to have been leveled down to the humblest capacity. The student, after his four years' attendance upon the ordinary academical course, might, if he saw fit, pursue his studies in the Divinity Halls for three full sessions and part of a fourth : or "without hearing a single course of lectures on theology, by his mere presence for a few days at one of the University seats in the course of six successive sessions, and by performing a few prescribed exercises, he might qualify himself for the ministry. Between these two, which may be regarded as the extreme methods, there were various ways adopted by students, and allowed by the church, of compounding together sessions of regular and irregular attendance upon the theological classes. The object of those with whom Dr. Chalmers now co-operated was to abolish altogether the six years' occasional attendance, to make a regular attendance for three full sessions to be in every case imperative, and to enjoin that at least two years' attendance should be given on the classes of Hebrew and Church History. The speech of Dr. Chalmers in the General Assembly of 1821, in favor of the proposed reformation, was one of the most brilliant which he ever delivered before the Supreme Court of his church. Its most powerful passages were afterward embodied in the 'Christian and Civic Economy of Large Towns,' and in his work on the 'Use and Abuse of Literary Endowments.' It was not till after many discussions and defeats that the object which Dr. Chalmers and his friends had in view was attained, and the standard of theological qualification for the ministry in the Church of Scotland permanently raised."

The latter case arose out of a presentation to the Inner High Church of Glasgow, issued by the Crown in favor of Dr. McFarlane, Principal of the University of Glasgow, a case of plurality which could not be defended by any plea of lightness of duty or inadequacy of support; for each of the offices thus proposed to be united in one person, were more than enough for all the labor of one, and both were amply endowed. If this case were admitted, it would be difficult to say upon what ground any plurality could be opposed. Through the influence of Dr. Chalmers and a few other clergymen of the city, who entertained as zealously the same views, the presentation was rejected by the Presbytery. Dr. McFarlane appealed to the Synod, which was to meet in October. In that body an attempt was made to represent the action of the Presbytery and of those who should sustain it, as resistance to the royal power, whence the presentation had emanated. After the legality of the course pursued by the Presbytery had been ably stated by his colleagues, Dr. Chalmers, in the close of his argument, nobly exposed the meanness and unconstitutionality of such a plea. "I would have said no more, but for one affirmation in the reasons of the appellant, even that this proceeding of ours is 'disrespectful to the Crown.' That is indeed a noble anecdote of British jurisprudence in the preface to De Lolme's 'Essay on the British Constitution. On his first arrival in London, he attended a court of law, when the cause happened to be a question between a subject and a prince of the blood. It was decided for the subject, and against the prince—a circumstance which in itself was quite enough to surprise the foreigner. But there was an accompaniment to the thing, which surprised him infinitely more than the thing itself; and that is, that no surprise whatever was either felt or expressed by the spectators—not even one movement of popular satisfaction, and no mobbish or tumultuary delight because of the poor man's triumph, and the great man's overthrow. And why? because the thing just happened in the even and ordinary course of English justice; it was but an everyday incident in the administration of law; and of the whole assembled public who were present, and had looked calmly and intelligently on throughout the whole of the process, not one discovered the slightest astonishment, not one betrayed any indecent exultation at the verdict, because it was precisely the verdict which, from the abstract merits of the case, they had been led to anticipate. It was this which gave to this enlightened stranger his profoundest sense of the excellence of our constitution; and this is the origin of far the soundest treatise which has appeared on the government and constitution of our highly privileged land.

"Now this is a noble anecdote. It has the moral sublime in it; and were I called to fix upon the thing that should be placed over against it in most direct and humiliating contrast, it should just be this reason of the appellant. It is a reason I could not have dared to utter in your hearing, lest you had rebuked me into silence for so presuming on the paltry and pusillanimous stuff which this venerable Court was made of. It is a bugbear to frighten children; and foreign as it is to all the habitudes of English justice, it would indeed sound most strangely in English ears. It smells of feudalism all over; and in politics, it is as unlike to the true spirit of British loyalty as in religion a driveling superstition is unlike to the homage of a rational and enlightened piety. Take my word for it, sir, that no feeling of the sort exists at head-quarters; nay, were the whole truth known, the feeling there would be exactly the reverse. In the hurry and hard-driving of the public offices, things are often done before the evil tendency is understood, and then a loop-hole of retreat is deemed of all things to be the most desirable. And were it only known with what fond, yet painful interest, the whole of Scotland was now looking on; were it known that our Kirk, with all its errors, was still the dearest object of our people's veneration; were it known how much it is that the righteousness of her measures is fitted to gladden all the land, and to pour the sunshine of an honest triumph into this very humblest of our cottages; were it known that, by this appointment, the most loyal magistracy in our empire have been thwarted, and the purest and most patriotic designs for the public weal are now placed on a brink of fearful uncertainty; were all this known, I feel sure, as of my existence, that the royal complacency would smile upon our calumniated labors, and not upon the men who could degrade their sovereign into a scarecrow, and prostitute his venerated name to the service of a hurtful and unhallowed usurpation."

The Synod affirmed the sentence of the Presbytery, and the matter was carried by appeal before the General Assembly of 1824. There Dr. Chalmers made another effort to avert from the church the dreaded evil; but that body was not yet prepared to appreciate the weight of his reasons. A large majority voted to reverse the sentence of Presbytery, and that "Dr. McFarlane should be admitted as minister of the High Church."

In the case of a man so variedly and successfully employed before the public, there is a natural curiosity which prompts us to inquire what were his private manners and habits, as if it would be gratifying to know how he compared with other men in matters wherein all men comport themselves into comparison with him.

To the pen of the Rev. Mr. Smyth, Mr. Irving's successor, in the assistantship of St. John's, we are indebted for a glimpse into the domestic life of Dr. Chalmers at this busiest period of his career:

" It was on Saturday, June 8th, 1822, that I joined Dr. Chalmers at Limekilns for Glasgow. I shall never forget the kindness which he showed me that day. Although a native of the west of Scotland, I had not been in the city of Glasgow since my childhood, and that merely for a few minutes. All was new and strange. My heart was full, and my anxiety was intense. Well do I recollect how thoroughly Dr. Chalmers made me acquainted with the localities through which we passed along the canal. 'Come, now, my dear, sir,' (I seem at this moment to hear the very words), 'and I will initiate you into the mystery of the locks,' a mystery which I had never seen before. At intervals he was busily occupied with the perusal of Sibb's 'Soul's Conflict,' a book which he greatly valued on account of its deep experimental character. We reached Glasgow on Saturday evening, and had a most affectionate welcome from the doctor's family, including his aunt Jean, as she was lovingly called, an 'old' lady with whom I afterward spent many happy hours. When we entered the dining-room for tea, my eye lighted on a table literally covered with letters, the accumulation of a few days. It appeared to me a most Herculean task for any man to address himself to the reading, how much more to the answering, of some fifty or sixty epistles on all varieties of subjects, public and private. It was Dr. Chalmers's practice at this time to reply to his correspondents, whenever it was practicable for him to do so, in course of post. In his answers he generally confined himself to the matter immediately on hand, waiving prefaces, and getting at once *in medias res*. In this way, although, perhaps, no man in Britain had a more extensive and multifarious correspondence he succeeded in never falling behind with his answers. I have repeatedly seen him reply to ten or twelve letters in the course of an hour. In this respect, as in others, our venerated friend was a striking example of the power of methodical adherence to a fixed system in accomplishing what to most men would have been an insuperable labor. Sabbath, June 9th, was the commencement of my public work in Glasgow. I preached in the school-house in the morning, and in the parish church in the afternoon, and heard Dr. Chalmers in the evening. The Lord was very gracious and helpful: I got through with calmness, and felt, I trust, thankful for better strength than my own. Arrangements were made for my continuance in Glasgow several weeks, and during that period I had ample opportunities of becoming well acquainted with Dr. Chalmers's 'manner of life,' as well as of his mighty enterprises for the temporal and spiritual welfare of men. Many have been under the impression that Dr. Chalmers was more a man of powerful impulses, who achieved wonderful things by fits and starts of burning zeal, than of systematic persevering application of mind. There never was a greater mistake. With all his transcendent genius, and talent, and philanthropy, I am satisfied that the main secret of his strength lay in his indomitable resolution to master whatever he undertook. What has been considered by some as a defect was indeed an excellence of no common order. When convinced that it was his duty to address himself to some course of study or of action, he concentrated on that his energies of mind and body, and with indefatigable assiduity completed his work, unless some urgent call of duty which did not admit of postponement, interfered. Dr. Chalmers devoted at least five hours each day to study; I use the word in its proper sense; he was thus studiously occupied partly before breakfast, and thereafter till one or two o'clock, in reading and composition. These were his hours, and it was understood that they were, except in the event of some special emergency, not to be invaded by friend or stranger. It being midsummer when I first resided under his roof he generally relaxed for two hours, taking some favorite walk, and kindly inviting me to accompany him. The Botanic Garden was a much loved resort. He luxuriated among the plants and flowers of the season, and delighted to examine minutely the structure and the beauties of some humble production that would have escaped the notice of a less practiced eye. He said to me one day, after he had been rapt in admiration of Nature and Nature's God — 'I love to dwell on the properties of one flower at a time; to fix my mind on it exclusively until I feel that it has taken complete hold of my mind. This is a peculiarity of my constitution. I must have concentration of thought on any given thing, and not be diverted from it.' My attention was arrested in the garden by a sunflower of large dimensions and exquisite coloring. He said, with deep emotion, 'Oh, that we could so open our hearts to the beams of the Sun of righteousness!' It was in such scenes that one not only saw but felt that the train of thought was heavenward—that his heart and his treasure were in heaven.

"He dined generally at half-past four o'clock; and it was Dr. Chalmers's practice to sally forth, as he playfully expressed it, after dinner, from his house in Windsor-place to St. John's parish, spending at least two hours several nights in the week among his parishioners. In these visits it was repeatedly my high privilege to accompany him. They were generally short but most instructive—*multum in parvo*. He possessed a singular power of stating the sum and substance of the gospel in a few comprehensive and most weighty sentences, and closed each visit with a most appropriate prayer. . . . . . The more advanced hours of the evening were spent in a less onerous way—letter-writing, or the literature of the day, or the society of friends who partook of his large-hearted hospitality and that of his beloved household. In no respect did Dr. Chalmers present a more attractive example of all that is kind and lovely than in the bosom of his own family. His children were young, but they were to him objects of daily and most affectionate interest; he was playful among them even to occasional romping. His smile of fatherly love was ever ready to encourage their approaches; and when absent for a few weeks he printed little letters for their acceptance. I can hardly trust myself, even at the distance of so many years, with detailed references to that once happy and precious home in which it was my lot to spend several months. The united heads of it have been removed from that household of which they were at once the ornament and the glory—revered—beloved—shedding down on children and domestics sweet and hallowed influences, binding all in one home-circle of warm and steadfast attachment. I may be permitted here to record my tribute of affectionate reverence for the memory of Mrs. Chalmers. To have been the wife of such a man afforded a strong presumption of qualities which *he* thoroughly estimated; and none who knew his lamented wife well could fail to be satisfied that she was in all respects a helpmeet for her distinguished husband. Possessed of talents decidedly superior, of large and varied information, of warm-hearted affections, and of what is infinitely better, enlightened and decided piety, Mrs. Chalmers commanded the esteem and the confidence of her family and her friends. Her judgment was calm, sound, and comprehensive. She possessed a tact and a delicacy of perception which fitted her for being a wise and faithful counselor. Dr. Chalmers had *unlimited confidence in her discretion.* He felt that her coincidence with him in opinion or in plans was of great value. She strengthened his hands and encouraged his heart in every labor of love. Nor did she ever forget the limits of a woman's sphere; exquisite feminine delicacy was united with great vigor and promptitude of mind. Habitually cheerful and happy, there was a sunshine of the soul which even the clouds of affliction did not obscure. Her health frequently suffered, but this trial served to bring out more fully the ornament of a meek and quiet spirit. Thoroughly conversant with Dr. Chalmers's views in regard to many exciting questions, she entered into his enthusiastic defenses and expositions of them with her whole heart; and with what gentle affection she poured a healing balm into the waters when ruffled, or in danger of being so, tendering some word in season that bound up the wound which ignorance or envy had inflicted. Her kindness to myself during my repeated sojournings I trust that I shall never forget. I experienced in her society much that was calculated to guide my inexperience, and to strengthen me for private and public duty. Her discernment of character was remarkable. It seemed as if by intuition she could at once discriminate between the true and the false-hearted, and yet there was the charity which hopeth all things. As a wife, a mother, a mistress, a friend, a disciple of Him who was meek and lowly in spirit, few are better entitled to affection's warmest tribute. It was my mournful privilege to be with her on that day which covered Scotland's church and people in sackcloth; and after the mortal remains of the husband who had been so many years the dearest object of love were deposited in the grave, not one murmuring or impatient word escaped her lips; all was lowly submission to her Father's good and righteous will — a widow indeed, but firmly trusting in the widow's God, and raising her agonized yet confiding heart to Him who was a man of sorrows and acquainted with grief. The conflict of nature was severe, but the victory of faith was not denied. Her sainted spirit had communion in its sorrows with the unsuffering inhabitants of heaven, and after a brief season of earthly tribulation, she, too, has entered the rest that remaineth for the people of God. May we be indeed followers of them who through faith and patience inherit the promises."

In all his correspondence with the various members of the family, while printing letters with his pen for the children, or meeting the caustic skepticism of his brother James as well as when responding to the piety of his mother, his wife and favorite sister, and while adapting his manner to the characteristics of each, and writing familiarly of those topics of most interest to his correspondent for the time, one topic is invariably urged either directly or indirectly, the great topic of peace with God through the Lord Jesus Christ.

His hospitality was large and genial. His social nature encouraged the visits of friends and parishioners; beside which his system of parochial instruction brought around him those numerous persons who contributed their voluntary assistance therein, and his reputation rendering him an object of popular interest brought multitudes of strangers as guests into his house. Though occasionally complaining of the latter intrusion, it was not in his nature to repel it. Provided only his hours of study were uninterrupted "there was scarcely any wearying of him by any succession of visitors however numerous or varied. There have been at times three different rooms full of people waiting for him, and when he issued from his retirement he had a cordial welcome ready for each one of them." No feature in his personal character was more prominent than his love of society and his large capacity for appreciating diversified phases of humanity; while enjoying the refinements of the highest and most polished, he could enter with the truest sympathy into all the humble joys and sorrows of the poor, and from the high pursuit of his own meditations he could enter with the most genial affection into the conversation of youth and its zeal in rudimentary knowledge.

"I think it was 1818, or 1819," says Mr. Colquhoun, "that Dr. Chalmers came to Killermont. I have received (for I was not then at home) an account of one incident of his visit from my friend Mr. Dundas, the sheriff of Selkirkshire, which is too characteristic to be omitted. Our family circle was then unbroken, and among them my eldest sister, who, to her many accomplishments, added the study of botany, attracted Dr. Chalmers's attention. With his usual warm interest in the pursuits of the young, he talked with her on that subject, and examined the flora which she had collected. One plant in the series was wanting, and he inquired why; on her telling him that she had not been able to find it, he said it was surely to be had in the neighborhood, and the subject dropped for that evening. The next morning, when the family assembled for prayers, Dr. Chalmers did not appear, and his bedroom was deserted. The family sat down to breakfast without him, nor was it till breakfast was half over that he came into the room, his hat in his hand, tired and heated from a long walk, but carrying with him the missing plant, which he presented to my sister. It is needless to say how much this trait affected the young hearts that were present, as it has remained impressed on Mr. Dundas to the present day.

"Dr. Chalmers's next visit to Killermont must have been in the summer or autumn of 1822, and we all recollect the interest which he showed in conversing with myself, then at Oxford, and with my brother, then quite a boy, on the subject of our respective studies. It was not the manner of a man who condescended to minds far his inferiors, but as if he became one of us, and our studies were as keenly relished by him, as if he were himself engaged in them. To my brother he talked eagerly of his boyish studies; of me, he inquired much of an Oxford course, and seemed to listen with as much delight to my account of Aristotle's ethics, which he compared with his favorite Butler, as though the Oxford student could give instead of gaining information; and in his walks with us his delights in nature were more keen than those of any of the party; and while rowing in the boat on the river Kelvin, gathering the water-lilies, of which I remember he had an intense admiration, his glee was as boyish as ours.

"Some years afterward, he passed several days at Killermont; our family circle was then sorely broken, and there remained only two of the sisters whom he had before seen, but I well remember that to one of these, who died the following summer, his conversation on religious subjects was of the utmost benefit. She saw, along with the greatness, the simplicity and tenderness of his mind, and was encouraged in some walks which she took with him, to confide to him her doubts and difficulties. I wish I had preserved the letter in which, after her death, he alluded to this, and spoke with characteristic force of the preparedness which he had noticed in her heart for the great change which was then before her. But, mixed with all that readiness to converse on religious subjects, was the same buoyant delight in literature, the arts, and the beauties of nature. I recollect his profound admiration for some casts from busts of the great painters and architects in the capitol at Rome, from which, he said, he took in great impressions—the exquisite enjoyment when, riding in the afternoon on a quiet pony, he was taken to see the distant views of Ben Lomond and Loch Lomond. His habit, I remember, was to go to his room after breakfast, and to remain there till one or two o'clock engaged in writing, at times telling us that he had written without intermission, and, at other times, that he had a blank morning, and had not done a quarter of an hour's work with his pen — his practice being, as he told me, after attempting some time unsuccessfully, to lay his pen down and take up a book upon some subject entirely different from that on which he was writing, until the inspiration of composition returned upon him, and he then resumed his work. His habits in society varied. Generally, when at his ease, and when his mind was not occupied with a train of thought, his conversation was full of interest, and it became so almost always when those who were with him touched upon a congenial subject, when he threw himself into it with all his peculiar strength and eloquence of language, combined with the most unaffected simplicity, but at times I have seen him perfectly silent, and wearing that blank look which he could throw into his countenance when the mind was otherwise engaged. I remember the late Lady Colquhoun gave me an instance of this, which, I imagine, must have occurred about the same time. He had gone, for the first time, to pay a visit at Rossdhu, and Lady C. awaited his arrival with great anxiety; when, however, he was shown into the drawing-room, after the first salutations were over, he sat perfectly silent, wearing his blank look. She tried a variety of subjects, but in vain, and he soon retired to his room. On coming down to dinner, he apologized, in the most amiable manner, for his silence, confessing, that a train of thought on the subject on which he was writing, had occurred to him on his journey to Rossdhu, and that he was terrified lest, if he entered into conversation, he should lose it before it was secured on paper."

The time was now drawing near for removal to his new field of labor, yet under the zeal of accomplishing his parochial improvements, no advance had yet been made in preparation therefor. In the summer of 1823, he was invited to occupy the house of Blochairn, in the neighborhood of Glasgow, that some leisure might be secured for that purpose ; but so strong was the hold of his parish upon his mind, that very little advantage was thereby gained. There was no falling off in devotion to the church occasioned by his connection with the university. He declared then, and his career afterward proved, that the church held still, and should always hold the highest place in his heart, and that the hope of serving the cause of the Redeemer more extensively, was his principal motive for the change.

" On Wednesday, the 5th of November, he laid before the

Presbytery of Glasgow his letter of resignation of the church and parish of St. John's, which, after many expressions of affectionate regret from different members, the Presbytery was pleased to accept." It was understood that his farewell discourse would be preached on the succeeding Sabbath. From the attraction of all his public appearances in Glasgow, it was to be expected that crowds would throng the church on that occasion. Indeed, for weeks beforehand, seats had been secured, and even the standing room in the aisles, on the pulpit steps, and round the precentor's desk, was already all engaged by tickets ; yet on the morning of that day entrance had to be secured to the holders of the tickets, by a company of police ; and finally; such was the number and persistency of the crowd, that a detachment of soldiers was stationed at the entrance of the church, to keep order and secure admission for the proper occupants of the pews; and after all, the house was crammed with twice the number it could comfortably accommodate. "The pew in which I sat," says one who was present, "contained fourteen sittings, but on that occasion twenty-six persons were crammed into it, some sitting, some standing on the floor, others standing on the seat." The confusion grew within as the pressure somewhat abated from without ; and it was no gentle or very Sabbath frame of spirit that prevailed. At length the preacher rose within that pulpit from which he was to address his hearers for the last time. In a moment the bustle ceased, and all the varied expressions of that great crowd of faces was turned into one uniform gaze of fixed and profound attention. After prayer and praise, the text, from Psalm cxxxvii, 5—6, was twice distinctly read, and its general lessons having been unfolded and impressed, and the preacher coming at the close to speak to those from whom, as their minister, he was now to be finally dissevered—" I will never forget," he said, " that it is your princely beneficence which has carried me forward in covering this parish with those institutions both of scholarship and piety that have done most to grace and to dignify the people of our beloved land. I will never forget the labors of that devoted band to whose union and

perseverance I still look for even greater services than they have yet rendered to the cause of christian philanthropy. I will never forget the unexpected welcome and kindness of my parochial families, among whom the cause, that to the superficial eye looks unpopular and austere, hath now found its conclusive establishment. I never will forget the indulgence and the friendly regards of this congregation; and I beg to assure each and all of them, that if a cold and ungenial apathy, whether of look or of manner, was all the return that they ever could obtain for their demonstrations of christian affection toward myself, it was not because I had not the conviction of that manifold good-will which was on every side of me, but that moving in a wide and busy sphere, and hurried in the course of a few moments from one act of intercourse to another, with more than a thousand of my fellows, my jaded and overborne feelings could not keep pace with it. There are hundreds and hundreds more whom in person I could not overtake, but whom in the hours of cool and leisurely reflection I shall know how to appreciate. And when I gaze on that quarter—the richest of all the wide horizon in the treasures of cordiality and grateful remembrance—then sweeter than to the eye are those tints of loveliness which the western sun stretches in golden clouds above it will be the thought of all the worth and the tenderness and the noble generosity that are there. Oh! I never can forget the city of so many christian and kindhearted men. I never will forget the countenance I have gotten from its upright and patriotic citizens..................
From the deep exhaustion — not incurred in the treatment of my parochial managements, for at all times was there a charm and tranquillity in these—but from the deep exhaustion of hurry and fatigue, and manifold distractions from without, have my footsteps been lured into a most congenial resting-place, among whose academic bowers Rutherford and Halyburton spent the evening of their days, and amid whose venerable ruins their bodies now sleep until the resurrection of the just. Should those high and heavenly themes on which they expatiated through life, and which shed a glory over their

death-beds, ever cease to be dear unto my bosom—should the glare of the world's philosophy ever seduce me from the wisdom and simplicity of the faith—should Jesus Christ and Him crucified not be the end of all my labors in expounding the law of righteousness, then let the fearful judgment of heaven blight and overcast the faculties that I have thus prostituted. 'If I forget thee, O Jerusalem—if I forget thee, O thou church and city of my God—let my right hand forget her cunning. If I do not remember thee, let my tongue cleave to the roof of my mouth : if I prefer not Jerusalem above my chief joy.'

When Dr. Chalmers descended from the pulpit it was entered by the Rev. Edward Irving, who invited the vast congregation to accompany him; as with solemn pomp and impressive unction he poured out a prayer for that honored minister of God who had just retired from among them. The church had been so closely packed that it took forty minutes to empty itself; and before the last of the hearers had left St. John's Dr. Chalmers, who had barely time to transfer himself from the statelier to the humbler edifice, had commenced the afternoon service in the chapel of Ease."

In his sermon before that audience, which was preached from Heb. iii, 13, he introduced a touching reference to the happy death of a poor weaver, who had been an infidel until within a few months of his death, in connection with which he quoted a few simple verses inscribed by the man upon a Bible presented to his son, and expressive of his dying wishes that his boy might be brought up in the fear of the Lord. Pursuing the train of thought suggested thereby, the preacher proceeded: "This, doubtless, is but one example, yet enough to prove how worthy of christian cultivation are those vast and untrodden spaces, that teem with families who are altogether beyond the pale of the word and of ordinances—enough to prove that there is not an aggregate of human beings through which a minister of the gospel might not ply his unwearied rounds, and earn the triumphs of a high and heavenly apostleship—enough to set at rest the obstinate incredulity of those who affirm of the cities of our land, that such is their hard-favored and impracticable resistance to all the endeavors, whether of kindness or of christianity, as to give the visionary character of a dream to the dear and delightful prospect of their ultimate reformation. I speak to the very poorest of my hearers: to you also belong the high capacities of an immortal spirit; to you belong all the elements of moral worth and moral greatness; to you the path of glory is open, and the exalted High Priest, who once sojourned in this world amid pains, and privations, and indignities more severe than all that any disciple of His is ever doomed to encounter, He, from the golden treasury of those gifts and graces wherewith He is invested, is ready even now to shower upon you everything that is needful either to bless you in time or to fit you for eternity. I can vouch for the comfort wherewith a minister of the gospel might move from family to family throughout the vicinities of this immediate population. I can vouch for the perfect graciousness of a kind and honest welcome from you all. I can vouch for the open door of access that there is in every house to the visitations of christian philanthropy; and that even in towns which are conceived to teem all over with loathsome dissipation and profligate companionship, there is a most warm and willing response to the familiar converse and the domestic services of the minister. May he who labors within these walls be enabled to verify this by his own personal experience. May the countenance of heaven rest upon all his ministrations, and while engaged in the Sabbath exercises of piety, or in the week-day intercourse with your families, may a blessing from on high attend every footstep of his progress in the midst of you. Meanwhile I will take leave of you. No breaking up of my official relationship will lessen that close and affecting relationship which I shall ever feel toward your families. If God be pleased to spare me, there is no house where I would more willingly resume, for a season, the ministrations of the word of life, no portion of the great vineyard of Christ in which I shall ever feel a more peculiar interest and property than that which is attached to it. May the blessings of God rest upon you all. May parents have great comfort of their children; and may children, brought up in the ways of piety, rise around their parents and call them blessed. Above all, may you be found in that way of pleasantness and path of peace which leads to heaven. A few years more and the storms of this changing life shall all have blown over us. Let our prayers often meet in the upper sanctuary; and when the morn of the resurrection cometh may we be found side by side at the right hand of our Judge and Saviour."

His multifarious labors for Glasgow were now brought to an end, and though he ceased not to keep an eye upon the operations he had set in motion, and sometime afterward put to a hand to help them on, he was no longer to be connected with them as a prime mover. Of the results of those remarkable eight years, Dr. Hanna presents the following summary: "A few months after his settlement in Glasgow, Dr. Chalmers had wept over the grave of his beloved friend, Thomas Smith, and a few weeks previous to his departure from Glasgow, he stood by the deathbed of this converted weaver. He saw the first and the last fruits of his Glasgow ministry seized by the hand of death, while ripening under the eye of the earthly husbandman, and laid up in the heavenly garner. But who could tell him of the numbers who, during the course of these eight years, and under that ministry, had been savingly impressed by Divine truth? We know of the thoughtless young officer, who, flaunting in idle vacancy through the city streets on a Sabbath forenoon, and attracted by the eager crowds which he saw pouring into the Tron church, turned into that church as he would have done into a theater, but found it to be indeed the house of God—to him the very gate to heaven. We know of the fashionable lady, full of taste and high refinement, but devoid of all earnest thought or care about her immortal soul, driving from her mansion in a neighboring county to be regaled by the eloquence of the celebrated orator, but found of Him whom she sought not, and turned effectually unto God. We know of the busy bustling merchant, immersed in all the calculations of this world's traffic, lifted to the sublimer calculations of eternity, and from the very whirl of this world's most powerful engrossments won over to a life of faith and devoted philanthropy. We know of the aspiring student, sent by thoughtless parents to college to prepare for the christian ministry — inflamed by literary ambition, but dead in heart to the love of Christ, awakened as from a trance, and made to feel the true nature of that office into which he had been heedlessly rushing, ushered into it fired with the fresh fervors of the all-constraining love. Of these we can not speak more particularly, nor can we offer any estimate of the number of those whose first religious impressions are traceable to the same earthly source, but we may be permitted to express the opinion, that with all the transient and tumultuous excitement of its mere pulpit oratory, there has rarely been a ministry of equal length as largely blessed of the Divine Spirit to the conversion of individual souls. The more general effects of that ministry, in its bearings upon the religious condition of Glasgow and of Scotland, lie open enough to observation. When Dr. Chalmers came to Glasgow, by the great body of the upper classes of society evangelical doctrines were nauseated and despised: when he left it, even by those who did not bow to their influence, these doctrines were acknowledged to be indeed the very doctrines of the Bible. When Dr. Chalmers came to Glasgow, in the eye of the multitude, evangelism stood confounded with a driveling sanctimoniousness or a sour-minded asceticism: when he left it, from all such false associations the christianity of the New Testament stood clearly and nobly redeemed. When Dr. Chalmers came to Glasgow, for nearly a century, the magistrates and town council had exercised the city patronage in a spirit determinately anti-evangelical: when he left it, so complete was the revolution which had been effected, that from that time forward none but evangelical clergymen were appointed by the city patrons. When Dr. Chalmers came to Glasgow, there and elsewhere over Scotland there were many most devoted clergymen of the Establishment who had given themselves up wholly to the ministry of the word and to prayer, but there was not one in whose faith and practice week-day ministrations had the place or power which he assigned to them; when he left it, he had exhibited such a model of fidelity, diligence and activity, in all departments of ministerial labor, as told finally upon the spirit and practice of the whole ministry of Scotland. When Dr. Chalmers came to Glasgow, unnoticed thousands of the city population were sinking into ignorance, infidelity and vice, and his eye was the first in this country to foresee to what a fearful magnitude that evil, if suffered to grow on unchecked, would rise: when he left it, his ministry in that city remained behind him in permanent warning to a nation which had been but slow to learn that the greatest of all questions, both for statesmen and for churchmen, is the condition of those untaught and degraded thousands who swarm now around the base of the social edifice, and whose brawny arms may yet grasp its pillars to shake or to destroy. When Dr. Chalmers came to Glasgow, in the literary circles of the Scottish metropolis a thinly disguised infidelity sat on the seats of greatest influence, and smiled or scoffed at a vital energetic faith in the great and distinctive truths of revelation, while widely over his native land the spirit of a frigid indifference to religion prevailed: when he left it, the current of public sentiment had begun to set in a contrary direction, and although it took many years, and the labor of many other hands to carry that healthful change onward to maturity, yet I believe that it is not over-estimating it to say, that it was mainly by Dr. Chalmers's ministry in Glasgow—by his efforts at this period in the pulpit and through the press—that the tide of national opinion and sentiment was turned.

And if Glasgow was honored in numbering Dr. Chalmers so long among her citizens, and in having been the sphere in which labors so eminently useful had been prosecuted, she proved herself not unworthy of the privilege. From her official men he always received the most courteous treatment, and to their kindness he was indebted for the facilities afforded him in carrying his plans into execution. Her citizens vied with one another in all kindly recognitions of one of whom all were proud, while among the narrower circle of his own congregation many personal attachments were formed, purer, deeper, and more lasting than any afterward created during a long lifetime of affectionate intercourse with his fellow-men."

Just before his departure a dinner was given in his honor, presided over by the Lord Provost, at which no less than three hundred and forty gentlemen sat down. The diversity of opinions and parties there represented, was a testimony to the recognized liberality of him, out of regard to whom they had come together. Upon the day after this entertainment, Dr. Chalmers set out for St. Andrew's, whither he was accompanied by a number of gentlemen from Glasgow, who, after attending at the ceremony of his installment into his new office, on Friday, the 14th, and upon his introductory lecture the next day, contributed to the harmony of the whole proceeding by entertaining at dinner the two principals, all the professors, and a number of gentlemen from the neighborhood of St. Andrew's.

Dr. Chalmers's family joined him toward the beginning of January. In the meanwhile he was pleasantly accommodated in the house of his friend, Mr. Duncan, then Professor of Mathematics in the University.

CHAPTER X.

THE labor upon which Dr. Chalmers had now entered was hardly less arduous than that which he had left behind. His previous occupations were such as to preclude any extensive preparation for succeeding duties. He consequently opened his course at St. Andrew's with lectures sufficient for only a week or two, and as he wished to keep his written compositions in advance of their delivery, it became an object of some anxiety to him to observe the distance between them narrowing as the time passed on. "I shall be lecturing," he writes in March, "for six weeks yet, and am very nearly from hand to mouth with my preparations. I have the prospect of winning the course, though it will be by no more than half a neck; but I like the employment vastly." "How like and yet how different this first session of Dr. Chalmers in the moral philosophy chair at St. Andrew's, and the first session of Dr. Thomas Brown in the same chair at Edinburgh. Both began their winter labors almost wholly unfurnished with written preparations; but the one came to them from the retirement of the country, and after a summer of quiet reading and reflection; the other from the whirl of city life, and from the tumultuous occupations of a different and most engrossing profession. Both under the excitement of the occasion, and with the same rare facility of rapid composition, threw off writings which scarcely required or admitted emendation, in which speculations the most original and profound were invested with all the charms of a fascinating eloquence. But Dr. Brown trusted much more than Dr. Chalmers to the spur of the moment. He seldom began to write his lectures till late in the evening of the day which preceded their delivery. Upon the subjects of many of them he had not reflected till he sat down, and many of his most ingenious theories occurred to him in the course of composition. Dr. Chalmers seldom began to write without a distinct and matured conception of the topics which he intended to discuss, and with certain broad outlines of thought laid down, which he seldom if ever traversed. From an early period in the morning he studied at regular intervals throughout the day, and the hour which saw Dr. Brown fastened to his midnight task found Dr. Chalmers relieved and at leisure to enjoy, with all the freedom and freshness of an unburdened mind, the society of his family and friends. One cannot follow the progress of either throughout their first session of professorial toil without the feeling that we are contemplating a singular intellectual feat, performed by a marvelously gifted operator. Yet to the mode of operation there attaches in the one instance a natural healthiness of tone and manner which belongs not to the other; and if to the *opus operatum* in the latter case there belongs a scientific completeness and finish which the other cannot claim, this may be attributed to Dr. Brown's greater antecedent familiarity with his subject, and to the well-digested plan upon which his labors were commenced and carried through."

Though pressed into the execution of such a task, and though yielding to the necessity, he enjoyed its excitement, Dr. Chalmers entertained no approbation of it as a feat, nay, he deliberately acknowledged the imperfections of his course, and that they were due to the want of adequate time in which to mature thought and select expression "I cannot," he said, "pretend to summon, as if by the wand of a magician, a finished system of moral philosophy into being in one or even in two years. There is a certain showy and superficial something which can be done in very short time. One may act the part of a harlequin with his mind as well as with his body; and there is a sort of mental agility which always gives me the impression of a harlequin. Anything which can be spoken of as a feat is apt to suggest this association. That man, for example, was a thorough harlequin, in both senses of the word, who boasted that he could throw off a hundred verses of poetry while he stood upon one foot. There was something for wonder in this; but it is rarely by any such exploit that we obtain deep, and powerful, and enduring poetry. It is by dint of steady labor—it is by giving enough of application to the work, and having enough of time for the doing of it — it is by regular painstaking and the plying of constant assiduities—it is by these, and not by any process of legerdemain, that we secure the strength and the staple of real excellence."

In addition to the regular moral philosophy class his lecture-room was always crowded with auditors drawn together by the reputation of his eloquence, and retained by the fascination of his views and manner. Their delight not finding sufficient utterance in the daily applause with which they greeted him, a design was contemplated of making him a valuable present, which coming to his knowledge was suppressed by his own kindly though firm discouragement.

No sooner had that session come to an end than he was busily employed in preparation for the approaching General Assembly, to which he had been elected as an elder by the borough of Anstruther. Several questions of interest were to come before that body. The first was that "respecting the admission of Principal Macfarlane as minister of the High church of Glasgow." In the debate which ensued on that subject, "the leading counsel for Dr. Macfarlane had quoted and laid much stress upon the Act of the Scottish parliament of 1592, by which Presbyteries were 'bound and astricted to receive and admit every qualified presentee.' Among the leading ecclesiastical authorities it had not hitherto been doubted that, in the exercise of her own inherent authority, either by a general law or by specific enactment, the Church could prevent such union of offices as that now contemplated. High legal authorities, however, now began to hint it as their conviction, that the Church could not do so without acting illegally, by violating the statute above alluded to. To the doctrine thus newly broached, Dr. Chalmers alluded in the close of his speech in words upon which after events impress a peculiar significance: "I do not at all enter into the question of your power to lay a veto on the presentation in this instance, for there can be no doubt of it: that presentation has had every justice done to it. The Presbytery received it to their notice, and with all the forms of court; they admitted it to lie upon their table, and then gave their full and deliberate regards to the fitness of the presentee. On the question that is always put and always must be pronounced upon in one way or other, whether the presentation shall or shall not be sustained, they did, but not till time and argument, and a fair and free debate were allowed to the consideration of it, come to a negative. For reasons strictly ecclesiastical, and for which these ecclesiastical guides and guardians can hold up an unabashed face in society, they laid their arrest upon the presentation by refusing to sustain it. They were reasons that bore to be canvassed before one of our superior judicatories, and for which that judicatory confirmed our decision. We now wait the sentence of our ultimate court; and we can never once dream that this final sentence, if given in our favor, is not to be effective. But if it could possibly be otherwise—if, on the plea that the Church hath overstepped her boundaries, it is found that there is a right and a force in the mere presentation which shall carry it over all your resistance, then I cannot imagine a feebler instrument, a more crippled and incompetent machinery, than our Church is for the professed object of its institution; nor do I see how, if struck with impotency like this, it can lift an arm of any efficacy to protect our Establishment from many great evils, or to stay the progress of a very sore corruption within her borders."

Though the reforming party in the Church were defeated on this point, they were not discouraged; for as the discussion had been left very much to themselves, their opponents having more confidence in their numbers than their arguments, many reasons unresponded to were favorably promulgated, and " when the question was relieved from the apparent invidiousness of resisting the claims of an individual, and put upon its broad and general grounds they were more hopeful than ever of success."

The subject of pauperism also came before the house in the

form of a resolution to petition against a bill then before parliament, proposing to do away with all poor-rates whatever. Though strongly opposed to that compulsory method of providing for the poor, which he believed to be calculated to increase the evil it was " designed to cure," Dr. Chalmers was not prepared for such a hasty and sweeping act of legislation, and therefore readily seconded the motion that the General Assembly should petition against the passing of the bill; and when the great opponent of poor-laws took such a course, there was no difficulty in obtaining a unanimous vote in favor of the petition.

The report of the committee upon the course of study to be required of students of theology, brought up another subject of debate. An overture insisting upon " one year's regular attendance at the Divinity Hall had been transmitted by the previous Assembly, to the different Presbyteries of the church." It was now reported that only six Presbyteries had sent in returns. This was represented as due to the little interest felt in the matter, and a motion was made that it should not be retransmitted. Drs. Cook, Inglis, Nicoll, and Mearns were in favor of such a step; but Dr. Chalmers, conceiving that the overture had been overlooked, being sent down mixed up with the general Acts of the Assembly, proposed that it should be retransmitted in a separate form. A stormy debate ensued, which resulted in giving a majority of one hundred and seventeen to seventy-four in favor of transmitting.

A fourth subject of discussion, also involving a cause of deep interest to Dr. Chalmers, was a petition praying for the erection of a new Gaelic chapel in Glasgow. It was opposed on the ground that those already existing were not filled. The leaders of the ruling party in the Assembly, Dr. Inglis, Dr. Mearns, Dr. Nicoll, and Dr. Cook, resisted the prayer of the Glasgow petitioners. " It had not, however, been in vain that Dr. Chalmers, in his eight years' labors, had exposed the spiritual necessity of thousands of the population, and pleaded for the multiplication of spiritual laborers among them. His words in the Assembly were few but weighty. The argument from unlet sittings he dealt with, when urged by those within the Establishment, in the very way in which he dealt with it afterward, when urged by those without. The broad outstanding fact—the true and firm basis of the petitioners' plea—was, that if they erected the new chapel, and filled it to overflow, there would still be a great overplus of Highland population in Glasgow unprovided for. There was no want of materials for crowding this and all the other chapels. To wait till all the existing chapels should be filled ere you raised another, were to take the surest way to augment indefinitely the numbers of those who lived wholly neglectful of all ordinances. To send another zealous laborer among that neglected and neglectful population, was to employ one of the most hopeful expedients for lessening the evil which of late years had been growing so rapidly. The question, grant or refuse the petition, was at last put, when it carried—grant, by a majority of ninety-nine to seventy-one."

On the first of June, the day after the close of the General Assembly, Dr. Chalmers, at the solicitation of Mr. Leonard Horner, took part in the annual meeting of the School of Arts, then in its infancy, and the first of its kind in that country. On this occasion he had the pleasure of being sustained by the co-operation of Sir Walter Scott, the only time in which these two great men "met on the same platform and were associated in the same work;" a fact due to the diversity of their pursuits alone, for certainly in many great features of character, they bore such a resemblance to each other, as must, upon more intimate acquaintance, have constituted the basis of mutual esteem. A graceful pen has lightly touched on some of these:

"You ask me to tell you about Dr. Chalmers. I must tell you first, then, that of all men he is the most modest, and speaks with undissembled gentleness and liberality of those who differ from him in opinion. Every word he says has the stamp of genius; yet the calmness, ease, and simplicity of his conversation is such, that, to ordinary minds, he might appear an ordinary man. I had a great intellectual feast about three weeks since — I breakfasted with him at a friend's house, and enjoyed his society for two hours with great delight. Conversation wandered into various channels, but he was always powerful, always gentle, and always seemed quite unconscious of his own superiority. I had not been an hour at home when a guest arrived, who had become a stranger to me for some time past. It was Walter Scott, who sat a long time with me, and was, as he always is, delightful; his good-nature, good-humor, and simplicity are truly charming: you never once think of his superiority, because it is evident he does not think of it himself. He, too, confirmed the maxim, that true genius is ever modest and careless ; after his greatest literary triumphs he is like Hardyknute's son-after a victory, when we are told,

> 'With careless gesture, mind unmoved,
> On rode he o'wre the plain.'

Mary and I could not help observing certain similarities between these two extraordinary persons (Chalmers and Scott) : the same quiet, unobtrusive humor, the same flow of rich original conversation, easy, careless, and visibly unpremeditated ; the same indulgence for others, and readiness to give attention and interest to any subject started by others. There was a more chastened dignity and occasional elevation in the Divine than in the Poet ; but many resembling features in their modes of thinking and manner of expression."

After about a fortnight's rest at St. Andrew's, Dr. Chalmers proceeded to Glasgow to watch over the progress of the new chapel which he had left in the "weakness of its infancy." Having announced his intention to preach there for six successive Sabbaths, and hold meetings during the intervening weeks, with all the different branches of the parochial agency, he plunged once more in that torrent of business which he had formerly set in motion and directed. The multitudes who assembled to hear him on the Sabbath were restrained by police

---

* Memoir and Correspondence of Mrs. Grant, of Laggan, vol. ii, page 167—169.

force, and none admitted except those who were provided with tickets. Beside other discourses, he delivered on those Sabbaths his lectures on Romans, from chap. viii, 31, to the 39th verse of the same chapter; as well as on the 22d of the eleventh, and 17th of the fourteenth chapters. Having thus strengthened the hands of his former fellow-laborers, and added considerably to their pecuniary resources, he turned his face homeward, taking the residence of Dr. Nicoll, at Costerton, in his way, where, in company with some other academic friends, Dr. Hunter, Mr. Duncan, and Mr. Gillespie, he spent a day of pleasant relaxation. To Prof. Duncan he was warmly attached, and in all their amusements we find these two friends preferring one another. In one of his journal letters Dr. Chalmers thus writes—" Had cordial greetings with the gentlemen in the library, then we sallied out to the premises, and had a very delightful forenoon saunter through the woods and lanes of Costerton. We fixed the situation of a future moss house, for which Dr. Hunter, I hope, will write an inscription; and I have left the fragment of a knife, broken by Mr. Duncan, in a spot which overhangs a bath to be made in a linn." " Before dinner we had a game at bowls in a green before the house. I and Mr. Duncan against Dr. Nicoll and Dr. James Hunter. We had the best of three games. Mr. Gillespie afterward took up Mr. Duncan and was beat by him." " Before supper there was family worship, when I was called to officiate. We were shown to our beds about twelve. I got the large bed-room in which Mr. Duncan was the night before, and he had a closet, with a small sofa-bed that communicated with the room. This arrangement was vastly agreeable to me; and we tumbled into our respective couches between twelve and one. I like him.

"*Friday.*— Got up about eight. Went to Mr. Duncan's closet, and got behind him in his sofa-bed, where I had a good purchase for jamming him out, and did so accordingly. Had cordial talk with him. Had a turn before breakfast, and agreed to find my way with him to Edinburgh by the help of coaches which go past this way. Dr. Nicoll, however, traversed this arrangement, he having so ordered it as to go to Edinburgh in his own carriage — to take Dr. Hunter and me along with him, and offered a place in the dickie to any other. I offered to take the dickie, but he would not hear of it; and as Mr. Duncan professed himself liable to giddiness, Dr. James Hunter sat beside the driver, and in this style we drove to Edinburgh. I had to explain and half apologize to Mr. Duncan for having deserted him, and he instantly saw that such an exclusive preference on our part for one another might hurt the feelings of our elders, and that it was far better to acquiesce in their plan. We set off between ten and eleven. But between that and breakfast, Mr. Gillespie, who is somewhat of a bluster, challenged me to a game at bowls, when, to the great satisfaction of all, I beat him, by thirteen to eight. On our way to Edinburgh, got in two newspapers at Dr. Nicoll's post-office, which we read in the chaise.

"*Anstruther, Sunday.*— Got up at nine, a good deal recruited, yet with the sensation that one good sleep required another. Had family worship after breakfast, and enjoyed my walking in the garden on the Sabbath morning. It recalled other days. The evening sermon began at six. The church was completely full, and many standers. Some had to go away. I preached the same missionary sermon that I had revised in the session-room, and which I have preached in Cupar, Perth, Edinburgh, Lanark, and Anstruther. It has done very well in that it has got £300 for the cause. I was very much tired."

The managers of a large Sabbath school at Stockport, for the purpose of liquidating a debt resting upon their building, had established an anniversary celebration, at which many eminent clergymen officiated, and at which, for the purpose of increasing the attraction, select and varied pieces of music were performed. In ignorance of these musical accompaniments, Dr. Chalmers complied with their request that he should preach the anniversary sermon. The appointment was for Sabbath, the 10th of October. Upon reaching Stockport, he was much annoyed by finding himself placarded, in regular theatrical style, as a prominent actor in a great musical and literary exhibition ; and managers and performers, in all the excitement of preparation, to turn the Sabbath into a day of entertainment and festivity. His disapprobation was distinctly, but without violence, expressed to the parties concerned. He had come, he said, from a great distance on their account, and had thereby purchased the privilege of telling them plain things, that they should have consulted him ere they made their arrangements, that what they had done stood in the same relation to what they should have done, that an advertisement of Dr. Solomon's did to the respectable doings of the regular faculty. On the Sabbath he sent for the principal manager with a view of obtaining some alteration in the exercises ; but that personage was then presiding at a dinner given before sermon to the "gentlemen of the orchestra," and in the midst of a speech to them. The prayers and the sermon were to have been mixed up with the music ; but Dr. Chalmers sent word that he would not be present at their music at all ; that his service should be separated altogether from their entertainment — that he should pray, preach, and pray again, in succession — not entering the pulpit till the moment of his beginning, and retiring from it as soon as he should have ended. This change was accordingly made, and at six o'clock in the evening, the time appointed for the sermon, he made his appearance. "Will you believe it ?" he writes, "an orchestra of at least one hundred people, three rows of female singers, in which two professional female singers, so many professional male singers, a number of amateurs : and I now offer you a list of the instruments so far as I have been able to ascertain them—one pair of bass-drums, two trumpets, bassoon, organ, serpents, violins without number, violoncelloes, bass-viols, flutes, hautboys. I stopped in the minister's room till it was over. Went to the pulpit — prayed, preached, retired during the time of the collection, and again prayed. Before I left my own private room they fell to again with most tremendous fury, and the likest thing to it which I recollect, is a great military band on the castle-hill of Edinburgh."

The collection taken up on the occasion of that sermon was £398, and on Monday it was augmented to £401.

CHAPTER XI.

FROM the multifarious labors of his summer vacation Dr. Chalmers returned to enter upon those of a session which constituted "the most brilliant epoch of his academical career at St. Andrew's." With more leisure for careful preparation than he had previously enjoyed, the encouragement of a numerous and attentive auditory was largely augmented. More than twice the number of students that ever attended the instructions of his most eminent predecessors crowded his lecture-room; some of older standing returned upon their course, and many gentlemen attached themselves to his class who had no other connection with the university. "The superior character and capacity of the students told upon the spirit and efforts of their professor. It was throughout one busy season of animating and most productive labor. His course of lectures on ethics was carried a stage further toward that condition of completeness, which however they were destined never to attain." In respect to that course it may be remarked that it departed from the boundaries previously set to the department in St. Andrew's and other Scotch universities. Under the head of moral philosophy they included both mental and moral science, as well as all that was taught of political economy. Dr. Chalmers rightly conceiving that morals are more intimately connected with religion than with metaphysics, ventured to set aside the whole branch of mental science and make his course one truly on moral philosophy, terminating in the doctrines of revealed religion and constituting a progressive approach to the study of christian theology. It was divided into those "moralities which reciprocate between man and man on earth," and those "which connect earth with heaven." The most valuable of his lectures were those belonging to the latter division, treating of natural theology. They were afterward remodeled and introduced into his course of theological instruction in Edinburgh " and will be found in the first and second volumes of his published works. In the fifth volume of the same series, the reader is presented with as many of the lectures in the first, or strictly ethical division of his course, as their author thought fit to publish.

Dr. Chalmers's method of instruction " was diffuse and illustrative. To facilitate the remembrance of his lectures, to give his students a distinct conception of the ground actually traversed, and to prepare them for that examination to which they were afterward to be subjected, he dictated a few succinct sentences, containing the leading topics of each lecture, so as to furnish his students with a condensed syllabus of his course. It would not have been easy for them, amid the excitements of that class, to have followed the old practice of the Scottish universities by taking notes during the delivery of the lecture. The very manner of that delivery would have been sufficient to have kept their eye fixed upon the lecturer. There was, beside, the novelty of many of the speculations, as well as of the garb in which they were presented; while the interest was at once deepened and diversified—at times, by some extemporaneous addition or illustration, in which the lecturer springing from his seat, and bending over the desk, through thick and difficult and stammering utterance in which every avenue to expression seemed to be choked up, found his way to some picturesque conception and expressive phraseology, which shed a flood of light on the topic in hand; and again, by some poetic quotation recited with most emphatic fervor, or by some humorous allusion or anecdote told with archest glee. It was almost impossible in such a singular class room to check the burst of applause, or to restrain the merriment. The professor did his best, and used many expedients for this purpose." But notwithstanding all, the pedestrian approbation was destined to accompany him "through the whole of his academical career."

To regular examination of his students upon the lectures ne delivered, Dr. Chalmers attached so much importance that he was in the habit of carefully writing out beforehand the principal questions. Yet one of his pupils informs us that "the examination was anything but formal. It was enlivened by questions first addressed to individuals, and then, if unanswered, cast abroad on the whole class. Each was anxious to distinguish himself by his replies. The same question found divers answers. In that diversity we found a new source of interest, and new lights were struck out. The excitement, the suspense of mind, and the successive approximations of one after another to the true and sufficient answer, created scenes of intellectual animation that I delight to recall. In the midst of these not seldom the professor himself broke in with some extemporaneous or half extemporaneous exposition on the topics that had come up. Nothing could be more genial than these gushes of fresh thought and vivid illustration. We called them his buds, and, like other buds, they were all the more interesting that they were not blown. In these excursions he often expressed himself with all the point, condensation, and terseness which every one must have observed in his conversational, as contrasted with his written, style. In a few emphatic and impassioned sentences he set before us the whole philosophy of a subject, and that in so compact and portable a form, that it was transferred not only to our note-books, but lodged for life in our minds, under the triple guardianship of the understanding, the imagination and the heart."

Political economy was too much of a favorite with Dr. Chalmers to be confined by him to the limited space it had previously occupied in the Scottish universities. According to an announcement made at the close of his first session at St. Andrew's, he opened, in November, 1826, a separate class for the study of that subject. This he did not teach by lecture, but by recitation, choosing "Smith's Wealth of Nations," as his text-book, and, in the course of examination, supplementing and illustrating the views therein presented. Of this method of instruction he thus expressed himself before the Royal Commissioners: "I must say that I feel great comfort in it, and am sensible of its great efficacy. I find that coming to close quarters with the juvenile mind upon subjects which they have previously read upon, is a very effective method of teaching them, insomuch that were I furnished with an unexceptionable set of text-books on moral philosophy, I should feel strongly inclined to adopt the same method in that class too."

Original investigation was also required of the students under his instruction. A topic belonging to the general subject under discussion was each Friday assigned to a portion of the class, who read respectively their essays upon it, in the lecture-room, on the Friday following. These productions were brief, not occupying more than eight or ten minutes in the delivery, but great latitude was permitted in treatment of the subjects assigned, or the choice of kindred ones. For the purpose of calling forth more strenuous effort, the subject for a prize essay was announced at Christmas, to be ready in the month of April. A new element in the philosophical class-room, introduced by Dr. Chalmers, was the daily prayer, whereby the work of the hour was opened, very short, but always impressive, and sometimes even sublime.

"Classes conducted by such an instructor, in which the methods now indicated were so vigorously prosecuted, could not but be effective. When he accepted the appointment to St. Andrew's, many a misgiving had been expressed as to his fitness for the new office, and many a sage reflection had been thrown out as to the opposite qualities that were required for the pulpit and for the chair. His lectures soon gave evidence that he could be profound as well as popular; and as to his mode of training the young, if the highest end of all good teaching be to awaken intellectual impulses, and stimulate to intellectual activity, that end was gained in a pre-eminent degree. An indescribable impulse was excited and sustained among the students. There was not a latent spark of intellectual enthusiasm in any breast that was not kindled into a glowing flame. It was impossible not to follow where such a leader led the way, and with many, as with himself, the pursuit became a passion. There was but one other professor in the Scottish universities who had been equally successful, though in a very different way, in calling the youthful intellectual energy into action, and he was now sinking into the sere and yellow leaf. 'If Professor Jardine, of Glasgow,' says one who was a student under both, 'had the art above most men of 'breaking the shell,' to use Lord Jeffrey's phrase, Dr. Chalmers excelled in tempting those whose shell was already broken, to prove their wings—in teaching them how to fly, and whither to direct their flight. Under Jardine we learned that we had an intellectual life; at St. Andrew's we were provoked to use it; and in the joy of its exercise, though we often mistook intellectual ambition for intellectual ability, time corrected that mistake, and meanwhile whatever was in us was drawn out of us by the intensive and enthusiastic spirit of our intellectual chief."

A part of the succeeding vacation was again occupied with the business of the General Assembly. The two principal subjects of debate were moved, the one by Dr. Thomson, the other by Dr. Chalmers. The former was a case of presentation to a Gaelic parish of a minister wholly unacquainted with the Gaelic language. The Presbytery had refused to sustain the presentation, the Synod had affirmed that decision, and the matter was now brought before the Assembly for final adjustment. Dr. Thomson moved, and Dr. Chalmers seconded the motion to instruct the Presbytery "not to proceed with such a settlement, and that this decision should be respectfully communicated to the officers of the Crown, in order that another and properly qualified individual might be presented." After a debate which called forth one of the most powerful speeches of Dr. Thomson, the motion was carried by a majority of 107 to 89. The motion presented by Dr. Chalmers was not so successful. It was aimed against the holding of college professorships by ministers at the same time retaining a pastoral charge—an evil at which he had, on other occasions aimed several sturdy blows. Though the motion was lost, the debate contributed to keep the subject before the public, and brought forward some more cogent arguments for reform. The most remarkable passage in it, was one touching the principal disputant himself. "Late in the afternoon of the second day's debate, a speech on the opposition side had been closed by a quotation from an anonymous pamphlet, in which the author asserted that, from what to him was the highest of all authority, the authority of his own experience, he could assert that, 'after the satisfactory discharge of his parish duties, a minister may enjoy five days in the week of uninterrupted leisure for the prosecution of any science in which his tastes may dispose him to engage.' As this passage was emphatically read, no doubtful hint being given as to its authorship, all eyes were turned toward Dr. Chalmers. The interposition of another speech afforded him an opportunity for reflecting on the best manner of meeting this personal attack. At the close of the debate, and amid breathless silence, he spoke as follows:

"Sir, that pamphlet I now declare to have been a production of my own, published twenty years ago. I was indeed much surprised to hear it brought forward and quoted this evening; and I instantly conceived that the reverend gentleman who did so, had been working at the trade of a resurrectionist. Verily I believed that my unfortunate pamphlet had long ere now descended into the tomb of merited oblivion, and that there it was mouldering in silence, forgotten and disregarded. But since that gentleman has brought it forward in the face of this house, I can assure him that I feel grateful to him from the bottom of my heart, for the opportunity he has now afforded me of making a public recantation of the sentiments it contains. I have read a tract entitled the 'Last Moments of the Earl of Rochester,' and I was powerfully struck in reading it, with the conviction how much evil a pernicious pamphlet may be the means of disseminating. At the time when I wrote it, I did not conceive that my pamphlet would do much evil; but, sir, considering the conclusions that have been deduced from it by the reverend gentleman, I do feel obliged to him for reviving it, and for bringing me forward to make my public renunciation of what is there written. I now confess myself to have been guilty of a heinous crime, and I now stand a repentant culprit before the bar of this venerable Assembly.

"The circumstances attending the publication of my pamphlet were shortly as follows: As far back as twenty years ago, I was ambitious enough to aspire to be successor to Professor Playfair in the mathematical chair of the University of Edinburgh. During the discussion which took place relative to the person who might be appointed his successor, there appeared a letter from Professor Playfair to the magistrates of Edinburgh on the subject, in which he stated it as his conviction, that no person could be found competent to discharge the duties of the mathematical chair among the clergymen of the Church of Scotland. I was at that time, sir, more devoted to mathematics than to the literature of my profession; and feeling grieved and indignant at what I conceived an undue reflection on the abilities and education of our clergy, I came forward with that pamphlet to rescue them from what I deemed an unmerited reproach, by maintaining that a devoted and exclusive attention to the study of mathematics was not dissonant to the proper habits of a clergyman. Alas! sir, so I thought in my ignorance and pride. I have now no reserve in saying that the sentiment was wrong, and that, in the utterance of it, I penned what was most outrageously wrong. Strangely blinded that I was! What, sir, is the object of mathematical science? Magnitude and the proportions of magnitude. But *then*, sir, I had forgotten *two magnitudes*—I thought not of the littleness of time—I recklessly thought not of the greatness of eternity!"

"For a moment or two after the last words were spoken a deathlike stillness reigned throughout the house. The power and pathos of the scene were overwhelming, and we shall search long in the lives of the most illustrious ere we find another instance in which the sentiment, the act, the utterance, each rose to the same level of sublimity, and stood so equally embodied in the one impressive spectacle."

During the remainder of this vacation, his time was more at his own disposal than it had been for many years, and the record of his spiritual condition is accordingly more full. Our limits admit only a few extracts.

"*Sunday, June 26th*, 1825.—After the interval of more than a twelvemonth have again recurred to my journal. Have not made progress during this interval, and find that I must just recur, as at the first, to the blood of Christ as my atonement—to the righteousness of Christ as my plea; but, oh! that under these principles I experienced more of the spirit of Christ in my heart, and anything like the satisfactory evidence of my having become a new creature."

"*28th.*—Had less of light and life in my devotional exercises this morning. Waited for some time, but without success. Surely in the absence of conception there may be faith and principle, and let me follow up a morning of darkness with a day of close and conscientious observation. Keep alive in me, O God, the love of thyself, and the love of my neighbor, and all will be right. Have gleams of sunshine in the reading of 'Romaine,' and find that I can get better on through the medium of tangible remarks and doctrines; and in what other way indeed but by the presentation of truth can good feelings be awakened? Oh, that I could appropriate Christ more simply, and then should I experience him to be the power of God for both a present and a future salvation!"

"*July 16th.*—Still the same glow of delight with 'Romaine,' but the same dissipation thereof and of all seriousness among the occupations of study and of society. What an argument for the Sabbath, for a day set apart to God's peculiar work, seeing that throughout the vast majority of the six days on which we do our work, we forget Him altogether. But should it be so? Should not this tendency be prayed against till it is prevailed over? Should not life be a perpetual Sabbath? Is there no way of impregnating all work with godliness? and is not the Lord's work that in which we should always be abounding?—O God, teach me this way and this work."

"*Sunday, 17th.*—This on the whole a prosperous day. Felt the charm of Sabbath, although perhaps too much taken up with Sabbath *business* to the exclusion of meditation and prayer. Read the sermon on the death of Mr. and Mrs. Philip Henry. Went to bed at eleven. I need more of unction in my Sabbath school, and a more thorough earnestness about the conversion of souls. Had some delicious and animating retirement in the evening when I thought I could descry what is meant by the glorious liberty of the children of God.—Let my regards be more cast henceforth on the things to be believed, and less on the act or manner of believing."

"*August, 19th.*—A quiet day at home. I feel heaviness, and there mingles with it a certain sense and feeling of decay, as if my imagination was less vivid, a haze overspreading all the objects of my contemplation, and far less both of interest, and I fear of power, whether in the walks of pathos or fancy, or even intellect. A fine topic this for religious exercise. Let me cultivate a closer fellowship with God, and be weaned from my own glory. O Heavenly Father! fill me with the desire of living altogether to thine: extinguish vanity, and the sinful lust of human applause."

The cold formalism of St. Andrew's was not without its effect upon his religious feelings. We find several such lamentations as these: "In a state of depression all day, arising partly from fatigue, and partly from the feeling of that uncongenial atmosphere by which I am surrounded." "Visited with melancholy thoughts when I dwell on the uncongeniality of my present neighborhood." And sometimes, under the weight of despondency, he conceived his talents sinking into decay, and his influence in the world diminishing. His plain dealing with himself is illustrated in an entry under the date of October 1st: "I am destitute of that spirit which prompted Christ to seek and to save that which is lost, of his compassionate zeal for the souls of men, of the patience wherewith he endured the contradiction of sinners *against himself*, and altogether of love either to God or men. Old things are not wholly passed away: the love of literature for *itself*, and the love of literary distinction, have not passed away. Let me love literature as one of those creatures of God which is not to be refused, but received with thanksgiving. Let me desire literary distinction—but let my desire for it be altogether that I may add to my christian usefulness, and promote the glory of

God—then, even with these, I would be a new creature. The impression of my defects is not such as to overwhelm me, but to stimulate. Objective christianity mixed its influence with the examination. The defects of my subjective should just lead me to cling faster to the objective; and I did feel a peace when I tried myself by the verse, that to them who believe He is precious. I was moved even to tears by a sense of my deficiencies; and, O God, let my peace be that of faith, and not of carnality. Let it be my incessant endeavor to heighten the characters of grace within, and then self-examination will become easier and more encouraging. Let me observe the temperance of this day, and that will make me more vigorous and unclouded in all my mental exercises."

The latter part of Dr. Chalmers's residence at St. Andrew's was clouded by the rise of several grounds of difference between himself and his colleagues.

By ancient law and usage the students of the United College were obliged to attend the Sabbath services in the old university-church of St. Leonard's. Notwithstanding an earnest remonstrance on the part of Dr. Chalmers, a college professor, whose hands were already full of his proper work, and who was otherwise unacceptable, had recently been appointed pastor of that church. The students were greatly dissatisfied, especially that part of them who esteemed the service of the Sabbath most highly, and presented a petition to the Senatus praying to be released from attendance there. Dr. Chalmers, although he thought some relief should be granted those whose religious feelings were thwarted by the existing law, did not consider it proper "to yield to the mere choice of youths, many of them of immature age;" but when the Senatus also rejected the expressed desire of their parents, he warmly espoused their cause, "both acts being alike revolting to him—that by which the Chancellor forced a minister upon the college, and that by which the college forced an attendance upon the minister." It was painful for him to take such a position, as he stood alone in doing so, and one of his fellow-professors was the very person in reference to whom the petition was drawn up; notwithstanding he firmly defended the right of parents to direct the religious education of their children. His conduct in this respect, as well as in permitting some of his family to attend a dissenting place of worship, gave great offense to the formal and establishment-loving community of St. Andrew's.

The second difficulty rose out of the administration of the college funds, a certain part of which it had long been customary for the professors to divide among themselves. When Dr. Chalmers came to take part in this transaction, he was naturally led to inquire into the legal authority for it, and finding good reason to believe that it possessed none, brought his objections before the Senatus Academicus. That body did not share in his scruples, and some of its members resented them as implying a charge of malversation. He declined receiving the portion assigned to him until he should see clearly his legal right to it.

In 1826, a commission was appointed to visit and report upon the colleges in Scotland. To their arbitration he submitted as a competent authority, and in May, 1829, received from them a decision authorizing him to receive the sums which had been allotted to him by the resolutions of the professors. These had now accumulated to the amount of £700. He thought no more of the matter until the publication of the Report of the Commissioners, in 1831, in which, without any mention of the part he had taken, it was stated as their conclusion that "the Principal and Professors appear to have made these appropriations without any authority." "Dr. Chalmers was utterly at a loss to reconcile this with the resolution under which he had been induced to accept of the dividends." He was placed in a most embarrassing position before the world, and resolved on a public vindication of himself. A few sentences from his letter to the Commissioners will give some idea of the power with which that defensive attack was made. After stating the facts of the case, he adds : " When receiving that money under your sanction, I did not understand that I had given up to you, in exchange for it, the power of aspersing my character and good name.

"I trust that I have made my own conduct perfectly distinct. The enigma of yours is now darker and more inscrutable than ever.

"I cannot divine what you think of these Candlemas appropriations. If you think them wrong, how is it that to me you have called evil good? If you think them right, how is it that to your Sovereign you have called the good evil?"

"After your act of May, 1829, I never once dreamed of any other sentence from your lips than that of a full, and open, and unqualified justification of the professors of St. Andrew's. Such a pronounced opinion upon them was the only consistent and honorable way in which you could follow up the permission you had given to myself; and, for their sakes, I honestly rejoiced in it. I never liked the practice they had fallen into of helping themselves, and was annoyed beyond measure by the obstructions which they threw in the way of my bringing the matter distinctly before you; but, after all, I could not but view the errors into which they had almost insensibly been led as being very much the errors of their position; and taking into account the exceeding smallness of their incomes, I, from the moment that your Act of 1829 was put into my hand, confidently looked for your declaration of entire acquittal and satisfaction with their conduct. But it appears that you have devised for them another species of consolation. Instead of telling the world that they were right, you have provided them with the comfort and the countenance of a larger companionship in wrong, and to enhance the favor, it is wrong which yourselves have created. You have not taken off the burden from their shoulders, but you have kindly introduced among them another offender of your own making, who, by sharing it along with them, might help to ease them of its pressure. After having vainly tried, among the relics of former visitations, to find for them a precedent, you have done what was next best—you have fastened upon me as the object of your seductions, and endeavored, by the conduct into which yourselves have misled me, to find for them an imitation. I can observe, gentlemen, that your taste is for uniformity, and that any discrepancy or contrast between me and my colleagues was an obnoxious spectacle in your eyes. To rid you of this, a work of assimilation had to be performed, that you might have the comfort of one simple and harmonious decision upon us all. British honor will know how to view such a proceeding. A British king and British parliament will know how to appreciate the moral judgments of men, who, instead of constructing their representation on the materials which they found, first adjusted the materials to suit their representation—who became the tempters first, and the accusers afterward—who, ere they would tell the fault, took aside the only professor who was free from it, and suggested, nay, authorized, the very deed which numbers him among the defaulters—who, such their love to virtue that nothing less than a monopoly of the article would serve them, cleared the field of its last remnant, that they might become the only examples and only expounders of it themselves."

But the cause which probably excited the greatest opposition to him in St. Andrew's, was his zealous endeavors to create around him a more profound religious feeling. He opened a Sabbath school in his own house, to which he admitted the members of the Moral Philosophy class who chose to attend. This beginning with five, continued to increase until his room was completely crammed. He had also a Sabbath class formed of the children of the poor in his neighborhood, and his old habits of visiting for the purpose of communicating religious instruction privately, were not laid aside. He marked out for himself a district among the destitute of the city of St. Andrews, to be regularly attended to as a pastoral care. In conducting his juvenile Sabbath school, he associated with himself Mr. John Urquhart, a young man of eminent piety and talents for instruction, and in the course of a short time other students of the university, fired by the zeal and counsel, and guided by the example of their professor, had established other Sabbath schools in different parts of the city. " Their common engagement in these evening schools led the students to hold Sabbath morning meetings for prayer and counsel — meetings at which the hallowed fire which glowed in every breast grew warmer at the touch of a congenial flame. Nor was this all. The visitation of their districts for the purpose of bringing out the young to school, had revealed a great and unexpected amount of religious indifference and neglect among the adult population, a discovery which, when made by ardent youths, panting to do good, was not long of being followed up by active efforts to relieve the destitution. The zeal, indeed, which embarked in these efforts, did not confine itself to St. Andrew's, but flowed out upon adjoining districts. 'There is a new system,' says Mr. Urquhart, ' of religious instruction which has been attempted in St. Andrew's this last session, and which, I think, is a most efficient system for evangelizing large towns. The plan is very simple. We first inquired after some persons residing in different quarters of the town who were religiously disposed. We called on these and requested the favor of a room in their house for a few of the neighbors to assemble in for religious purposes. We expected a little group of eight or ten persons to assemble, but were astonished to find the attendance increase in some of the stations to fifty or sixty. Many of these never went to church. We generally read and explained a passage of Scripture, and read some extracts from such books as we thought were most striking and useful. You understand we never called it *preaching* : and accordingly Dr. Haldane gave his consent that the young men in the Established Church should engage in the work. Churchmen and dissenters all went hand in hand, and we forgot that there was any distinction ; and this must be the case more universally ere the cause of our great Redeemer go triumphantly forward. I do think this a most plausible method of getting at that class of the community who do not attend the public services of the gospel. I may mention that we have a Mr. H. here, a Baptist minister from London, of whom, perhaps, you may have heard. He has come to attend Dr. Chalmers, and has been very useful here. He and my friend Mr. A., have established several preaching stations in the country round where the people seem eager to hear the gospel."

As president of a missionary society, composed of Christians of different denominations, Dr. Chalmers also accomplished a labor of extensive usefulness. Holding monthly meetings for the communication of missionary intelligence, he took the duty of collecting and presenting that information upon himself. The interest attaching to these meetings drew such crowds that he at last had to obtain the Town Hall for their accommodation; and the interest so awakened contributed to encourage and sustain a similar society among the students, which produced fruits of no common value. From that society, formed in the midst of a worldly-minded community, and at first relying for support chiefly upon the known disposition of Dr. Chalmers, went forth Mr. Nesbit to Bombay, "the oldest Scottish missionary on the field of India," Mr. Adams to the valley of the Ganges, and that most laborious and successful of all missionaries, Dr. Alexander Duff, to Calcutta, whither he was soon followed by others from the same circle of influence. At its first formation that students' society was peremptorily refused the use of any room in the university, and by some of the professors was regarded as *thoroughly unacademical*. With difficulty could a place of meeting be obtained in town; but after the labors of Dr. Chalmers had progressed for some time, so greatly was the feeling changed, that some of the professors became openly favorable to it, while the rest relinquished all actual opposition. In the language of Dr. Duff, one of the young men by whose efforts it was founded, "Whatever may have been the *extent* of *inward* spiritual renovation, no one could question the extent of *outward* visible amelioration in the religious aspect of things. Religion, which had long settled down at zero, or many degrees below it, was sensibly raised in its temperature, and, in some instances, kindled into an inextinguishable flame. The long repose of stagnation and death, with its teeming brood of corruptions, was effectually disturbed; and out of the strife and conflict of hostile elements a new progeny, fraught with life and purity, began to emerge; and in the missionary libraries and assemblies, the prayer-meetings, the Sabbath schools, and preaching stations in town and country, an extensive machinery was erected for the diffusion of life-giving influences all around. And all this suddenly springing into existence from the presence of one man!"

During the winter 1825-6, Dr. Chalmers completed the third volume of his "Christian and Civic Economy of Large Towns," and in the succeeding vacation again took his seat in the General Assembly, where he had the satisfaction of seeing his measure, regarding theological education, carried; but was doomed to another defeat on the subject of pluralities, on which the Assembly declined all further discussion until the Royal Commissioners, to visit the Scottish Colleges, should issue their report. That report, when it did appear, in 1831, was entirely favorable to Dr. Chalmers's views. In the course of the summer he delivered "a lecture before the School of Arts at Haddington, preached four successive Sabbaths in Glasgow, and spent a week or two with a sister who had lately married the Rev. Mr. McLellan, minister of Kelton in Kircudbrightshire." In the latter excursion he accomplished two other objects very gratifying to his feelings, a visit to the old parish church of Anwoth, consecrated by the memory of Samuel Rutherford, and to the birthplace, as well as the grave, of Dr. Thomas Brown. He also saw with warm interest many of the scenes associated with the genius of Robert Burns.

Next winter was marked to him by the death of his sister Isabel, on the 4th of December, and of his mother on the 14th of February following, both "full of the hope of eternal glory, believing in, and trusting to, the righteousness of Jesus Christ." Of his mother's latter days he afterward remarked that "Hers at length was a perpetual feast of pleasing thoughts and pleasing emotions, and the serenity within was pictured forth on her whole aspect. She resisted our attempts to bring her forth of her solitude, preferring to reside in Anster by herself, to being with us, even after all her family had left her; and such was the sufficiency of her internal resources, that never was there spent a solitude of greater independence and greater enjoyment, divided as it was, between little schemes of usefulness to the poor families around her, and those secret exercises of reading, and meditation, and prayer which have so ripened her for heaven. My impression of her in early life was, that she was more remarkable for the cardinal than the softer virtues of our nature. But age, and the power of Christianity together, had mellowed her whole character; the mildness of charity, and the peace which the world knoweth not, threw a most beautiful and quiet light over the evening of her days."

On the 26th of February, 1827, Dr. Chalmers received an offer of the Professorship of Moral Philosophy in the London University, which, however, especially, it would seem on account of its exclusion of theological instruction, he finally concluded not to accept. "In the meanwhile, having an urgent application from the Rev. Edward Irving, to open the new church then being erected for him in London," as soon as the session closed, he hastened up to the metropolis, where he had repeated conferences with several of the patrons of the new university.

On this occasion he spent some time in the company of Coleridge, of whom he remarked, as did every one who knew that eminent man in his later days, that "his conversation, which flowed in a mighty stream, was most astonishing," while he confessed, that to him a great part of it was unintelligible. The reply of Mr. Irving to this objection was highly characteristic. "Ha! you Scotchmen would handle an idea as a butcher handles an ox. For my part, I love to see an idea looming through the mist."

Returning to Edinburgh in time to take part in some of the business of the General Assembly, Dr. Chalmers delivered one of his ablest speeches in defense of Mr. McLeod, of Bracadale, who for refusing to perform the ordinance of baptism, in a number of cases, owing to some conscientious scruples, had been suspended from the office of the ministry by the vote of his Presbytery. Appeal had been made to the Assembly, where now, through the efforts chiefly of Dr. Chalmers, the case was brought to an agreeable termination.

In midsummer of that year the Royal Commissioners visited St. Andrews, to investigate the state of the university. Their queries suggested to Dr. Chalmers a great many other topics of interest in relation to educational matters: and after answering before that body all their questions as fully as proper, he pursued the subject further in a treatise "On the Use and Abuse of Literary and Ecclesiastical Endowments," which was completed with the close of the year. This work, the Quarterly Review pronounced "one of the most vigorous and eloquent defenses of such endowments that ever proceeded from the press—a treatise which would alone have been sufficient to immortalize its author;" yet nowhere more distinctly than in that treatise did he denounce the evils resulting from maladministration of their patronage.

"Certain it is, that, by a corrupt and careless exercise of patronage, much has been done to call forth, if not to justify, even the warmest invectives that have been uttered upon this subject. When one thinks of the high and the holy ends to which an established priesthood might be made subservient, it is quite grievous to observe the sordid politics which have to do with so many of our ecclesiastical nominations. Endowments cease to be respectable when, in the hands of a calculating statesman, they degenerate into the instruments by which he prosecutes his game of ambition; or when, employed as the bribes of political subserviency, they expose either our church or our universities to be trodden under foot by the unseemly inroads of mere office-mongers. It is thus that a land may at length be provoked to eject from its borders the establishment either of an indolent or immoral clergy, wherewith it is burdened, and to look, without regret, on the spoliation or the decay of revenue in colleges. It is truly not to be wondered at, if the poverty neither of lazy priests, nor of lazy and luxurious professors, should meet with sympathy from the public. The same generous triumph that was felt on the destruction of the old monasteries, still continues to be felt on the destruction of every old and useless framework; so that, when either a church becomes secularized, or universities, instead of being the living fountain-heads, become the dormitories of literature, they will, sooner or later, be swept off from the country by the verdict of popular condemnation."

Elevation of the standard of scholarship in the Scottish universities was a subject urged in the same work, with all its author's power of argumentation, and from the statements therein made, it appears that some effort of the kind was greatly needed. The whole college course extended to four years; but the yearly attendance was limited to one session of six months. On entering, " the student was subjected to no preliminary examination. It was required that he should be acquainted with the rudiments of the Latin, but he might be, and he generally was, altogether ignorant of the Greek language. The junior Latin class, in a Scottish university, scarcely ranked higher in its exercises, than the head form in any of the best English schools, while the professor of Greek had to begin his pupils with the alphabet of that tongue." Dr. Chalmers proposed as an improvement, " that a gymnasium or school of the highest grade, in which mathematics and the classics should be taught by one or more tutors, with salaries higher than those of the ordinary schoolmaster, and lower than those of the professor, should be attached to each of the universities; that by these tutors all such instructions should be supplied as had been hitherto communicated in the earlier Latin, Greek, and mathematical classes of the university; that in order to test that capability of translating the simpler Latin and Greek authors, and that acquaintance with the elements of geometry, which should be required of every student before admission to the university, an entrance-examination should be instituted. He did not propose that attendance upon the gymnasia connected with the colleges should be made imperative. It would be sufficient if the candidate for entrance proved himself to be possessed of the necessary qualifications, whether these had been attained under the training of the college tutors or under any ordinary schoolmaster." It is difficult to conceive how the obvious necessity of some such reformation could fail to actuate the friends of liberal education in Scotland; and yet strange to say, we are informed that, down to the present day, though great advances have been made in the higher schools of the country, within the walls of the universities no alteration as to the junior classes has ever been attempted.

Yet Dr. Chalmers, while censuring Scottish professors for tolerating a very humble degree of scholarship among their pupils, takes occasion to pay a just tribute to the literary talent and industry prevalent among themselves. "The truth is," he observes, "that greatly more than half the distinguished authorship of our land is professorial; and, till the present generation, we scarcely remember, with the exception of Hume, in philosophy, and Thomson in poetry, any of our eminent writers who did not achieve, or at least germinate, all their greatest works while laboring in their vocation of public instructors in one or other of our universities. Nay, generally speaking, these publications were the actual product of their labor in the capacity of teachers, and passed into authorship through the medium of their respective chairs. Whatever charges may have been preferred against the methods of university education in Scotland, it is at least fortunate for the literary character of our nation, that the professors have not felt, in conducting the business of their appointments, as if they were dealing altogether with boys. To this we owe the manly, and original, and independent treatment which so many of them have bestowed on their appropriate sciences, and by which they have been enabled to superadd one service to another. They have not only taught philosophy; they have also both rectified its doctrines, and added their own views and discoveries to the mass of pre-existent learning. They, in fact, have been the chief agents in enlarging our country's science; and it is mainly, though not exclusively, to them that Scotland is indebted for her eminence and high estimation in the republic of letters."

In September, Dr. Chalmers made a rapid tour through the north of Ireland. Upon his return, the living of St. Cuthbert's,

Edinburgh, one of the most desirable in Scotland, and then vacant by the death of Sir Henry Moncrief, was made to him, but declined, from a conviction of the superiority of a professorship in point of usefulness.

But little more than a month afterward another attempt was made to secure his services in Edinburgh, which was destined to be more successful. On the 31st of October, 1827, the town council and magistrates of Edinburgh, unanimously elected Dr. Chalmers to the professorship of Systematic Theology in their university. "As the appointment took place so close upon the opening of the collegiate session, it was arranged that he should not enter upon the duties of his new office, till November, 1828. The year thus given for preparation was most diligently improved." The composition of his theological lectures was commenced immediately, and the treatise on Political Economy, on which he had been at work for some time previous, was laid aside to make way for the more urgent demand. Yet his time was far from being all his own. A continual influx of visitors absorbed a large portion of each day: nor was it without pleasure that he conducted them round among the memorials of the past, which abounded in the neighborhood—objects which operated upon his imagination, as border legend did upon that of Sir Walter Scott." St. Andrew's was the first place in Scotland which the light of the gospel had visited; and the Tower of St. Regulus still survived as an impressive relic of primitive christianity—a tall, square, solid column, upon which the storms of ten centuries or more have spent themselves in vain. In Roman Catholic times, St. Andrew's had been the seat of the primacy—its castle tenanted by the heads of a lordly hierarchy—its cathedral, upon which the labor of one hundred and sixty years was expended, the largest and stateliest ecclesiastical edifice in the kingdom. Its university, the most ancient in Scotland, was the cradle of the Reformation. In front of St. Salvator's College was the hallowed spot where Hamilton expired among the flame, and close by the castle was the scene of Wishart's martyrdom. From the deck of a French galley, while his feet lay in irons, the spires of St. Andrew's were pointed out to John Knox. 'Yes,' said he, 'I know it well, for I see the steeple of that place where God first opened my mouth in public to His glory; and I am fully persuaded, how weak soever I now appear, that I shall not depart this life till that my tongue shall glorify His godly name in the same place.' The very pulpit from which his fervid tongue fulfilled that prophesy is still shown at St. Andrew's, while the removal of every vestige of Popery, and the ruins of castle and cathedral, remain to tell us of the preacher's power. In still later days, Henderson and Melville, Rutherford and Halyburton, had wandered through the college gardens, meditating those acts, or musing over those writings which have so extensively contributed to mould the character of the Scottish people. Amid localities so rich in hallowed remembrance, Dr. Chalmers reveled with intense delight. He studied the histories connected with each. Again and again did he return to them, and with a growing enthusiasm gaze on the venerable relics. At one or other more sacred spot he might be seen at times standing lost in thought, heedless of notice or salutation. His power of vivid conception had rebuilt the ruined walls, had repeopled the silent area, had raised the stake, and brought up the martyr's form as he stood heroic amid the flames. It was a sentiment far deeper than that of mere antiquarianism which absorbed him. He had that sentiment. It glowed round every relic with which any tale of olden time was linked. But it was a deeper and more powerful emotion which filled his breast, when, on the very ground they trod, and in the places where they received their noblest vindication, he communed with the men and sympathized with the principles of the Scottish Reformation. An hour's walk was sufficient for visiting the most remarkable localities, and whoever came to him, Dr. Chalmers was always impatient till he had them off to a 'round of the ruins.' If the many groups thus guided had been chronicled, we should have a long and strange array of British peers and Glasgow merchants, burghers of Anstruther, and cottagers of Kilmany, escorted with equal delight, and having lavished upon them an equal attention. Each fresh eye that looked upon those ruins, gazed, he fancied, with a feeling kindred to his own, and it revived and redoubled his own enjoyment to communicate such a pleasure. During the later period of his residence in St. Andrew's, Dr. Chalmers lived in a house which had formed part of St. Leonard's College, and he had great delight in announcing to his guests that they were under the roof which covered the small upper chamber—approachable then only by a ladder—which had been the study of the celebrated Buchanan, and that they were in the dwelling where Dr. Samuel Johnson being asked by one of the professors whether he had been satisfied with the dinner which had been provided for him, returned the fierce reply: 'Sir, I came to Scotland, not to eat good dinners, but to see savage men and savage manners, and I have not been disappointed.'"

Upon the termination of his last session at St. Andrew's, his students once more pressed upon him the acceptance of a testimonial of their esteem; and that which he correctly declined in the course of his labors, he could with perfect propriety accept, at their close. The appropriate gift consisted of a copy of Walton's Polyglot, with Castell's Lexicon. The last lecture of his course was delivered on the 24th of April, and was closed with a valedictory to his class, brief, but very appropriate and beautiful.

"I will pursue the connections of moral philosophy with Christianity no further at present. So much am I impressed with the unity of the two subjects, or rather with the way in which the one graduates into the other, that I scarcely feel myself translated to another walk of speculation by the removal which is now before me from an ethical to a theological chair. There is, at least, nothing violent in the transition, for I feel it as if but a step in advance from the rudiments to the higher lessons of the same science. But though mentally there may be little or no change implied by this transference of my duties, yet personally I must confess that it cannot be accomplished without a feeling of painful laceration, insomuch that I dare hardly trust myself with the expression of one parting homage to a place all whose localities, from its classrooms even to the remotest corner of its area, are interwoven with the remembrances of early boyhood. There is one experience, gentlemen, to which the history of my various changes in life has peculiarly, and, I will even say, has painfully exposed me, and that is, how little a man gains, or rather, indeed, how much he loses, in the happiness of natural and healthful enjoyment, by passing from a narrower to a wider, and what some may call, a more elevated sphere. There is not room in the heart of man for more than a certain number of objects, and he is therefore placed far more favorably for the development of all that pleasure which lies in the kind and friendly affections of our nature, when the intimacy of his regards is permitted to rest on a few, than when, bustled through an interminable variety of persons and things, each individual can have but a slender hold upon the memory, and a hold as slender upon the emotions. It is thus, that on looking back upon my city experience I have little more than the dazzling recollection of a feverish and troubled dream, while athwart this medium and at a larger distance in the retrospect, I can enjoy the sweet prospect of a country parish, all whose scenes and cottage families are dear to me. I know that I am to repeat this experience, and am quite sure that amid the din, and the confusion, and the crowded attendance of that larger theater to which I go, I shall often look back with a sigh on the closer and the kindlier fellowships that I have held with the students within these walls. Be assured, gentlemen, as you would of any moral certainty, that there is nothing in the busier scenes which are now before me that is fitted to displace you from my recollections, but, on the contrary, to enhance all my regrets and all my regards, when on contrasting the students of St. Andrew's with those of Edinburgh, I shall think of my connection with you as a peculiar and a more tender relationship."

In the succeeding General Assembly the principal business in which Dr. Chalmers figured was the address on the Test and Corporation Acts, moved by himself in the following terms: "That the General Assembly should present an address to

His Majesty, of their high satisfaction at the Act which had obtained the sanction of the legislature, for repealing so much of several acts of Parliament which imposed the necessity of taking the sacrament as a qualification for entering upon office." His remarks in support of this motion constitute valuable material to one tracing the progress of his mind. "There is one most appropriate topic for a place in our address, and that is the Repeal of the Corporation and Test Acts. It were certainly not in good taste for us to specialize with any degree of minuteness such events as are merely political. But the measure to which I now refer is not of that character. It is not a secular but a sacred interest which is involved in it. It were strange, I do think, to pass over in silence, or even to pass over slightly, a matter so connected as this is with religious liberty and the rights of conscience; more especially, as what our government has actually done upon this question is so fitted to rejoice every enlightened friend of Christianity, and in particular to call forth the acknowledgments and gratulations of the Church of Scotland.

"We have heard the repeal of these Acts spoken of as the removal of a stigma from our church. I am not sure if this expresses my precise feeling upon the subject. The truth is, I look upon the whole history of this matter as in the highest degree honorable to the Scottish Establishment, and as fitted to demonstrate the native stability of that basis upon which she rests. It has now become experimentally palpable that she stands in need of none of those securities wherewith her fearful sister in the south thought it necessary at one time to prop up what she must then have felt to be her frail and precarious existence. Instead of such securities for us, we ourselves were the objects of jealousy to the hierarchy of England, and thrust, along with its general body of sectarians, to an outfield place beyond the limits of her guarded inclosure. And what has been the result? A striking lesson, if blind intolerance would but learn it. In virtue of our inherent strength, we, in the midst of disabilities, have stood and prospered; and the motto of our northern church—'Nec tamen consumebatur'—

blazes in characters as fresh and undefaced as ever upon her forehead. The truth is, that our provincial Establishment bids as fair for sound and vigorous endurance as does the great national Episcopacy of these realms; and at this moment it must be palpable to every eye that, wanting all her artificial protections, we yet outpeer her far in the love and reverence of our country's population.

"On the subject of the difference between the two Establishments, I have but one word to offer on the question where it is that the stigma lies. In walking through a street the eye is sometimes arrested by the sight of large wooden props leaning obliquely on the walls of one of the houses, and obviously placed there for the purpose of upholding it. Is it possible, sir, to resist the impression of that being the craziest edifice along the whole pavement? The fabric of the English Church with her Test and Corporation Acts, incurred the whole discredit of such an appearance; and she has inconceivably strengthened herself, both in reality and in public estimation, by the taking of them down. The only blunder is, that to please the fancy of the eye of certain of her devotees, long accustomed to the sight of some such projections, and whose taste would have been offended by the want of them, she has erected in their place a buttress of stucco, in the shape of a declaration. It was proposed at first that the Kirk of Scotland should have been conjoined with the Church of England in this declaration. That, sir, I would have felt to be a stigma; and if anything in the progress of this most delightful bill was more satisfactory than another, it was that upon this part of the subject they took another thought, and resolved to keep the whole of this stigma to themselves.

"And now, sir, I have just to crave your toleration for one word more, in order to a very short insertion which I would humbly propose in this part of your address. You are aware that the philosophy of our age is all in favor of free trade, and that the extension of this principle to christianity carries an inference along with it unfavorable to religious establishments. Now, sir, in the masses and the large movements which take place among the parties and proceedings of a state, opinion is apt to be taken by whole bodies of men in the bulk, and without any reference had to certain important modifications which it is dangerous to lose sight of. I feel convinced, sir, that on this very question there is the want of a most necessary discrimination between the use of these artificial securities for an Establishment which have now been abolished, and the use of an Establishment at all. And, therefore, now is the time, when felicitating our monarch on the abolition of the one, that we, in one short and emphatic sentence, should lift our strenuous testimony in behalf of the other. It follows not because there should be a full equality between churchmen and sectarians in every civil and political right, that therefore a church and an Establishment are uncalled for. Believing, as we do, that without the maintenance of a national clergy, all the zeal, and effort, and activity of dissenters could not save our land from lapsing into a tenfold grosser heathenism than it otherwise would do; and fearful as we at the same time are, that some may be counting on the last glorious triumph of liberality as a step in advance toward the overthrow of religious establishments, we are all the more imperiously called upon to distinguish between the things which differ; and while we rejoice in the wider door that has now been opened for sectarians to all the privileges of citizens, to accompany this with our pointed declaration in behalf of a church to which I heartily believe that Scotland stands mainly indebted for the religion and the worth of her people.

"I can truly say that I feel as much in earnest for the public testimony in behalf of the latter sentiment, as in behalf of the former; for the appeal by us on the side of a religious Establishment, is an appeal on the side of that law of toleration which has recently been extended to all sects; and I think that a united testimony in favor of both these principles would come with peculiar grace and propriety from the Church of Scotland—from that church which, on the one hand, is a living instance of the uselessness of those restrictions which have now been done away, and, on the other hand, has made such ample returns for the protection of the state in the worth of her services; and I further think, sir, that such a manifestation on our part were not only in the highest degree becoming, but considering the aspect of the times, were in the highest degree seasonable. With all my predilections on the side of freedom, I do not apprehend so much of danger to our land from the advances of liberality, as from the over impetuous career of a headlong and unguarded liberalism. I have spoken with frankness of the Church of England, but most assuredly, without the slightest feeling of disrespect; conceiving, as I do, that to put forth upon her the invading hand of a destroyer, were, instrumentally speaking, to reach the deadliest possible blow at the Christianity of the nation."

The motion was lost, but the liberal party could at least console themselves with the fact that they had thereby obtained an "expression of the Assembly's approval of the repeal."

Mr. Irving was at the same time in Edinburgh, delivering a series of lectures on prophesy. "He is drawing," says Dr. Chalmers, "prodigious crowds. We attempted this morning to force our way into St. Andrew's Church, but it was all in vain. He changes to the West Church for the accommodation of the public."

"*Monday, 26th.*—For the first time heard Mr. Irving in the evening. I have no hesitation in saying that it is quite woeful. There is power and richness, and gleams of exquisite beauty, but withal a mysticism and an extreme allegorization which I am sure must be pernicious to the general cause. This is the impression of every clergyman I have met, and some think of making a friendly remonstrance with him upon the subject. He sent me a letter he had written to the king against the repeal of the Test and Corporation Acts, and begged that I would read every word of it before I spoke. I did so, and found it unsatisfactory and obscure, but not half so much so as his sermon of this evening."

The rest of this summer Dr. Chalmers devoted entirely to preparation for his theological lectures in Edinburgh, upon which he entered in the beginning of November. His inauguration took place on the 6th, and the introductory lecture was delivered on the following Monday at eleven o'clock in the forenoon. " The morning of that day was singularly unpropitious, showers of snow and hail sweeping through the college courts; yet from so early an hour as nine, those who had secured that privilege were passing by a private entrance into the class-room, while so great a crowd besieged the outer door, that a strong body of police found it difficult to restrain the tumult.

" It was a day," says Mr. Bruce Cunningham, " as you will easily believe, of no common expectation and excitement, not only among those who were professionally required to become his pupils, but also to not a few of the worthiest citizens of Edinburgh, who having once and again listened with impassioned wonder and delight to his mighty words as a preacher of the gospel, scarcely knew what to expect from him as an academic expounder and disciplinarian in the science of theology. If I may judge of other minds from the state of my own feelings at the time, I may safely state, that at no time, either before or since, has a tumult of emotions, so peculiar and intense, agitated the hearts of the many who waited for his first appearance in the chair of theology. I well remember his look as he first came from the vestry into the passage leading to the desk. He had an air of extreme abstraction, and, at the same time, of full presence of mind. Ascending the steps in his familiar resolute manner, he almost immediately engaged in his opening prayer: that was most startling, and yet deeply solemnizing. In closest union with a simple, forcible antithesis of intellectual conception, clothed in still more antithetical expressions, there was a deep vital consciousness of the glory of the divine presence. The power of the dialectician restrained and elevated by the prayerful reverence as of some prophet in ancient Israel, imparted a most remarkable peculiarity of aspect to his first devotional utterance, in the class. On his discourse I shall not presume on your patience by anything like detailed remark. All felt far more deeply than they could worthily declare, that it was a most glorious prelude, and that at once and forever his right to reign as a king in the broad realms of theological science, and to rule over their own individual minds as a teacher, was as unequivocal as his mastery over a popular assembly. Personally I always feel, in recalling that scene, as if, by some peculiar enchantment of association, I had listened, all unconscious of the present world, to one or other of Handel's most sublime efforts of harmony. To this hour I dwell with all the mysterious delight that is awakened by some grand choral symphony on some of his novel expressions, which, borrowed from physical science, directly tended, by almost more than the force of his best diagrams, to make his noble thoughts all our own."

The rapturous applause which hailed the opening of the course continued, with scarcely a sensible abatement, throughout the session. The lecturer was dealing with his favorite subjects—Natural Theology and Evidences of Christianity—and eagerly seized the opportunity of presenting thereupon the results of long continued and mature reflection. "And he had much to animate him in the audience he addressed—an audience altogether unique within the walls of a university, embracing in addition to his own regular students, distinguished members of the various professions, and many of the most intelligent citizens of Edinburgh." This latter class, very properly feeling that something more than applause was due from them to one who had contributed so much to their instruction, and delight, at the end of the course, presented him with an addition to his salary of more than two hundred pounds.

Before the end of that same session, Dr. Chalmers found himself called upon to take part in the great political question of Catholic Emancipation. A letter from Sir James Macintosh, of the 22d February, 1829, urging the importance of making public his views on the subject, which were known by his friends to be liberal, drew forth one of his most brilliant efforts, not, however, as Sir James had suggested, in the form of a sermon or pamphlet, but of a speech before a meeting of the citizens of Edinburgh, in order to petition in favor of the Catholic Emancipation Bill. That speech had tremendous effect on the cause at the time, and for the broad, liberal and truly

Protestant spirit which imbued it, merited the applause it received. The last paragraph is especially worthy of everlasting remembrance.

"It is not because I hold Popery to be innocent that I want the removal of these disabilities; but because I hold, that if these were taken out of the way she would be tenfold more assailable. It is not because I am indifferent to the good of Protestantism that I want to displace these artificial crutches from under her; but because I want that, freed from every symptom of decrepitude and decay, she should stand forth in her own native strength, and make manifest to all men how firm a support she has on the goodness of her cause, and on the basis of her orderly and well laid arguments. It is because I count so much—and will any Protestant here present say that I count too much?—on her Bible, and her evidences, and the blessing of God upon her churches, and the force of her resistless appeals to the conscience and the understandings of men; it is because of her strength and sufficiency in these that I would disclaim the aids of the statute-book, and own no dependence or obligation whatever on a system of intolerance. These were enough for her in the days of her suffering, and should be more than enough for her in the days of her comparative safety. It is not by our fears and our false alarms that we do honor to Protestantism. A far more befitting honor to the great cause is the homage of our confidence; for what Sheridan said of the liberty of the press, admits of most emphatic application to this religion of truth and liberty. 'Give,' says the great orator, ' give to ministers a corrupt House of Commons; give them a pliant and a servile House of Lords; give them the keys of the Treasury and the patronage of the Crown; and give me the liberty of the press, and with this mighty engine I will overthrow the fabric of corruption, and establish upon its ruins the rights and privileges of the people.' In like manner, give the Catholics of Ireland their emancipation; give them a seat in the Parliament of their country; give them a free and equal participation in the politics of the realm; give them a place at the right ear of majesty, and a voice in his counsels; and give me the circulation of the Bible, and with this mighty engine I will overthrow the tyranny of Antichrist, and establish the fair and original form of Christianity on its ruins.*

"The politics of the question I have left to other and abler hands. I view it only in its religious bearings; and I give it as my honest conviction, and I believe the conviction of every true-hearted Protestant who knows wherein it is that the great strength of his cause lies, that we have everything to hope from this proposed emancipation, and that we have nothing to fear."

"The effects of that speech," says Mr. Ramsay, "have been described as something very remarkable. An excitement and enthusiasm pervaded the large and closely crowded assemblage seldom witnessed in modern times. I heard our most distinguished Scottish critic (Lord Jeffrey), who was present on the occasion, give it as his deliberate opinion, that never had eloquence produced a greater effect upon a popular assembly, and that he could not believe more had ever been done by the oratory of Demosthenes, Cicero, Burke or Sheridan."

---

* We have in this case a curious example of the contrast sometimes existing between the judgment of an author and that of the world upon his production. "The delivery of this splendid passage, which was given with prodigious force, elicited a burst of applause so deafening and enthusiastic, that the effect was altogether sublime. The shouts and huzzas were thrice renewed, and it was with difficulty the speaker could proceed."—*Caledonian Mercury, March,* 1829.

"The conclusion of the reverend Doctor's speech was greeted with renewed shouts and huzzas, the whole audience standing and waving their hats in the air. This lasted several minutes, and it was not without difficulty that the tumult of admiration was allayed."—*Ibid.*

"I was quite uncomfortable in speaking, from my excessively high pitch of voice, beneath which I could not fall. It was well received, notwithstanding. I have uniformly experienced the insincerity of that pleasure which is afforded by the praise of others."—*Journal, March* 14*th*, 1829.

The same subject Dr. Chalmers also presented at a meeting of the Presbytery of Edinburgh, entering more fully into his reasons for advocating the removal from Roman Catholics of all civil disabilities.

In the midst of these exciting occupations, he received information of the death of his youngest and favorite brother, Alexander, on the 22d April, 1829. On the day of the funeral he entered these words in his journal letter to Mrs. Chalmers: "This is the fifth time within these few years that I have been chief mourner, and carried the head of a relative to the grave. But this has been far the heaviest of them all." Again, on the next day: "*25th April.*—I alternated my employments within doors by walks in the little garden, where all the objects exposed me to gushes of mournful remembrance. The plants—the petrified tree—the little cistern for water-plants—the rain-gauge—all abandoned by the hand which had placed them there, and took such delight in tending them. I could even fancy the dog to have a certain melancholy air from the want of customary attentions. I this day visited the grave, exposed to full sunshine. I have never felt any bereavement so much."

The succeeding summer vacation Dr. Chalmers spent, with little exception, in the quiet of a country retirement, at Penicuik. And from the routine of professorial duties he withdrew during the winter holidays of 1829–30 to St. Andrew's, where it was most gratifying to find that the asperity of feeling which had existed toward himself was entirely done away. The intercourse of those few days was unproductive of anything to mar the pure delight associated with the beloved scenes of his youth.

The Church of Scotland was that winter greatly embarrassed by the errors and wild fancies of some of her members. Thomas Erskine, Esq., of Linlathen, and the Rev. Mr. Campbell, of Row, had both presented views of the atonement naturally leading to the doctrine of universal salvation; and Mr. Irving had begun to promulgate those strange delusions which threw so deep a shade over the latter part of his otherwise illustrious career. The miraculous gift of tongues, which those men united in defending as real, created then quite as great a sensation as the spirit-rappings and revelations of later times. The respectability of the circumstances under which it appeared, was, however, greatly superior. The persons now mentioned had, for sometime previous, held that the miraculous gifts of Pentecost were no longer conferred only on account of the feebleness of modern faith, and had made it a subject of prayer that the faith of Christians might be increased until it should be consistent with God's will to send down such a sign of his favor. "At last the startling announcement reached the public ear, that the miraculous gifts of the day of Pentecost had reappeared. On a Sabbath evening in the end of March, Mary Campbell was lying on a bed of weakness, and what seemed likely to prove a bed of death. Her sister, a female friend, and one or two of the household, were engaged along with her in prayer, when suddenly she was visited by a mysterious impulse, and with almost superhuman strength and in a loud exalted tone, she poured forth in some unknown tongue, 'a volume of majestic sound.' Occasionally, in moments of inspiration, seizing pen or pencil, and writing with lightning speed, she covered scraps of paper with strange characters, said to be of an unknown language. Not long after, at a prayer-meeting in Port-Glasgow, the same pretended gift of tongues was exercised by a person named M'Donald, and there as elsewhere, miraculous cures were alleged to have been wrought."

Both Mr. Erskine and Mr. Irving declared publicly their conviction of the reality of those utterances as the work of inspiration.

In the controversies which ensued, Dr. Chalmers took no part; but spoke always with the kindest consideration of the gentlemen principally concerned. Regarding the gift of tongues, he took the most effectual method, by obtaining one of Mary Campbell's written revelations, and subjecting it to the investigation of skillful linguists. One of these he took with him on a journey to England, for the purpose of having it examined by some of the Oriental scholars of the metropolis. The result was, what, doubtless, he expected, a distinct verdict that the pretended tongue was an unmeaning jargon, and the whole affair an imposition. The journey to London alluded to, was undertaken at the solicitation of Mr. Spring Rice, as chairman of a committee of Parliament, on the condition of the Irish poor. The opportunity which an appearance before that committee afforded for an exposition of his views on the subject of pauperism, was such as Dr. Chalmers could not suffer to pass unimproved. The examination to which he there submitted, drew forth, in the plainest and most direct manner, views which, taken in connection with what has since befallen Ireland, are possessed of too much interest to admit of much abridgment. After stating his objections to poor-laws in general, and his own experience on the subject in Glasgow, and replying to some preliminary questions respecting the application of his principles to Ireland, the examination proceeded as follows:

"In what respect do you consider the assessment principle would be productive of evil under such circumstances?"—"I think it would just add to the recklessness and improvidence of the people, and so land the country in a still greater population without increased means of maintaining them. If I may be permitted, I will advert to a principle which I think may be called the pervading fallacy in the speculations of those who advocate the establishment of a poor-rate in Ireland, and is founded on the observation of a connection between a high state of character and a high state of economic comfort. It is quite palpable that so it is in fact; but there seems to be an important mistake in the order of causation. It is often conceived that comfort is the cause and character is the effect; now I hold that character is the cause and that comfort is the effect. It does not appear that if you lay hold of a man thirty or forty years old, with his inveterate habits, and improve his economic condition, by giving him, through a poor-rate or otherwise, £9 or £4 a year more, it does not appear to me that this man will be translated thereby into other habits or higher tastes, but he will dissipate it generally in the same reckless and sordid kind of indulgence to which he had been previously accustomed; whereas if, instead of taking hold of the man and attempting to elevate him by the improvement of his economic condition, you take hold of the boy, and attempt to infuse into him the other element, which I conceive to be the causal one, by means of education, then you will, through the medium of character, work out an improvement in his economic condition. What I should advise is, that education be made universal in Ireland, and that you should weather for a season the annoyance of Ireland's mendicity, and the annoyance of that pressure which I conceive to be altogether temporary. This appears to me the only principle upon which Ireland can be securely and effectually brought to a higher standard of enjoyment, and into the state of a well-habited and well-conditioned peasantry. I think that if patiently waited for, very great results might be looked for ere another generation pass away; but then the establishment of a poor-law would throw a very heavy obstruction indeed on that educational process, to which alone I look for a permanent improvement in the state of Ireland."

"You have stated that you conceive the tendency of the principle of assessment would be to increase population, and to create or to increase habits of improvidence and inconsiderate marriages; now, if it is shown that in Ireland the population has increased more rapidly, and that greater improvidence exists than in Britain, how would you reconcile those two statements, your statement of principle, and this statement of facts?"—"I am quite sensible of the effect which this complication of the problem has had in casting what may be called a general obscuration over it. If the only element upon which the standard of enjoyment depended was a poor-rate, and if in point of fact we saw in a country where a poor-rate was established, a much higher standard of enjoyment than in a country where there was no poor-rate, the inference would be a very fair one—establish the poor-rate there, and we shall bring the people up to a higher standard. But the whole matter is mixed and complicated with other influences ; there are other elements than the poor-rate which enter into the question of a nation's prosperity, and have a deciding influence on the taste and condition of the people. The low standard of enjoyment in Ireland is attributable not to the want of a poor-rate, but to other causes—to misgovernment and to imperfect education. On the other hand, there has been a gradual elevation of the people of England, keeping pace with its commerce, its growth in general opulence, its pure administration of justice. The better condition of its people is no more due to its poor-rate, than it is to its national debt. Its high standard of enjoyment is not in consequence of its poor-rate, but in spite of its poor-rate. I believe that had there been no poor-rate in England, there would have been a higher standard of enjoyment than there is now ; and, on the other hand, that if there had been a poor-rate in Ireland, there would have been a lower standard of enjoyment there than there is at present. In a word, had the condition of the two countries, with reference to the single circumstance of a poor-rate, been reversed, there would have been a still wider difference between them in favor of England and against Ireland, than there is at this moment."

"You conceive that if you were to add to the causes which have tended to increase rapidly the population of Ireland and to produce improvidence and recklessness on the part of the people, an additional cause tending in the same direction, namely, the establishment of a poor-rate, you conceive the evils already existing would be very much augmented?"— "They would. If it is intended to introduce the system of poor-rate into Ireland with a view of elevating the standard of enjoyment, or elevating the general condition of the families of Ireland, this is an aim far different from the ordinary purpose of a poor-rate. The aim of the present system of poor-rate is to rescue a fraction of the people from extreme wretchedness ; but should it aim at the still more magnificent object of raising the general population above the level and the rate of its present enjoyments, the very expense of such an achievement, extending to a million families in Ireland, would seem to fasten upon the scheme the charge of being utterly impracticable, beside utterly failing in its object, for that is really not the way of raising a people to higher tastes and habits of enjoyment."

"Do you not consider that the improvidence of the people, and their recklessness in consequence of the increase of their numbers, will be found in a direct proportion to their misery and degradation, provided the misery is not of that cast which immediately affects human life?"—"I think that the causal and antecedent influence in the whole matter is a moral one. The people are in an uneducated state, with perhaps no great infusion of Christian principle in their minds; it is this which produces misery and a low economic condition, and if brought out of this by direct educational means, it will operate favorably upon their providential habits so as to restrain the tendency of the country to over-population."

"Are you of opinion that a measure of colonization upon an extended scale, applied as a national effort to the pauperism of the United Kingdom, especially of Ireland, would be a beneficial measure, facilitating the introduction of amended laws, and of a more judicious management of the poor, and if blended with a judicious education, would produce improved habits of thinking on the part of the lower classes, especially the younger portions of them?"—"I think it would be beneficial; but I do not think that the application of the general cure should wait for the scheme of colonization, though I think that such a scheme might operate as an auxiliary to the cure. In this view, a scheme of colonization might be very useful."

The following extracts from Dr. Chalmers's examination in reference to the report of a committee on the education of the lower orders, are also too important to be omitted, presenting, as they do, his opinion of the place which the Bible should occupy in education, while proving the breadth of his own liberality:

"What observations would you make to the Committee upon the principles laid down in that Report, which, while it connects religious instruction essentially with the principles of national education, in order to meet the difficulties of a mixed community, leaves that religious instruction which is rendered absolutely necessary, under the supervision of the respective ministers of the various denominations?"—"My approbation of the leading principle in that report depends upon the construction which is given to it. 'Resolved, That this Committee, with reference to the opinions above recorded, consider that no system of education can be expedient which may be calculated to influence or disturb the peculiar tenets of any sect or denomination of Christians.' If it be meant by this clause that there shall be no compulsion on Catholics to attend the Scriptural class, I quite agree with it; but if it be meant by this clause that in deference to any principle or inclination of theirs there shall be no Scriptural class open to the demand of every parent who may choose that his children may attend it, to that I would not agree, and on this matter I would hold no negotiation with any party whatever; but substituting a school on what I judge to be the best constitution for one, I would hold it forth to the free choice of all the parochial families, and I think that a Scriptural class should be the integrant and indispensable part of every such school."

"Are the Committee then to understand that you consider the system of education would be incomplete without the establishment of a Scriptural class in each school, but that you consider it would be inexpedient to render the attendance upon such Scriptural class compulsory upon the parties?"—" I would not have any part of the education given at the parish school made compulsory; they should no more be compelled to attend the Bible class than to attend the reading or arithmetic class, and the Bible would of course fall to be read by the more advanced scholars. I can not answer for what the Catholics will do, though I have a very strong opinion upon what they ought to do. If they do not attend the Scriptural reading that is going on in a school so constituted, then I think the districts which they occupy should be laid open to the influence of all that general religious activity that is now expatiating freely over the length and the breadth of Ireland. My idea of the perfection of an ecclesiastical system lies in this, that in the first instance there should be an establishment, but that establishment constantly operated upon, stimulated and kept on the alert by the zeal and activity of an energetic, active, and unconstrained dissenterism; and I have a parallel idea to this in reference to a scholastic system, that there should be an apparatus of stationary schools, but if those stationary schools are not working the effect which is desirable, and which effect is, that the whole young population of the country should be leavened with Scriptural knowledge, then I say that with reference to those districts of country where this deficiency prevails, there should be free scope and encouragement given to the same sort of active and zealous exertion on the part of religious philanthropists, whether acting individually or in societies, and that in all such places there should be full and free encouragement given to the talents, and the energy, and the competition of private adventurers."

"By a Scriptural class, do you mean a class meeting on ordinary school-days, and at ordinary school-hours, or would you apply that denomination to a class which met on special days fixed for that purpose?"—"I would greatly prefer that the Scriptural class should be taught every day of the week; I should consider it very defective to confine the reading of the Scriptures to one or two days of the week."

"But whether upon one or more days of the week, or every day, do you still think that no compulsion ought to be used, and no regulation enforced by authority to render the attendance upon that class a *sine qua non?*"—"Certainly not."

"Had you at Glasgow any portion of your parishioners in St. John's of a religion differing from the Established Church of Scotland?"—"A good many; it was one of those parishes in which, from the population having outstripped the established means for their instruction, there were very few indeed who belonged to the Established Church of Scotland."

"Were there any Roman Catholics?"—"A good many Roman Catholics."

"Were any of those Roman Catholics in the progress of education within your view?"—"There happened to be one school very numerously attended, to the extent of 300 scholars, within the limits of the parish of St. John's; it was a school which, along with two others, was supported by the Catholic School Association that was formed in Glasgow, and we made what we thought a very good compromise with the Catholic clergyman; he consented to the use of the Bible, according to the authorized version, as a school-book, we consenting to have Catholic teachers, and upon that footing the education went on, and went on I believe most prosperously, and with very good effect. From the mere delight I had in witnessing the display and the exercise of native talent among the young Irish, I frequently visited that school, and I was uniformly received with the utmost welcome and respect by the schoolmaster. I remember, upon one occasion, when I took some ladies with me, and we were present at the examination of the school for about two hours, he requested, at the end of the examination, that I would address the children. I felt a kind of momentary embarrassment at the proposal; I was resolved, however, to address them as I would any Protestant children, and accordingly did address them, for perhaps a quarter or nearly half an hour, urging upon them that Scripture was the alone rule of faith and manners, and other wholesome Protestant principles. The schoolmaster, so far from taking the slightest offense, turned round and thanked me most cordially for the address I had given."

"That schoolmaster being a Roman Catholic?"—"That schoolmaster being a Roman Catholic; it really convinced me that a vast deal might be done by kindness, and by discreet and friendly personal intercourse with the Roman Catholics. I may also observe, that whereas it has been alleged that under the superintendence of a Catholic teacher there might be a danger of only certain passages of Scripture being read, to the exclusion of others, as far as my observations extended, he read quite indiscriminately and impartially over Scripture; I recollect that day in particular, I found him engaged with the first chapter of John."

"Did you meet with any contradiction on the part of the

Roman Catholic clergy of Glasgow?"—" Not in the least, for the clergyman was a party in the negotiation; he attended our meetings, and there was a mutual understanding between the clergyman and the members of the committee: nay, a good many members of the committee were themselves Roman Catholics; and I remember when I was asked to preach for the Roman Catholic School Society, the committee came and thanked me for my exertions and more particularly the Roman Catholic members of that committee, who were present at the sermon."

It is not to be supposed that Dr. Chalmers ever regretted the liberality of his sentiments, but he lived long enough to see that his expectations here expressed were unfounded—to have abundant evidence of a kind which has been rapidly accumulating since his death, that no liberality on the part of others, that no kindliness of personal intercourse with its subjects, any more than its own professions, can divest Popery of its inherent intolerance.

Dr. Chalmers availed himself of his presence in London to enjoy another conversation with Coleridge, of which we have only a brief indirect summary. The poet-philosopher, as usual, took the reins of discourse in his own hands. "He began—in answer to the common inquiries as to his health— by telling of a fit of insensibility in which, three weeks before, he had lain for thirty-five minutes. As sensibility returned, and before he had opened his eyes, he uttered a sentence about the fugacious nature of consciousness, from which he passed to a discussion of the singular relations between the soul and the body. Asking for Mr. Irving, but waiting for no reply, he poured out an eloquent tribute of his regard—mourning pathetically that such a man should be so throwing himself away. Mr. Irving's book on the 'Human Nature of Christ,' in its analysis, was minute to absurdity; one would imagine that the pickling and preserving were to follow, it was so like a cookery-book. Unfolding then his own scheme of the Apocalypse—talking of the mighty contrast between its Christ and the Christ of the gospel narrative, Mr. Coleridge said that Jesus did not come now as before—meek and gentle, healing the sick, and feeding the hungry, and dispensing blessings all around, but he came on a white horse; and who were his attendants?—famine, and war, and pestilence."

Of another conversation, occurring that same day, a fuller account has been preserved by the rapid pen of Mr. J. J. Gurney, who was one of the company, embracing also Dr. Sumner, Bishop of Chester, Dr. Lushington, Mr. Buxton, and Mrs. Fry, with whom Dr. Chalmers dined at Mr. Hoare's. "The conversation during dinner, turned to the subject of capital punishments. Lushington, in the warmest terms, expressed his abhorrence of the system, and declared his opinion, that the poor criminal was thus hurried out of life and into eternity, by means of the perpetration of another crime, far greater, for the most part, than any which the sufferer himself had committed. He even indicated a feeling that the worse the criminal, the more improper such a punishment. Buxton rallied him, and restated his argument with great pleasantry: 'The Dr. assures us, that if your lordship was condemned to the gallows, or you, Dr. Chalmers, were about to suffer the *ultimum supplicium*, he would be the last man to prevent the execution of the law, or prevent the translation of the virtuous to a happier state; but to terminate the probationary existence of the most degraded of our race—the worst of robbers, or the most outrageous of murderers—was opposed at once to all the feelings of humanity, and to all the principles of religion.' After all, however, there is a great deal of truth in Dr. Lushington's statement, and substantially we are all agreed."

"After dinner a brisk discussion arose respecting the comparative religious condition of the Long Parliament, and of our representatives in the present day of latitudinarianism and laxity. Lushington contended that the advantage lay on the side of our modern senate, and that the looseness of the present was a less crying evil than the hypocrisy of past times. The bishop and Chalmers took the other side, and not only demonstrated the religious superiority of the Puritans, but strongly insisted on the great principle, that it is godliness which exalteth a nation, and which can alone impart true strength and stability to human governments. Chalmers stated the points of the argument with great strength and clearness, and the bishop confirmed what he said. In the evening Joanna Baillie joined our party, and after the bishop and others were gone, we formed a sociable circle, of which Chalmers was the center. The evidences of Christianity became again the topic of conversation. I rather think the harmony of Scripture, and the accordance and correspondence of one part with another were adverted to. This evidence of accordance is one to which Dr. C.'s mind is obviously much alive. He knows how to trace in the adaptation between one branch of truth and another, and especially between *God's religion* and man's EXPERIENCE, the *master-hand* of perfect wisdom and goodness.

"CHAL. 'The historical evidences of Christianity are abundantly sufficient to satisfy the scrutinizing researches of the learned, and are within the reach of all well educated persons. But the internal evidence of the Truth lies within the grasp of every sincere inquirer. Every man who reads his Bible, and compares what it says of mankind with the records of his own experience—every man who marks the adaptation of its mighty system of doctrine to his own spiritual need as a sinner in the sight of God, is furnished with practical proof of the divine origin of our religion. I love this evidence. It is what I call the *portable evidence of Christianity*.'

"On the following morning he read the Scriptures to the family circle, and selected the latter half of John, xiv. The verse which peculiarly attracted his attention was verse 21:—'He that hath my commandments, and keepeth them, he it is that loveth me: and he that loveth me shall be loved of my Father, and I will love him, and will manifest myself to him.'

"When our conversation was concluded, my brother, Samuel Hoare, took me with him on the box of his chariot, and drove Dr. Chalmers and his highly pleasing wife, to Wilberforce's, at Highwood Hall, beyond Hendon. Dr. C. and his lady were engaged to stay some days there, and we were glad of the opportunity of enjoying the company of the *senator emeritus*, together with that of Dr. C. for a few hours. Our morning passed delightfully. Chalmers was indeed comparatively silent, as he often is, when many persons are collected, and the stream of conversation flowed between ourselves and the ever lively Wilberforce. I have seldom observed a more amusing and pleasing contrast between two great men than between Wilberforce and Chalmers. Chalmers is stout and erect, with a broad countenance — Wilberforce minute, and singularly twisted: Chalmers, both in body and mind, moves with a deliberate step—Wilberforce, infirm as he is in his advanced years, flies about with astonishing activity, and while, with nimble finger, he seizes on everything that adorns or diversifies his path, his mind flits from object to object with unceasing versatility. I often think that particular men bear about with them an analogy to particular animals: Chalmers is like a good-tempered lion—Wilberforce is like a bee: Chalmers can say a pleasant thing now and then, and laugh when he has said it, and he has a strong touch of humor in his countenance, but in general he is grave; his thoughts grow to a great size before they are uttered—Wilberforce sparkles with life and wit, and the characteristic of his mind is 'rapid productiveness.' A man might be in Chalmers's company for an hour, especially in a party, without knowing who or what he was— though in the end he would be sure to be detected by some unexpected display of powerful originality. Wilberforce, except when fairly asleep, is never latent. Chalmers knows how to vail himself in a decent cloud—Wilberforce is always in sunshine. Seldom, I believe, has any mind been been more strung to a perpetual tune of love and praise. Yet these persons, distinguished as they are from the world at large, and from each other, present some admirable points of resemblance. Both of them are broad thinkers, and liberal feelers: both of them are arrayed in humility, meekness, and charity: both appear to hold self in little reputation: above all, both love the Lord Jesus Christ, and reverently acknowledge him to be their only Saviour."

The respectful kindness of Sir Robert Peel was manifested toward Dr. Chalmers in procuring for him an appointment as one of His Majesty's chaplains in ordinary in Scotland.

With the view of enjoying a few days' intercourse with Mr. Hall and Mr. Foster, Dr. Chalmers consented to open for public worship, an independent chapel in the neighborhood of Bristol; after which he turned his face northward, and on the 10th of July was again in Edinburgh. A few weeks later, his kind attentions to Mr. Gurney, confined by sickness in his neighborhood, gave occasion to another series of valuable reminiscences. "I have found his visits," writes Mr. Gurney, "like two things of which I have lately experienced the vast importance—a tonic for the faint, and a crutch for the lame. The new revolution in France, and the commotions which have since taken place in other parts of Europe, have, of course, been the subject of daily thought, meditation, and converse. 'I think,' said Dr. Chalmers, 'the Scriptures afford us good reason to believe that the ultimate diffusion of pure Christianity in the world must be preceded by commotion, and confusion, and distress of nations. Look at the new French revolution—there is much that one approves at present both in its tendency and its results. But you see it has been effected by the growth of merely human intelligence—by the working of the unregenerate mind without a particle of christian principle. It is just the striving of the natural wisdom and the pride of man after that which we are apt to conceive to be the consummation of our happiness—*a condition of independence.* I am not one of those who underrate the value of civil and political liberty; but I am well assured that it is only the principles of Christianity which can impart true security, prosperity, and happiness, either to individuals or to nations. I am prepared to expect, that on the efforts which are now making in the world to regenerate our species, without religion, *God will impress the stamp of a solemn and expressive mockery.*'

"It is evident that Dr. Chalmers is deeply impressed with the opinion that an overwhelming tide is but too likely, erelong, to sweep down many of our civil, literary, and religious institutions. The spirit which prevails abroad he apprehends to be in somewhat active preparation at home, and he ascribes its existence and increase to the wide dissemination of *superficial* knowledge. Chalmers is a great advocate for religious establishments.

"CHAL. 'I like to see the *earth* helping the *woman*. I do not plead very earnestly for any particular church, but I would have a well formed machinery fixed in every country—ducts of irrigation—through which the predominant religion, whatever it is, may diffuse its streams of christian instruction. I do not perceive that when such a provision is absent, men are prone to supply the deficiency for themselves: and the practical effect appears to be that a large proportion of the populalation is left without any religious instruction at all.

"' The population in England and Scotland has immensely outgrown the provisions of the two Establishments—and what becomes of the surplus? They do not provide themselves with religious privileges, but are more than content to continue without them. I was furnished with a picturesque argument for Establishments, on the top of St. Paul's. When I looked eastward over the city of London, I beheld it dotted with spires—for the city was built at a time when the church was able to meet the demands of the inhabitants. But westward the eye roams over a comparatively new town and new population, and a spire is hardly to be seen. On the whole, I conclude, that unless the law of the land provides churches, and a corresponding administration of the Gospel, it is in vain to expect that the people will provide them for themselves.'

"I told Dr. Chalmers that this was almost the only subject that I knew of, on which I did not sympathize with him. Nevertheless, I fully unite in sincerely deprecating the fall of any of our religious institutions by the rude hand of anarchy and infidelity. It ought to be remarked, that Dr. Chalmers's views on this subject are connected in his mind, not with a bigoted attachment to any particular form of religion, but only with an earnest desire for the *maintenance of Christianity itself*.

" CHAL. ' The Scotch Establishment has one great advantage over that of England. It acknowledges no temporal head, and admits of no civil or Parliamentary interference with its doctrine and discipline. The State helps to support it, but has nothing to do with the conduct of its ministrations. This devolves solely on its Synod. It is not so with the Church of England ; but I would not demolish the Church of England on that account—I would only restore to her her own Convocation. Were some little poisonous stream to find its way into the sources of the Nile, by which all the waters of the river were rendered insalubrious, it would be a foolish remedy to cut up and destroy the dykes by which those waters are conveyed through all the plains of Egypt. Good sense would dictate—*only*, the *stopping up of the small polluting fountain.*'

"Dr. Chalmers's conversations with us have been much more frequently about *things* than *persons ;* and indeed he has too much intelligence and power of mind to descend to a species of conversation commonly called gossip—which is the frequent refuge of many whose understandings are meagerly stored with information. Persons, however, who, from the combination of talent and oddity, have made a noise in the world, must lay their account for being the subject of conversation in all sorts of companies. Such a man is Edward Irving, who once acted as an assistant preacher to Dr. Chalmers, in the Tron church at Glasgow.

" CHAL. 'When Irving was associated with me at Glasgow he did not attract a large congregation, but he completely attached to himself, and to his ministry, a limited number of persons, with whose minds his own was in affinity. I have often observed this effect produced by men whose habits of thinking and feeling are peculiar or eccentric. They possess a *magnetic* attraction for minds assimilated to their own."

"Nevertheless, I observed, eccentricity, especially in people of serious religion, is extremely undesirable. I much prefer those broad, intelligible qualities which attract the mass of mankind.

"Chal. 'Yes, truly—after all, *gravitation* is much better than *magnetism*.

"'I undertook to open Irving's new chapel in London. The congregation, in their eagerness to obtain seats, had already been assembled about three hours. Irving said he would assist me by reading a chapter for me in the first instance. He chose the very longest chapter in the Bible, and went on with his exposition for an hour and a half. When my turn came, of what use could I be in an exhausted receiver? On another similar occasion he kindly proffered me the same aid, adding, "I can be short." I said, how long will it take you? He answered, "ONLY ONE HOUR AND FORTY MINUTES." 'Then,' replied I, 'I must decline the favor.'

"Craig. 'My friend, Mr. P., invited a party to supper. Some of his guests had three miles to walk home after the meal. But *before* its commencement, Mr. P. requested Irving, who was one of the party, to read the Bible and expound. He began and continued a discourse, which manifested not even a tendency toward termination until midnight. The supper was of course either burnt up or grown cold. When the clock struck twelve, Mr. P. tremblingly and gently suggested to him that it might be desirable to draw to a close. "Who art *thou*," he replied, with prophetic energy, "who darest to interrupt the man of God in the midst of his administration?" He pursued his commentary for some time longer, then closed the book, and, waiving his long arm over the head of his host, uttered an audible and deliberate prayer that his offense might be forgiven.'

"The last accounts which I have heard from the 'West Country' indicate a *progressive descent* into the absurd and preposterous. I was struck with the simplicity of mind and genuine charitableness which Dr. Chalmers displayed in conversing on this subject, before its issue was quite so apparent as it is at present.

"Chal. 'Were Erskine at home, I should be very happy

---

* The Rev. Mr. Craig of Edinburgh.

to bring you together. He is a most amiable and pleasing person, and one whose consistency of conduct proves the genuineness of his piety. It is true, however, that his imagination overpowers his other faculties. He assures me, that a quarter of an hour's personal examination on the spot would convince me of the truth of the West country miracles. Incredulous as I am respecting it, I do not presume to determine what may or may not be included within the infinite variety of Divine dispensation. I just hold myself open to evidence.'

"One morning, while Dr. Chalmers was with us, and was speaking with great liberality of certain Christians who differ from him in sentiment, Dr. —— joined our party; an amiable and pious man, about my own age, once well known and loved by some members of our family. Unhappily he has now fallen into a religious system the very opposite to Chalmers—a system of the most rigid exclusiveness. So strangely is his spiritual vision perverted, that while he condemns all denominations of Christians as fatally erring, he appears to presume that the true *universal* church of Christ consists of himself and a few other individuals, who, while they reject the Sabbath, occasionally meet together in this place for devotional purposes. After Chalmers was gone, he began to unfold his views to me, which appear to be simply these: that the Church of Christ is ONE; and that since he and his friends were the only persons who exactly conformed themselves to the model of the New Testament, they, and they only, were that ONE Church. I can hardly describe the odd feeling it gave me, just after I had been expatiating in the broad fields of Dr. Chalmers's heart and intellect, to be thus suddenly thrust into the narrowest of imaginable corners. The contrast was instructive, and enhanced my value for that mighty stream of Divine love and charity which overleaps all the barriers of pride and prejudice. May I ever be preserved from becoming a latitudinarian in religion! but while I am deeply convinced that on no other foundation can any man stand with safety, but *Jesus Christ*, I never more clearly saw than I do at present, that this foundation has a *breadth* proportioned to its stability. Christianity is a law of liberty. It may be said to teem with the riches of a divine *liberality*. God 'giveth to all men LIBERALLY, and upbraideth not.' I am disposed to think that the *breadth* of every system of religion, which has Christ for its basis, is one of the best tests by which we may try its genuineness and its truth. I afterward told Chalmers what had passed between Dr. —— and myself. He put on a countenance of great good humor. 'It reminds me,' said he, 'of an elderly gentleman, of whom I once knew something, who was fully persuaded that true Christianity was exclusively to be found in himself and an *old wife*. When the old lady died the universal church was restricted to his single person.'

"I mentioned a work, popular among the Unitarians, which solves all the attributes of God into pure *benevolence*—denominates sin 'moral evil'—ascribes it to the direct appointment of God, and presumes to infer, that it not only promotes the general good, but, taken in connection with its corrective consequences, in the end enhances the happiness of the sinner. Hence it follows, that if a man murders his parents, or flays his children alive, he will be the better for it in *the long run*.

"CHAL. 'It is a dangerous error to reduce the Divine attributes to the single quality of goodness. Our best metaphysicians (especially Brown) teach us, that the *ethical virtues* are in their nature unalterably independent. Justice is an ethical virtue, distinct in its origin, character, and end, and must not be confounded with any other. These principles apply to the moral attributes of God.' Yes, I said, they are blended, but not confused.

"CHAL. 'There is union in them, but not unity. The harmony, yet distinctness, of the Divine moral attributes, is most instructively *inscribed* on the atonement of Christ.' Truly, I replied, that is a point where justice and benevolence meet—where God has displayed at once His abhorrence of sin, and His mercy to the sinner.

"CHAL. 'Brown had very low and inadequate views of the character of God. The same may be said of Paley—witness his founding his system of morals on expediency. This was indeed a degradation in a Christian and moral philosopher, and the more so, as even a Cicero could declaim against 'utilitas' as the basis of morals.' I mentioned an anecdote which I have heard of Paley in his last illness, which is said to have had the authority of William Hey, the late noted surgeon at Leeds, and which, if true, is remarkably consoling. When not far from his end, Paley, in conversing with some of his family or friends, took a calm review of his several works. He expressed the deep regret and dissatisfaction which at that awful time he felt in the recollection of his 'Moral Philosophy.' He was happy to believe that his 'Natural Theology' and 'Evidences of Christianity' were sound and useful works; but the book on which his mind then dwelt with the greatest pleasure was his 'Horæ Paulinæ.'

"CHAL. 'I am not surprised at this. It is an admirable statement of evidence, and displays a more masterly hand than any of his other works.' Our Lord has declared, that except we are 'converted, and become as little children,' we shall 'in nowise enter the kingdom of heaven.' I have heard that this lucid and powerful writer became a little child, in the best sense of the terms, before he died. I have also heard it stated, on what appeared to be good authority, that had his posthumous sermons been chronologically arranged, they would have displayed a gradually progressive change from a sort of semi-Pelagianism, to a sound and evangelical view of Christianity. It is delightful to be able to *ascribe* such a man as Paley to the company of true believers in a crucified Redeemer."

Again, in the month of October, Dr. Chalmers appeared in London as one of the deputation of the Church of Scotland, to present a congratulatory address to William IV, upon his accession to the throne. The account of his presentation to the king, and of the various festivities of the occasion, was contained in letters written for the entertainment of his children:—"*London, October* 28*th*, 1830.—MY DEAR MARGARET— This is the big and busy day. Got up at seven. Went out to order the loan of a court hat, which is promised me by twelve. A general dressing, and anxiety on all hands to be as snod* as possible. A breakfast, at which all the members of the deputation were present; Dr. Singer, Dr. Cook, Dr. McKnight, Dr. Lee, myself, Mr. Paul, Mr. Sinclair, Sir John Connel. We are, beside, to have Sir Henry Jardine, Mr. Pringle of Yair, and Dr. Stewart of Erskine, as attendants. A vast deal of consultation anent our movements to and from. We are all on edge. We have to make three bows; and the question is, whether we shall all make them on moving toward the throne, or after we have spread ourselves before it, and there is such a want of unanimity and distinct understanding about it, that I fear we shall misbehave. However, time will show, and I now lay down my pen till it is over.

"We assembled in our hotel at one. The greatest consternation among us about hats, which had been promised at twelve, but had not yet arrived. There were four wanting; and at length only three came, with the promise that we should get the other when we passed the shop. We went in three coaches, and landed at the palace entry about half-past one. Ascended the stair; passed through a magnificent lobby, between rows of glittering attendants all dressed in gold and scarlet. Ushered into a large anteroom, full of all sorts of company, walking about and collecting there for attendance on the levee: military and naval officers in splendid uniforms—high legal gentlemen with enormous wigs—ecclesiastics, from archbishops to curates and inferior clergy. Our deputation made a most respectable appearance among them, with our cocked three-cornered hats under our arms, our bands upon our breasts, and our gowns of Geneva upon our backs. Mine did not lap so close as I would have liked, so that I was twice as thick as I should be, and it must have been palpable to every eye at the first glance, that I was the greatest man there—and that, though I took all care to keep my coat unbuttoned, and my gown quite open: however, let not mamma be alarmed, for I made a most respectable appearance, and was treated with the utmost attention. I saw the Archbishop of York in

---

* *Anglicé,* neat.

the room, but did not get within speech of him. To make up for this, however, I was introduced to the Archbishop of Canterbury, who was very civil; saw the Bishop of London, with whom I had a good deal of talk, and am to dine on Friday; was made up to by Admiral Sir Philip Durham; and was further introduced, at their request, to Sir John Leach, Master of the Rolls, to Lord Chief Justice Tindall, to the Marquis of Bute, etc. But far the most interesting object there was Talleyrand—whom I could get nobody to introduce me to—splendidly attired, as 'the French embassador, attended by some French military officers. I gazed with interest on the old shriveled face of him, and thought I could see there the lines of deep reflection and lofty talent. His moral physiognomy, however, is a downright blank. He was by far the most important continental personage in the room, and drew all eyes. I was further in conversation with Lord Melville, Mr. Spencer Percival, and Mr. Henry Drummond. The door in the middle apartment was at length opened for us, when we entered in processional order. The Moderator first, with Drs. Macknight and Cook on each side of him; I and Dr. Lee side-by-side followed; Mr. Paul and Mr. George Sinclair, with their swords and bags, formed the next row; then Sir John Connel and Sir Henry Jardine; and last of all, Mr. Pringle, M. P., and Dr. Stewart. We stopped in the middle room—equally crowded with the former, and alike splendid with mirrors, chandeliers, pictures, and gildings of all sorts on the roof and walls—for about ten minutes, when at length the folding-doors to the grand state-room were thrown open. We all made a low bow on our first entry, and the King, seated on the throne at the opposite end, took off his hat, putting it on again. We marched up to the middle of the room, and made another low bow, when the King again took off his hat; we then proceeded to the foot of the throne, and all made a third low bow, on which the King again took off his hat. After this, the Moderator read his address, which was a little long, and the King bowed repeatedly while it was reading. The Moderator then reached the address to the King upon the throne, who took it from him and gave it to Sir Robert Peel on his left hand, who in his turn gave the King his written reply, which he read very well. After this, the Moderator went up to the stool before the throne, leaned his left knee upon it, and kissed the King's hand. We each in our turn did the same thing; the Moderator naming every one of us as we advanced; I went through my kneel and my kiss very comfortably. The King said something to each of us. His first question to me was, 'Do you reside constantly in Edinburgh?' I said, 'Yes, an't please your Majesty.' His next question was, 'How long do you remain in town?' I said, 'Till Monday, an't please your Majesty.' I then descended the steps leading from the foot of the throne to the floor, and fell into my place in the deputation. After we had all been thus introduced, we began to retire in a body just as we had come, bowing all the way with our faces to the King, and so moving backward, when the King called out, 'Don't go away, gentlemen, I shall leave the throne, and the Queen will succeed me.' We stopped in the middle of the floor, when the most beautiful living sight I ever beheld burst upon our delighted gaze—the Queen, with twelve maids of honor, in a perfect spangle of gold and diamonds, entered the room. I am sorry I cannot go over in detail the particulars of their dresses; only that their lofty plumes upon their heads, and their long sweeping trains upon the floor, had a very magnificent effect. She took her seat on the throne, and we made the same profound obeisances as before, advancing to the foot of the steps that lead to the footstool of the throne. A short address was read to her as before: and her reply was most beautifully given, in rather a tremulous voice, and just as low as that I could only hear and no more. We went through the same ceremonial of advancing successively and kissing hands, and then retired with three bows which the Queen returned most gracefully, but with all the simplicity, I had almost said bashfulness, of a timid country girl. She is really a very natural and amiable looking person. The whole was magnificent. On each side of the throne were maids of honor, officers of state, the Lord Chancellor, a vast number of military gentlemen, and among the rest the Duke of Wellington. My next will be to Helen. God bless you, my dear Margaret.—I am, your affectionate father,

"THOMAS CHALMERS."

"*London, October 29th*, 1830.—MY DEAR HELEN —I did not finish my description of our interview with the Queen in my letter to Margaret, for after we left the grand state-room we remained in the middle room ; and after us the Corporation of Dublin, a very large body, went with addresses to the King and Queen. There were some very magnificent people among them ;. and as a great number had to be introduced, it took up a long time, so we had to wait half an hour at least in the middle room till the levée began, when the two inner doors between the middle and great state-rooms were thrown open. The King, instead of being upon the throne, now stood on the floor. There was an immense number of people introduced to him, going in a very close and lengthened column from the outer room by one corner door of the great state-room, passing the King, and retiring through an avenue of state attendants by the other corner door. I kissed his hand the second time, and was named both by him and Sir Robert Peel. After this we remained in the middle room a considerable time, and at length left the Palace. We had to wait a long time in the door lobby till our coaches drew up for us. The crowding and calling of coaches had a very animating effect. We got to our hotel at four—waited there half an hour. Our coaches came for us again to take us to the Mansion House where we were to dine with the Lord Mayor. This is a magnificent house, and has a very noble dining-room. The Lord Mayor himself was unwell, and could not be with us. His chaplain did the honors for him. There were about fifty. We assembled in the drawing-room. There were about six ladies ; and I was very graciously received by the Lady Mayoress and the Lady Mayoress Elect, the latter of whom I had the honor of leading to the great dining hall. The Lady Mayoress elect will be Lady Mayoress at the great civic feast to their Majesties, so that I had the honor of leading the very lady to dinner whom the King will lead to the great Guildhall dinner in about a fortnight. It was truly a civic feast. I had the honor of sitting second on the right hand from the Lady Mayoress, there being the Lord Mayor elect between me and her, so that I sat between the Lord and Lady Mayor elect, to be Lord and Lady Mayor in a few days. They were both as kind and cordial to me as possible, as was also the Lady Mayoress. There are some venerable customs handed down from very remote antiquity, which I took great delight in witnessing and sharing in. After dinner one of the portly and magnificent waiters stood behind the Lady Mayoress with a large flagon having a lid that lifted, and filled with the best spiced wine. He then called out 'silence,' and delivered the following speech from behind the Lady Mayoress, with the great flagon in his hand: 'Commissioners of the Church of Scotland, the Lord Mayor, the Lady Mayoress, the Lord Mayor elect, the Lady Mayoress elect, my masters the Sheriff and Aldermen of the good city of London, bid you hearty welcome to this our ancient town, and offer you a cup of love and kindness, in token of good feeling and good fellowship.' I have not done justice to the speech, for those Aldermen present were named in it, among the rest the famous Alderman Waitman and Sir Claudius Hunter. After this speech by the crier, the cup was given to the Lady Mayoress, who turned round with it to her neighbor, the Lord Mayor Elect; he lifted the lid and kept it in his hand till she drank, both standing; she then gave it to him, but not till she wiped with a towel the place she had drunk at; he put on the lid, and turned round to me who rose; I took off the lid, he drank, wiped, gave the cup to me; I turned round to my next neighbor, the Lady Mayoress elect, she rose and took off the lid, I drank, wiped, and gave the cup to her who put on the lid, turned to her next neighbor, etc., and so the cup, or great flagon rather, went round the whole company. Another peculiar observance was, that instead of hand glasses for washing, there was put down an immense massive plate of gilt silver, with a little rose water poured into it, and placed before the

Lady Mayoress; she dipped the corner of her towel into it, and therewith sponged her face and hands, and said plate went round the table, and each of us did the same. It was most refreshing. Then came toasts and speeches. The Moderator gave one in reply to the Church of Scotland; and the Lady Mayoress declared she would not leave the room till I spoke, so there was a particular toast for me, and I had to make a speech, which I concluded with a toast to the Lady Mayoress. Mr. George Sinclair was asked by her Ladyship to return thanks in her name, which he did with a speech, etc. After the ladies retired I sat between the Lord Mayor, who took the chair, and Alderman Sir Claudius Hunter, who was particularly kind to me. We drank tea with the ladies; and I had much cordial conversation with the *eminentes* who were there, as Alderman Waithman, Mr. Hartwell Horne, author of the 'Introduction;' Mr. Alexander Chalmers, author of the 'Biographical Dictionary;' Sir Peter and Lady Laurie, etc. I should have mentioned that I gave a second little speech in compliment to Mr. Horne, whom I offered as a toast. We went off in our carriages about ten, much delighted with the day's work, and retired to bed soon after our arrival.

It was during this visit that he saw Mr. Irving for the last time. The incident is thus recorded by himself: "Had a very interesting call from Mr. Irving between one and two while I was in bed. He stopped two hours, wherein he gave his expositions; and I gave at greater length and liberty than I had ever done before my advices and my views. We parted from each other with great cordiality, after a prayer which he himself offered and delivered with great pathos and piety."*

"*The remonstrances of Dr. Chalmers had no effect in dislodging from the mind of Mr. Irving his implicit faith in the restoration of miraculous gifts to the Church. How strong this belief remained with him to the last, will appear from the following affecting extract from a paper drawn up by his father-in-law, the late Dr. Martin of Kirkaldy:

"Of his implicit obedience to what he believed to be the voice of Jehovah, one of the most striking instances was what led to his dying in Glasgow. His medical advisers had recommended him to proceed

In the General Assembly of 1831 the errors of Mr. Irving were taken under consideration, and resolutions adopted emphatically condemning them, and instructing " any presbytery before which he might appear, claiming the privileges of a licentiate or minister of the Church of Scotland, to call him to its

---

before the end of autumn to Madeira, or some other spot where he might shun the vicissitudes and inclemency of a British winter. But some of the oracular voices which found utterance in his church had proclaimed it to be the will of God that he should go to Scotland, and do a great work there. Accordingly, after an equestrian tour in Wales, by which his health appeared at first to be improved, but the benefit of which he lost through exposure to the weather and occasional preaching, contrary to the injunctions of his physician, he arrived at Liverpool on his way to the north. In that town he was taken alarmingly ill, and was unable for several days to quit his bed; but no sooner could he rise and walk through the room, than he went, in defiance of the prohibition of his medical attendant, on board a steamboat for Greenock. From Greenock he proceeded to Glasgow, delighted at having reached the first destination that had been indicated to him. From Glasgow it was his purpose to proceed to Edinburgh; but this I need not say he never accomplished. So much, however, was his mind impressed with its being his duty to go there, that even after he was unable to rise from his bed without assistance, he proposed that he should be carried thither in a litter, if the journey could not be accomplished in any other way, and it was only because the friends about him refused to comply with his urgent requests to that effect, that the thing was not done. Could he have commanded the means himself, the attempt at least would have been made. Nor, though his frame of mind was that of almost continual converse with God, do I think that he ever lost the confidence, that after being brought to the very brink of the grave, he was still to mark the finger of God in his receiving strength for his Scottish mission, till the last day of his life was far advanced, when one of the most remarkable and comforting expressions which he uttered seemed to intimate that he had been debating the point with himself, whether he should yield to the monitions which increasing weakness gave him of approaching dissolution, or retain his assurance that he should yet be re-invigorated for his distant undertaking. 'Well,' said he, 'the sum of the matter is, if I live, I live unto the Lord; and if I die, I die unto the Lord; living or dying, I am the Lord's;'— a conclusion which seemed to set at rest all his difficulties on the subject of his duty. So strongly had his confidence of restoration communicated itself to Mrs. Irving, that it was not till within an hour or so of his death that she entertained any idea of the impending event."

bar." At the same time, Mr. McLean and Mr. Scott, two licentiates, who had adopted his or similar views of the character of the Saviour, as having taken on him fallen human nature, were deprived of their license, and Mr. Campbell of Row, was deposed for teaching the doctrine of universal atonement, and that assurance is of the nature of faith. Dr. Chalmers was not in the Assembly in which these questions were agitated, yet we find reason to believe that his opinions were not without weight in their settlement.

The Church of Scotland had now lost one upon whose judgment and activity she had long been accustomed to repose much confidence. Only about two months before the meeting of that Assembly, Dr. Andrew Thomson had fallen by a stroke unusually sudden. On the 9th of February, 1831, in full vigor of mind and body, he had taken part in the business of presbytery, and returning home in animated conversation with a friend, reached his own door, fell down and expired. Immediately after the event, Dr. Chalmers was among the friends who hastened to the spot, but found every effort to restore the functions of life, in vain. No death could have been so gravely felt throughout Scotland, save that of Dr. Chalmers himself. They had co-operated, for a long series of years, in the same noble cause. They had stood side by side in the front of evangelization. The theological lecture of next day closed with a tribute to the memory of Dr. Thomson.

"I meant, gentlemen, to have expatiated on this subject at a greater length, and perhaps would have done so with greater vigor, but I must confess that the sad and saddening event of yesternight has unhinged me out of all strength for the requisite preparation. At the ordinary time employed in framing a lesson for others, I was called away to be a learner myself— to read a lesson which of all others is the oftenest told, yet the oftenest forgotten—to gaze upon features which a short time before were instinct with living energy, but which were then fast locked in the insensibility of death. I should not have felt myself justified in thus adverting to it, had it only stood connected with personal griefs or personal interests of my own, but, gentlemen, it is an event of deepest interest to the members of a theological school, and more especially to those who are now training for the Church of Scotland, standing apprised, as I doubt not you all are, of the heavy loss that Church has sustained in the noblest and most distinguished of her ministers. A time of deep emotion is not the time for analysis; yet the characteristics of Dr. Thomson's mind stood forth in such bold and prominent relief, that it needs but the bare enumeration to be recognized by the most superficial observer. The first and foremost of these characteristics was a dauntless, uncompromising honesty in the maintenance of all which he deemed to be the cause of truth and righteousness. But, gentlemen, I must spare myself the execution of this task, for I feel the wound to be greatly too recent, and that the afflicted heart keeps all the other faculties of the soul in abeyance. At present I have no steadiness of hand for drawing a portrait, every lineament of which opens a fresh and bitter recollection. There is still an oppressive weight on the subject, which makes all attempts at delineation impossible; and rather far than sketch the likeness of one who, with a suddenness so extraordinary, has been drawn away from us, would I now mingle in sympathy with his friends, or weep with his deserted family."

The hand which here refused to draw the beloved portraiture, a few days afterward executed it in a manner worthy both of itself and of the illustrious subject. The funeral sermon, of which it forms a part, will be found in the collection of Dr. Chalmers's published works.

CHAPTER XII.

In November, 1830, the speculations on Political Economy, which had been suspended to make way for the preparation of his theological lectures, were resumed. It had long been an object of ambition with him to produce a work on that subject which might constitute a suitable starting point for a series of publications on Moral Philosophy and Theology. Through the whole session of 1830–31, he pursued the subject in weekly lectures before his class, and the succeeding summer was spent in throwing his long accumulating materials into the form of a regular methodical treatise. The work was published in January, 1832. This, the favorite child of his intellect, was doomed to meet, at first, with a scanty share of public favor. The time was unpropitious. All minds were engrossed with the Reform Bill, which was then before Parliament, and the grand object of popular desire. Dr. Chalmers, though decidedly liberal in his views, and though his best efforts had been given to the cause of the poor, was not in favor of that bill. The measures therein proposed he deemed inadequate, and the hopes thereby created fallacious. His book was written with the express design of sifting and exposing the insufficiency of all such, and of preparing the way for his future proof that a moral and religious reform was needed as the basis of all permanent improvement in the condition of the lower classes. In proportion, therefore, to the cogency of its reasoning was its necessary unpopularity before the then existing state of public feeling. Some of the Reviews were abusive, designating the doctrine of the work "most portentous and abominable," and "a miserable sophism," and the author as one "incompetent to reason on the subject;" but Dr. Chalmers having committed the full expression of his views to the public, as usual, withheld from all controversy with opponents in defense of them.

The death of Dr. Meiklejohn had left the chair of Church History, in the University of Edinburgh, vacant. In the canvass which ensued, it was most gratifying to the feelings of Dr. Chalmers that the new professor was appointed out of respect to his recommendation, and from entire confidence in his judgment, and still more so that one of so congenial a spirit as the excellent Dr. Welsh became thereby his fellow-laborer.

In the month of October he received a letter from the Bishop of London, informing him of that article in the will of the Earl of Bridgewater, setting apart eight thousand pounds for the purpose of procuring " a treatise or treatises to be written in proof of the wisdom and benevolence of the Deity as manifested in the works of creation," and requesting him to undertake a portion of the work. The department assigned to him being the " Adaptation of External Nature to the Moral and Intellectual Constitution of Man," fell in with a favorite train of thought, and was accordingly accepted with delight, and pursued with alacrity. The summer months of 1832 were given up to the composition of this work which was published in the succeeding year. The Quarterly Review, hostile not only to all liberal thought, but to all works of liberal thinkers, attempted to prejudice the public mind in regard to it, but failed to obstruct its deserved popularity. " Two editions of fifteen hundred were disposed of as soon as published. In 1834, a third edition of the same number of copies was called for," after which it ceased to appear as a Bridgewater Treatise, being incorporated into the series of its author's works.

While Dr. Chalmers's feelings were truly liberal his political views led him to adhere chiefly to the conservatist party.; he consistently disapproved of the Reform Bill, and refusing to join in the illumination on the occasion of its success, suffered the penalty of having his windows shattered by the mob. The stormy spirit exhibited at that time by the lowest class of the people in burning of grain, in machine breaking, and destructive riots, was indeed enough to deter any good and brave man from giving his support to the party to which it belonged.

In reality however, he was less a conservative than a reformer, whose schemes were above the reach of ordinary whig politics; and while the radicals were for leveling all things down to themselves, he proposed to level all classes up toward the standard of the Gospel.

The aproach of the cholera in January, 1832, threw the whole country into a state of terror and dismay. The Presbytery of Edinburgh, at their meeting on the 25th of January, resolved that the 9th of February should be observed as a fast-day within their bounds; but afterward learning that the government intended to appoint a general fast, another meeting was called to reconsider their resolution. The remarks of Dr. Chalmers, especially as far as pertaining to his practical views of prayer, are too valuable to be omitted. "My first, my main reason, indeed, for wishing an earlier presbyterial fast, and not waiting for a later national one is, that in every case of urgent and immediate danger I should like the speediest and promptest application of the remedy that is suited to it. For the averting of disease I believe in the healing virtue of medicine, but for the averting of disease, I believe also in the healing virtue of prayer. I would rather, therefore, have a fast in a few days, than a fast in a few weeks, on the very principle that I would rather take the proper medicine in an hour, than delay taking it till to-morrow. I hold that religion is a mockery, and the church and the priesthood are but a solemn imposition on the world, if there be no substantial efficacy in prayer—if there be no such process as that of a real and actual interchange between Heaven and earth, of ascending petitions on the one hand, of descending mercies and fulfillments on the other. But believing, as I do, in the doctrine of prayer, in the plain and literal import of it, as being an asking on the one side and a receiving on the other, I would have the speediest possible day for public and social prayer, and that for the business object of laying the speediest possible arrest on the progress of the destroyer. When once this principle takes full possession of the mind all other considerations are of a subordinate and secondary character. If only confident of the effect of prayer in propitiating the favor of God, one cares less and thinks less of the effect it may have upon men.

"And yet this latter object ought not to be undervalued, nor am I at all unwilling to enter on the question of the effect which any measure of ours may have on the minds and feelings of general society. There is no subject on which men are more apt to go astray, than when pronouncing on the state of the public taste or the public sentiment in regard to any given question. Each man takes his impression from that part of the public wherewith he himself has personally and immediately to do; and perhaps it will be just set down as my individual variety of opinion on this matter, but I must confess it to be my strong, indeed, my confident impression, that by our perseverance in the resolution of last Presbytery on the subject of the fast, by our holding it even in the prospect of another which we are bound to hold with equal solemnity and reverence, we shall earn the blessings and the grateful acknowledgments of all that is best principled and best conditioned among the families of Edinburgh.

"On this question I do feel for the character and independence of our church. The inconvenience of a double fast is a bagatelle when compared with the permanent stain that we shall inflict by this method of avoiding it. Did ever the ecclesiastical give way to the civil in such a manner before?—and shall we compare the temporary awkwardness that will soon be got over, with the perpetual mischief of the conspicuous precedent, held forth by this metropolitan Presbytery, in the sight of all the land? I hailed, with delight, the presbyterial appointment, though from my absence on the day of its being made, I had no share in it; and I hail with equal, perhaps with surpassing delight, the promise of a national appointment. I rejoice in the public recognition of God by our rulers, whether in church or state; and there are thousands and tens of thousands among us, who will most cordially do honor to both.

"It has been said that men will not suspend their secular business on the presbyterial fast-day; and that, in particular, the civil authorities will not acknowledge it. Our services will not be the less interesting, and, I may add, not the less effective, though none but simple and spontaneous worshipers — the worshipers of the heart — are found to share in them. The strength of our church lieth not in the countenance of power, it lies in the religion of our people ; and I promise, if our appointment for Thursday shall stand, such a general response to it on the part of the population, as will cause every lover of our Establishment to rejoice. And if the civil authorities do refuse their countenance to it, we, I trust, shall never be wanting in all loyalty and respect to them. The men who do profoundest homage to the presbyterial fast, will, do profoundest to the national fast also. We shall do the one, and most assuredly not leave the other undone."

The Presbytery resolved to keep their original appointment, " and in the general and devout observance of the day, Dr. Chalmers's anticipations were more than verified." The national fast was observed on the 22d of the same month. In the interval, many outbreaks of popular prejudice and violence, stimulated by the force of terror, had occurred. Mobs had assailed the cholera hospitals and insulted some of the most eminent and benevolent of the physicians ; while there had been found in parliament some members who ridiculed the proposal which recognized the hand of God in the pestilence. To these facts allusion was made by Dr. Chalmers in his prayer while conducting in St. George's church the solemnities of the day of national humiliation. The words of the prayer were taken down by one of the audience, a copy was also solicited from Dr. Chalmers, and widely circulated in the public papers.

"Do Thou, O Lord, ward off from us the further inroads of that desolating plague, which in its mysterious progress over the face of the earth has made such fearful ravages among the families of other lands. Hitherto, O God, Thou hast dealt mildly and mercifully with the city of our own habitation. Do Thou pour out the spirit of grace and supplication upon its inhabitants, and spare them, if it be thy blessed will, the inflictions of that wrath which is so rightfully due to a careless and ungodly generation.

"We pray, O Lord, in a more especial manner, for those patriotic men whose duty calls them to a personal encounter with this calamity, and who, braving all the hazards of infection, may be said to stand between the living and the dead. Save them from the attacks of disease; save them from the obloquies of misconception and prejudice; and may they have the blessings and acknowledgments of a grateful community to encourage them in their labors.

"Above all, we pray, O God, that the infidelity which places all its reliance on secondary causes may never sway either the councils of this city, or the councils of this nation. May there at all times be the public recognition of a God in the midst of us. And let not the defiance or the levity of irreligious men ever tempt us to forget that mighty unseen Being, who has all the forces of nature at his command—who sits behind the elements that he has formed, and gives birth, and movement, and continuance to all things."

The practical efficacy of prayer was a subject more fully and systematically treated in the sermon preached on the same occasion, and which is now included in the series of his works.

In accordance with a recommendation made by a committee of the House of Commons, the government in 1831, resolved to adopt a system of popular instruction for Ireland, which was expected to meet the wants and gratify the feelings of the various parties in that portion of the United Kingdom. A board was to be constituted, of persons professing different religious opinions, and which was to exercise a complete control over all the schools erected under its auspices. For four or five days in the week, moral and literary education only was to be given in these schools, and the remaining one or two set apart for such religious instruction as the clergymen of the respective persuasions should approve. "The board was also to 'permit and encourage the clergy to give religious instruction to the children of their respective persuasions, either before or after the ordinary school hours in the other days of the week.'"

The Bible was not to be employed in the common instruction of these schools, but a book of Scripture extracts was drawn up for that purpose. A register was also to be kept of the attendance of the children at their different places of worship on the Sabbath.

This scheme was vehemently opposed in Ireland. The Kildare Street Society, the most active in the work of popular instruction, in whose schools the Bible was daily read and attendance on that exercise imperatively enjoined, rose against it. The Protestants generally, considered themselves injured by it, and the Orangemen, viewing it in a political light, took a large part in the opposition. Petitions against the measure flowed in upon the House of Commons from all parts of the country; and in this movement of protestant Ireland, Scotland was at first disposed to join. At an extraordinary meeting of the Presbytery of Edinburgh, held for the purpose of considering this subject, it was moved that the Presbytery should petition Parliament against the proposed plan of education for Ireland. Dr. Chalmers was not favorable to that motion. "We all know, Moderator, said he, " that this has been a question very keenly agitated elsewhere ; that it has given rise in many quarters to a very busy fermentation; and that certainly one ingredient of this fermentation is, I trust, what will never be admitted within the limits of any ecclesiastical court in the Church of Scotland. The fact is too glaring to be denied, that often, very often, there has been a great deal more of politics than of religion in this opposition to the scheme of education in Ireland; and that thousands are the individuals who care not a straw for Christianity, who have gladly seized upon the topic, and now wield it as a mere instrument of annoyance, and, they hope, of eventual overthrow to the existing administration. I trust that the very respectable movers of the question in this place, will give me full credit when I acquit them, as I do, most cordially, of any sinister, any secondary design of this sort ; indeed, we should all, I am firmly persuaded, feel it a sad prostitution of our Presbytery to be made the organ of any State party whatever. But now that the matter is brought before us, it is our part rightly to entertain it, and feeling purely and proudly independent, whether on the politics of the ministry, or the politics of the opposition, calmly and conscientiously, as best we may, to give upon it a sound and christian-like deliverance. Certain it is that government is now engaged with a problem of great difficulty ; and our becoming part is not in a factious spirit to embarrass, but in a friendly, and withal frank and honest spirit, to lay our sentiments before them. And I have no scruple in avowing it as my own sentiment, that in the instance chiefly complained of, they have made a most unfortunate departure from right principle. Their great error—which they share in common with their predecessors — the error, in fact, into which our rulers were betrayed, even anterior to that measure of emancipation which I happen to have most cordially approved of, and in which error they seem to have persisted ever since, is to have made the Catholics, or any other class of subjects whatever, parties in the negotiation. All along, they have been far more anxious to find out what would please the Catholics, than to find out what was in itself right. Now, instead of treating either with Catholics or Orangemen upon this question, it would have been far better had they, in the exercise of their independent wisdom, framed their own independent measure, adopting not what at the time was the most popular, but what, in the light of abstract and immutable truth, was the best constitution of a school, and then held it forth as the only constitution they would stand by, and which they offered to the acceptance of the population." Dr. Chalmers proceeded to state what it was in the constitution actually adopted for the schools, which appeared to him to be objectionable. This new board was to charge itself with the attendance of the pupils in the churches of their various denominations. He could conceive nothing more unseemly — nothing more calculated to obstruct the light making its way in the darkened mind—than such a board thus setting itself up, and declaring that the children of Catholics should go only to their own place of worship, and that the children of Protestants should go nowhere but to theirs. To the employment of

Scripture extracts in school instruction, there could be no general objection; but to a book framed by a mixed Board, and intended to supersede the entire word of God, he had an insuperable repugnance. His confidence was strong in the efficacy of a Bible circulated with no other seal upon it than the seal of its own inspiration—no other sanction upon it than the high name and authority of heaven; but "let it but undergo a process of distillation through the alembic of a human council or human commission, and, however slightly it may have been changed, it sustains a damage; it comes out to public view in the character of a book moulded by human hands, so that priests might approve, instead of standing forth in the character of a book which neither priests nor people dare to meddle with. The original authority is overshadowed by the political or ecclesiastical; and, in place of being listened to as the voice that speaketh from heaven, it is listened to as a voice proceeding from a conclave of fellow-mortals upon earth." His main, however, and capital objection, lay against the exclusion of the Bible from the work of ordinary instruction. A daily Bible class—a class not for half-learned children, but for full and finished readers—a class not compulsory on any, but optional to all, he held to be an integral and indispensable part of all rightly-constituted schools, and that part the Government had unwisely and unrighteously repudiated. But notwithstanding these objections, he was not prepared to approach the Legislature with a summary condemnation of the measure. Before taking such a step, it was his anxious desire that the Presbytery should not only be decided on the principles of the question, but conversant with all its details, that they should so fully inform themselves, and be so thoroughly prepared, that any remonstrance they might make to government should be at once worthy of them to offer, and of importance for the government to receive. He moved, therefore, that in the meantime a committee should be appointed to prosecute inquiry. This motion was unanimously agreed to. A committee was appointed, with Dr. Chalmers at its head, which was instructed to use all diligence and to report to the next meeting of

Presbytery. Dr. Chalmers lost little time in placing himself in communication with many influential individuals, both among the favorers and opponents of the government scheme. Two days after the meeting of Presbytery we find the following entry in his Journal:

"Writing many letters as convener of the Irish Education Committee;" and a few days afterward, "overwhelmed with letters on the subject of Irish schools." Lord Melbourne informed him that he had so far misapprehended the meaning of the regulation as to a register of attendance at church, that it was not intended to oblige the children to attend the churches of their own denomination; but that all difficulty as to this regulation was likely to be removed by its withdrawal. Shortly afterward, the Archbishop of Dublin, as a member of the Board, announced that the measure of registering the attendance of children at the different places of worship was relinquished. Dr. Chalmers had put the following query:—' In the controversy on this question I observe it affirmed on the side of government, that all Protestant children may have daily reading in the whole Bible if they will, but is not this only if the clergyman, or teacher employed by him, other than the regular schoolmaster, be daily at his post, and is not this attendance very precarious?' Lord Melbourne's reply to this query was, 'The parents of the children and their religious teachers, may make any arrangement they please for the children reading the Bible out of school-hours;' an answer which obviously implied that the Board was not to charge itself in any way with the matter. To the leading Parliamentary opponent of the scheme Dr. Chalmers put this query, ' If it were made part of the regular schoolmaster's duty to have a whole Bible class for all advanced scholars who chose to be taught, not out of school-hours, but during some part or other of the regular school diet, would not that satisfy the Protestants?' The answer was, ' I can have no hesitation in saying that it would not satisfy the Protestants.' In the Kildare street Society's schools the daily reading of the Holy Scriptures was authoritatively and universally enforced, no child being allowed the benefit of the other lessons of the school without taking part in this, and nothing short of this would satisfy those whose opinions this member represented. Dr. Chalmers discovered here that form of ultraism, in the endeavor to avoid which the government had but fallen into another. He objected to force being used, whether that force was employed for or against the daily reading of the Bible in the schools. Of that intermediate method which he was disposed to recommend, he found a perfect and very interesting example in those schools which the General Assembly of the Church of Scotland had established in certain districts of the Highlands where a Catholic population prevailed. In these schools a daily Bible class was taught, but the teachers were instructed 'not to press on the Catholic children any instruction to which their parents or their priest objected as interfering with the principles of their own religion. To the schools established upon this principle, Roman Catholic children were sent without reluctance, mingling in the same classes with Protestants, without jealousy or distinction, and not unfrequently joining in the exercises of the Bible class.

" The effect of that full and special examination to which the government system was subjected was to enhance rather than extenuate Dr. Chalmers's repugnance to it; and when, on the 26th of April, he came before the Presbytery with the Report of the Committee, which he had drawn up, he prefaced it by saying, ' I was bound to make all possible inquiries, and after giving my best attention to the scheme, I am obliged to confess myself more averse to its character, and more fearful of its consequences, than before.' In reviewing the most important provisions of the plan, that Report observed, ' The first of these provisions which the Committee would notice, is that by which in the general and joint education of the scholars, consisting both of Protestants and Catholics, for four or five days in the week the use of the Bible as a school-book is prohibited, and that not because of its literary unfitness for this office, but because of its religious unfitness, in the estimation of the Catholic priesthood, for being employed as a book of juvenile or popular education. The most common, because perhaps the most obvious, objection to this regulation, is the privation of Scriptural instruction to which it subjects the Protestant children; but, to the minds of your Committee, there appears another strong objection against it, and which could not be done away though other days were specified and other methods were pointed out by which the privation might be compensated or made up for to the children of Protestants. The religious unfitness of the Bible for free and general use, whether in schools or through society at large, is, we are aware, the prevalent conception of the Romish priesthood; but should the regulation in question be adopted, the conception will be embodied in British law, and it does appear a signal departure from the spirit of that legislation which has obtained in this country for several generations, if, for the first time, an express restriction be laid on the use of Scripture by the authority of the State. . . . . . . It does not appear to your Committee that a book of Scripture extracts is at all unsuitable for schools, but all depends on the purposes for which such a book may have been formed. It essentially changes the character of such a compilation, when, instead of being given as a specimen of the Bible, it is given as a substitute for the Bible; or when, instead of certain parts of Scripture being admitted for the literary object of easy reading, or of adaptation to the gradual advancement of the learners, certain parts are excluded because of a religious objection by the priests, as members of any denomination. It is this surrender of the truth and wisdom of God to the partialities or the prejudices of men which vitiates the transaction. Nor do we escape from the evil however indefinitely near the substance and doctrine the book of extracts may be to the whole Bible. If any part of Scripture, however small, have been given up in deference to a religious antipathy, if any words, however few, have been taken out of this book because they are offensive to the principles or feelings of a particular sect, then, in concession to the demands of that sect, the integrity of Heaven's Record is violated, and the same malign character adheres to the principle of the compromise, whatever is the material extent, whether great or small, to which it may be carried. . . . . . The only remaining feature of this scheme to which we would direct the attention of the Presbytery, is that by which the toleration of the Catholics on the part of the government has advanced toward positive favor. On the days for separate religious instruction the clergy of both denominations are not only permitted, but permitted and encouraged, to give religious instruction to the children of their own persuasion. . . . . . This seems to proceed on the ground that the mere existence of a sect, irrespective of all consideration of its tenets, is in itself a sufficient reason not merely for its being permitted, but for its being fostered and patronized. In such a policy of a like treatment of different denominations, however opposed they may be in their pretensions and principles, there is a virtual surrender of the great reason on which a Protestant establishment is upheld either in this or in any other land."

The Report concluded with stating it as the opinion of the Committee, that if it should be deemed proper to approach the government on the subject, their petition should be one as much of suggestion as of censure, and giving all due credit to the patriotic purposes of those who had undertaken so arduous a task. The Report was approved and petition forwarded, the chief prayer of which was that a daily Bible class, optional to all the children, should be instituted in each school, and that the book of extracts and the setting apart of separate days for religious and secular instruction should be relinquished. The subject was taken up in the succeeding General Assembly. In the meanwhile a correspondence on the subject took place between Dr. Chalmers and Mr. Stanley, wherein it appeared that the principal ground of difference between them lay in this, that the latter would have had the Protestant children to meet half an hour earlier, or wait in school half an hour later, than the regular hours, to have the Bible read, while the former preferred that the Bible reading should take place in usual school hours, leaving the Catholics perfectly free to attend it or not. "In the one way of it," as Dr. Chalmers pithily expressed it, "the Bible was made to skulk from the Catholics, and in the other, the Catholics were made to skulk from the Bible."

The succeeding General Assembly learning, in the course of debate arising on this subject, the chief secretary saw no objection to a daily Bible class imperative on Protestants and optional to Catholics, contented themselves with petitioning in terms equivalent to those employed by the Presbytery of Edinburgh:

"The Presbyterian Church in Ireland, influenced by the same considerations, assumed at first the same attitude of hostility. But her interest in obtaining such a modification of the defects, as would place within her reach the obvious benefits of the scheme, was much more urgent; and her negotiations for this object were finally successful. At an early stage, if not from the period of their compilation, the use of the Scripture extracts was left optional. At first every school receiving Government aid was bound to adhere strictly to the regulations drawn up by the Board. Latterly, where the school-house has not been built by the Board, which in the north of Ireland is the usual case, the local patrons draw up their own regulations, submit them to the Commissioners, and, if approved of, are bound only by them—central control yielding thus to local authority. At an interview with the Lord Lieutenant of Ireland, in the year 1840, a deputation from the Presbyterian Church submitted a model constitution for these schools, which received the sanction of the Government. That constitution contains the following clause: " The times for reading the Holy Scriptures, and for catechetical instruction, are so arranged as not to interfere with or impede the scientific or secular business of the school; and no child, whose parents or guardians object, is required to be present or take part in these exercises, and no obstruction shall be offered to the children of such parents receiving such instruction elsewhere as they may think proper." For the children of their own and other Protestant communions, the Presbyterian Church has secured all that Dr. Chalmers desired. In their schools the day for separate religious instruction is done away. The Bible is read during the ordinary school-hours; "the extent of its use subject to no control but the will of the parents, expressed through committees of their own free choice, and the greatest convenience of the attending scholars." Subject to the provision that instruction in them be not forced, the Westminster Catechisms are also freely used during the ordinary school hours. The schools under the General Assembly of the Irish Presbyterian Church, enjoying the advantages of the Government bounty, are thus in their constitution and practice identical with those schools in the Highlands under the General Assembly of the Scottish Establishment, to which Dr. Chalmers pointed as a "beautiful and perfect example, unexceptionable in its principles, and most beneficial in its results."

Dr. Chalmers as Moderator of the Assembly of 1832 could, of course, take no part in its debates; yet there were some features which honorably distinguished his connection with it. The daily public dinners given by the Royal Commissioner who represents the Crown in General Assemblies of the Scottish Church, as well as the daily public breakfasts given by the Moderator, it had long been customary to keep up through both Sabbaths occurring during the sitting of the Assembly. This custom Dr. Chalmers resolved to break through. The breakfasts he could discontinue by his own authority; and as soon as he perceived the certainty of his election, he wrote a respectful note to the Commissioner, Lord Belhaven, requesting that his presence at the Sunday dinners, to which the Moderator was always specially invited, might be dispensed with, and suggesting the propriety of suspending the entertainment on that day. Both the request and the suggestion were favorably received, and the latter being acted on, constituted a precedent which has been observed ever since.

One of the subjects brought before that Assembly was destined afterward to enlist the utmost efforts of Dr. Chalmers, and ere it was settled to shake the Scottish Establishment to its foundations. It was introduced by overtures presented from eight Presbyteries and three Synods, supplicating the Assembly to devise some means for preventing the settlement of ministers over congregations to which they were unacceptable, and for giving efficacy to the call of the people. In order to comprehend the merits of this question it is necessary to know the process whereby a minister is inducted, according to usage of the Church of Scotland. For every parish there is some person or persons possessing the right of presenting a minister to the church when vacant. In some cases this person is the monarch, in others, a land-owner of the parish or some corporate body. Whoever possesses such a right is called the patron of that parish, a relic of the preceding evils, which the Reformation did not succeed in removing ; lay patronage was long and firmly resisted by the people and Church of Scotland. By the Revolution Settlement in 1699, it was abolished, but was restored by an Act of Parliament passed under the artful management of Bolingbroke, in 1711. It was then, however, added to a procedure already perfect in itself, and from which patronage might be at any time removed without leaving a deficiency behind. By a deed of presentation laid before the Presbytery, the patron nominates the minister whom he chooses. The purport of this document is that he requires the Presbytery "to make trial of the qualifications" of the presentee, "and having found him fit and qualified for the functions of the ministry, at the said parish of——— to admit and receive him thereto and give him his act of ordination and admission in due and competent form." In pursuance of this requirement, the first thing done by the Presbytery, is to enjoin the presentee to preach in the vacant church, on one or two appointed Sabbaths, that the people over whom he is to be ordained may have some knowledge and trial of his qualifications. Thereafter a day is fixed, of which due intimation from the pulpit is given to the parishioners, on which the Presbytery assembles in the church of the vacant parish, for the purpose of moderating in, or presiding at the call. At this meeting, after public worship conducted by the member of Presbytery appointed to preside, a paper is presented, the tenor whereof is as follows : "We, the heritors, elders, heads of families, and parishioners of the parish of ——, within the bounds of the Presbytery of ——, and county of ——, taking into consideration the present destitute state of the said parish, through the want of a gospel ministry among us, occasioned by the death of our late pastor, and being satisfied with the learning, abilities, and other good qualifications of you, Mr. A. B., and having heard you preach to our satisfaction and edification, do hereby invite and call you, the said Mr. A. B., to take the charge and oversight of this parish, and to come and labor among us in the work of the Gospel ministry, hereby promising to you all due respect and encouragement in the Lord. We likewise entreat the reverend Presbytery of —— to approve and concur with this our most cordial call, and to use all proper means for making the same effectual, by your ordination and settlement among us, as soon as the steps necessary thereto will admit. In witness whereof, we subscribe these presents." etc. This document the people are invited to subscribe in presence of the Presbytery, and the signatures having been completed, and the Presbytery, sitting in judgment upon the call as now presented to them, having sustained it as sufficient, entered thereafter upon the trial of the literary and theological attainments of the presentee. Having satisfied themselves as to these, they appoint a Sabbath for *serving the edict*, as it is termed, or for publicly announcing to the congregation of the vacant parish, the proposed day of ordination; to which announcement the notification is appended, that if any one knows any reason against the admission of the presentee, he is to present himself before the Presbytery and give in the same. On the day fixed for the final and solemn act of ordination, before proceeding to the religious services, the report of the member who served the edict is called for and received, and again by public proclamation of the officer of the Court, the opportunity is offered to any who have objections to the life or doctrine of the presentee to come forward and substantiate them. No such objections having been tendered, after public worship the presentee is required to stand up, and in presence of the congregation, to answer a series of questions, the last of which is as follows : "Do you accept and close with the call to be pastor of this parish, and promise through grace to perform all the duties of a faithful minister among this people?" After an affirmative reply to this and the preceding queries, in not one of which is any allusion made to the patron or his presentation, the Presbytery, by prayer and the laying on of hands do solemnly set him apart to the office of the holy ministry."

The Church remonstrated on the occasion of the restoration of Patronage, and repeated her protest for years, but without effect. It remained notwithstanding, in her power gradually, by the quiet accumulation of precedents, to render the presentation of little weight; indifference however gradually prevailing in the church itself, and the deference shown to patronal rights, came to throw all the weight of authority into the act of presentation, while the parts performed by the Presbytery and congregation ceased to be anything more than empty form. Many remonstrances had been raised against this course of usage, and several General Assemblies, from 1575 to 1736, had attempted to arrest it by declaring it to be a principle of the Church of Scotland " that no minister shall be intruded into any parish contrary to the will of the congregation." Latterly, however, the evil got such foothold that the advocates of intrusion possessed an overwhelming majority in the Assembly, and it was acted upon as law that the will of the people, howsoever expressed, should not constitute any barrier in carrying out the preseutation. Some Presbyteries, to whose lot it fell to ordain a minister in opposition to the general wish of the people, remonstrated ; but in vain. The supreme ecclesiastical court peremptorily commanded procedure according to the presentation ; and at least one example was given of a minister deposed from office for refusing to comply.

The people finding that no relief was to be obtained by appealing to the General Assembly, made various attempts at relieving themselves, and many settled down in silent discontent, attending upon church as a matter of respectable form, but in which their heart had no longer any interest. Others united themselves with various dissenting bodies, thus drawing from the establishment, in fifty years, more than one hundred thousand of the most pious and energetic Christians of the country.

A few attempts were made to meet force with force or with stratagem. Upon the day of ordination sometimes the members of Presbytery would be seized on the way and carried off to some distant place, and the intrusive presentee coming to the church would find himself ingloriously alone. Sometimes the church doors would be found barricaded and guarded by a mob who would not suffer the Presbytery to proceed. Such means naturally led to a still more offensive step of intolerance, " and the unseemly sight was witnessed, of Presbyters going forward to the ordination service guarded by dragoons—of ministers placed in their parishes at the point of the bayonet." The party through whose majority these violent and unwise measures were taken, assumed to themselves the very modest name of Moderates, while the small minority, who advocated non-intrusion—or, in other words, return to the original intention of their ecclesiastical constitution, were represented as extravagant radicals.

The translation of Dr. Thomson to a prominent church in Edinburgh, and the conversion of Dr. Chalmers, gave a new strength to the evangelical party. The herculean labors of the latter in Glasgow, and of the former in the metropolis, enlisted much of the best intellect of both cities, and extended their influence to large numbers who never listened to the sound of his voice. Dr. Chalmers's career afterward, as a professor, operated still more directly in changing the state of feeling among the ministers of the church. The strength of the evangelical party continued rapidly to increase, and that increase both those great men tested from year to year by the proposal of various and gradual measures of improvement, some of which, as those regarding ministerial education and pluralities, have already been mentioned. The grand test, however, was that of the settlement of ministers, and although the gradual increase of their number, was a motive with the evangelical party, for putting off the consideration of that question until the time, which seemed near at hand, when it could be settled according to their views with little resistance, the state of public feeling would suffer it to be postponed no longer. The dissatisfaction was not like that of the ignorant rabble, to be silenced by the strong arm of force, it was that of the best and wisest in the land, with whom force could avail only to drive into more cautious and effective means of attaining their end. A society had been constituted sometime previously, under the auspices of Dr. Andrew Thomson, for the purpose of buying up the rights of presentation, but had latterly changed its ground to that of requiring the entire abolition of patronage, in which it was extensively sustained by the voice of the public. Another society was framed, called the Voluntary Church Association, with the design of working the overthrow of all religious establishments. The number of petitions sent into Parliament begging the interference of the legislative authority in this matter gave occasion to the appointment of a Parliamentary Committee of Inquiry. It had distinctly become necessary to the very existence of the Scottish Establishment to remove the abuses connected with patronage.

Dr. Chalmers seeing clearly that the final adjustment of the difficulty could not be much longer postponed, prepared himself by careful study of all its points and relations, for his part in the coming discussion. As had been expected, the consideration of the subject was urged upon the Assembly of 1833, by still greater weight of authority than before, no less than forty-two of the inferior courts of the church having overtured respecting it; and so strong had the non-intrusion party become, that nothing but union among themselves, upon a specific measure, was necessary to carry it.

The course which Dr. Chalmers deemed the best, and which he laid before a private meeting of influential ministers, held prior to the sitting of the Assembly, was for the church simply to recur to the original intention of the existing plan, and, instead of giving undue weight to the presentation, by a series of acts, to continue to give proper importance to the call of the people, until the non-intrusion principle should be fairly established by precedent. Thus, all question of right and of legislation would be avoided. The present emergency, however, was too urgent for a plan of such slow development, and it was not adopted. Instead of it, they resolved to propose "that by some act of legislation controlling the proceedings of the inferior courts, the General Assembly should at once establish a uniform practice." His second proposal was, that, concurrently with their own legislation, application should be made to the government, so that the civil sanction might be conferred upon their act. This, from deference to the opinion of that eminent lawyer and friend of the Scottish Church, Lord Moncrieff, who asserted that it was undoubtedly within the legalized functions of the church to deal with the matter as proposed, he also yielded, though he afterward regretted that he had done so. As to the particular act of legislation to be proposed, it was agreed that the expressed "dissent of the majority of the parishioners should be held as a bar to settlement." The measure thus agreed upon was committed to Dr. Chalmers to bring before the General Assembly. In his speech on that occasion, he endeavored to reconcile the opponents of patronage, and to bring into the very temperate measure, which he sustained, those of his own party who would have preferred something more radical. After directing some remarks against the system of popular election, he proceeded: "I am aware of the theoretical partiality which many of my friends have for the whole system of our ministerial appointments being out-and-out ecclesiastical, which it would be if, as by the Act of Assembly 1649, the nomination were vested in the session; and the power of objecting in the people, and the final judgment, where these two parties were at variance, in the Presbytery. Even the Act of Parliament 1690, by which the nomination is vested, not in the elders alone, but in the elders and heritors, might be accommodated to this theory by the single qualification of heritors being communicants. Whether the same qualification applied to our existing patrons, that they should be in communion with the church, and so within our own ecclesiastical pale, and under our own ecclesiastical control—whether this would reconcile them more to the present system of patronage, I do not know. But however much we may differ respecting the initiative, I not only feel inclined to go as far, but would even go further than the advocates, either for the Act of Parliament 1690, or for the Act of Assembly 1649, respecting the safeguard or the check. The great complaint of our more ancient Assemblies, the great burden of Scottish indignation, the practical grievance which, of all others, has been hitherto felt the most intolerable and galling to the hearts of a free and religious people, is the violent intrusion of ministers upon parishes. An effectual provision against this enormity, this unfeeling outrage, which, in the exercise of a reckless and unprincipled patronage has so often been perpetrated in our beloved land, an outrage by the appointment of an ungodly pastor on the rights of conscience and the religious sensibilities of a sorely aggrieved people, a provision against so deep and so wide a moral injury as this to the families of a parish, I should feel the most valuable of all the legislative expedients or devices which could be proposed on the present occasion, and would welcome it all the more cordially if we had not to go in quest of it without the limits of our actual ecclesiastical constitution, or, in other words, if instead of enacting a new law we had but to declare our interpretation of an old one. Now the law of Calls places such a facility in our hands; and, as I feel I must not take up the time of the Assembly, let me state at once, and without further preamble, my own preference as to the best way of restoring significancy and effect to this now antiquated, but still venerable form—and this is by holding the call a solid one which lies, not in the expressed consent of the few, and these often the mere driblet of a parish; but larger than this, which lies in the virtual or implied consent of the majority, and to be gathered from their non-resistance or their silence. In other words, I would have it that the majority of dissentient voices should lay a veto on every presentation.

"In this power of a negative on the part of the people there is nothing new in the constitution or practice of the Church of Scotland. It is the great barrier, in fact, set up by the wisdom of our forefathers against the intrusion of ministers into parishes. It could make no appearance in the First Book of Discipline 1560, where it was provided that the people should have the initiative, or that the ministers should be appointed, not with their consent, but by their election. But after the probation of eighteen years, we have the Second Book of Discipline 1578, where the election is made to proceed by the judgment of the eldership and with the consent of the congregation, and care is expressed that 'no person be intrusit contrar to the will of the congregation or without the voice of the eldership.' This interdict by the people is further recognized and ratified in the Act of Assembly 1649, and of Parliament 1690. It is, in fact, the appropriate, the counterpart remedy against the evil of intrusion. If we hear little of the application or actual exercise of this remedy during the times it was in force, it was because of a great excellence, even that pacific property which belongs to it of acting by a preventive operation. The initial step was so taken by the one party as to anticipate the gainsayers in the other. The goodness of the first appointment was, in the vast majority of instances, so unquestionable as to pass unquestioned; and so this provision, by its reflex influence, did then what it would do still—it put an end to the trade of agitation. Those village demagogues, the spokesmen and oracles of a parish, whose voice is fain for war, that, in the heat and hubbub of a parochial effervescence, they might stir up the element they love to breathe in, disappointed of their favorite game by a nomination which compelled the general homage, had to sheathe their swords for lack of argument. It was like the beautiful operation of those balancing and antagonist forces in nature which act by pressure and not by collision, and by means of an energy that is mighty but noiseless, maintain the quiescence and stability of our physical system. And it is well when the action and reaction of these moral forces can be brought to bear with the same conservative effect on each other in the world of mind, whether it be in the great world of the state, or in the little world of a parish. And the truth, the historical truth, in spite of all the disturbances and distemper which are associated with the movements of the populace, is, that turbulence and disorder were then let loose upon the land, when this check of the popular will was removed from the place it had in our ecclesiastical constitution, and where it was inserted so skillfully by the wisdom of our fathers, that, instead of acting by conflict, or as a conflicting element, it served as an equipoise. It was when a high-handed patronage reigned uncontrolled and without a rival, that discord and dissent multiplied in our parishes. The seasons immediately succeeding to 1649, and 1690, when the power of negation was lodged with the people, not, however, as a force in exercise, but as a force in reserve—these were the days of our church's greatest prosperity and glory, the seasons both of peace and of righteousness. Persecution put an end to the one period, and unrestricted patronage put an end to the other.

"But the last element in the composition of this affair, and to which I have scarcely yet adverted, is the power of the church. For let the ancient privilege of a negation be again given to the people, and there will come to be a tripartite operation ere a minister shall be fully admitted into a parish—not a business, however, unmanageably complex on that account, else whence the rapid, and smooth, and practicable working of the British Legislature? And here the question at once occurs, whether shall the objection taken to the presentee by the majority of the people be submitted for review to the Presbytery, as by the Acts of 1649 and 1690, or shall it be held conclusive so as without judgment by us to set aside the presentation? My preference is for the latter, and I think that I can allege this valid reason for it. The people may not be able to state their objection, save in a very general way, and far less be able to plead and to vindicate it at the bar of a Presbytery, and yet the objection be a most substantial one notwithstanding, and such as ought, both in all christian reason and christian expediency, to set aside the presentation. I will not speak of the moral barrier that is created to the usefulness of a minister by the mere general dislike of a people—for this, though strong at the outset, may, being literally a prejudice or a groundless judgment beforehand, give way to the experience of his worth and the kindness of his intercourse among them. But there is another dislike than to the person of a minister—a dislike to his preaching, which may not be groundless, even though the people be wholly incapable of themselves arguing or justifying the grounds of it— just as one may have a perfectly good understanding of words, and yet, when put to his definitions, not be at all able to explain the meaning of them. This holds pre-eminently of the Gospel of Jesus Christ manifesting its own truth to the consciences of men, who yet would be utterly nonplused and at fault, did you ask them to give an account or reason for their convictions. Such is the adaptation of Scripture to the state of humanity — an adaptation which thousands might feel, though not one in the whole multitude should be able to analyze it. When under the visitations of moral earnestness, when once brought to entertain the question of his interest with God, and conscience tells of his yet uncanceled guilt, and his yet unprovided eternity—even the most illiterate of a parish might, when thus awakened, not only feel most strongly, but perceive most intelligently and soundly, the adjustment which obtains between the overtures of the New Testament and the necessities of his own nature. And yet, with a conviction thus based on the doctrines of Scripture and the depositions of his own consciousness, he, while fully competent to discern the truth, may be as incompetent as a child to dispute or to argument it; and when required to give the reasons of his objection to a minister at the bar of his Presbytery, all the poor man can say for himself might be, that he does not preach the Gospel, or that in his sermon there is no food for his soul. It were denying the adaptation of Christianity to human nature, to deny that this is a case which may be often and legitimately realized. With a perfect independence on the conceits and the follies, and the wayward extravagance or humors of the populace, I have, nevertheless, the profoundest respect for all those manifestations of the popular feeling which are founded on an accordancy between the felt state of human nature and the subject-matter of the Gospel. But in very proportion to my sympathy and my depth of veneration for the christian appetency of such cottage patriarchs, would be the painfulness I should feel when the cross-questionings of a court of review were brought to bear upon them; and the men, bamboozled and bereft of utterance by the reasonings which they could not redargue, or, perhaps, the ridicule which they could not withstand, were left to the untold agony of their own hearts—because within the Establishment which they loved, they could not find, in its Sabbath ministrations or week-day services, the doctrine which was dear to them. To overbear such men is the highway to put an extinguisher on the Christianity of our land—the Christianity of our plowmen, our artisans, our men of handicraft and of hard labor; yet not the Christianity theirs of deceitful imagination, or of implicit deference to authority, but the Christianity of deep, I will add, of rational belief, firmly and profoundly seated in the principles of our moral nature, and nobly accredited by the virtues of our well-conditioned peasantry. In the olden time of Presbytery—that time of scriptural Christianity in our pulpits, and of Psalmody in all our cottages — these men grew and multiplied in the land; and though derided in the heartless literature, and discountenanced or disowned in the heartless politics of other days, it is their remnant which acts as a preserving salt among our people, and which constitutes the real strength and glory of the Scottish nation."

The eloquence of the speaker did not succeed in reconciling all the party to his motion. It was lost by a majority of twelve against it. After a year had given full opportunity for deliberation, in an Assembly of which Dr. Chalmers was not a member, it was again brought forward by Lord Moncreiff and carried by a majority of forty-six. "Moulded into the form of an 'Overture and Interim Act on Calls," Lord Moncreiff's motion was expressed in the following terms :—"*Edinburgh, May 31, 1834.*—The General Assembly declare, That it is a fundamental law of the church, that no pastor shall be intruded into any congregation contrary to the will of the people; and in order that the principle may be carried into full effect, the

General Assembly, with the consent of a majority of the Presbyteries of this church, do declare, enact, and ordain, that it shall be an instruction to Presbyteries, that if at the moderating in a call to a vacant pastoral charge, the major part of the male heads of families, members of the vacant congregation, and in full communion with the church, shall disapprove of the person in whose favor the call is proposed to be moderated in, such disapproval shall be deemed sufficient ground for the Presbytery rejecting such person, and that he shall be rejected accordingly, and due notice thereof forthwith given to all concerned; but that if the major part of the said heads of families shall not disapprove of such person to be their pastor, the Presbytery shall proceed with the settlement according to the rules of the church: And further declare, that no person shall be held to be entitled to disapprove, as aforesaid, who shall refuse, if required, solemnly to declare in the presence of the Presbytery, that he is actuated by no factious or malicious motive, but solely by a conscientious regard to the spiritual interests of himself or the congregation."

"Such was the Veto Law. Intended as a final and pacifying measure, it was proposed after the maturest deliberation. After a year's interval, in the course of which it was subjected to the severest scrutiny, it came before the General Assembly of 1834, approved by the most eminent legal advice, and sanctioned by the authority of the legal and political advisers of the Crown in Scotland. It was carried, before any of the chapel-ministers had been introduced into the church courts, by a clear majority of all the different constituencies of which the General Assembly is composed; and two months after its passage, it had this judgment pronounced upon it in the House of Lords, from the lips of Lord Brougham, at that time Lord Chancellor of England:

"'My Lords, I hold in my hand a great number of petitions from a most respectable portion of His Majesty's subjects in the northern part of this island, all referring to one subject—I mean church patronage in Scotland, which has greatly and powerfully interested the people of Scotland for many months past, and respecting the expediency of some change in which there is hardly any difference of opinion among them. The late proceedings in the General Assembly (viz., in passing the Veto Law), have done more to facilitate the adoption of measures which shall set that important question at rest, upon a footing advantageous to the community, and that shall be safe and beneficial to the Establishment, and in every respect desirable, than any other course that could have been taken; for it would have been premature if the Legislature had adopted any measure without the acquiescence of that important body, as no good could have resulted from it. I am glad that the wisdom of the General Assembly has been devoted to this subject, and that the result of its deliberations has been these important resolutions (viz., the Veto Act), which were passed at the last meeting.'"

CHAPTER XIII.

In the summer of 1833, Dr. Chalmers sought the recreation and rest from intellectual labor, which he so much needed in a two months' tour; one object of which was the gratification of a long cherished whim of seeing and ascending to the top of all the cathedrals of England. The records of that tour were contained in journal letters to his children, constituting some of the most delightful of his published correspondence. Thus to his daughter Grace he describes some of the subterranean wonders of Derbyshire: "After breakfast, ordered the gig, and was carried to the Bagshaw Cavern, recently discovered, and full of crystallized minerals, stretching along the walls or depending in icicles from the roof. The exploration of it is very fatiguing; first, the descent of 126 steps under the earth; second, a passage often narrow and requiring a very low stoop; third; steps and scrambles to the lateral cavities that we meet with on our way. This is perhaps the greatest natural curiosity in Derbyshire, though more of a scientific than spectacular character; and this, combined with its difficulty of access and distance from the inn causes it to be less frequented. The poor man who shows it is evidently a man of talent and humor—has seen better days, and wrote an account of his cave which is now all sold off. He tells me that it was an elaborate work, and written with more humor than was ever brought into play before on any subterranean subject, and that it has gained him a great reputation. He begged me to speak in favor of his cavern, which was too little visited. Its great peculiarity is, that out-and-out it is completely natural, not a tool being lifted within it, save in the construction of its descending steps. In one place the passage widens into a chamber called paradise, all in a sparkle with large and beautiful crystals, then contracts again, and winds laterally and by a scrambling ascent into another chamber, at least equal to the former and more lofty, called Calypso's Cave, then terminates in a third, which, though it receives no name, is nearly as good as the two former. Walked our fatiguing way back again and welcomed the light of day. We had three candles, each of us holding one. I should have mentioned that I had to put on another coat and hat at the guide's house; and a worse coat or worse hat I never saw on the back or head of any carter or scavenger in the land, insomuch that I was a spectacle to the children of the village, who shouted and laughed behind me; and even the driver of my gig, though a grave, silent, and simple lad of twenty-two, could not restrain his merriment. By the way, though it is a little more expensive, I always take him to the sights along with me; first, because I found a great ignorance of Derbyshire curiosities in Huddersfield, and I want to make him more enlightened and enlarged than his fellow-citizens; second, because I always feel a strong reflex or secondary enjoyment in the gratifications of other people, so that the sympathy of his enjoyment greatly enhances my own; and thirdly, because I get amusement from the remarks of his simple wonderment and not very sagacious observation; and it has now passed into a standing joke with me, when leaving any of our exhibitions, that 'there is no such fine sight to be seen at Huddersfield.' Drove back to the inn at Castleton, where after a short excursion to the castle immediately above the Peak Cavern (and which, by the way, belonging of old to the Knights of Peveril, gave birth to Sir Walter's novel of 'Peveril of the Peak'), I dined about three. After dinner, I walked with my companion of the gig to Speedwell Mine, a very noble curiosity, where, after a descent into the bowels of the earth of 106 steps, we entered a boat which carried us along a subterranean canal of nearly a mile, one half of which only is described by us. We have a regular archway over our heads, cut out for the convenience of the miners, and which still remains though the work is abandoned. The two boatmen propel us by pushing with their hands against the sides of the tunnel. They placed some candles along the tunnel on each side near the entrance, and which were seen by us all the way, and with their reflection in the water had a very pretty and pleasing effect—at the distance of nearly half a mile they shrunk into the appearance of distant stars. But how shall I describe the scene at the termination of our voyage?—a scene to the description of which I fear that even your pen would be inadequate, yea, even in its sublimest mood, when set to an exercise in composition that shall bear off the palm of victory from all your class-fellows. The canal is crossed about half way by a mighty chasm which reaches to an unknown height above us, and an unknown depth beneath us. An arch has been thrown over it on which we alight at the termination of the first half of the canal, and might, if we so chose, pass on to the second half, and be carried forward in a boat another quarter of a mile. But as it is just the same with the last quarter of a mile, we therefore go no further than to this arch, guarded by a strong iron railing to keep us from being precipitated into the mysterious abyss below. Here we stood; and as we were under a hill many hundred feet high, there was room for an altitude above our heads of invisible termination, while the termination of the horrible pit beneath our feet was alike invisible. Down this tremendous chasm there thundered a roaring water-fall; and we were furnished with blue lights that we might be enabled to trace its way as far as possible. The man ascended a ladder along the side of the cataract, and placed a gunpowder preparation on one of the crannies, which blazed and sparkled and shot up gleams of illumination for several minutes, which left unrevealed, however, the roof that was over us. And then more fearfully glorious still, he descended a ladder and placed another light beneath us, and by the side of the foaming cataract, which shed momentary radiance far and wide and deep among the Plutonic recesses of this scene of wonders, but left the secret of its bottom untold. I never took in so powerful an impression by the eye from any spectacle as from this last one, though the one above us too was particularly fine. Sky-rockets have been thrown up without reaching the roof, or bringing it within the observation of human eyes. We returned from this impressive scene in the boat, and by the way put fire to a blast which had been prepared for our entertainment, when, after passing it for a few minutes, it whizzed and exploded with a noise which made the vaulted tunnel to ring and reverberate all over. And could I describe the effect with the eloquence, or in the terms of a boarding-school Miss, I would say that such a roar of cannonading never bellowed or bounded so majestically on the auditory organs of awe-struck and astonished hearers. When we made our egress up the steps and again returned to the light of day, I made my gig driver acknowledge, and I am sure with perfect sincerity, that 'no such thing is to be seen or heard at Huddersfield.' Returned to the inn at Castleton. Took our gig there and drove on to Bakewell, fourteen miles distant, over a fine upland country, but which at length on our approach to Bakewell, on the banks of the Wye, assumed another character, and presented a very fine specimen of English comfort and beauty. Got at Bakewell into a spacious, elegant, but withal most civil and comfortable inn, under the sign of the Rutland Arms, a little after eight. Was ushered into a very snug sitting-room, with a bedroom immediately off it, and went to my needful repose between ten and eleven. I am, my dear Grace, yours most affectionately. "THOMAS CHALMERS."

After visiting the magnificent seat of the Duke of Devonshire at Chatsworth, and what he felt to be more impressive in its old baronial grandeur, the noble residence of Kedlestone, he proceeded to London and then to Cambridge, where he declared himself dizzied with the number of introductions to men of eminence in science and learning. His interest in the old universities of England amounted to enthusiasm, and his reception by the learned men then resident in Cambridge, and some of whom still continue to adorn it, must have been highly gratifying. Thus, in a letter to Mr. Chalmers, he writes of one of those pleasant days: "Professor Sedgwick sent me a message that he would accompany me to breakfast with Professor Airy, who lived a mile from Cambridge, at the Observatory. Had a delightful walk with him thitherward. He took me to the roof of the Observatory, and explained to me all its chief instruments. Breakfasted with the very *élites* of the nation in philosophy — Sir John Herschel, Sir David Brewster, men from Oxford, men from Cambridge, etc. A celebrated optician showed us some experiments, after breakfast, in his department. Took a cordial leave of his party at eleven. Walked to Cambridge well accompanied. Met a letter brought by a messenger, on the way, from Professor Forbes, who had tried to find me out, but could not, among the assembled hundreds the night before. Disturbed by learning from Mr. Sedgwick that at the public dinner to-day the Universities of Scotland were to be drunk, and that I was expected to reply. This set me conning a speech. Went to hear what was going on in the Section of Physics. Saw Professor Forbes there, and heard on the subject of light the argumentations of Herschel and Airy. After the work of the Sections was finished we had our concluding general meeting in the Senate Hall, quite filled with ladies and students; and on the elevated platform, around the President's chair, a brilliant assemblage both of aristocratic and literary grandees. I was beckoned to go among them, and sat immediately behind the President, and by the side of Dr. Lloyd of Trinity College, Dublin. After the Report had been read we had many speeches, from Lord Fitzwilliam, the Marquis of Northampton, Dr. Robinson of Dublin, etc., the last named of whom delighted me with his defense of the high mathematics in opposition to a remark of Lord Fitzwilliam on the Reports being too abstruse for the comprehension of a general audience. At the breaking up of the meeting had many greetings, from Mr. Malthus, his lady, and daughter, Dr. Buckland of Oxford, whom I knew before, Dr. Somerville, the husband of the famous authoress, etc. Transferred ourselves to the dining-hall of Trinity College, where sat at least six hundred. My ticket took me to table A, near the President, where I had the good fortune to be within conversation of Mr. Malthus. Much noble speaking, chiefly from the

President Sedgwick, Marquis of Northampton, Brunel, Buckland, Vernon, son to the Archbishop of York, whom we met when we were together in London, etc. When our Universities were given, the chairman delivered a very high personal eulogy on myself, and nothing could exceed the deafening reception which I met with. The burden of my short speech was Sir Isaac Newton, a pupil of this College; and my toast was, " Trinity College, and long may the science of Newton, and the Christianity of Newton, be enshrined within her walls." I was received with great partiality and favor; and whereas there is a dread in such a mixed company of philosophers of any allusion to Christianity, my pointed allusion to the sacred faith and philosophy of Newton was received with a cordiality which nothing could exceed. Brunel's speech kept them in a roar of laughter for half an hour, though neither he nor any of us could reach perhaps to more than half the company. When we broke up, walked about with Mr. Jones, Professor of Political Economy, King's College; then called on Mr. Simeon, by whom I was very kindly received; then met in his room at Trinity the son of Mr. Hoare, of Hampstead Heath, who had made himself known to me before; along with him were Mr. Perry, senior wrangler, and Mr. Goulburn, son to the quondam Chancellor of the Exchequer. Talked congenially with them, and walked with the young men in moonlight among the courts and cloistered beauties of Trinity College. Ever believe me, my dearest Grace, yours most affectionately.

"THOMAS CHALMERS."

Returning to London he visited the House of Commons and met with several of the legislative notorieties, among whom, in a letter to his daughter Anne, he specially mentions Mr. Daniel O'Connell, " who," he says, " shook me most cordially by the hand, complimenting me on my evidence about the Irish Poor-Laws, saying that he was a disciple of mine upon that subject, and not of his own priest, Dr. Doyle; and I, on the other hand, glad of good being done whatever quarter it came from, and knowing him to be an influential personage, expressed myself much gratified with the view that he had taken on that question. I am sure it would have done your heart much good to have seen how closely and cordially Mr. Daniel O'Connell and your papa hugged and greeted each other in the Lower House of Parliament."

After visiting the cathedral of Canterbury, he went to Kingston with Mr. Bartlett, the rector, of whom he writes: "On the whole, he is one of the most delightful and intelligent persons I have met with among the clergy of England. I stand indebted to him for three high gratifications—*first*, in that his lady is the great-grandniece of Bishop Butler, author of the Analogy and Sermons; and through her he is in possession of certain of this great man's relics, which he showed me and put into my hands, as a snuff-box of antique fabrication, and a small jotting-book for the receipts and other little transactions of his clerical office; and lastly, a Greek New Testament with his annotations, all in his own handwriting, and on which last Mr. Bartlett did me the honor of asking me to record in my handwriting, the opinion I had of this great champion of Christianity. *Second*, less than a mile from Mr. Bartlett's parsonage-house, is the church and house where the great Hooker lived and labored and died. Thither we went, though in a pour of rain, and entered the church, where we saw his burial-place and monument, as also the house where he spent so many years of his life, and breathed his last."

A week more was spent "in the very thick of London society," at the end of which he took his way to Norwich. At the outskirts of Ipswich, the Rev. Mr. Bridges was in waiting for him with his gig and took him to his own house. Of Mr. Bridges' family he remarks: "The breath of heaven is here; without, a scene of beauty that to the eye of sense is altogether delicious—and within, a sanctuary of love and holiness. After breakfast took me to an adjoining field, where, under the foliage of a spreading tree, the infant school was assembled. I was asked to address them, and did it. Mrs. Bridges visits the houses of the parish with the view to a Christian effect, and is a mighty help to her husband. He took me to his church and a few of his cottages, and I never witnessed such closeness and efficiency of pastoral work as he exemplified in his addresses to the mothers of families. He makes a real business both of the Christianity of his own soul and the Christianity of his family and parish, watching over the souls of all as one who must give an account."

Mr. Bridges took Dr. Chalmers to the house of Mr. J. J. Gurney. Of his visit to that excellent quaker family, "an abode," as he has himself called it, " of friendship and piety," we cannot withhold an extract or two : " Mr. Bridges left us, but not without leaving on my heart a profound sense of his christian devotedness and worth. After he went out, Mrs. Francis Cunningham, the lady of one of our best English clergymen, came in, and has been an inmate during my abode at Earlham. She is sister to Mr. Gurney, and is really a very attractive person, for simplicity, and christian principle, and elegant accomplishment, and withal high intelligence and cultivation. But last of all, another lady, who dined and spent the night—now aged and in quaker attire, which she had but recently put on, and who in early life was one of the most distinguished of our literary women, whose works, thirty years ago, I read with great delight—no less a person than the celebrated Mrs. Opie, authoress of the most exquisite feminine tales, and for which I used to place her by the side of Miss Edgeworth. It was curious to myself, that though told by Mr. Gurney, in the morning of her being to dine, I had forgot the circumstance, and the idea of the accomplished novelist and poet was never once suggested by the image of this plain looking Quakeress, till it rushed upon me after dinner, when it suddenly and inconceivably augmented the interest I felt in her. We had much conversation, and drew greatly together, walking and talking with each other on the beautiful lawn after dinner. She has had access into all kinds of society, and her conversation is all the more rich and interesting. I complained to her of one thing in Quakerism, and that is, the mode of their introductions : that I could have recognized in *Mrs. Opie*, an acquaintance of thirty years' standing, but that I did not and could not feel the charm of any such reminiscence when *Joseph John* simply bade me lead out *Amelia* from his drawing-room to his dining-room. I felt, however, my new acquaintance with this said Amelia, to be one of the great acquisitions of my present journey; and this union of rank, and opulence, and literature, and polish of mind, with plainness of manners, forms one of the great charms of the society in this house. Had much and cordial talk all evening; a family exposition before supper, and at length a general breaking up, somewhere about eleven o'clock; terminated this day at once of delightful recreation and needful repose.

"THOMAS CHALMERS."

"*Saturday, July 27th.*—Mrs. Opie left us early, and we parted from each other most cordially. Went with Mr. Gurney in his carriage to Norwich—first to his bank, where I acquitted myself with all proper bows and civilities of pleasant remark to the partners and other members of the establishment whom I was brought into converse with; secondly, through the town, ancient and respectable, with no less than thirty-six parish churches, several of which I entered, and was solemnized by their grandeur; thirdly, to the castle, around whose walls we walked, and where I eyed with delight the number of ecclesiastical towers that arose from the general mass of buildings; fourthly, to the cathedral, where I was introduced to Prebendary Wodehouse, who took charge of me, and conducted me in person through the cathedral. But I must first mention the call which I and Mr. Gurney made on the venerable bishop, now in his ninetieth year. He received us with great courteousness; had just finished the reading of my last book, which he complimented, and gave us most entertaining anecdotes of other days, and I felt particularly interested in his personal acquaintanceship with Bishop Warburton. We stopped a quarter of an hour with the venerable old prelate — a perfect gentleman, and of a mild and benevolent spirit, and great suavity withal. I was much pleased with the cathedral and its precincts, through which Mr. Wodehouse, who kept by me for two hours, conducted me. There is a great predominance of Saxon in the cathedral. I, as usual, ascended to the top of the tower, and dragged the Prebendary after me. The chief points of attraction and interest are the cloisters, beautifully groined; Erpingham's gate, an entrance to one of the courts of the cathedral, with a small and graceful sweep of arch, and great exquisiteness without exuberance of ornament; the tower, perhaps the finest part of the general building; and, lastly, the monuments, not so much for their architecture, as for the celebrity of the men to whom they are dedicated, being no less than Bishop Hall, Bishop Horne, and Dean Prideaux."

Of this visit to Earlham, Mr. Gurney has preserved lengthened memoranda, from which we give the following extracts:

"*Earlham, 7th Month, 24th,* 1833. — As we were sitting in the drawing-room rather late on the evening of the 18th instant, Dr. Chalmers entered with our friend, Chas. Bridges, Vicar of Long Newton, Suffolk, as his companion. Dr. Chalmers is a man peculiarly susceptible of being pleased—looking at objects which surround him through a favorable medium.

"CHAL. 'I have been traveling through Kent, Essex, and Suffolk, and now through Norfolk, the agricultural garden of England. It is a delightful country—varied in its surface, and clothed in greenness. As to the *moulding* and *statuary* of the scenery, we excel you in Scotland; but when I look over the fields of your country, I seem to be no longer looking through my naked eye, but through an eye-glass, tinged with green, which throws a more vivid hue over nature than that to which I am accustomed.'

"On the following morning we conversed on the subject of the great minds with which he had been brought into contact. I asked him who was the most talented person with whom he had associated, especially in power of conversation. He said Robert Hall was the greatest proficient he had known as a converser, and spoke in high terms of his talents and of his preaching. 'But,' said he, 'I think Foster is of a higher order of intellect; he fetches his thoughts from a deeper spring; he is no great talker, and he writes very slowly; but he moves along in a region far above the common intellectual level. There are passages in his Essays of amazing depth and beauty, especially in that on 'Popular Ignorance.' I am sorry to say, however, he is disposed to radicalism, and would scarcely object to substitute for the machinery of Oxford and Cambridge—those endowed seats of religion and learning—factories worked by steam.'

"In the course of the morning, Dr. Chalmers accompanied me to Norwich. As we were going into the market-place, he was arrested by catching a view of the steeple of 'St. Peter Mancroft Church,' (as it is called), which he thought a noble structure. He is fond of ecclesiastical architecture; and it was entertaining to observe the pleasure which he enjoyed while we were examining the building without and within.

"The next objects of our attention were the hall called 'St. Andrew's' originally used for public worship, and built by Sir Thomas Erpingham, as a penance for his sins; the beautiful gateway to the cathedral, which bears the name and image of the same Sir Thomas; the cathedral itself, of which the almost unrivaled tower was of course pointed out; and the elegant ruin in the Bishop's garden. No young or ardent traveler could derive more pleasure from such sights than the doctor. We then called on the venerable bishop, now in his ninetieth year, and very delightful was our interview. The dear old man was in good heart and health, reading without spectacles, hearing without the smallest difficulty, and able to talk with his old vivacity. He was evidently much animated by seeing Dr. C.; on the other hand, Dr. C. was *charmed*, as well he might be, with the bishop.

"BISHOP. 'Dr. Chalmers, I am very glad to be introduced to you; I have just been reading your Bridgewater Essay with great satisfaction. I am especially pleased that you have insisted so much on the views of Bishop Butler, whom I have always reckoned to be one of the best and wisest of writers.'

I remarked, that it was strange that a writer of so liberal and comprehensive a cast should be accused of Popery.

"BISHOP. 'There is no ground for it — people will always call names; they will tell you (addressing Dr. C. with a smile), that my friend Joseph here is a wicked fellow.' They then conversed on Dr. Adam Smith's theory of moral sentiments.

"BISHOP. 'I am sorry to find from your work, that his splendid passage respecting the necessity of a mediator was omitted in the second edition.'

"CHAL. 'The omission was probably owing to his intimacy with Hume.' I asked the bishop whether he had not been acquainted with Hume.

"BISHOP. 'O yes, I used to meet with him at the old Lord Bathurst's; he was fond of a game of whist, to which I, too, had no objection, and we have sometimes played together. He was a very good-natured man; but I have heard him say cutting things about *us*—I mean the clergy.'

"The bishop then repeated part of the passage from Dr. A. Smith, with peculiar accuracy and feeling. I do not precisely recollect whether the bishop quoted the whole of this extract; but he told us, that the passage had been fixed in his memory since his early manhood. When he afterward spoke, in his usual terms, of his painlessness of body, and peace of mind, the latter more particularly was adverted to, I think, by Dr. Chalmers, as a subject of especial gratitude and satisfaction. 'The more so,' I added, 'because it is grounded, as I trust, on that great doctrine of Christianity, to which even Adam Smith has so feelingly alluded.' 'Oh yes,' said the bishop, in a decided and emphatic tone, 'that is the *only thing*—there is no *other* way.' This acknowledgment precisely corresponded with what I had before heard from him, and was very grateful both to myself and to Dr. Chalmers. The bishop afterward drew a lively picture of the talented but hot-headed Atterbury, Bishop of Rochester, who was well known to his uncle, Lord Bathurst; and also of the mighty Warburton, in whose diocese he had once held a living, and with whom he was familiarly acquainted. He described him a giant in conversation, and a fearless champion against Hume and other infidels; 'I have no liking for the men,' said he, 'and no fear of their talents.' With the exception of Lord Bathurst and a few others, he indulged in a sort of scorn against the nobles of the land. 'As for you *lords*,' said he, in the bishop's hearing, 'your venison is but a poor repayment for the fatigue of listening to your conversation.' I suppose that, like Johnson, he imagined himself privileged to be a bear.

"BISHOP. 'His wife, too, had a spirit of her own—she used to call her husband Brigadier Moses!'

"I was glad to hear Chalmers and the bishop fully according in the praise of Warburton's 'Julian,' which surely contains important and specific, though somewhat indirect, evidence of the truth as it is in Jesus. After our friend C. W. had conducted the doctor to some others of our ecclesiastical remains, we returned home to dinner. It is always pleasant to watch the noble expressions of Dr. C.'s countenance; but he is often very quiet in a large party. I never saw a man who appeared to be more destitute of vanity, or less alive to any wish to be brilliant.

"In the course of Monday morning the Doctor and I walked down to a fir grove at the extremity of the park, where a colony of herons have lately formed a settlement. He was as much interested and pleased as a schoolboy would have been in watching the singular appearance, gestures, and sounds of these birds. His mind seemed quite occupied by the fitness between the length of their necks and that of their legs, and also by the circumstance, that as they swim not, but only stand in the waters, they do not, like other aquatic birds, require webs to their feet—and therefore have none.

"CHAL. 'The great fear I entertain respecting the operation of the Reform Bill is, lest it should throw the legislative power into the hands of men of business—already full of all kinds of occupation—to the exclusion of men who have leisure for deep study and reflection, and are therefore able to cope with great principles on the various subjects of legislation. There is a fine passage in Ecclesiasticus, on the danger of intrusting with the arcana of government, men whose hearts and hands are full of the common business of life. I wish we were more alive to the principles which are there unfolded. It is an alarming fact, that in order to effect a paltry saving of a few thousand pounds per annum, that great work, the trigonometrical survey of Great Britain, was on the point of being left incomplete. It was saved by a majority of only two votes in a committee of the House of Commons.'

" The passage to which Dr. C. alluded, and which we forthwith read together, is well worthy of notice. It is in chap. xxxviii., and begins as follows : ' How can he get wisdom that holdeth the plow, and that glorieth in the goad, that driveth oxen, and is occupied in their labors, and whose talk is of bullocks ? He giveth his mind to make furrows, and is diligent to give the kine fodder.' The writer then goes on to describe in a vivid manner, the work of the carpenter, the seal-cutter, the smith, and the potter ; and adds, ' without these can not a city be inhabited, and they shall not go where they will, nor go up and down. They shall not be sought for in public council, nor sit high in the congregation : they shall not sit on the judge's seat, nor understand the sentence of judgment, and they shall not *be found where parables are spoken.*'

" CHAL. ' I take great delight in the book of Ecclesiasticus. Were I to speak merely from my own judgment of the internal evidence, I should say that it contains almost equal marks of inspiration with the book of Proverbs. But the New Testament gives no countenance to such an opinion. There are few books in the Old Testament more often quoted by the evangelists and apostles than the book of Proverbs : but they take no notice of Ecclesiasticus.'

" The more we became familiarized to Dr. C.'s company, and observed the remarkable union which he presents of high talent and comprehensive thought, with an almost childlike modesty and simplicity, the more we admired him, as one notable example of that exquisite divine workmanship which so much fills his own contemplations. I may also add, that the more we became acquainted with his thorough amiability, the more we loved him.

"I must not conclude without just remarking, that our dear and honored friend is a man of prayer. The prayers which he uttered in our family circle, on some solemn occasions, were concise, emphatic, and comprehensive—indicative of a very reverent sense of the holiness of God, and of the all-sufficiency of the one appointed mediation. I find myself often recurring to some of his concluding words—'These petitions we humbly offer unto Thee, in the name of Him whom Thou hearest always. Amen.'"

In style, as well as subject, the letters of Dr. Chalmers to his children are invariably suited to the age of his correspondent. Such, for example, is the manner and subject of a letter printed with the pen for his little daughter, Fanny. "Set off at twelve in a coach for Beverley, open, and drawn by Mr. Venn's own horses. He accompanied me along with Mr. Scott and another clergyman, whose name I have strangely forgotten. It was a most kind and respectable convoy for nine miles. The object was that I might see Beverley Minster, not a regular cathedral, but really as splendid and noble an edifice as I could desire to see, and that would rank high among the cathedrals of England. In taking up Mr. Scott, at the outskirts of Hull, made a short call on his interesting family, consisting of a wife and a good many children; one son in orders, and several grown up daughters. Before examining the cathedral minutely, visited the minister of Beverley. His name is Mr. C., and as I wrote Helen in my last letter about the biggest bell I had ever seen in my life, let me now write little Fanny about the biggest man I ever saw. He is so heavy that he cannot walk; he would weigh more than two of your papa. We found him sitting on an arm chair that could have been made into a bed for you and Helen sleeping in. When he goes to the church to preach, which he does very often, he gets upon a wooden horse called a velocipede, which runs upon wheels, and with this he moves through the streets, and through the church till he gets to the foot of the pulpit; and then two great strong men-servants push him up the stair and through the door of the pulpit with their backs and their shoulders, when he sits squash down upon an immense cushion and preaches sitting to the people, for to do it standing would be impossible. He received us with great politeness, is a literary and gentlemanly person, and so much esteemed that his odd movements in public excite no ridicule, he being very much respected and sympathized with. On my stating how desirable it is to have a printed guide for all great objects of curiosity, he made distribution among us four of a small work that he himself had drawn up on Beverley Minster, furnished with which we made a most satisfactory survey of the magnificent, highly adorned, and carefully kept structure, used as a parish church, but having no less than £1400 a year of revenue for keeping it in order.—I am, my dear Fanny, your affectionate papa, "Thomas Chalmers."

Proceeding on his leisurely journey northward, on Sunday, the 11th of August he preached at Belford and Norham, though eighteen miles asunder. Another notion of this tour was from Norham to Woodhouselee to "speel along the border on foot, with one leg, wherever it was possible in England, and another in Scotland." This manner of traveling was obstructed by the kindness of friends, and the only approach to the realization of his plan of a solitary ramble, was one day when he "proceeded down the Liddel, in company with George Thomson, of seventy years of age, a genius and a character; and as he walked slow, and I kept back with him for the sake of his information, we took just four hours and a half to our twelve miles' ride. He gave me much intelligence regarding all the hills and localities within sight—being a pure Liddelsdale man, and thoroughly imbued with the spirit and tastes of a Scottish Borderer, beside being a botanist, and, I suspect a poet also. He pointed out to me Mangerton Pillar, round which I went; Mangerton House, on the other side of the Liddel; the site of Jock o' the Side's house; the direction where Pudding-burn House lay; Stangarth Castle, etc.; all famous in Border story. He represented himself as a relative of the poet Thomson, whose father, by the way, died minister of Hopekirk, and is buried there. He recounted to me various Border exploits, and had the traditionary knowledge of many Border rhymes.

Reaching Woodhouselee in the afternoon of Saturday, he thus closes his letter on the Border country : " The end of the week brought me to the end of the Border line. The only revisitation I should like to make along the whole length of it, is to the Hermitage river, that runs into the Liddel from the N. W., and that for the sake of Hermitage Castle. I cannot but remark it as unexpected and strange, that I should, without my being previously aware of them, have been so handed from one acquaintance to another, and from one horse or carriage to another, so in fact as not to have been suffered to foot it along any part of the journey. I, all the week, in fact, have had the services done to me which I recollect in my younger days, done to those beggars who were carried about in barrows ; lifted at Norham, and let down at Kirknewton—lifted at Kirknewton, and let down at Sprouston—lifted at Sprouston, and let down at Edgerston—lifted at Edgerston, and let down at Wolflee—lifted at Wolflee, and let down at Hindlee—lifted at Hindlee, and let down at the Rowe—lifted at the Rowe, and let down at Woodhouselee. I will not, when I consider the length and arduousness of the way, say it was hard to be disappointed of my pedestrian speculation; but rather, when I look back to all the accommodation I have had, and to the kindness which prompted it, I cannot but feel a grateful emotion, which for once in this classic and inspiring region, I shall give vent to in poetry—

" Good people, my thanks,
   For thus haining my shanks."

CHAPTER XIV.

The established Church of Scotland is supported by a regular charge upon the rent of land paid by the owners, and not by the imposition of a burden upon the industry of the country. The city of Edinburgh is an exception, the established ministers of that city drawing their income from an annual impost of six per cent. on the rental, payable not by the owners, but by the occupiers of "the several dwelling-houses, chambers, booths, cellars, and all other houses high and low." This is called the Annuity tax, and from the payment of it, "all the members of the College of Justice, comprising the Bench, the Bar, and the whole body of Writers or Attorneys, are by law exempt." A burden so unequally imposed, naturally gave much dissatisfaction, which increased with the growth of dissent, and was stimulated to greater activity by the progress of political reform. Very unkindly and unfairly, instead of applying to the head of authority to have the evil corrected, the people of Edinburgh endeavored to throw the obloquy upon the ministers, who had no hand in establishing the system, and had come to the city in dependence upon the pay that was guaranteed to them by those from whom they received the call. By refusing to pay the assessment, it was thought that the ministers would either relinquish their income, or by attempting to obtain it in course of law, bring disrepute upon both the system and themselves : in other words, the tax payers, instead of applying for a change of the law, determined either to starve or disgrace the excellent men who depended upon their honor. The ministers admitted of great reductions of their salaries, by having the impost laid upon only four-fifths of the rental, and by excusing all whose rent amounted to only five pounds and under, as well as by freely giving certificates of exemption to such as plead inability to pay. Still, the illegal resistance prevailed, until the Town Council, at last, who ought to have done so at first, took the matter in hand. The measure proposed by that body evinced as little wisdom as Christianity. It was, in brief, to abolish the Annuity tax, reduce the number of city ministers from eighteen to thirteen, collect their salary from the pew rents, and supply whatever deficit there might be, by an assessment laid partly upon the landlord and partly upon the tenant. A consultation with the Presbytery was necessary. After frequent conferences were held between committees of the two bodies, at last a set of queries was submitted by the Council, to which authoritative answers were requested from the Presbytery. Dr. Chalmers was appointed to draw up those answers, which he could do with the better grace, as not being personally concerned, and Wednesday, the 23d of January, was appointed for the final decision. The crowd which assembled, both from interest in the case and desire to hear Dr. Chalmers, was immense. The speech was one of its author's ablest productions. Going over their queries in order, when he came to reply to the proposal for reducing the number of the ministers, his answer was: " The Presbytery cannot give their consent to any arrangement which shall have the effect, either immediately or in future, of reducing the number of clergymen. On this subject, the Presbytery would, in the first place, appeal to those days in the past history of Edinburgh, when, as in 1668, there were twelve ministers, with a population, it is understood, of less than 20,000, or in 1722, when there were sixteen ministers, with a population of about 25,200. The numbers at present are eighteen ministers to a population of upward of 55,000; and the Presbytery never can consent to aggravate still further the disproportion between the former and present ecclesiastical provision for the city, by a reduction in the number of city ministers. They are the more strenuous in this resistance, that the evil has been fearfully increased by an inundation of hearers in the city churches from the suburbs and surrounding neighborhood of Edinburgh, in virtue of which it will be found that many thousands within the city itself, now wandering like sheep without a shepherd, have been denuded of that rightful property which they once had in the Sabbath ministrations and week-day services of their respective clergymen. The Presbytery never will consent to a reduction in their number, so long as the peculiar service of reclaiming these outcasts remains unaccomplished—a service of the utmost importance to the moral and christian interests of the community, and which, under the present system of seat-letting, and of general congregations, is utterly impracticable."

Having commented largely on the answers to the remaining queries, Dr. Chalmers proceeded: "I will not speak of the ecclesiastical burdens of the city, because the effort of the clergymen is to deliver the city from a tenfold heavier burden of pauperism, profligacy and crime. The two terms of the alternative are the luxury of the higher classes, and the instruction of the lower, and I stand up as the friend of the lower classes when I stand up for the maintenance of that fund which is the subject of your deliberations. Our cause, despite of the obloquy which has been heaped upon it, is emphatically the cause of the unprovided — it is the cause of the poor against the rich—of the many who should reap the benefits of the Establishment in the lessons of christian instruction, against the comparatively few who would refuse to pay the endowments, or who would retain what is not theirs, and who, for their own private uses, would appropriate that which ought to be expended on the best and highest objects of patriotism." After quoting a passage in favor of Establishments, from the writings of William Cobbett, Dr. Chalmers concluded thus:

"I have already professed myself, and will profess myself again, an unflinching, an out-and-out — and I maintain it, the only consistent radical. The dearest object of my earthly existence, is the elevation of the common people — humanized by Christianity, and raised by the strength of their moral habits to a higher platform of human nature; and by which they may attain and enjoy the rank and consideration due to enlightened and companionable men. I trust the day is coming when the people will find out who are their best friends, and when the mock patriotism of the present day shall be unmasked by an act of robbery and spoliation on the part of those who would deprive the poor of their best and highest patrimony. The imperishable soul of the poor man is of as much price in the sight of heaven, as the soul of the rich; and I will resist to the uttermost—I will resist even to the death—that alienation which goes but to swell the luxury of the higher ranks, at the expense of the Christianity of the lower orders."

"The Reverend Doctor," the reporter adds, "throughout this long address, spoke with marked energy and emphasis, and at the conclusion, in particular, his manner was characterized with unusual animation. On sitting down, a burst of applause rose from the spectators, which lasted for several minutes."

His exertions had indeed overtasked his strength, and on the way home, he was affected with a stroke of paralysis, which, without entirely disabling, confined him to his room for several weeks. A slight return of the attack some time afterward, pointed out the propriety of entire cessation of labor for some time. Accordingly, the summer of 1834 was spent in quiet country retirement, with healthful exercise and easy reading, without more writing than was involved in keeping up a pretty extensive correspondence. That, however, amounted to what a man of ordinary industry would deem an overwhelming task. For, in addition to his own private letters, he had now fully entered upon his vast scheme of church extension, and was employed in making it known, and recommending its objects, and suggesting measures of advancing them in all directions. The religious wants of his countrymen, had, at least from the time of his first explorations in Glasgow, never been absent from his mind, side by side with many other ideas for the benefit of mankind, that one had retained its place and given evidence of its activity in his various labors in the Tron and St. John's parish, in his Sabbath schools for the poor, and missionary efforts in St. Andrew's, and, since his removal to Edinburgh, the condition of a large portion of that population had attracted his christian sympathy. Near his residence, the suburban village of Water of Leith, was distinguished for irreligion and disorder. Of its thirteen hundred and fifty-six inhabitants, only one hundred and forty-three had seats in any place of worship. With the aid of a few friends, he " provided a missionary for it, who in six months had collected a congregation of between three and four hundred, most of whom had been utter strangers to the ordinances of the gospel." He had also set on foot a scheme for creating a new parish and church in the Cowgate, one of the most destitute portions of the city. In 1817 he had asserted that twenty more churches were needed to meet the religious wants of Glasgow. The estimate was then deemed extravagant ; but such had been the progress of correcter views, chiefly as the result of his own teaching, that now among his former parishioners of that city, a plan was adopted for actually realizing the suggestion. Mr. Collins, still pursuing that noble career of christian benevolence upon which he had entered, together with his former pastor, was at once the originator and the principal agent in the accomplishment of the scheme : but so extensive and weighty was the co-operation, that in 1841, the last church of the twenty was completed.

The same spirit also more extensively pervaded the body of the Scottish clergy. A committee had been appointed to take means of increasing the usefulness of the church as early as 1828 ; but without any results, until the Assembly of 1834 furnished it with some new powers and placed Dr. Chalmers at its head.

The design of the Scottish established Church is to furnish religious instruction to every individual throughout the land, who has not chosen it for himself in some dissenting body. But the increase of churches since the Reformation had fallen far behind that of the population, and now hundreds and thousands, especially in the large cities, were utterly unprovided for. The views of the evangelical party contemplated no innovation. It was only the self-development which the establishment should have maintained all along. There were formal impediments, it is true. New parishes were subject to the patron of the original parish, and when chapels of ease were erected the ecclesiastical courts refused to admit their ministers to a place with their brethren, or to grant them a Kirk session to aid in their ministerial work, while they were dependent for pecuniary support wholly upon the pew-rents. A bill passed by Parliament in the summer of 1834, did away with the former obstacle, and an Act of Assembly of the same year admitted all the existing chapel ministers to the full standing of the parochical clergy.

The way was thus prepared for the better execution of the design long contemplated by Dr. Chalmers. In pursuance of the objects of the committee he now made it his business to awaken the co-operation of men of standing all over the country. His plan was to build new churches by the free gifts of the people, depending not so much upon the donations of the wealthy as the penny-a-week contributions of the poor. To the latter he attached very great importance, not only for the large pecuniary results it was capable of giving, but also because thereby the feelings of that class whom it was designed to benefit, would be enlisted in the enterprise. The ministers of the new churches were to be provided for from the pew-rents, which at the same time were to be put low enough to be within the means of the poorest. In order the better to attain that end it was thought desirable to have small endowments for each of them. The intention is thus presented in Dr. Chalmers's own language : " The whole peculiarity of our scheme lies in this ; and, while this is kept out of sight, we shall never have done with the unintelligent crudities of those by whom we are made the objects of a perpetual misrepresentation. The church is planted for the express benefit of certain unprovided families occupying a given district that has been previously explored, and whose limits have been previously determined ; and the specific thing on which we rest, and are willing to rest exclusively the merits of our cause, is the footing upon which the relation is established between this church and these families. (1.) We provide them with a church *near enough,* else they are still unprovided families. (2.) We are laboring to provide them with a church at *seat-rents low enough,* else they are obviously still unprovided families. (3.) We take care that *the district be small enough,* and its families few enough to be thoroughly pervaded by the week-day attentions of a clergyman; else in one most important respect these families would still be unprovided, because not provided with a minister who might assume the pastoral superintendence, and discharge it so fully as to become the counselor and Christian friend of one and all of them."

Application was accordingly made to government for an endowment, and met, at first with much favor; but the dissenters seeing the progress of the scheme (for in one year under the management of Dr. Chalmers, no less than sixty-four new churches had been or were being built), and fearing lest it should interfere with their own advancement, united their efforts to defeat it. Earnest and numerous remonstrances were addressed to Parliament against the intended grant, the result of which was the appointment of a committee of investigation into the means of religious instruction. Their report, submitted at the end of two years, fully sustained the representations made of the spiritual wants of the country, but no measure followed of a nature to supply them.

No such external discouragements, however, could impede the progress or extinguish the zeal of the indefatigable mind, now laboring for the religious instruction of Scotland's poor. Amid disappointments and opposition, both out of the church and in it, he pressed on with unflagging devotion, maintaining a voluminous correspondence, issuing circulars and pamphlets, directing agents and stirring up the active benevolence of the people by the wonderful power of his voice. No less than four pamphlets in relation to the subject were published by him in the months of April and May, 1835; and not content with all his own voice could effect, he, in 1836, under sanction of the General Assembly, instituted a system of meetings over the country at which various well instructed deputies were appointed to "plead the cause in the most popular and effective manner." Nor were the fruits disproportioned to the labor expended. At the end of four years, Dr. Chalmers had to report to the General Assembly the addition of nearly two hundred churches, "for the erection of which upward of two hundred thousand pounds had been contributed." A proof not only of his own energy, but of the truth with which he had divined the wants of his countrymen. In his own words, "Had the operations of the Committee not harmonized with the sentiments of the country, they never could have commanded an amount and continuance of pecuniary support altogether without a precedent in the history of christian beneficence in this part of the British empire. Nor is there any premonitory symptom yet of declining fervor in this cause among the people of Scotland. The work is still far from its termination. It has only, so to speak, begun. The cases of most helpless and affecting destitution still remain to be overtaken. There are wastes of poverty, irreligion, and crime, which have still to be redeemed, and which nothing but the aggressive operation of a territorial establishment, wisely, and strenuously, and perseveringly conducted, is adequate to subdue; and until every such moral wilderness is explored and reclaimed, and the whole country present the aspect of a field which the Lord hath blessed, and is causing to bring forth the fruits of righteousness, the Committee may not rest from their labors, nor the people from their hearty and zealous co-operation. At the glorious era of the church's Reformation, it was the unwearied support of the people which, under God, finally brought her efforts to a triumphant issue; in this era of her extension—an era as broadly marked, and as emphatically presented to the notice of the ecclesiastical historian, as any which the church is wont to consider as instances of signal revival and divine interposition—the support of the people will not be wanting; but by their devoted exertions, and willing sacrifices, and ardent prayers, they will yet testify how much they love the house where their fathers worshiped—how much they reverence their

Saviour's command, that the very poorest of their brethren shall have the gospel preached to them."

Dr. Chalmers, in the midst of his many occupations in the winter of 1835-6, prepared, from survey made by himself and agents of his own appointment, a statement of the condition in respect to religion, of districts in Edinburgh, embracing a population of twenty thousand, for presentation before the Commissioners of Religious Instruction; and in his examination by that body, he also took occasion to set forth the grounds and principles of the church extension scheme. The opponents of that enterprise, especially the Rev. Dr. Lee, of Edinburgh, upon examination, endeavored to make impressions of a contradictory nature. This circumstance, together with an attempt afterward made to give weight to their party by the election of Dr. Lee as Moderator of the next Assembly, led to a public controversy and some unpleasant feelings, which it took years to reconcile. Thereby, however, the cause of reformation was promoted, and the opposition, defeated in their attempt, were made to feel the increasing strength of those convictions they had so long succeeded in suppressing.

CHAPTER XV.

LITERARY societies now vied with each other in honoring one whose name conferred more honor than it received in connection with any society. In January, 1834, Dr. Chalmers was elected a Fellow of the Royal Society of Edinburgh, and nearly at the same time, a corresponding member of the Royal Institute of France, and in the summer of 1835, he received the degree of Doctor of Laws, from the University of Oxford. The second of these he justly acknowledged as the proudest of his literary honors, and respecting the last, which was conferred during a visit to London in June, 1835, we have the following reminiscence from the pen of Lord Elgin: "I retain a very pleasing impression of Dr. Chalmers's visit to Oxford in 1835. I do not know that I ever saw him enjoy himself more thoroughly than he seemed to do on that occasion. With the exception, indeed, of the degree conferred upon him by the University, Dr. Chalmers's visit to Oxford was not marked by any very striking incident. What was chiefly interesting to one who esteemed and admired him, was to witness the heartiness with which he entered into the spirit of the place, and the almost boyish delight which he seemed to experience, after the toils of his sojourn in London, in suffering his imagination to expatiate among scenes of academic grandeur and repose. I well remember his coming to my apartment at Merton, before eight o'clock one morning, and telling me of a sequestered court which he had found in a college, into which he had strayed on his way from Christ Church, and the earnestness with which he claimed credit for having thus discovered for himself a spot of surpassing beauty, which could, he assured me, be known to few. I remember, too, the serious manner in which, while we were strolling in the college garden, on the afternoon of the day on which his degree was conferred on him, he apologized for the extravagance of which he had been guilty in purchasing the robes of a Doctor of Civil Law, notwithstanding the precautions I had taken to relieve him from this necessity, saying, 'You see I could not bring myself to leave the place, without carrying away with me some memorial of the academic costume.'

"On the day following his arrival at Oxford, I was requested to endeavor to ascertain whether it would be agreeable to him to receive an honorary degree from the University; and I had afterward the satisfaction of being present when it was conferred on him. Rarely have I witnessed as much enthusiasm in the Oxford theater, as was manifested when he presented himself to go through the ceremony of admission. This was the more gratifying, because it was notorious that on some by no means immaterial points, his views were not coincident with those which obtained at the time with an influential section of the Oxford University public. Indeed, the only expression of regret which fell from him in my hearing during the course of his visit, had reference to the reserve which characterized, as he thought, the manner of some eminent men, connected with a certain theological party, to whom he was introduced, and which prevented him from touching, in conversation with them, upon topics of highest import, with the frank and genial earnestness which was natural to him. This was, however, only a passing remark. Most assuredly there was no indication of lack of cordiality in his reception by Convocation. Dr. Chalmers was himself deeply affected by the warmth with which he was greeted; and I think I might almost venture to say that he looked upon this visit to Oxford as one of the most pleasing incidents in his career."

While thus laboring for the spiritual well-being of his countrymen, and receiving the highest honors of his profession, both at home and abroad, he was still struggling, in his own affairs, with the difficulties attendant upon an office poorly paid.

The theological professorship, previously connected with a

city pastoral charge, when such pluralities were abolished, retained a very inadequate endowment. At Dr. Chalmers's first connection with it, the salary was only one hundred and ninety-six pounds, paid by the Town Council, no fees being taken from theological students. A few years later, this was entirely dried up by the insolvency of the Town Council, and the only remedy provided, was the exaction of a small fee from those who attended the lectures. Dr. Chalmers was thus left dependent upon a precarious income, amounting, on an average, to about four hundred pounds a year, while occupying a place in society involving an outlay of more than eight hundred. Not only for his own sake, but also on account of his successors in office, he felt some effort to obtain an adequate endowment for the professorship to be incumbent on him. A memorial presented to government on the subject, however, failed of success. Consequently, compelled to adopt some method of eking out his insufficient resources, he fell in with a proposal from his publisher, of issuing, in quarterly volumes, a cheap edition of his works. This enterprise was begun in January, 1836. Many of the treatises were greatly enlarged in the course of republication, and most of the first five volumes were entirely new material.

One of the great questions then agitating the British public, was the propriety of religious establishments. An almost universal conviction existed of the necessity of reform in the Church of England and Ireland, and a large party advocated the abolition of the system entirely. This party was largely represented in Parliament. Commissions of inquiry were appointed to look into the matter, who, beginning with the Irish Establishment, led to a reduction in the number of its bishops, and proposals to alienate a large amount of its revenue. The friends of the English church were aroused to their utmost efforts: and among the means adopted by them for defense, a society was organized in London, designated The Christian Influence Society. Early in 1837, Dr. Chalmers was solicited to deliver, before this association, a course of lectures, as the opening of a series devoted to an exposition of its peculiar objects. Viewing this in the light of a most favorable opportunity of bringing forward in didactic, rather than controversial form, his idea of a church establishment, he agreed to undertake the task, but postponed the execution of it until the following spring. The time and care expended in the preparation of these lectures, were amply repaid; none of his productions were received with greater favor, or told with more effect upon their cause. The first of the course was delivered in the Hanover Square Rooms, London, on Wednesday, the 25th April, 1838. None were admitted except those who had received tickets from the society, whose choice had brought together an audience of the highest rank, and most refined education: and yet the effects recorded of the lecturer's power were not inferior to those he had produced upon larger and promiscuous assemblies. The enthusiasm of attendance continued to increase through the whole course. An American clergyman, the Rev. J. A. Clark, who was present at the fourth and fifth, says in regard to them: " The hour at which the lecture was to commence was two o'clock. I thought it necessary to be beforehand in order to secure a seat. When I arrived, I found the hall so perfectly crammed, that at first it seemed impossible to gain admission, but by dint of perseverance I pushed my way onward through the dense crowd, till I had reached nearly the center of the hall. Though the crowd was so great, it was very obvious that the assembly was made up principally of persons in the higher walks of life. Dukes, marquises, earls, viscounts, barons, baronets, bishops, and members of Parliament, were to be seen in every direction. After some considerable delay and impatient waiting, the great charmer made his entrance, and was welcomed with clappings and shouts of applause, that grew more and more intense, till the noise became almost deafening." The concluding lecture was graced by the presence of nine prelates of the Church of England. The tide that had been rising and swelling each succeeding day now burst all bounds. Carried away by the impassioned utterance of the speaker, long ere the close of some of his finest passages was reached, the voice of the lecturer was drowned in the applause, the audience rising from their seats, waving their hats above their heads, and breaking out into tumultuous approbation. Nor was the interest confined to the lecture-room. "Nothing," says Dr. Begg, "could exceed the enthusiasm which prevailed in London. The great city seemed stirred to its very depths. The doctor sat when delivering his lectures, behind a small table; the hall, in front, being densely crowded with one of the most brilliant audiences that ever assembled in Britain. It was supposed that at least five hundred of those present were Peers and members of the House of Commons. Sir James Graham was a very constant attender. The sitting attitude of Dr. Chalmers seemed at first irreconcilable with much energy or effect; but such an anticipation was at once dispelled by the enthusiasm of the speaker, responded to if possible, by the still more intense enthusiasm of the audience; and, occasionally, the effect was even greatly increased, by the eloquent man springing unconsciously to his feet, and delivering with more overwhelming power the more magnificent passages, a movement which, on one occasion, at least, was imitated by the entire audience, when the words, 'the king cannot—the king dare not,' were uttered in accents of prophetic vehemence, that must still ring in the ears of all who heard them, and were responded to by a whirlwind of enthusiasm, which was probably never exceeded in the history of eloquence. Some of us sat on the platform beside the doctor, and near us were the reporters. One seemed to leave the room every five minutes with what he had written, so that by the time the lecture was finished, it was nearly all in print. On the day of the first lecture, which commenced at two o'clock, and terminated about half-past three, some of us went round by the city, and when we reached our dinner table at five o'clock, we were able to present Dr. Chalmers a newspaper, I think the 'Sun,' or 'Globe,' containing a full report of his lecture. Nothing was more striking, however, amidst all this excitement, than the child-like humility of the great man himself. All the flattery seemed to produce no effect whatever on him; his mind was entirely absorbed in his great object; and the same kind, playful, and truly christian spirit, that so endeared him to us all, was everywhere apparent in his conduct. I had the honor afterward, to be introduced to the Duke of Cambridge. He immediately introduced the subject of Dr. Chalmers. 'What does he teach?' said his Royal Highness, rapidly. I intimated that he taught theology. 'Monstrous clever man,' said the duke, 'he could teach anything.'. I have heard Dr. Chalmers on many great occasions, but probably his London lectures afforded the most remarkable illustrations of his extraordinary power, and must be ranked among the most signal triumphs of oratory in any age."

The lectures were immediately published in authentic form; and notwithstanding the anticipations by the newspapers, eight thousand copies were circulated within a year. They were afterward inserted in the series of his works and constitute the most complete embodiment of his ideas " upon the establishment and extension of national churches as affording the only adequate machinery for the moral and christian instruction of a people."

"From the time of his appointment as one of its corresponding members, Dr. Chalmers had cherished the intention of reading a paper before the Royal Institute of France. In execution of this design he left England for Paris early in June, 1838, accompanied by Mrs. Chalmers and two of his daughters. Lady Elgin, Sir John and Lady Hay, Lady Shaw Stewart, and Mr. Erskine, all of whom were there, vied with each other in affording him every opportunity for thoroughly exploring Paris; and to the same kind friends he was indebted for more than one interesting glimpse into the interior of French Society." Superior to the prejudices of nationality, he seems to have carried with him everywhere a heart prepared to be pleased. In the records of his first sight of Paris, he declared himself much impressed with its beauty and lightness up and down the Seine, and delighted with the Tuilleries garden ; its sculpture, its shaded walks,-its groups of pedestrians ; and goes on to note " how much more still and leisurely every thing moves here than in London. All in Paris is within a manageable compass;

and I was not prepared for its being so much less busy, and populous, and extensive, than our own metropolis. It is more a city of loungers; and life moves on at a more rational pace. Its buildings are more impressive."

After spending between two and three weeks in Paris, reading his paper on the Distinction, both in principle and effect, between a legal charity for the relief of indigence, and a legal charity for the relief of disease, before the Royal Institute, making the acquaintance of M. Guizot, and various other eminent literary characters, he made an excursion through the provinces, in the course of which he visited the Duc de Broglie, to whom he had been introduced in Paris, and who had invited him to spend a few days at his country residence. One of the days spent there was a Sabbath, of which we find the following record: "Found the morning worship party in the library at eleven. The Duke read a chapter of the French Bible, the tenth of John, at a table; the Duchess, opposite to him, read sermon, one of Audebez's. We then all knelt, and she uttered a French prayer; could not follow it, but her frequent 'O, Seigneur,' in a most devotional tone, went to my heart. Whether the prayer was extemporaneous or learned by heart, I know not. At three, a small party. Conversed in the Duchess's own apartment, when I read a chapter and expounded. My topic was appropriation, from the tenth chapter of Romans. It gave rise to a brief conversation, chiefly on the part of Mademoiselle Ponnarrie, who must in part have understood me. She is the same I met in Lady Elgin's and who was spoken of to me as likely to translate my 'Natural Theology.' Madame de Stael said I had given her much comfort. All here are Catholics but the Duchess and Madame de Stael. Was shown Diodati's translation of my St. John's Sermons. Family worship in the evening, consisting of a chapter and the Lord's Prayer, at which we knelt, the Duchess officiating; about seven domestics present in the morning, and fifteen in the evening."

Not many months afterward that noble and pious lady was numbered with the dead. In his letter addressed to the Duke on that melancholy bereavement, Dr. Chalmers remarked of her as the most exalted and impressive of all the acquaintances he had made for many years.

From Broglie he and his traveling companion, Mr. Erskine, proceeded to Alencon. " The variety and amount of sweet and engaging landscape, as we pass along quite baffling. A church to the right, another to the left, another onward, projected to the sky. The succession of loveliness prodigious. I now understand the beauty of Normandy." Reaching Tours they ascended the Loire to Orleans, and thence to Pithiviers and Malesherbes, then to Fontainbleau and again to Paris. Looking back upon this tour, he says of it, " a most interesting journey, by which my opinion of the actual state of property in France, and also my views of its eventual, have been made more favorable. Much, however, must be left to time and experience. Have been greatly enlightened by the conversation of the Duc de Broglie.

From a desire to spend the last years of his life in a manner entirely devotional, Dr. Chalmers now put forth all his strength to bring his plans for Church extension to maturity, that he might consign the continuance of them in successful operation to the hands of others, at the General Assembly of 1840, about which time he would conclude his sixtieth year. "It is a favorite speculation of mine," he says, " that if spared to sixty, we then enter on the seventh decade of human life; and that this, if possible, should be turned into the Sabbath of our earthly pilgrimage, and spent sabbatically, as if on the shore of an eternal world, or in the outer courts, as it were, of the temple that is above—the tabernacle in heaven. What enamors me all the more of this idea, is the retrospect of my mother's widowhood. I long, if God should spare me, for such an old age as she enjoyed, spent as if at the gate of heaven, and with such a fund of inward peace and hope as made her nine years' widowhood a perfect feast and foretaste of the blessedness that awaits the righteous."

This, designed to be his last great effort for the cause in which he had spent his strength so long, was to embrace oral addresses in all important places throughout the land. On the 18th of August, 1838, "he began a tour through the south-western districts of Scotland, in the course of which ten Presbyteries, embracing one hundred and seventy ministers, were visited: and addresses on church extension were delivered in Stranraer, Wigton, Greenock, Dunoon, Kilmarnock, Ayr, Paisley, Dumbarton, Hamilton, Lanark, and Biggar. It was a new sphere of effort which Dr. Chalmers had now entered. He was unpracticed in extempory speaking; and yet, without a considerable admixture of this form, he found that he could not adapt himself to the varied and promiscuous audiences which he addressed. He had never taken part in any platform discussion, yet in such public meetings as he now undertook to address, hostile collisions might occur. But he would do all, and dare all, for a cause that was so dear."

About the same time a proposal was made to him by Mr. William Campbell, of Glasgow, which promised greatly to hasten the execution of his plans. In view of many cases of extreme destitution, and of the scanty funds at command of the committee, rendering it necessary to raise most of the money for each new church in the place for which it was erected, Mr. Campbell "suggested that a new fund be created, especially intended to meet cases of extreme destitution; and that this fund should consist of contributions of one pound or upward, for each of the next hundred churches that should be built. If one thousand such subscribers could be obtained in Scotland, then one thousand pounds, a sum adequate to defray the whole cost of the edifice, would be available for each of the new buildings. Mr. Campbell himself offered twenty-five pounds for each such church, coming thus under personal obligation for twenty-five hundred pounds. Dr. Chalmers hailed the proposal with delight, and resolved to devote the whole summer of 1839 to an effort to carry it into execution. The brief interval between the close of the college session and the meeting of the General Assembly, was filled up by visits to Dundee, Perth, Stirling, and Dunfermline. The General Assembly was scarcely dissolved when he resumed his tour, addressing influential audiences at Brechin, Montrose, Arbroath, and making his way to Aberdeen, where a peculiarly brilliant reception was given to him. His progress was interrupted by a summons which called him instantly to London; but the busy and anxious negotiations, in which he there for a time took part, directed though they were to a new and most embarrassing subject, did not divert him from his summer project, for again, and after only a few days of rest in Edinburgh, on his return from the metropolis, we find him setting out on what he called his great northern tour."

On this journey he visited the most important places in the Highlands of Scotland, awakening an active interest wherever he appeared. At Inverness, no less than two thousand pounds were raised for the cause ; yet, upon the whole, the results of this tour of Scotland, did not meet his expectations. He had set out with the confident hope of raising £100,000, and of making another addition of one hundred churches ; but the increasing opposition to establishments, and the conflict with the civil authorities defeated the design. The whole sum raised was not more than £40,000. Upon presenting his report to the General Assembly in 1840, he concluded in the following words:—" The convener of your committee, who has prepared the above report, craves permission to close it with one brief paragraph which is personal to himself. He finds that the labors and requisite attentions of an office which for six years he has so inadequately filled, have now become a great deal too much for him ; and for the sake of other labors and other preparations, more in keeping with the arduous work of a theological professorship, as well as with the powers, and, he may add, the prospects and the duties of advanced life, he begs that he may now be suffered to withdraw. While he rejoices in the experimental confirmation which the history of these few years has afforded him of the resources and the capabilities of the Voluntary system, to which, as hitherto unfostered by the paternal care of Government, the scheme of Church Extension is indebted for all its progress, it still remains his unshaken conviction of that system notwithstanding, that it should only be resorted to as a supplement, and never but in times when the powers of infidelity and intolerance are linked together in hostile combination against the sacred prerogatives of the church, should it once be thought of as a substitute for a national establishment of Christianity. In days of darkness and disquietude, it may open a temporary resource, whether for a virtuous secession, or an ejected church to fall back upon; but a far more glorious consummation is, when the State puts forth its hand to sustain but not to subjugate the church, and the two, bent on moral conquests alone, walk together as fellow-helpers toward the achievement of that great pacific triumph — the christian education of the people. He to whom you assigned so high and honorable an office as the prosecution of this object, and who now addresses you in the capacity of its holder for the last time, will not let go the confident hope, that, under the smile of an approving heaven, and with the blessing from on high, glorious things are yet in reserve for the parishes of Scotland; and though his hand, now waxing feeble, must desist from the performances of other days, sooner will that hand forget its cunning, than he can forget or cease to feel for the church of his fathers."

'At the earnest entreaty of the Assembly, Dr. Chalmers continued at the head of the Extension Committee for another year, nor did he retire from the great field of labor till two hundred and twenty churches—more than one-fifth of its whole complement — had been added to the churches of the Establishment.'

CHAPTER XVI.

Under the Divine blessing, the efforts of Dr. Chalmers had succeeded in working a great revolution in public feeling, in favor of practical Christianity. A spirit of devotion and religious inquiry prevailed, which refused any longer to sit down contented under the empty and drowsy pulpit performances of previous times. The younger clergy had also for years been carrying forth over the land the progressive spirit of their beloved professor, and had given to the evangelical party a strong preponderance in the councils of the church, which went far to repair the corruptions of a century. An end was put to the ordaining of elders merely with a view to holding a seat in the General Assembly; candidates for the ministry were subjected to a closer examination, and their course of instruction enlarged: a stricter supervision was exercised over the conduct and doctrine of ministers; that act of the Assembly of 1799, whereby the ministers of all other denominations were excluded from occupying a pulpit of the Establishment on any occasion, was set aside, and ministerial communion restored with the English and Irish orthodox Presbyterians, one entire body of seceders was received into the national church, and great advances had been made in the cause of foreign missions and of home education. "In 1835, fresh from his field of labor in the east, the church's own first and most honored missionary, Dr. Duff, presented himself before the Assembly, and to his fervent pleadings on behalf of missions, the whole House gave back one unbroken response of direct and grateful acquiescence. Hitherto it had been only on educational destitution existing in the Highlands and Islands of Scotland that the General Assembly had fixed its attention. But now its more wakeful eye was fastened on the like but more fatal destitution existing in the large towns and more populous districts of the Lowlands; and under the counsels of Dr. Welsh, and the vigorous agency of Mr. David Stow, of Glasgow the best basis was laid for an improved and extended national education in the institution of Normal Schools. In 1836, widening still further the embrace of her sympathies and efforts, a scheme was organized, and an annual collection in all the churches was ordered, for the promotion of Christianity in the British colonies, where so many of our expatriated countrymen, through want of the means of grace, had fallen into spiritual forgetfulness. The year 1838 was distinguished by the appointment of a Commission of Inquiry into the state of the Jews, in execution of which Dr. Keith and Dr. Black, Mr. McCheyne and Mr. Bonar, journeyed over Europe to Palestine—furnishing that report upon which a new Scheme for the Conversion of the Jews was added to those formerly existing, and which received from the christian public a general and cordial support. Altogether, in evidence of the rekindled zeal and redoubled energy with which all her public christian enterprises were prosecuted, we can point to the church's collective annual revenue for these objects in the year 1839, as being *fourteen times greater* than it had been in 1834. Speaking of this brief but brilliant period, Dr. Chalmers says:—"We abolished the union of offices—we are planting schools—we are multiplying chapels—we are sending forth missionaries to distant parts of the world—we have purified and invigorated the discipline—we are extending the church, and rallying our population around its venerable standard—we are bringing the sectaries again within its pale—and last, though not least, we have reformed the patronage; and our licentiates, instead of a tutorship in the families of the great as their stepping-stone to preferment, now betake themselves to a parochial assistantship or to a preaching station, with its correspondent home-walk of christian usefulness among the families of the surrounding poor, as the likeliest passage to a higher place in their profession, even as it is the best preparation for the duties of their high calling. And not only is there the visible glow of this great and wholesome reform abroad over the country, or in the outer department of the church, but in the business of its courts and judicatories, in the General Assembly itself, there is the same great and obvious reformation: so that, instead of the ecclesiastico-political arena which it once was, more at least than half its time is taken up with the beseeming cares of a great moral institute, devising for the christian good and the best interests of men both at home and abroad."

It was not possible to proceed far in such a course without coming athwart some self-seeking move of politics or favoritism.

The history of the first collision of that kind shall be retained in the language of Dr. Hanna: "A few months after the passing of the Veto Law by the Assembly of 1834, a presentation was issued by the Earl of Kinnoul to the vacant parish of Auchterarder, in Perthshire. Mr. Young, the presentee, was not in orders, holding only a license from his Presbytery, which permitted him to preach as a candidate for the holy office. After he had preached on two successive Sabbaths in the pulpit of the vacant church, a day was appointed for moderating in a call—that is, for inviting the people to express their concurrence in his settlement. In a parish containing three thousand souls, only two of its inhabitants came forward upon that day to sign the call; and when, in obedience to the recent Act of Assembly, an opportunity was afforded to those male heads of families whose names were on the attested communion roll, of tendering their dissent, out of the three hundred entitled to use this privilege, two hundred and eighty-seven, or more than five-sixths of the whole number, gave in their names as dissentients, and all expressed their readiness to make the solemn declaration, that they were actuated by no factious or malicious motives, but solely by a conscientious regard to the spiritual interests of themselves and the congregation. To afford them time for reconsideration, and an opportunity, if they chose to avail themselves of it, to withdraw their names, the Presbytery adjourned for a fortnight; but at the adjourned meeting, without one exception, they all adhered to their dissent. Before any final judgment was given, in consequence of objections taken to some parts of the Presbytery's proceedings, the case went by appeal before the Synod of Perth and Stirling, and afterward before the General Assembly of 1835. Having repelled the objections which had been taken to the actings of the inferior Court, the Assembly remitted the case to the Presbytery, with instructions 'to proceed in the matter in terms of the Interim Act of last Assembly.' Acting under these instructions, the Presbytery, on the 7th July, 1835, rejected Mr. Young, 'so far as regarded that particular presentation.' Against this rejection the presentee entered an appeal to the Synod, which he afterward abandoned; and it was with mingled curiosity and alarm that the church learned, that in conjunction with the patron he had raised an action against the Presbytery before the Supreme Civil Court, the Court of Session. As the action was originally laid, the Court was asked to review the proceedings of the Presbytery solely with the view of determining the destination of the benefice, and declaring that the just and legal right to the stipend still lay with the rejected presentee. The case, however, had not been in Court more than a few weeks when an ominous change was made upon the whole character of the action. This change, technically denominated 'an amendment of the libel,' was effected by the introduction of new clauses, in which the court was asked to find and declare that the rejection of Mr. Young, expressly on the ground of a veto by the parishioners, was illegal, being contrary to statute, and that the Presbytery was still under statutory obligation to Mr. Young upon trial, and if found qualified to ordain him as minister of the parish. The case, the novelty and importance of which began now to be universally appreciated, was ordered to be heard before all the judges. The pleadings began on the 21st November, and closed on the 12th of the succeeding month. On the 27th February, 1838, and on six subsequent days, the judges delivered their opinions, deciding, by a majority of eight to five, in favor of the pursuers and against the church. The majority was composed of the Lord President (Hope), Lord Gillies, the Lord Justice-Clerk (Boyle), Lord Meadowbank, Lord Mackenzie, Lord Medwyn, Lord Corehouse, and Lord Cunninghame. The minority consisted of Lord Fullerton, Lord Moncrieff, Lord Glenlee, Lord Jeffrey, and Lord Cockburn. The judgment of the Court, delivered on the 8th March, did not cover the whole of the conclusions craved by the pursuers; but after repelling the objections which had been taken to the jurisdiction of the Court, and the competency of the action, restricted itself to finding, that in rejecting Mr. Young, 'on the sole ground that a majority of male heads of families, communicants in the said parish, have dissented, without any reason assigned, from his admission as minister, the Presbytery have acted illegally and in violation of their duty, and contrary to the provisions of certain statutes libeled on.'

"Throughout all the lengthened arguments delivered at the Bar and from the Bench, the two leading questions which were carefully distinguished from each other, and subjected to separate discussion, were,—1. The legality of the Veto Law,— whether the church, under statute or otherwise, was legally competent to enact such a law, and whether, in enacting it, she had violated any statute of the realm; and, 2. The competence of the Court of Session to interfere, in case it should find the Veto Law to be illegal, for any other purpose, and to any other effect, than simply to regulate the destination of the benefice. The pleadings at the Bar, as well as the opinions delivered from the Bench, left a certain amount of obscurity resting upon both these leading topics. It sometimes seemed as if the alleged illegality of the Veto Law lay exclusively in the conclusive force bestowed upon an arbitrary dissent of a majority, and in the church having thereby transferred to the people a privilege which, though possessed by herself, she was not at liberty to alienate; so that if taking Mr. Young upon trial, and looking upon his non-acceptability as a disqualification, she were on that ground by her own authority and upon her own judgment to reject him, she would be guilty of no breach of any statute. In the arguments, again, by which the competency of the Court of Session to adjudicate upon this case was sustained, it was difficult to know whether it was affirmed or not, that over all such actings of church Courts as directly or indirectly carried civil consequences, the Court of Session claimed the same authority which it possessed and exercised over all the inferior civil tribunals of the kingdom, or whether any separate standing and exclusive jurisdiction was allowed to the ecclesiastical judicatories. The Court of Session had considered itself competent to declare that a Presbytery which, acting under the explicit directions of the supreme ecclesiastical tribunal, had done nothing but carry out a law of the Assembly, had done an illegal act. But was it prepared to do here what, in every like case of a purely civil character, it was its right and duty to do—to order the Presbytery to proceed as it directed; and holding the Veto Law as a nullity simply because it, the Court of Session, held it so, to take the necessary steps toward the presentee's ordination: and in case of the Presbytery's disobedience, was it prepared by the ordinary compulsitors of law—by fine or imprisonment—to enforce obedience to its edict? In itself the sentence pronounced by the Court was equivocal. Declaring what the Presbytery had done to be illegal, it stopped short of declaring or prescribing what the Presbytery should do. That sentence might have been given though all that the Court meant to interfere with was the appropriation of the stipend. One thing alone was clearly and conclusively determined by it, that should the Church persist in rejecting Mr. Young, she incurred thereby the forfeiture of the benefice. It was to prevent, if possible, this forfeiture that, at its meeting in May, 1838, the General Assembly instructed its law officer to appeal the case to the House of Lords. That there might be no misunderstanding, however, of the position relative to the Civil Courts assumed by the church; the same Assembly passed a very memorable resolution. The church's separate and exclusive spiritual jurisdiction, though not yet actually invaded, was most seriously menaced. Opinions had been uttered, both at the Bar and from the Bench which went to strip her of all those liberties and privileges, which, given her by her Great Head, she believed had been amply guaranteed to her by statute, and which, except in the darkest periods of her persecution, she had freely exercised and enjoyed. The blow had not yet been struck which should lay her prostrate beneath the secular power, but the arm was lifted, and there seemed no want of will to strike. Calmly, solemnly, resolutely, in front of the impending danger she took up her ground — ground from which she never swerved. By a majority of 183 to 142 the General Assembly of 1838 resolved—

"That the General Assembly of this church, while they unqualifiedly acknowledge the exclusive jurisdiction of the Civil Courts in regard to the civil rights and emoluments secured by law to the church and the ministers thereof, and will ever give and inculcate implicit obedience to their decisions thereanent, do resolve, that as it is declared in the Confession of Faith of this National Established Church, that the Lord Jesus Christ is King and Head of the Church, and hath therein appointed a government in the hands of church officers distinct from the civil magistrate, and that in all matters touching the doctrine, government, and discipline of the church, her judicatories possess an exclusive jurisdiction, founded on the Word of God, which 'power ecclesiastical (in the words of the Second Book of Discipline) flows from God, and the Mediator, Jesus Christ, and is spiritual, not having a temporal head on earth but only Christ; the only spiritual King and Governor of his Kirk;' and they do further resolve, that this spiritual jurisdiction and supremacy, and sole headship of the Lord Jesus Christ, on which it depends, they will assert, and at all hazards defend, by the help and blessing of that great God who, in the days of old, enabled their fathers, amid manifold persecutions, to maintain a testimony even to the death, for Christ's kingdom and crown: And, finally, that they will firmly enforce obedience to the same upon all office-bearers and members of this church, by the execution of her laws in the exercise of the ecclesiastical authority wherewith they are invested."

"Nearly a year had elapsed ere the Auchterarder case was heard before the House of Lords. Lords Brougham and Cottenham having delivered their opinions on the 2d and 3d May, 1839, and their opinions substantially agreeing, the sentence of that court was passed, dismissing the appeal and confirming the deliverance of the Court of Session. For one thing, at least, the Church of Scotland had to thank these noble Lords: their speeches cleared away all the ambiguity which had rested upon the discussion of the court below. It was by a simple and very short line of argument that they each arrived at their interpretation of the law of Patronage. By the concluding clause of the Act of Queen Anne restoring patronages, the Act 1592 had been revived, and became the governing statute upon this subject. That statute ordains 'that all presentations to benefices be directed to the particular Presbyteries, with full power to give collation thereupon, and to put order to all matters and causes ecclesiastical within their bounds, according to the discipline of the Kirk; provided the aforesaid Presbyteries be bound and astricted to receive and admit whatsoever qualified minister presented by His Majesty or lay patrons.' According to the interpretation put upon this statute by Lords Brougham and Cottenham, the sole province of the church in the matter of collation, beyond which she cannot travel without subjecting herself to civil coercion, is to judge of the personal qualifications of the presentee, and in so judging she must strictly limit herself to an inquiry into his life, literature, and manners. 'With respect to qualification,' said Lord Brougham, 'I am somewhat surprised to find in the very able and learned arguments from the Bench below, an attempt made to show that qualification is of such extensive meaning, that within its scope may be brought the whole of the matter at present in dispute—namely, the acceptableness and reception of the party presented by the congregation as finding favor in their sight. * * * I am going to show your Lordships that no such meaning can possibly, by the law of Scotland, be given to the word 'qualified.' It is a technical word in this question; it is not the word 'qualified' used in its general sense, as you talk of a man's qualities—of his capacity—of his abilities—of his merits, which are all general phrases, and none of them technically defined. The word 'qualified' is as much a known word of the law, and has as much a technical sense imposed upon it by the statutes—by the law authorities—by the opinions of commentators—by the dicta of judges—as the word 'qualification' has when used to express a right to kill game, or when used to express a right to vote in the election of a member of Parliament. * * * It means a qualification in literature, life, and morals, to be judged of by the Presbytery; and no one talks of interfering with that right of so judging by them.' The Lord Chancellor was equally explicit: 'But if it be clear, as it certainly is, that the qualifications referred to in the statutes are personal qualifications—'literature, life, and manners'—'there can be no ground for contending that the dissent of the majority of the heads of families is a disqualification within the meaning of the statutes. * * * The absolute right of patronage, subject only to the rejection of the presentee by the adjudication of the Presbytery for want of qualification, which is secured by the statute, is inconsistent with the exercise of any volition by the inbahitants, however expressed.' Such an interpretation confined the jurisdiction of the church to the one single topic of judging of the presentee's life, literature, and manners, and deprived the congregation or general body of communicants of all standing, weight, and influence in the settlement of ministers. It was an interpretation altogether new—new to every party of churchmen in Scotland, and inconsistent with the whole current of hitherto unchallenged laws and actings of the church. When a patron happened to present a clergyman already ordained, upon whose personal qualifications the church had already passed approving judgment, in such a case, and according to this interpretation, no ground or liberty of rejecting him remained. Lord Brougham, referring expressly to such a case, declared that nothing so wild had ever been urged as the supposition that the church could claim or exercise such a right; and yet up to this time, neither among the lawyers nor the ecclesiastics of Scotland had there ever been a doubt as to the church's possession of this right—her whole proceeding in the instance of the translation of ordained clergymen from one parish to another was based upon its existence—in innumerable cases had it been exercised, ordained presentees having been rejected, and yet never once, whether in court civil or ecclesiastical, had this power of rejection been challenged. In 1817, Dr. Hill, the leader of the Moderate party, introduced and carried a measure in the General Assembly, by which the union of a professorship in a college and the ministerial charge of a country parish was prohibited. By this new version, however, of the law of Patronage, such a measure was *ultra vires* of the Assembly, and any professor rejected upon the ground of this prohibition had only to bring his case before the Civil Court to have his right to admission confirmed and enforced. So universal was the conviction that the church's prerogative extended beyond a mere adjudication upon life, literature, and morals, that when, in 1833, Dr. Chalmers first introduced the Veto Law, Dr. Cook's motion, which on that occasion was carried, declared it competent for the heads of families to give in objections, of whatever nature, against the presentee, and for the Presbytery, if they thought such objections to be well-grounded, to reject him. In the discussion which then took place, Dr. Cook strenuously affirmed ' that the church regarded qualification as including much more than learning, moral character and sound doctrine—as extending, in fact, to the fitness of the presentees, in all respects, for the particular situation to which they were appointed."

" Had the interpretation now put upon the Law of Patronage, been known in the preceding century, to what an amount of ecclesiastical litigation about calls would it have put an immediate and final termination. For many years in the earlier part of that century, and so long as that party still predominated which was resolved to carry out the principle, which the church had so often declared to be a fundamental one, that no pastor should be intruded into any congregation contrary to the will of the people, cases continually occurred in which presentees were rejected on no other ground whatever, than the insufficiency of the call — their want of acceptability to the people; but there never was a case of any such rejected presentee having recourse to the Court of Session, because neither in the Parliament House nor in the Assembly, had this new view been broached, of the unfettered right of the patron. When the Moderate party, under the able guidance of Lord Brougham's distinguished relative, Principal Robertson, began that course of policy, which, after many a painful conflict, finally reduced the call to a mere dead form, the struggle was restricted entirely to the Church Courts, which it certainly would not have been, had it ever been imagined that so summary a method of settlement was available as that supplied by the decision of the House of Lords.

"The mere novelty, however, of this interpretation of a single law, was not nearly so alarming as were those general views as to the constitution of the church, and the nature and consequences of her connection with the State, upon which that interpretation obviously and ostensibly was based. The church's power, in this single case, had been limited to such narrow boundaries, because no statute could be found which distinctly and specifically bestowed upon her any other or wider range of action. It was in vain that the church's advocates spoke of powers and privileges — of a constitution and polity possessed by her, not in virtue of any donation by the State, but in virtue of her divine institution by Christ. It was in vain that they pointed to the many express statutory recognitions and ratifications of her government and discipline, as flowing to her from her great spiritual head. It was in vain that turning to that very Act of 1592, by help of which the right of the patron was to be carried triumphantly over all those defenses against the intrusion of unacceptable ministers, which the church had erected, they quoted the clause which gave the church full power to put order to all matters and causes ecclesiastical, *according to the discipline of the Kirk.* It was in vain that they quoted another portion of this same statute, in which, referring to and repealing a previous Act, which had asserted the Royal supremacy over all persons and causes ecclesiastical, it was declared that it " should no ways be prejudicial, nor derogate anything from the *privilege that God has given* to the spiritual office-bearers in the Kirk, concerning heads of religion, matters of heresy, excommunication, *collation or deprivation of ministers*, or any such like censures specially grounded and having warrant of the Word." The statute had spoken only of judging of the presentee's qualifications, and beyond that the church must not proceed. If in her judicial capacity she had frequently prevented the settlement of ministers, against whose " life, literature, and manners," nothing could be alleged ; if in her legislative capacity she had passed many laws, imposing other restrictions upon patronage than the single one now allowed, her judgments were illegal, her laws were impotent. Instead of her own old conception that she had all freedom, except that which statute specifically denied, the new conception was that she had no freedom except that which statute specifically granted. Adopting this conception, ' one-half, and more than one-half, of the privileges of the church would be disallowed; and she would be rendered more bare of honor and prerogative, than even any ordinary corporation, whose privileges may be asserted and ascertained by an appeal to the general practice of the constitution.'

" In their sentence, the Court of Session had refrained from laying any order upon the Presbytery, and the House of Lords did nothing more than simply affirm that sentence. In the forwardness of his zeal, however, Lord Brougham volunteered to instruct the Court of Session as to their future course. 'And then,' said his lordship, ' may come this question, What is the Court of Session to do upon the petitory part of the summons, supposing that shall be insisted upon ? Enough it is for me to-day to observe that this is not now before us. But suppose it were, I should have no fear in dealing with it. I should at once make an order upon the Presbytery to admit, if duly

qualified, and to disregard the dissent of the congregation; and if they did not admit, they broke the laws, they acted illegally, and were liable to the consequences, civil and other, of disobeying the positive and clear order of a statute.".....
"Still, it is affirmed that the Presbytery may persist in refusing. My lords, it is indecent to suppose any such case. You might as well suppose that Doctors' Commons would refuse to attend to a prohibition from the Court of King's Bench; you might as well suppose that the Court of Session, when you remit a cause with orders to alter the judgment, would refuse to alter it."

Never once during all that period when litigations about conflicting presentations, and the settlement of ministers thereupon, had been so numerous, had the Court of Session ventured upon such an act as that which they were now so heartily counseled to perform. They had been once asked to do a kindred deed, but they had refused to interfere, "because that was interfering with the power of ordination, or the internal policy of the church, with which the lords thought that they had nothing to do." Should the Presbytery persist in refusing to settle Mr. Young, one clause of the very act upon which so much was grounded, might have suggested to Lord Brougham another alternative than the one which he had suggested: "Providing always, in case the Presbytery refuses to admit any qualified minister presented to them by the patron, it shall be lawful to the patron to retain the whole fruits of the said benefice in his own hands." If Presbyteries were under statutory obligation to admit qualified presentees, and by the ordinary compulsitors of the law could be forced to fulfill such obligation, how came such a clause as this into that very Act, by which, as it was alleged, that very obligation was imposed? That clause, indeed, stands upon the statute-book as a perpetual protest against that series of encroachments upon the spiritual prerogatives of the church, upon which the Court of Session was now hastening to embark, and a perpetual vindication of that position, which, as the sequel will indicate, the church felt herself compelled to occupy.

"The speeches of Lords Brougham and Cottenham were delivered early in May, 1839, and had great influence in determining the proceedings of the General Assembly, which commenced its sittings on the 16th of that month. They effected a very important change in that course of policy which Dr. Chalmers had been prepared to advise. He was in no way particularly wedded to the Veto Law. Regarding it only as one mode of gaining a certain end—the hindering of bad, and the promoting of good, appointments—he was ready to make any change in the mode, if only the same end could be realized. The decision of the Court of Session had made it clear that whenever a rejection under the Veto Law took place, a forfeiture of the temporalities of the living would ensue. But up to the time when the Lord Chancellor and Lord Brougham had delivered their opinions, he had been convinced that if relinquishing the form of procedure established by the Veto Law, and falling back upon her own intrinsic powers, the church were to sit in judgment upon each case of settlement as it occurred, she would be able to prevent all improper intrusion of parties upon reclaiming congregations. He had been prepared, therefore, to advise that the Assembly should repeal the Veto Law; and, with a general declaration of a resolution to maintain the principle of Non-Intrusion, should commit the whole matter in the first instance to the Presbyteries of the Church. These speeches of the two chancellors taught him that a veto by the Presbytery would now be held to be as illegal as a veto by the congregation; and that to repeal the Veto Law would bring them no nearer to the effecting of such a harmony between the law of the State as interpreted by the highest legal functionaries of the realm, and the law and practices of the church, for the prevention of intrusion, as should hinder the dissevering of the benefice from the cure of souls. Assuming that the church were to stand firm in her purpose, to take no part in the ordination of men whom she conscientiously believed to be unfit for that particular charge to which they had been presented, it was obvious that the desired harmony could be attained only through the intervention of the Legislature. A direct and immediate application to the Legislature seemed, therefore, the fittest, if not the only course for the church to pursue. For six years past, Dr. Chalmers had not been a member of the General Assembly, and with the exception of reading his annual report on Church Extension, he had taken little part in the general management of church affairs. But a truly momentous crisis had now arrived, before which his strong purpose of retirement gave way, and every energy of his nature was devoted to the guidance of the church through the troubled and perilous passage. He entered the conflict with an anxious but unembarrassed spirit. Mere party ties had but little hold on him. With many of the opinions held, and many of the sentiments uttered by some of the most prominent evangelical leaders, he had no sympathy. He did not participate in the conviction that the right to choose their own ministers, belonged, by divine donation to the people. He disliked when the contest on which the church had now fairly entered was represented as a contest for the rights of the christian people; nor could he approve of the phraseology, rife now in some quarters, according to which the privileges of communicants, in the matter of the appointment of their religious instructors, was spoken of as part of the liberty wherewith Christ had made his people free. Believing in the existence of no divine right, wedded to no abstract theory, his position was, that the church should be left to carry out her own conscientious convictions—should be left unbribed and unfettered to do what she thought best for the christian good of the people ; and, as his own convictions most cordially went along with what the church had declared to be a fundamental principle of her policy, he was prepared at any hazard, to take any necessary step, at once for the preservation of the church's general freedom, and the protection of the church's humblest congregations. The General Assembly, upon whose deliberations and decisions so much was now depending, met at Edinburgh on the 16th of May, 1839. Scarcely had the necessary preliminaries been concluded, when Dr. Cook, the leader of the Moderate party rose to say that there was one question of such pre-eminent importance, that he wished the day for its discussion to be fixed without delay; intimating, at the same time, his intention to submit a resolution regarding it to the House. On the following Monday, three motions were read and tabled; one by Dr. Cook, one by Dr. Chalmers, and one by Dr. Muir. The discussion was fixed to be on Wednesday, and for several hours before the Assembly convened upon that day, the house was crowded in every corner. The days were past when the Edinburgh public suffered an Assembly to go by with little other notice than that which the military cortège of the Commissioner excited. Interests were now at stake, in which Scotland's remotest extremities were concerned; and the great heart of the body ecclesiastic, beat fuller and stronger as each returning Assembly came round. Participating in those deep and solemn feelings, which had gathered many a group of the faithful over the land around the throne of grace, the General Assembly, before the debate began, called upon the venerable minister of Kilsyth to engage in prayer. Dr. Cook opened the discussion. His motion was to the effect that the Assembly should hold the Veto Law as abrogated, and proceed as if it never had passed. Dr. Chalmers's motion consisted of three parts. The first embraced an acknowledgment of, and acquiescence in, the loss of the temporalities of the living of Auchterarder; the second contained the expression of a resolution that the principle of Non-Intrusion was not to be abandoned; and the third proposed the appointment of a committee to confer with the Government, in order to prevent any further collision between the civil and ecclesiastical authorities. The magnificent oration in which Dr. Chalmers supported this motion, occupied three hours in its delivery; and so great and exhausting was the effort, that he had to retire from the court immediately, nor was he able to return to give his vote at the close of the debate. The discussion had commenced at twelve o'clock on Wednesday the 22d, and at two o'clock, on the morning of the following day, when it was announced as the result of the vote, that Dr. Chalmers's motion was carried by a majority of forty-nine, the irrepressible cheer that burst from the galleries, told in what direction, and how strongly, the popular current was running."

Consequent upon this vote a committee was appointed with Dr. Chalmers at its head, whose first effort " was to obtain from the Legislature a confirmation as to civil consequences of the Veto Law." As the best way of opening negotiations, they concluded to send a large deputation to London, and Dr. Chalmers was induced to interrupt his northern tour, in order to assist in it. In company with Dr. Gordon, Dr. Dewar, Dr. Candlish, and others, he accordingly proceeded to wait upon the members of the cabinet, and some of the more eminent parliamentary leaders. Lord Melbourne, who was then premier, had, on the occasion of a former deputation on the subject, expressed, in his own refined style, a hope that " that d—d fellow Chalmers was not among them," and now, while treating Dr. Gordon and the rest with respectful attention, most carefully avoided Dr. Chalmers. The sifting which his vacillating conduct in relation to the question of new endowments received, had made him cautious of coming in contact with the same strong intellect again.

Upon the whole, the deputation felt encouraged by their reception, having received the assurance, from several members of the government, " that they were fully impressed with the importance of the subject, and would give it their most serious consideration, and that they would give instructions to the Lord Advocate to prepare, along with the Procurator, a measure to be submitted to the cabinet," and that, " in the disposal of those livings which are at the nomination of the Crown, its patronage will most certainly be exercised in accordance with the existing law of the church, a resolution which applies to nearly one-third of the parishes of Scotland."

In 1835 another case of conflict between the civil and ecclesiastical powers occurred. The Crown, as patron of the parish, presented Mr. Clark as assistant and successor to the aged and infirm minister of Lethendy. In conformity to the veto of the congregation, the Presbytery refused to ordain, and the case being carried by appeal before the General Assembly, the Presbytery was sustained. Afterward, Mr. Clark brought an action against the Presbytery in Court of Session. The minister of Lethendy in the meanwhile died, and the Crown finding the parish still vacant, issued another presentation in favor of Mr. Kessen; the Presbytery, when about to ordain him, were served with an interdict from the Court of Session, forbidding them to proceed. Craving advice of the General Assembly, which met in 1838, they were by an almost unanimous voice of that body, ordered to go forward with the ordination. Upon the day appointed for that purpose, when the Presbytery had assembled, " the agent of Mr. Clark sought and obtained leave to read an opinion from an eminent lawyer in Edinburgh. It came from the Dean of Faculty, the leading counsel and chief adviser in all the legal measures taken against the church. It was sufficiently startling, and had the ministers who sat to listen to it been men of infirm principle or yielding purpose, it might well have shaken their determination, for it hung over them the weightiest terrors of the law. 'The members of the Presbytery,' said the dean, 'will most infallibly be committed to prison, and most justly.' It had been said, that in acting as he had done, Mr. Clark had been guilty of contempt of the church, and some had even spoken of depriving him of his license, so as to take from him the ground that gave him his legal standing. The dean at once placed the rights of Mr. Clark upon what seemed to him a broader and surer basis. 'The deliverance of the Assembly attempts illegally to trample on Mr. Clark's rights as a British subject; for *any man in this country who adheres to its doctrines, is entitled to be a member of the Established Church.* The rights of Mr. Clark as a probationer, in this respect, are as sacred as those of a layman. He was legally entitled to his license, and he holds it as a British subject.' Perhaps it was their clear conception of the length to which such a doctrine would go in exposing the whole discipline, as well as the whole government, of the church to secular dictation and control, which helped to fortify this Presbytery against all the arguments and threats by which they were assailed. Unmoved by these, they ordained Mr. Kessen to be minister of Lethendy. They had now to face a more trying ordeal. The act of ordination had no sooner been consummated than a complaint was lodged against them for a breach of interdict, and they were summoned to appear at the bar of the Court in Edinburgh, on the 14th June, 1839. In itself, it was a formidable enough matter to be dragged from their quiet country charges and to be pilloried for public observation in an uncongenial court, and before an unsympathizing bar. But it was as criminals, guilty of a contempt of constituted authorities — it was for punishment as such that they were to appear. The dean had pledged his word that they should be imprisoned, and there were not wanting other tokens that his prophesy might be verified. A very deep sympathy on their behalf was excited, and one or two of the leading clergymen of Edinburgh resolved to accompany them to the bar. The day arrived. When the twelve judges took their places on the bench, they had a court room before them crowded densely to the door. The Presbytery was summoned to appear. They entered, accompanied by a few friends. The crowd through which they passed had already closed, when once more it opened, and with meek, but dignified demeanor, Dr. Gordon stepped forward to place himself at their side. There was something singularly appropriate in the act. No minister of equal talent had been more unobtrusive, or shown a stronger aversion to popular agitation, or anything like public display. But now that clergymen, who had mingled in the strife of parties as little as himself were called to suffer for conscience' sake, he felt compelled, in the most public manner to countenance and support them.

" 'Gentlemen,' said the Lord President, after their names had been read over, and the citation read, ' I have to ask you, one and all, whether, by yourselves or counsel, you have anything to say, and what you have to say, in explanation or vindication of your conduct ?'

" 'As my name,' said the Rev. Mr. Stirling, of Cargill, ' is the first on the list, and as I happen to be the senior minister present, I have been intrusted by my brethren with the statement which they wish to make to the court.' The following statement was then read by him : 'My Lords—We appear in obedience to the citation of your lordships, inasmuch as we hold it to be the duty of all subjects to render their personal compearance when cited by the civil courts; and being deeply impressed with the obligation of giving all honor and reverence to the judges of the land, we disclaim any intention of disrespect to the court in what we have done. But in ordaining to the office of the holy ministry, and in admitting to the pastoral charge, to which, in our procedings complained of, we strictly limited ourselves, we acted in obedience to the superior church judicatories, to which, in matters spiritual, we are subordinate, and to which, at ordination, we vowed obedience.' Mr. Kessen, having read a similar statement, the judges retired for consultation, and the court adjourned. By a narrow majority the clergymen escaped imprisonment, and were subjected only to the solemn censure of the court. In pronouncing the censure, the Lord President took occasion to say—'I am directed by the Court to signify that it was not without considerable difficulty their Lordships brought themselves to adopt this lenient measure; but they desired me to state, that if you or any other Presbytery of the church were ever brought before them again under similar circumstances, you and they will be dealt with in a very different manner. The ordinary punishment for disobedience to the law, by a breach of interdict, is imprisonment ; and I am directed to say, that if a case like the present should occur again, that punishment will be resorted to.' "

The church and the civil authority were now in direct conflict, each claiming to be in the exercise of their constitutional rights. The matter was about to come before the Legislature for decision, and had the church enjoyed the harmonious support of her own members, the judgment in her favor might have been less doubtful; but the party called Moderate, though now in the minority, were still struggling to the utmost of their power to retard that progress, which they could not entirely obstruct. When Dr. Chalmers, on the 14th of August, 1839, presented before the Assembly's Commission the report of the deputation, no sooner had he sat down than Dr. Cook "rose to declare that the announcement just made that the Government of the country intended to exercise their patronage in conformity with the Veto Law, appeared to him to be nothing short of a violation of the law on the part of the Crown. In the leading case which came before the court, he put forth all his strength of argument to prove that the Veto Law was now defunct — the decision of the civil courts had blotted it out of the statute-book of the church. The casting of such an imputation on the Crown, and the continuance of a vigorous opposition in the church courts, though calculated to increase the existing embarrassments, may have appeared to the Moderate party necessary for the vindication at once of their principles and their consistency. We can offer no such excuse for the next step taken by the Dean of Faculty. If not, as generally believed, the prompter, he had been the vigorous promoter of all the litigation by which the church had been harassed. The struggle had now been carried to a different arena, where his interference was less called for, and, perhaps, not so appropriate. He had power, however, even in that quarter to hinder the church's getting what she asked; and with the laborious diligence which distinguished all his doings, he exerted that power in the production of an enormous pamphlet, given to the public soon after the close of the Commission." An able response from the pen of Dr. Chalmers was issued within the same year. But this difference among the professed friends of the Church of Scotland must have operated unfavorably upon the minds of men, such as most of the members of Parliament were, ignorant of the real nature of her constitution and claims.

"In June, 1837, Mr. Edwards was presented to the church and parish of Marnoch. Having acted previously, for a period of three years, as assistant to the former incumbent, he was well known to the parishioners, and so unacceptable were his ministrations, that at their urgent and almost unanimous desire, their aged pastor had dispensed with his services. In a parish whose population was about 2800 souls, his call was signed by one solitary communicant, the keeper of the inn at which the Presbytery were wont to dine. Out of 300 heads of families whose names were on the communion-roll, 261 tendered their dissent. Acting under special direction of the General Assembly 1838, the Presbytery of Strathbogie rejected Mr. Edwards; and on this rejection being intimated to the patrons, the trustees of the Earl of Fife presented another individual to the charge. Upon the issuing of this second presentation, Mr. Edwards applied for and obtained an interdict from the Court of Session, prohibiting the Presbytery from proceeding with the settlement. After due consideration of this document, and with the declared principles and recent practice of the church before them, the Presbytery resolved ' That the Court of Session having authority in matters relating to the induction of ministers, and having interdicted all proceedings on the part of the Presbytery in this case, and it being the duty of the Presbytery to submit to their authority regularly interponed, the Presbytery do delay all procedure until the matters in dispute be legally determined.' This judgment was brought under review of the General Assembly of 1839. The circumstances being precisely similar to those which had occurred at Lethendy, the Presbytery might have been enjoined to take the same course which had been prescribed to the Presbytery of Dunkeld. Instead of this they were simply instructed to suspend all further proceedings in the matter till the following General Assembly. Avoiding all immediate and direct collision between the Presbytery and Court of Session, this decision was one which even those who disapproved most vehemently of the recent actings of the church could have no difficulty in obeying; and it was framed so as to lay the least possible pressure upon the majority of a Presbytery well known to be so affected. While the church was dealing thus tenderly with her own children, under the first indications of a refractory and rebellious spirit, Mr. Edwards was pressing on the action which he had raised against the Presbytery in the Court of Session; and in June, 1839, he obtained a judgment in his favor, by which it was declared that, notwithstanding the veto put by the people on his appointment, the Presbytery were still bound to take him upon trial with a view to ordination. As this judgment was purely a declaratory one, unaccompanied by any such order as Lord Brougham had suggested as the proper means of enforcing obedience, the Presbytery with perfect safety, and without violating their own convictions, might have delayed, at least till the compulsitors of law had been applied. Their newborn allegiance, however, to the Court of Session was too ardent to admit of delay, and no sooner was its sentence notified, than, with needless haste, and with a violence and irregularity of movement which found no defender, even among the leaders of the Moderate party, by a majority of seven to three, they resolved to bid open defiance to their ecclesiastical superiors, and to proceed forthwith to settle Mr. Edwards as minister at Marnoch. It was in these circumstances that the case came before the Commission of Assembly on the 11th December, 1839. In vain were the seven refractory clergymen asked to reconsider their extraordinary resolution; in vain were they assured that if they would only desist procedure, and in the meantime do nothing, all judgment upon their contumacy would be waived, and the Commission would be content simply to remit the matter to the General Assembly in May. They would make no concession. They would neither express any regret for the past, nor give any promise as to the future. Its authority thus openly defied, its laws and decisions thus daringly trampled on, what was the church to do? In the way of prevention rather than of punishment—to take from them for a season that power which they had openly declared it to be their purpose to employ in a manner so flagrantly unlawful—it was resolved that they should be suspended from exercising the functions of the holy ministry. In a speech of extraordinary ability, Dr. Candlish moved this resolution," which was warmly supported by Dr. Chalmers, and carried by a majority of a hundred and twenty-one to fourteen. The refractory majority of the Presbytery of Strathbogie being thus suspended from office, the minority were instructed to take measures for supplying the vacant parishes with ministerial services. A deputation of committee appointed to open a friendly correspondence with the suspended ministers appointed Aberdeen as a place of meeting, but on arriving there, were met by "a legal agent who put into their hands a paper signed by the seven clergymen, in which they declined the interview. Already, indeed, had proof too palpable been afforded that all hope of reconciliation was gone. On the day after that on which the sentence of suspension was passed, and while the Commission was still sitting, a notarial protest, at the instance of these ministers, was served upon that court; and a few days thereafter, as if no judgment against them was in force, they assembled as if in Presbytery, and proceeded to take Mr. Edwards upon trial. The protection sought for and relied upon was that of the Civil Court, to which they presented an application, in which they called upon the court to suspend the sentence of the Commission—to prevent its intimation and execution—to prohibit the minority from acting as a Presbytery, and to interdict all clergymen of the church from preaching or discharging any of the functions of the ministry in any of their parishes. The demand was so broad and startling that even the Court of Session for the moment drew back. 'In this case,' said the Lord President, 'the Court are prepared to grant the interdict, but not to the full extent prayed for. The complainers prayed the court to interdict and prohibit the parties complained of from preaching in the respective parishes of the complainers. Now, the court could not prevent any man preaching in these parishes. Any one might preach in the open air, for instance. The court had jurisdiction only over the parish churches, the churchyard, the schoolroom, and the bell.' Taking in the meantime this limited view of its jurisdiction, the court interdicted the minority of the Presbytery, and all others, from using, in executing the sentence of the Commission, any of the places and buildings specified by the Lord President. Acknowledging as it so fully did, the court's right of entire control over all its temporalities, the church yielded immediate compliance with this interdict. The clergymen appointed to intimate the judgment of the

Commission either preached in the open air or under such shelter as some neighboring shed or barn could furnish. Then and afterward an opportunity was opened for the effective preaching of the gospel over a wide district of country. Some of the ablest ministers of the church were deputed by the Commission to officiate in the parishes of the suspended clergymen. In Marnoch, and the seven parishes in its neighborhood, their warm and zealous ministry gathered around them crowds of attentive and devout hearers. 'I have no words,' wrote one of these clergymen, 'to describe the scenes of yesterday at Marnoch. Never in my life has it been my privilege to witness such intensity of feeling as in that congregation. Men and women were bathed in tears; numbers rose to their feet, and stood in breathless attention, and at the close of the service all seemed unwilling to retire.' In proportion, however, to the interest excited among the people must have been the annoyance to the suspended clergymen. Unsatisfied with the exclusive possession of their churches, churchyards, and schoolhouses, they renewed their application to the Court of Session, which, on the 14th February, by a decision which outran all its predecessors, granted to its full extent the prayer of their primary petition. In doing so, that court not only suspended a spiritual censure passed by the proper ecclesiastical authorities, being guilty thus of a direct interference with the spiritual discipline of the church, but by drawing a fence round a whole district of the country, and by prohibiting any member of the Establishment from preaching or administering the sacraments within its bounds, it at once deprived such of the people as remained true to the church, of all freedom to worship God according to their conscience, and it assumed the right of dictating to the church where, and where only, by whom and to whom, the ordinances of the gospel were to be administered. It was an open invasion of the most sacred territory of the church, and it met with a resistance at once prompt and decisive."

Repeatedly were interdicts served upon those clergymen who had received appointments to preach in the "banned district," but they, conceiving that the Civil Court had transcended its legitimate powers in forbidding them to preach, paid no attention to what proved to be but empty threats. For notwithstanding what had been previously asserted of punishment, the Court of Session did not feel safe in risking its authority so far. "To give their brethren the sanction of their example, Dr. Chalmers, Dr. Makellar, Dr. Gordon and others of like standing in the church, in the face of interdicts served personally upon each of them, went and preached in the district of Strathbogie." . . . "It was a state of things, however, too anomalous to be suffered to continue." The call for legislative intervention was imperatively demanded. After the excitement of considerable expectation and a delay of eight months, the Government declared themselves unable to introduce a bill to Parliament on the subject. Finding that to be the case, Lord Aberdeen, who had previously corresponded with Dr. Chalmers and others concerned, determined to attempt a remedy for the evils, and on his own responsibility, and without any communication with the Non-intrusion party, save a note to Dr. Chalmers, on the 5th of April, 1840, brought in a bill before the House of Lords, which he conceived would effect that end; but which unfortunately only led to further disappointment. By this bill parishioners were allowed to state objections of all kinds to the presentee; "but it obliged them to state the grounds and reasons of their objections. It allowed the Presbytery to take all these objections into consideration, but it permitted them to give effect to them only when personal to the presentee, when legally substantiated, and when sufficient, in their judgment, to warrant his rejection. It altogether excluded a dissent without reasons; it disallowed unacceptableness to the people as a disqualification. It refused to the Presbytery the power of giving effect in any instance to the popular opposition simply as such, no matter how general or how strong that opposition might be. That which the Veto Law had said should be done in every instance, it said should be done in none. It left the judgment of the House of Lords in the Auchterader case untouched; and it offered no protection whatever against such aggressions on the part of the Court of Session as it had recently committed. Even within the limited domain conceded to the church, the Court of Session would be the final judges whether the objections on which a Presbytery rejected were such as the Bill allowed, and whether they had been sufficiently substantiated. The Presbytery might have the strongest possible conviction that, acting within the provisions of the Bill, they were bound to reject; yet if the Court of Session thought otherwise, they would be bound to ordain, and if they refused, all the ordinary consequences of disobedience to the common law of the country would follow. It was nominally as a remedy for an existing evil that this Bill was introduced, yet it left that evil just where it found it. New legislation was asked for and required; yet it professed to be merely a declaratory enactment, and did not propose to effect any alteration in the Law of Patronage, as interpreted by the two Chancellors."

The Non-intrusionists were perfectly sensible that all the objections of a congregation, however substantial, would go for nothing, if admitted only upon those conditions. Repeatedly had Dr. Chalmers declared their doctrine on that point. In his reply to Dr. Cook in the General Assembly on the 22d of May, 1839, he had said:

"I am fully prepared for all the wanton ridicule which has been cast on a popular antipathy without reasons, or such reasons as can be stated before a bench of Judges for them to judge upon. The Dean of Faculty, in his pleading before the Lords of Session, makes repeated and contemptuous allusions to this mystic and incomprehensible something, too shadowy for expression, too ethereal to be bodied forth in language, and on which we would reject the presentee — grounding our rejection on a veto, itself without grounds, or at least such grounds as are capable of being set forth and made intelligible to the minds of other men. Now, if there be one thing of which we are more confident than another, it is that we have all philosophy upon our side, and all that is sound in the experience of human nature. Not in Christianity alone, but in a thousand other subjects of human thought, there may be antipathies and approvals, resting on a most solid and legitimate foundation — not properly, therefore, without reasons deeply felt, yet incapable of being adequately communicated. And if there be one topic more than another on which this phenomenon of the human spirit should be most frequently realized, it is the topic of Christianity—a religion, the manifestation of whose truth is unto the conscience; and the response or assenting testimony to which, as an object of instant discernment, might issue from the deep recesses of their moral nature, on the part of men with whom it is a felt reality—able, therefore, to articulate their belief, yet not able to articulate the reasons of it. There is much, and that the weightiest part by far of the internal evidence for Christianity, that rests on the adaptations which obtain between its objective truths and the felt necessities or desires of our subjective nature—adaptations powerfully and intimately felt by many a possessor of that nature, who is yet unable to propound them in language, far less to state or vindicate them at the bar of judgment. And if ever the prerogatives of the human conscience were at one time more cruelly trampled on than at another, it has been within the last century, and at the bar of this House—when the collective mind of a congregation, who both knew and loved the truth as it is in Jesus, has been contemptuously set at naught; and the best, the holiest feelings of our Scottish patriarchs, by lordly oppressors sitting in state and judgment over them, were barbarously scorned. In that age of violent settlements, these simple, these unlettered men of a rustic congregation, could say no more, yet said most truly of the intruded minister, that he did not preach the Gospel, and that in the doctrine he gave there was no food for the nourishment of their souls. I cannot image a more painful spectacle than such men as these, the wortheis of the olden time, at once the pride and the preserving salt of our Scottish commonwealth, placed under the treatment and rough handling of an able, jeering, ungodly advocate; while coarse and contemptuous clergymen, booted and spurred for riding committees, were looking on and enjoying the scene; and a loud laugh from the seats of these assembled scorners completed the triumph over the religious sensibilities of men, who could but reclaim with their hearts and not with their voices. This was the policy of Dr. Robertson, recently lauded in high places— a policy which has dissevered our population from our church, and shed most withering influence over the religion of the families of Scotland. Re-enact this policy if you will, and you place your Kirk, as a National Establishment, on the brink of its sure annihilation. Have a care, ye professing friends of order and loyalty, have a care lest, by a departure from the line of resolute and unswerving principle, you strip the church of all moral weight in the eyes of the community. Think of the deadly enemies by whom we are encompassed; and have a care lest, by one hair-breadth of deviation from the path of integrity and honor, you cause the hearts of these Philistines to rejoice.

"This discernment of the Gospel, this just perception of truth on the part of a home-bred peasantry, though unable to assign the principles or reasons, is not more marvelous than is their just perception of beauty, though unable to assign the philosophy of taste. Hear the most philosophical of all our poets, Akenside, who, in his 'Pleasures of Imagination,' bids us

"'Ask the swain
Who journeys homeward from a summer day's
Long labor, why, forgetful of his toils
And due repose, he loiters to behold
The sunshine gleaming as through amber clouds
O'er all the western sky. Full soon, I ween,
His rude expression and untutor'd air,
Beyond the power of language, will unfold
The form of beauty smiling at his heart,
How lovely, how commanding!'—'Heaven,
In every breast hath sown these early seeds
Of love and admiration.'

"In the one case our peasant feels, and correctly feels, an admiration, which, unskilled in metaphysics, he cannot vindicate; in the other, he knows the truth, though, unskilled in logic, he can neither state, nor defend the reasons of it.

"'It has been frequently remarked,' says Dugald Stewart,

'that the justest and most efficient understandings are often possessed by men who are incapable of stating to others, or even to themselves, the grounds on which they proceed in forming their decisions.'—' An anecdote which I heard many years ago, of a late very eminent judge (Lord Mansfield), has often recurred to my memory, while reflecting on these apparent inconsistencies of intellectual character. A friend of his who possessed excellent natural talents, but who had been prevented, by his professional duties as a naval officer, from bestowing on them all the cultivation of which they were susceptible, having been recently appointed to the government of Jamaica, happened to express some doubts of his competency to preside in the Court of Chancery. Lord Mansfield assured him that he would find the difficulty not so great as he apprehended. 'Trust,' he said, ' to your own good sense in forming your opinions ; but beware of attempting to state the grounds of your judgments. The judgment will probably be right ; the argument will infallibly be wrong.' "

" I would take the verdict of a congregation just as I take the verdict of a jury, without reasons. Their judgment is what I want, not the grounds of their judgment. Give me the aggregate will; and tell me only that it is founded on the aggregate conscience of a people who love their Bibles, and to whom the preaching of the cross is precious ; and to the expression of that will, to the voice of the collective mind of that people, not as sitting in judgment on the minor insignificancies of mode, and circumstance, and things of external observation, but as sitting in judgment on the great subject-matter of the truth as it is in Jesus—to such a voice, coming in the spirit, and with the desires of moral earnestness from such a people, I for one would yield the profoundest reverence."

Such were the antagonistic positions of Lord Aberdeen's Bill and the Veto Law of the Church of Scotland, and all efforts to reconcile them were ineffectual. A correspondence between Dr. Chalmers and Lord Aberdeen served only more clearly to define the boundary over which neither of them could pass. The General Assembly of 1840, by a majority of 221 to 134, "resolved, that in its then existing form they could not acquiesce in the Bill, and that it was the duty of the church to use every method to prevent its obtaining the sanction of the Legislature." The Bill was subsequently withdrawn before it had finally passed the House of Lords. The fruitlessness of all attempts to obtain a recognition of their rights from men who either would not or could not understand or appreciate their principles, deeply grieved those who had been the most zealous friends of the Establishment. In this time of their embarrassment, a pamphlet by Dr. Chalmers appeared, with the title, "What ought the Church and People of Scotland to do now? being a pamphlet on the Church Question, with an Appendix on the Politics of the Church Question." In that appendix the following sentences occur: "After all, I now owe an act of justice to the Whigs. I understand justice in the same sense as equity (*æquitas*); and I am now bound to say, that if on the question of church endowments I have been grievously disappointed by the one party—on the question of church independence I have been as grievously disappointed by the other. Of course, I speak on the basis of a very limited induction; but, as far as the findings of my own personal observation are concerned, I should say of the former, that they seem to have no great value for a church Establishment at all—and of the latter, that their great value for a church Establishment seems to be more for it as an engine of State than as an instrument of christian usefulness. The difference lies in having no principle, or in having a principle that is wrong. In either way they are equally useless, and may prove equally hurtful to the church; and though the acknowledgment I now make to the Whigs be a somewhat ludicrous one, if viewed in the character of a peace-offering, I am, nevertheless, bound to declare, that, for aught like church purposes, I have found the Conservatives to be just as bad as themselves.

"It is for the church now to renounce all dependence upon men; and persevering in the high walk of duty on which she has entered, to prosecute her own objects on her own principles—leaving each party in the State to act as they may."

The danger now threatening the church was the same as that with which she struggled in earlier days, and the majority were prepared to meet it in the spirit of their fathers. Unlike the Church of England, that of Scotland recognizes no temporal head. Her constitution, from the days of Knox, has recognized "the right to a free and uncontrolled self-government" in all matters ecclesiastical. Times of sloth and defection indeed occurred in her early history: "but from these temporary disgraces she nobly redeemed herself. Under the tyranny of the Stuarts, four hundred of her clergymen voluntarily resigned their livings, rather than acknowledge the royal authority supreme within the house of God. And true to the same principle, their scattered flocks were driven into exile, shot down in the wild morass, or executed on the scaffold, till thousands perished." And the contest ended only with the Revolution, which acknowledged the church's independence.

Another long period of inactivity and spiritual coldness had been attended by gradual submission to the secular powers, until the more worldly-minded already viewed the entire control of these powers established by prescriptive right. "It was no false alarm which visited the heart of Dr. Chalmers, when at the Bar and from the Bench he heard the Church of Scotland pronounced to be a creature of the State, and the civil supremacy over her actings so unhesitatingly and unlimitedly affirmed. That alarm was heightened when, for the discharge of a purely spiritual act, a Presbytery was summoned to the bar of the Civil Court and rebuked; and it received a full confirmation when the preaching of the Word and the administering of sacraments was prohibited in a whole district of the land. At an early stage of the conflict the paramount importance of the question, as to the church's spiritual jurisdiction, revealed itself to his eye. It was when exercised in defense of the privileges of the people, that this jurisdiction had been in the first instance assailed, and the two topics of Non-intrusion and spiritual independence had come thus to be implicated together. He was most anxious to distinguish and keep them separate, that its proper place and its own right relative importance might be assigned to each. In principle he was opposed to all violent settlements, as hurtful to the efficacy of the christian ministry, and prejudicial to the interests of true religion. In no circumstances, and under no force of compulsion would he ever have taken part or given any sanction to such an ordination as that of Mr. Edwards in the parish of Marnoch; but he was fully aware, notwithstanding, that the ideas prevalent in Scotland as to the nature of the pastoral relationship, and as to the conditions under which the church should establish it, were, to some extent, peculiar to his country, and that what might be ruinous to the interests of religion there might not have the same effect elsewhere, and that the obligations, therefore, resting upon the Church of Scotland might not rest equally upon all other churches in all other circumstances. It was different with the other principle brought now into jeopardy. In his estimate it was a broad, a general, a universal truth, free from all accidents of place and time—a truth for all ages, and all countries, and all churches—that however placed toward, and however indebted to, the civil power, the church of Christ, while giving her services, should never part with her liberties—while receiving State support should never submit to State control, save in the disposal of the State's emoluments." Under the force of this conviction, he was led, in opening the debate on Lord Aberdeen's Bill, in the General Assembly, to speak as follows:

"Now, sir, looking on this part of our case, keeping a steadfast eye on the question of our spiritual independence, and putting out of view for a moment the question of Non-intrusion altogether, there are many, I trust very many, who think variously on the law of patronage and its modifications, and yet would harmonize and enter into one conjunct and firm phalanx for the vindication of our church's outraged privileges; and if there ever was a crisis in our history—ever a period of those manifold and sore controversies, among which from infancy our church has been cradled, when courage and consistency have been more called for, it is the day on which we have now fallen—when the poison of false and hollow principle is undermining our strength from within, and thousands of our deadliest enemies from without are on the tiptoe of high expectancy for a coming overthrow. Sir, it is a leading principle of our Presbyterian constitution, that there is a distinct government in the church, which the State, of course, must approve ere it confers upon us its own temporalities; or, in other words, that we have as uncontrolled a management of our own proper affairs as if we received not one farthing out of the national treasury; that when in the act of becoming an Establishment, we, in the brief and emphatic deliverance of my friend, Mr. Gray, 'gave them our services, but not our liberties,' getting at their hands a maintenance for our clergy, and engaging in return for the christian education of the people; a conjunction, we think, fruitful of innumerable blessings both to the church and to society, but in which the value given is many hundred-fold greater than the value received. Still, if the State be not satisfied with the bargain, they can at any time give us up. If, over and above our services in things spiritual, they must also have our submission in things spiritual, in these we have another Master, to whom, and to whom alone, we are responsible; and we utterly repudiate, as we should an accursed thing, the sacrilegious bribe that would tempt us from an allegiance to Him; for that in these things He has the sole and undivided mastery, is a principle which lies at the very foundation of the Church of Scotland; and on her giving up this, as by the loosening of a corner or a keystone, the whole fabric will tumble into ruins. The establishment of this, as the principle of our church, is the peculiar glory of Scotland, the fruit of a hard-won victory, after the struggles, and the persecutions of more than a hundred years. A principle which has cost us so much we are not now willing to let go; and if the State will insist on our surrender of it, or the forfeiture of our endowments, we are willing to try the experiment, and to brave the same cost over again. It is a principle, sir, that we have not forgotten, though it has been renounced by a few declarationists among ourselves, and although it has faded away from the recollections and feelings of general society, like an old charter which might slumber in its repositories for generations, while its articles remain unbroken, but which the rude hand of violence will recall from its oblivion, and quickening it anew into vigor and vitality, will bring back, as if by resurrection, on the face and to the observation of the world. It is even so with the grand, the fundamental principles of our church—its own inherent liberty in things ecclesiastical—familiar as household words, Bishop Burnet tells us, even to the humblest of our peasantry, but which, suffered to lie quiet for a century and a half, because let alone, had ceased at one time to be spoken of, and so fallen away from the memory, even from the understandings of men. From 1688 to 1838—from the time of the Revolution- settlement to the time when the Court of Session gave forth its interdict against the Presbytery of Dunkeld in the case of Lethendy—no civil power ever attempted to interfere with the steps of our ecclesiastical procedure, or to meddle with our Establishment in aught but the temporalities which belong to her. It was the disturbance given then which has aroused the church, and will at length arouse the nation, from its dormancy. It threw us back on the first elements of a question, which, from the days of our great-grandfathers, had been settled and set by. When conjured up again, it sounded like an antique paradox on many an ear; but minds are gradually opening to the truth and sacredness of our great principle, and we doubt not that the very agitations of this controversial period have flashed it more vividly and convincingly on the understandings of men than heretofore. Our ark is now in the midst of conflicting billows, but so that its flag is all the more unfurled by the storm which has raised them, and the inscription there, now spread forth and expanded in the gale, is making the motto of our Establishment patent to all eyes, that 'the Lord Jesus Christ is the only head of the Church of Scotland.' Sir, we have nailed this color to the mast, and will keep by it in all its fortunes, whether of tempest or of sunshine, through which the winds of heaven may carry it."

Though greatly to be regretted, it is certainly not to be

wondered at that the Assembly failed of unanimity in this matter. When was so large a body ever found in which all were capable of duly appreciating so noble a principle, or of incurring the risk of losing all their earthly possessions in defense of it? The Moderates, now commonly called by all but themselves, the Intrusionists, did not withhold their hands from contributing to break down that independence for which their colleagues were contending. The degree of their opposition appeared when the case of the Strathbogie ministers came before the Assembly, when in laying upon the table the reasons for their dissent from the final judgment of the court, whereby the act of the Commission in suspending was sustained, they affirmed that the conduct of those ministers in taking their orders from the civil rather than the ecclesiastical court was "conformable to the clearest principles of reason, and the express injunctions of Scripture," and that in their opinion "the sentence passed upon them was unconstitutional, illegal, and invalid." In the month of June succeeding, "a private circular, signed by Dr. Cook and others, was sent among their friends inviting them to form an association, based upon the reasons of dissent already alluded to, and requesting that a general meeting for the purpose of maturing the plans of the association should be held in Edinburgh on the morning of the 12th of August." On that same day the regular meeting of Commission was held, in which Dr. Chalmers, speaking of the difficulties by which the church was then surrounded, and referring to certain ungenerous remarks thrown by Lord Aberdeen and Sir Robert Peel, in Parliament, referring the conduct of the Non-intrusion party to irritated feeling, proceeded to say:

"We must stand out against this series of aggressions thus rising in magnitude one above the other, else the most sacred of the church's territories, the very innermost recesses of her sanctuary, will lie open to invasion, and be trodden under foot. I know the obloquy which will be heaped upon us; I have heard the odious names which are given to this resistance, and am prepared for them. If not an impartial public, at least an impartial posterity will judge aright between us and our adversaries, and tell whether it is we who have been the rebels, or they who have been the persecutors. And here I may say one word in reference to those who express the hope—and I observe that Sir Robert Peel is among the number—that we shall give up our personal feelings and submit. What these personal feelings are, he has not specified, whether irritation or a false sense of honor—the pride of men who have committed themselves and gone too far to retreat without shame and degradation. Never was an appeal made so utterly wide of the object to sensibilities which have no existence, or if they have, it is in so slight a degree, that they are overshadowed by principles of such depth and height, and length and breadth, as to engross and occupy the whole man. These principles, whether comprehended or not by our adversaries, are the only moving forces that tell or have told on the proceedings of the General Assembly. The free jurisdiction of the church in things spiritual—the Headship of Christ—the authority of His Bible as the great statute book, not to be lorded over by any power on earth—a deference to our own standards in all that is ecclesiastical—and what is more, a submission unexcepted and entire to the civil law in all that is civil;—these are our principles—*these*, and not personal feelings, are what you ask us to give up, by giving in to those adversaries who have put forth an unhallowed hand upon them. And is there no room for a similar appeal being made to them? Have *they* no personal feelings in this matter—no feeling of ignominy in the anticipation of defeat—no feeling of triumph in the anticipation of victory—no mortification of disappointed vanity should their own battle-cry, 'that what firmness has done before it will do again,' be rolled back by a resolute and unyielding church on the head of her haughty persecutors?"

These last words created a tremendous sensation among both the members and the crowd who had assembled to listen to the discussion. One of the court "abruptly and impetuously called Dr. Chalmers to order;" but the roar of tumultuous approbation drowned all opposition, and for a few minutes no speaker could be heard. When it ceased, Dr. Chalmers continued:

"Is there no inward chagrin among Parliamentary friends, who now mourn over their own abortive attempts at legislation; and, let me add, is there no sense of offended dignity among the functionaries of the law, should it be found that law—no impossible thing, surely—has for once in one hundred and fifty years gone beyond its sphere? Which of these two rival elements, we ask, in all conscience and equity, ought to give way? whether the feelings of men who, free from all hazard, lose nothing, in whatever way the contest is terminated, or the principles of men who risk their all for these principles, and who, though many of them now in the winter of life, will, rather than abandon them, brave the prospect of being driven from their comfortable homes, and cast with their helpless and houseless families on the wide world? 1 ask, is it well for Sir Robert, from his elevated station and seat of silken security, to deal forth such a lesson to the church and the people of Scotland; and while he spares the patrician, the lordly feelings, of all in rank or in office who have leagued to bear us down, to make no allowance for the consciences of men who, though humble in condition yet high in sentiment, are, like their fathers before them, prepared to renounce all for the integrity of that church which is at once the glory and the bulwark of our nation?"

From this harassing warfare, Dr. Chalmers's attention was for a time diverted by another agitation of the subject of poor laws, awakened by Dr. Alison's book, advocating the principle of assessment. Dr. Chalmers defended his own views before the meeting of the British Association, in Glasgow, and afterward, in a series of lectures, which were published, but failed to convince his countrymen of the superiority of his method. In September and October, 1840, he delivered a short course of lectures on education, before the Mechanics' Institute in Greenock. About the same time he was, by some friends, put in nomination for the chair of Theology in the University of Glasgow, then vacant; but such was the opposition to him now among conservatives, that all their influence was employed to prevent his election. Sir James Graham, Lord Rector of the University at the time, undertook a journey to Glasgow for the sole purpose of voting against him. Of course, the rejection detracted as little from the reputation of Dr. Chalmers, as the election would have added to it; but it served to show the bitterness of political rancor.

Their knowledge of this state of feeling may have encouraged the seven suspended ministers of Strathbogie to the step which they afterward took. Disregarding the citation of the General Assembly, and meeting each judgment of that tribunal with an edict of the Civil Court, they continued to represent themselves as the Presbytery of Strathbogie, and as such proceeded to take Mr. Edwards upon trial, and found him qualified. Mr. Edwards himself obtained from the Court of Session an order to ordain him, though what right the Court of Session had to such an ecclesiastical act, it is difficult to understand. The seven, however, declared themselves satisfied with it, and appointed a day, Thursday, the 21st of January, 1841, to put it in execution. "A heavy snow-gale had passed over the country, choking up the public roads, and covering the earth to the depth of two feet and upward. Stormy, however, as Wednesday had been, and few more stormy days had been experienced for many years—deep as the snow lay on the face of the earth, and gathered as it was in large and almost impassable wreaths on every highway and byway in Banff and Aberdeenshire, early on Thursday morning little bands of men from all the neighboring parishes, moving on in lines, the stoutest in advance breaking up a path for his companions who followed him, were seen wending their way to the church of Marnoch. In two or three carriages drawn by four horses each, the clerical actors and their law agents were conveyed to the same spot. A singular assemblage was gathered there to greet their approach. Upon the trampled and slushy ground around the kirk, two thousand men were standing. The church doors were opened, and the church was instantly and densely filled—thick groups gathering about doors and windows, who could not obtain admittance. The lower part of the building was reserved for the parishioners, and the galleries for strangers. The court having been opened by prayer, the following dialogue occurred :

"Mr. Murray, one of the elders of the parish—'I wish to ask you by whose authority you have met here?'"

"The Rev. Mr. Thomson, of Keith, the Moderator of the Presbytery—'By the authority of the National Church, and in the name of the Lord Jesus Christ.'"

"Mr. Murray—'Have you any proof to show that you came here by the authority of the National Church?'"

"Mr. Thomson—'The meeting must be first constituted by the clerk reading the minutes, and we shall then answer your question.'"

All the necessary documents having been read, the Moderator remarked that they had one-party at the bar, and asked if there were any other individuals who wished to appear as parties in the case. The question called up Mr. Murray, and the interrupted dialogue was resumed, the law agents of the respective parties taking now a part in it.

"Mr. Murray—'Came you here by the authority of the General Assembly? I ask you that, before answering your question.'"

"Mr. Thomson—'We will give any information to parties at the bar, but not to any other. Do you intend to sist yourself as a party at the bar?'"

"Mr. Murray—'No, sir; but at any rate I should first require to know by what authority you came here?'"

"Mr. Peterkin, of Edinburgh—'It is impossible that any person can be heard who does not appear as a party at the bar, and is entered on the minutes a party there.'"

"Mr. Duncan—'As agent for the elders, heads of families, and communicants of the parish of Marnoch, and particularly for Mr. Murray, I put again the question, which has been as yet refused an answer. We cannot appear as parties at your bar, till we are convinced of your authority.'"

"Mr. Thomson—'Although we do not admit the right of

any party to question us on our authority for meeting here, yet I have no objection to say that we are here as the Presbytery of Strathbogie, a part of the National Church, assembled in the name of the Lord Jesus Christ.'"

"Mr. Duncan.—'Do you appear here by the authority of the General Assembly, or against its authority?'"

"Mr. Thomson.—'We are sent here as the Presbytery of Strathbogie, and under the protection of the law of the land.'"

"Mr. Duncan.—'Do you give me no reply to my question?'"

"Mr. Thomson.—'No, no.'"

"As the authority of the Presbytery was not recognized by the people, the only alternative left to Mr. Duncan was, as their agent, and in their name, to read two protests, the one signed by all the elders, and the other by four hundred and fifty communicants. In the first of these, the protesters, addressing themselves to the ministers, said, 'It is with extreme pain and disappointment that your personal position as suspended ministers of the Church of Scotland precludes us from appearing before you to lodge objections against the settlement of Mr. Edwards, which have been prepared, and are ready to be substantiated before any competent Church Court. These objections we solemnly declare to be such, affecting as they do the qualifications, life, and doctrine of Mr. Edwards, as, in our opinion, to cause his deposition even if he were an ordained minister, and to preclude him from admission in his character of a licentiate claiming ordination as presentee to our parish * * * We earnestly beg you to consider the above, and avoid the desecration of the ordinance of ordination; but if you shall venture to disregard this representation, we do solemnly, and as in the presence of the great Head of the church, the Lord Jesus Christ, repudiate and disown the pretended ordination of Mr. Edwards as minister of Marnoch. We deliberately declare, that if such proceedings could have any effect they must involve the most heinous guilt and fearful responsibility in reference to the dishonor done to religion and the cruel injury to the spiritual interests of a united Christian congregation.'"

"Having read the protest," we quote now the words of an eye-witness, " Mr. Duncan 'said 'As agent for the elders, male heads of families, and communicants of Marnoch, I have now only to say, that they take no further part in these unconstitutional proceedings. They wait a better time and another court. They can have no further business here, and they will, I believe, all accompany me from the church, and leave you to force a minister on a parish against the people's will, but with scarcely one of the parishioners to witness the deed.' The people of Marnoch immediately arose from their seats in the body of the church : old men, with heads white as the snow that lay deep on their native hills, the middle-aged, and the young who were but rising into life. Gathering up their Bibles and Psalm-books, which in country churches often remain there for half a century, they left the church, once free to them and theirs, but now given up to the spoiler. They went out, many in tears and all in grief. No word of disrespect or reproach escaped their lips. They went away in the strong conviction that their cause was with the most Powerful, and that with Him rested the redress of all their wrongs. Even those who sat in the pew—the only pew representing Intrusionism, were moved—they were awed. 'Will they all leave?' we heard some of them whispering. Yes, they all left, never to return."

"When they left the church, the people of Marnoch assembled in a snowy hollow, at the foot of the hill on which the church was built, and having listened to a short address from Mr. Duncan, in which he strongly urged that everything should be done with order, unity, and peace, they separated, and, with a rare exercise of self-denial retired to their different homes. The place left vacant by them in the church was immediately filled by a rush of strangers from without, and a disgraceful scene of riotous disorder ensued, which it required the presence of a magistrate to check. When peace had been restored the act of ordination was completed. It was an ordination altogether unparalleled in the history of the church, performed by a Presbytery of suspended clergymen, on a call by a single communicant, against the desire of the patron, in face of the strenuous opposition of a united Christian congregation, in opposition to the express injunction of the General Assembly, at the sole bidding, and under the sole authority, of the Court of Session.

"The conduct of the people, so decorous on the day of this ordination, was equally judicious and becoming afterward. To provide for the existing emergency they resolved to erect a place of worship for themselves in a village three miles from the parish church, and where, whatever might be the issue, a church would be required. Many meetings were held over Scotland to express sympathy with them in their painful position, and to aid them in the erection of this church." Only the feeble state of his health prevented Dr. Chalmers from being present at the meeting held for that purpose in Edinburgh, his views were however expressed in a letter to the chairman. The same cause also, withheld him from all public appearances on behalf of the church until the meeting of the Assembly in May, 1841, and even then, he had to restrict himself to two efforts; in one of which, treating of the general question, he declared an alteration in his sentiments, "reconciling him to a public movement for the total abolition of lay patronage; and in the other, he moved that the Assembly find the seven ministers of Strathbogie guilty of offenses involving deposition." In addressing the Assembly on this motion, he said, "We are told by the friends of these gentlemen, that in all they have done they have been actuated by a sense of duty, or by the impulse of a conscience stirring within them, and which they found to be irresistible. We will not deny this, and we have no interest in denying it; but I would ask, when we deposed Mr. Irving, the other year, for an alleged heresy, did we make our decision turn upon his conscience? or did we take evidence on the consciences of Mr. Maclean and Mr. Dow, when we took his license from the one, and his parochial charge from the other? or were we arrested by the conscience or the conscientiousness of that holy and excellent person, Mr. Campbell of Row, when we ejected him from his status as a minister of the

Church of Scotland? Sir, I know not what the inward principle of the ministers of Strathbogie may have been, nor will I attempt any conjecture on this subject; but I do know, that when forbidden by their ecclesiastical superiors to proceed any further with Mr. Edwards, they took him upon trials; and when suspended from the functions of the sacred ministry by a commission of the General Assembly, they continued to preach and to dispense the sacraments—that they called in the aid of the civil power to back them in the exclusion from their respective parishes of clergymen appointed by the only competent Court to fulfill the office which they were no longer competent to discharge; and lastly, as if to crown and consummate this whole disobedience—as if to place the top-stone on the Babel of their proud and rebellious defiance, I know that, to the scandal and astonishment of all Scotland, and with a daring which I believe themselves would have shrunk from at the outset of their headlong career, they put forth their unlicensed hands on the dread work of ordination; and as if in solemn mockery of the church's most venerable forms, asked of the unhappy man who knelt before them if he promised 'to submit himself humbly and willingly, in the spirit of meekness, unto the admonitions of the brethren of the Presbytery, and to be subject to them and all other Presbyteries and superior judicatories of this church;' and got back from him an affirmative response, along with the declaration that 'zeal for the honor of God, love to Jesus Christ, and desire of saving souls, were his great motives and chief inducements to enter into the functions of the holy ministry, and not worldly designs and interests.' Sir, I repeat I am not able to go into the depth and the mysteries of men's consciences; but this I am able to perceive, that if in heresy this plea were sustained, the church would be left without a creed; and that if in contumacy this plea were sustained, the church would be left without a government, both doctrine and discipline would be given to the winds, and our National Church were bereft of all her virtue to uphold the Christianity of the nation, when thus helpless and degraded, she was alike unable to correct the errors, however deadly, or to control the waywardness, however pernicious and perverse, of her own children.

"The Church of Scotland can never give way, and will sooner give up her existence as a National Establishment, than give up her power as a self-acting and self-regulating body, to do what in her judgment is best for the honor of the Redeemer and the interest of His kingdom upon earth. We can see no other alternative. If these men do not humble themselves, their deposition is inevitable. The Church of Scotland cannot tolerate, and what is more, it could not survive the scandal of quietly putting up with a delinquency so enormous as that into which these brethren have fallen. If the vindication of her outraged authority is indeed to be the precursor of her dissolution as a National Church—if, in the recent language of an offended nobleman within these walls—if this is to be the last knell of the Presbyterian establishment in Scotland, only let the Legislature say so : and then let it be seen whether or not the church of our fathers be prepared to abjure her connection with the State, rather than, bereft of all her respect, and so of all her usefulness, she will submit to be vilified into a thing of naught."

"Dr. Cook moved, in opposition, that all proceedings against these clergymen should be set aside as incompetent, and they should be declared to be in the same situation in all respects as if no such proceedings had ever taken place." After a long debate, "Dr. Chalmers's motion was carried by a majority of ninety-seven in a house of three hundred and forty-seven members." The suspended clergymen then, by one of their own number, read a paper justifying their conduct, and retired from the Assembly. The sentence of deposition was solemnly pronounced upon them, after that Dr. Cook had read a protest, in which for himself and as many as chose to join him, he declared, "We regard it as binding upon every member of a church established by law to be subject to the civil power in all matters declared by the supreme civil authorities of the country to affect temporal rights, and that for conscience' sake ; and firmly convinced as we are that the said ministers have acted in conformity to this obligation, and that they have done nothing which is not sanctioned both by ecclesiastical and civil law, we cannot, without violating what we owe to the Church and State, cease to regard these men as still ministers, just as if the proceedings against them had never been instituted." On next day, the Moderates, finding, perhaps, that their protest of the evening before had gone too far, intimated that they would make no opposition to the motion that was made not to receive it. On the evening of the following day a messenger at arms appeared at the door " to serve upon the Assembly an interdict against their proceeding to carry the sentence of deposition into effect." Some little delay having been occasioned by sending for the Royal Commissioner, who happened to be absent from the house, the interdict was left with the officer in attendance at the door. It was laid upon the table and the Assembly adjourned. "On Monday, a series of resolutions, carefully reciting all the circumstances as they had occurred, and declaring the attempt thus made to be a flagrant breach of the privileges of the National Church, were framed, and ordered to be transmitted to her Majesty the Queen in Council, and without further notice of the interference, the business of the Assembly was resumed."

In the beginning of the Parliamentary session of 1841, Lord Melbourne, who was then Premier, intimated that it was not the intention of government to propose any measure for altering the Law of Patronage in Scotland; but to enforce that already existing. The manner of enforcing it which they had adopted, was singularly indirect, for men professing to feel themselves safely within the limits of their legitimate authority. It appeared in the influence exerted against Dr. Chalmers in the Glasgow election, and in the rejection of Dr. Candlish as a candidate for the new chair of Biblical Criticism in Edinburgh, on the declared ground of his belonging to the non-intrusion party, or as they expressed it, of his setting himself in opposition to the law. Without daring to inflict the penalty of the law, the civil powers, it seems, had determined upon a system of petty annoyance and persecution of individuals. "Had the law-officers of the Crown received instructions to proceed in ordinary course to vindicate the authority of the law; had complaints against any or all of those clergymen who had preached in Strathbogie been lodged in Court and the common compulsitors of law — fine or imprisonment—been put into operation; had the church even authoritatively been told by the government, that she must either retrace her steps, undo what she had done, and submit to all the adverse sentences of the Court of Session, or be visited with all the common penalties which an infraction of law incurred, she would have known better what to do. As it was, her position was so painful, that it occurred to some ministers in Greenock and its vicinity, that instead of waiting till interminable litigation from without, and a wider anarchy from within, rendered it impossible for her to carry on her government, she should go forward to the Legislature, and insist either that her spiritual independence should be recognized and secured, or that the connection between her and the State should be dissolved. This proposal was communicated by the Rev. Mr. Smith of Greenock to a few of the leading friends of the church in Edinburgh." It met with the hearty approbation of Dr. Chalmers; but from a belief that many of the non-intrusionists would yet regard it as premature, he advised its postponement. This occurred in the month of March, 1841, and on the 5th of May, a new Bill for the settlement of the Scotch Church question was introduced into the House of Lords, by the Duke of Argyll, a bill that granted all that the church laid claim to, differing from the " Veto Law only by extending the right of dissent to all male communicants, instead of restricting it to the male heads of families, and by making specific provision for the Veto being set aside, whenever it could be proved to have sprung from factious motives or causeless prejudices." The General Assembly, by a majority of more than two to one, declared its approval of this bill; but before the time for the second reading of it arrived, a new ministry was in power, a new Parliament was elected, and the active hostility of the minority within the church, had their deputation in London to contradict the voice of the majority. Some of the advice volunteered by that deputation to the government was to the purport that less timidity should be exercised in inflicting the penalties of the law upon their brethren, that harsher treatment would certainly succeed in breaking the spirit of independence in the church, intimating in the following language, how very agreeable such a course would be to themselves. "If the responsible advisers of the Crown shall be prepared to instruct their law-officers to maintain in the Civil Courts the cause of the ministers of Strathbogie, and of others who may be placed in similar circumstances, and *to prosecute for breach of interdict, etc.*, those who may in opposition to interdicts granted by the competent courts, invade the rights of such parties, the minority of the last General Assembly, and the large body of office-bearers of the Church of Scotland, who hold views in common with that minority, *will have much reason to be satisfied.*"

The degree of resistance to the General Assembly, by its own minority, amounted in more than one instance to gratuitous insult. Some of them proceeded to the length of assisting at the celebration of the Lord's Supper by the deposed ministers. Upon information of this act of insubordination, the Commission " instructed the Presbyteries to which the offending ministers belonged, to take such steps as were necessary for vindicating the authority of the church, and proposed that a 'solemn remonstrance and warning' should be prepared and addressed to them. When the resolution to this effect was carried, Dr. Cook gave in reasons of dissent, the second of which was as follows :—' Because the resolution now sanctioned, puts an end to all hope of devising any measure by which the members of the church might be united, and imposes upon us, and upon all who agree with us in the opinion which we have repeatedly expressed as to our present distressing condition, to take such steps as may appear most effectual for ascertaining from competent authority, whether we who now dissent, and they who concur with us, or they who continue to set at naught the law of the land, and the decisions of the Civil Courts in what we esteem a matter of civil right, are to be held by the Legislature of the country as constituting the Established Church, and as entitled to the privileges and endowments conferred by statute upon the ministers of that church.' Instead of the question coming before the Legislature as one between the church and the Civil Courts, Dr. Cook desired to present it as one between two parties in the church who could not longer remain united, one or other of which must be repudiated by the Legislature. If actually entertained in that form by the administration of Sir Robert Peel, there could be no doubt of the decision being in favor of that party to which Dr. Cook was attached. The prospect of so speedy a settlement demanded the most prompt and vigorous measures; and a special meeting of the Commission was summoned to meet on the 25th August. Dr. Chalmers, who had not been at the previous meeting, resolved to be present upon this occasion, that he might sound the key-note of preparation for that event which he now believed to be almost, if not altogether inevitable. 'As to the war of argument,' he said, 'that is now over; seeing the time has come when the strife of words must give place to the strife of opposing deeds and opposing purposes. In this, the ministers of the other side have set us the example. They have begun with deeds which we must disallow; and they now tell us that they mean to call on the Legislature for their declaration, which of the two parties is henceforth to be the Established Church of Scotland. It is but justice both to the public and to the government, that they should know how it is that we stand affected by such an intimation. There has, I fear, been a strange incredulity all along, in regard to the strength of our principles, or at what hazard, and to what extent of sacrifice, we have resolved to maintain them. The necessity is now laid upon us, that we should make a distinct and articulate reply to this question, and my fondest prayer, even as for the salvation both of the country and of the church, is for the response of an unshrinking and undiminished majority that the principles on which they have hitherto acted they are resolved to abide by, whatever be the hazard, and whatever be the sacrifice. * * * It is our solemn duty to do all we can for the averting of such a catastrophe (the breaking up of the Establishment), and heaven forbid that it should be hastened on by any indiscretion, still less by any disrespect, or any deed of violence on our part. * * * I will proceed no further, and for this single reason, lest the language of determination should be interpreted into the language of defiance. Most assuredly I have no desire that the breach should be any further widened: and yet it is of the utmost importance— of the utmost practical importance for the right settlement of this question—that the state of matters should be plainly understood, for nothing can exceed the misconception, cherished especially by the higher classes, both in this country and in London. Be it known unto all men, then, that we have no wish for a disruption, but neither stand we in the overwhelming dread of it. We have no ambition, as has pleasantly been said of us, for martyrdom of any sort, but neither will we shrink from the hour or the day of trial. In short, let it be distinctly known, both over the country at large, and more especially in the camp of our adversaries, that, whatever the misgivings might be in other quarters, among us there are no falterings, no fears. Should what has been termed the crisis, arrive, we know of a clear, and an honorable, and withal a christian outgoing; confident in the smile of an approving heaven from above, and that confidence not abated when we look around ou the goodly spectacle of our friends and fellow-christians—the best and worthiest of Scotland's sons—in readiness to hail and to harbor the men who are willing to give up all for the sake of conscience and of christian liberty. The God whom they serve will not leave them without help or without a home."

"To be prepared for the worst, the Commission appointed a large committee, with instructions to bring 'the principles and privileges of the church, as well as the dangers that may threaten us, before the government, the Legislature, and the country at large, by deputations, public statements, meetings, and such other means as may appear expedient.' The first public meeting held in fulfillment of this resolution took place in the Church of St. Cuthbert's, Edinburgh, on the evening of the day on which the Commission met. That church exhibited on this occasion an extraordinary spectacle. Fourteen hundred ministers and elders were crowded together in the lower part of the building, while from the double tiers of galleries as many spectators as could force their way into the edifice were gazing down upon the scene. The Rev. Dr. Gordon occupied the chair, and a resolution to adhere at all hazards to the principles upon which the church had taken her stand was unanimously adopted by the vast assemblage. The alternative of separation from the Establishment, to which so many ministers might speedily be forced, was steadily contemplated, and the first hint thrown out of that peculiar method of sustaining them in their new positions which Dr. Chalmers had already designed. He was the first to give up all hope of a satisfactory Parliamentary adjustment; he was the first also to busy himself both with the design and the execution of the practical measures required by the approaching disruption. This meeting in Edinburgh was followed up by similar meetings all over the country, in which a spirit of equal energy and resolution was manifested. This general attitude of determination and preparedness had its temporary effect. The threatened appeal to the Legislature was not persisted in, and the government made a friendly instead of a hostile movement toward the church. Taking the earliest opportunity of addressing the new administration, Commissioners, appointed by the church, had waited on Sir Robert Peel, and presented a memorial to the government. Almost immediately thereafter a proposal was made by Sir George Sinclair to the Non-intrusion committee for effecting a final adjustment of the question, by adding a clause, which he had drawn up, to the bill of Lord Aberdeen. Understanding that this clause recognized the right of the Church Courts to give effect to the objections of the people, if found to be insuperable, in every case in which they considered it to be their duty to do so, the committee, while carefully guarding themselves against a positive approval of such a settlement, stated that it was one to which they could conscientiously submit." Upon further discussion it appeared that the meaning attached to the clause by the committee, was not that which it was construed as bearing by the leading men of the other side, and it never came before Parliament.

Dr. Chalmers was now withdrawing himself, as much as circumstances would permit, from the conflict of public business, reserving his strength for the emergency of a disruption, which he foresaw to be inevitable, and dedicating his days, according to a long cherished design, to exercises of devotion. To this his journal, now resumed in its former fullness, bears abundant evidence, in a number of passages of such a spirit as these:

"*March* 17*th*, 1840.—Entered the seventh decade of my life. I have looked long at this birth-day as a great moral and spiritual epoch. My God, enable me by prayer and performance to make it good. Quite sure that the acceptance of Christ, with a full reliance on Him and the confident appropriation of His righteousness, is the transition step to a life of happy and prosperous obedience. O my God, give me to hold this fast, and to realize by it a present salvation—the light and liberty and enlargement of one of thine own children. O that my heart were a fountain of gracious things, which might flow out with gracious influence on the hearts of my acquaintances, and more particularly of the members of my family.

"*April* 15*th*.—O for quiet! Great need of repose. Gleams, too, of right and religious feeling. Think of my creatureship, but not habitually, not closely enough. What a revolution would it be if I had just an adequate and practical sense of the God who made me! The very sense of being made by another, how it should annihilate the sovereignty of self—how it should subordinate and keep in check the waywardness of one's own will. What hast thou, O man, that thou didst not receive?

"*April* 17*th*.—Growing distaste for the burdens of public business. Pray for wisdom amid the manifold difficulties of my position. Visit me, O God, with light and love from thy sanctuary.

"*May* 6*th.*—Sadly agitated about church matters, and things looking very doubtful. But saddest of all is the distress and decay of religious feeling, and the want of a system of practical self-discipline.—O my God, enable me to wait upon thee without distraction; and I pray for wisdom to clear my way through the difficulties by which I am encompassed. My retrospects of the day that is past are exceedingly dim; and the work of self-examination therefore, in that proportion, unsatisfactory. Search me and try me, O God.

"*November* 9*th.*—Yesterday being Sabbath, I employed in part, as usual, in the perusal of difficult theology, when I was visited by a sense of the injunction—' Thou shalt not do *any* work.' On that day let me rest, and let it be a day not of study, but of sentiment and of sentiment allied with repose, such as resting in God, having peace and joy in believing, waiting on God, rejoicing in hope, patient under injuries or in any sort of tribulation.—O grant that by a right use of the weekly Sabbath my old age may be mellowed into the Sabbath of my life; and let me experience that in the quietness and confidence of the seventh day there is a recruiting of strength for the duties and the exercises of the other six.

"*Sunday, May* 16*th.*—Was heavy when I awoke this morning; but did experience relief and elevation by the effort of a simple faith. Have adopted a new system of Sunday readings, confining myself to a prayerful reading of Scripture. Last Sunday began with John i, and to-day John ii. Have had two pleasant, and, let me hope, two spiritual Sabbaths, to some degree, in consequence. Was much delighted by my ordinary Bible passage this morning in 1 Sam. ii,—Hannah's prayer, ' For by strength shall no man prevail.' Still very deficient in my attention as a hearer at church, though to-day better than usual. Feel now that to be spiritually-minded is life and peace—at least, of this very certain, that I shall have no peace without it; and let me hope that this experience will shut me more up to a life of religion. Find that sermons from the pulpit or chapters in the Bible which would fail to interest me were I only bestowing a cursory attention upon them, become interesting when I make an effort to realize the objects of which they treat. Familiarize me, O God, more and more with the things of faith and eternity.

"*Sunday, 23d.*—Had my Sabbath Bible exercise, and mean to persevere in it. The chapter of the day was John iii. My chief thought was on the efficacy of faith as apart from conception, and faith too in the naked word, either with or without a lively manifestation of the archetype : our safety and spiritual health hanging on the first ; our sensible comfort mainly depending, I should imagine, on the second. Let me here record my prayer to God for sustenance and succor and guidance through the fatigues and difficulties of the coming week (General Assembly); and O that He would lead me back to this retreat in safety, and enable me to write of His gracious answer to the voice of my supplications. Hide me in thy pavilion, O God, from the strife of tongues. Give me the preparation of the heart and answer of the mouth. Cause my way to please thee, that enemies might be at peace. And, O defend the church, and bring her out of all her perils into a haven of security and quietness. Let me be without carefulness, rolling the whole burden of my anxieties upon God.

"*July 23d.*—Have great need of the life of faith. I have sad infirmities of temper. My God, help me to overcome all the obstructions which lie in the way of my perfect observance of the second law. How miserably deficient in the grace of endurance. Help me, O God!

"*September 27th.*—Began this day my Institutes of Theology. I pray for God's blessing upon the work, and that faith and His glory may be the single aim of my heart. I have great comfort in quiet and leisurely and thorough study.

" *October 3d.*—Began my regular Biblical devotions this day— I trust with good to my soul. The result so far has been a feeling of comfort and satisfaction. Prosper this enterprise, Almighty Father ; and bless it to my eternal welfare."

The Biblical exercises alluded to, constitute what have been published since his death under the names of "Horæ Biblicæ Qnotidianæ," and "Horæ Biblicæ Sabbaticæ." Of the former he has himself said that they "consisted of his first and readiest thoughts clothed in the first and readiest words, which occurred to him," and Dr. Hanna remarks that the latter might "be described as the Sabbath diary of the last six years of Dr. Chalmers's life." They were continued with unbroken regularity to the day of his death.

CHAPTER XVII.

IN January, 1842, another stage was reached in the Non-intrusion controversy, in a series of resolutions offered before the Presbytery of Edinburgh, by Dr. Gordon, affirming " the propriety of seeking the abolition of the Law of Patronage, as especially in the construction now attempted to be put upon it, involving a violation of the constitution of the church and kingdom, secured at the Revolution, and unalterably ratified by the Act of Security and Treaty of Union." Dr. Chalmers had hitherto strongly resisted the anti-patronage movement, but now, hopeless of harmonizing the conflicting elements, contributed his cordial support to the resolutions.

In a letter to the Duke of Argyll, dated February 9th, he thus expresses his opinion of the ground then occupied by the church:

1st. The church may acquiesce in, she never will approve of, a mere *liberum arbitrium;* and it will have little or no effect in laying an arrest on the anti-patronage movement.

" 2d. The church, in my opinion, would accept of your grace's bill, and that not as a step to ulterior changes, but for the purpose of working it honestly and faithfully, with the view to an efficient ministration of the gospel in Scotland. Many of us, and myself in particular, do not think that it comes up to the *beau ideal* of a best possible constitution for the appointment of clergymen. But we shall be content to wait for this being realized by a gradual and pacific march of improvement, and have no sympathy with those who talk of installments, and would keep the church and the country in a state of incessant turmoil and agitation.

" But, 3d, and most important of all, the church, I fondly hope and pray, will never consent to be cast down by any power on earth beneath the *liberum arbitrium*. If the right of the patron, on the one hand, is to carry it over the judgment of the ecclesiastical courts that it is not for the christian good of the families in a parish that his presentee, unacceptable to them, shall be admitted their minister; the church, on the other hand, never will submit to the mandate of any court under the sun calling on them to ordain and admit that man. On this head I trust that our majority will present an unbroken phalanx of resistance to the violence that would offer such an invasion upon our liberties; and should the further violence be perpetrated of driving us, because of this, from our own rightful patrimony, we shall in hundreds, I trust, quit the endowments of a church thus Erastianized, and, under God, cast the support of our righteous cause on the people of Scotland."

In the meanwhile another instance had occurred of Presbyterial insubordination sustained by the Court of Session. The Rev. Mr. Middleton, for some time assistant to the minister of Culsalmond, " obtained at last a presentation to that parish. The Presbytery of Garioch met on the 28th October, 1841, to moderate in the call. A majority of the communicants on the roll dissented from the appointment. According to the recent regulations of the church, the Presbytery was not bound to give immediate effect to that dissent by rejecting the presentee, but was required only to stay procedure, and report to the next General Assembly. The Presbytery resolved, however, to proceed immediately to the ordination. A minority of the court appealed to the superior judicatories, but this appeal was set aside. The people then came forward with special objections to the presentee, but the Presbytery refused to consider them. The parishioners and the minority in the Presbytery protested separately against this resolution, and appealed to the Synod. There is a standing order of the church that no Presbytery shall ordain in face of an appeal. Trampling upon this order, and setting all the common forms of procedure at defiance, the Presbytery resolved to meet again at Culsalmond on the 11th November, for the purpose of completing the settlement. It was another bleak, wintry, snowy day such as that which occurred about a year before in the neighboring parish of Marnoch, and another such crowd assembled. But the same wise counsels did not prevail, nor was the same spirit manifested by the people. The rapid and imperious movement of the Presbytery had created the feeling that they were stealing a march upon the people, and trying to do the deed before legal check of any kind could be imposed. Rashly and most unwisely the people took the check into their own hands. When the doors were opened, a motley crowd, principally composed of strangers from a distance, rushed in, and took such complete possession of the building, that it was with extreme difficulty, and by the help only of the officers of justice, that the Presbytery could find their way into the church. It was to no purpose that they found an entrance; for no sooner was the attempt made to commence the proper business of the court, than loud discordant clamors, rising from all quarters, drowned their voices, and effectually prevented all further progress. They waited for an hour or more — again and again making the effort to proceed, but making it in vain. They retired at last to the manse, and there, in a private room, and within locked doors, this unhappy ordination was consummated. The parishioners complained to the Commission of the arbitrary and irregular conduct of the Presbytery, and that court, which met on the 17th November, cited the parties complained of to appear before the ensuing General Assembly, and in the meantime, until the protests and appeals which had been made were judicially disposed of, prohibited Mr. Middleton from officiating in the parish of Culsalmond, and instructed the minority of the Presbytery of Garioch to provide for the administration of sacred ordinances in that parish. The sentence of the Commission was purely and exclusively spiritual: it touched no civil right—it carried with it no civil consequence. It had grounds to rest on disconnected with any question about the legality of the Veto Law. Mr. Middleton, however, and the majority of the Presbytery, applied to the Court of Session to suspend it, and to prohibit its intimation and execution. Lord Ivory, to whom, as Lord

Ordinary, their petition was in the first instance directed, refused to grant its prayer, on the grounds 'that there was no question now before the court as to the legality of the Veto Law; that the civil rights, whether of the patron or presentee, would stand perfectly unscathed, notwithstanding all that had yet been done by the Commission: and that the only question here was, shall this court interfere with the proceedings of a proper church Court, when that court, acting within its own province, is dealing with a proper ecclesiastical cause, and this too, while that cause is still actually depending before them?' The case went before the first division of the court, and the majority of the Judges reversed the decision of the Lord Ordinary. On the 10th March, 1842, the Suspension and Interdict were granted as craved. In delivering his opinion, the Lord President declared that it was quite sufficient to bring this matter within the jurisdiction of the court—'that a gross stigma had been fixed on Mr. Middleton's sacred character as a minister of the gospel,' by his being forbidden for a time to officiate; and that the majority of the Presbytery had been 'degraded from their status and functions as established ministers, and their general usefulness and respectability affected' by their being overlooked, and the minority appointed to supply all the ministerial services which the parish of Culsalmond required. At the beginning of this controversy, it was alleged in defense of the Court of Session, that it had interfered only when such civil rights as are properly the subjects of civil action were immediately involved. As broader and deeper invasions of the church's territory were made, the defense was widened by its being affirmed that the Civil Court was warranted to interfere in all cases where civil rights were directly or indirectly affected. But now the Court of Session, speaking through its President, had given it broadly to be understood, that if any one conceived that by the sentence of an ecclesiastical court, any injury had been done to his reputation, or respectability, or usefulness, that was in itself enough to justify the court in reviewing, and if it saw reason, in reversing the sentence of which he complained. No act of discipline could the church perform ; no spiritual censure or sentence of condemnation could she pronounce, which, upon this ground, did not lie open to revisal or reversal by the Court of Session. By assuming this prerogative, that court constituted itself as the court of last appeal in all such cases; and the church lay stripped of any supreme or exclusive jurisdiction.

"A broad and patent way to the Court of Session had been opened, and where Presbyteries had gone before them, individual ministers could find no difficulty of approach. The minister of Stranraer had been accused of various acts of fraud, and his Presbytery were proceeding in his trial, when he applied to the Civil Court ' to suspend the whole proceedings of the Presbytery ;' and ' further to prohibit, interdict, and discharge the said Presbytery from taking cognizance of the pretended libel.' The minister of Cambusnethan had been found guilty of four separate acts of theft, and the Presbytery were about to depose him, when he raised an action of reduction in the Court of Session, and obtained an interdict against their proceeding. Mr. Clark, the presentee to Lethendy, who was living in the manse of which he had taken possession, was accused of repeated acts of drunkenness, and the Presbytery of Dunkeld had entered upon the investigation of these charges, with a view to deprive him of his license. But he too had recourse to the great Protector, and an interdict against the Presbytery had been issued."

The time had fully come for a final declaration of principle and purpose, and corresponding firmness of action. The next Assembly was looked forward to as the fitting scene of such declaration, if only a suitable form could be adopted. On this point Dr. Chalmers declared it to be his opinion that the church should put forth a claim of rights, with a statement of what they held to be their duty, and their determination to adhere to it, and that their true ground was that of spiritual independence, and not of non-intrusion alone. The letter in which this opinion was advanced and sustained was circulated among the leading friends of the church in Edinburgh, and met with their warmest approbation, and when Mr. Dunlop, to whom that work was intrusted, drew up the claim of rights, he adhered as closely as possible to the principle advocated in Dr. Chalmers's letter.

The Assembly of 1842 was one of great interest to the enemies as well as the friends of the Church of Scotland. Upon making up the roll of members it appeared that the deposed ministers of Strathbogie had also sent their representative, and when Mr. Dunlop moved that their return be disregarded, he was warmly opposed by Dr. Cook, who strenuously asserted that these seven ministers should not be held as deposed. Dr. Chalmers, who seldom took part in the minor business of the Assembly, could not keep silence on hearing this extraordinary proposition. "Moderator," he said, "this is the first time in my life that I ever heard it asserted, that the dissent of a minority superseded the sentence of a court passed by an overwhelming majority. The proposition is in substance, that those deposed by the General Assembly of 1841, shall, nevertheless, be allowed to sit as members in the General Assembly of 1842. Why, Sir, the proposition is so very monstrous, and so fully comes in conflict—so palpably and immediately comes in conflict—with a first principle, that I cannot hold it to be a case for argument at all. But that such a proposition should be made, that such a proposition should ever be thought of, is a very instructive fact. It discovers to what a fearful extent of anarchy and disorder the enemy within—whether by the instigation and encouragement of the enemy without, I cannot say —are resolved to plunge the Church of Scotland; how they are resolved to strip her of the last vestige of that authority which belongs to every distinct body, governed by distinct office-bearers. Never, Sir, would I say, has the character of the outrage inflicted upon the Church come out in such bold relief as at the present moment, when we have just met under the countenance of Her Majesty; when we have been ushered to our places with the form and circumstance of a great national Institute; and when we are now holding our deliberations in the presence and hearing of Royalty, represented by one of the most respected of our noblemen. We are now congregated in this our first meeting of the present Assembly, by the authority and appointment of the last General Assembly. And, Sir, in these circumstances, what is the first thing we are called upon to do ? Why, to pluck from our archives the most solemn deed of that most solemn convocation, and to trample it down under our feet as a thing of insignificance or a thing of naught. It is under the authority of last General Assembly that we now hold our places, and are now met as a deliberative body ; and I must say that if there is anything more than another which could unsettle all men's notions of order and authority, it would be the success of the present proposition. It would truly be an egregious travesty, it would make a farce of the proceedings of our General Assembly, a complete laughing-stock of our Church, were there left her no authority to enforce obedience from her own sons. It would present a strange contrast between the impotence of our doings, and the pageantry of our forms—between the absolute nothingness of the Assembly, and the mighty notes of preparation—the imposing cavalcade which accompanied us—the pealing of the clarionets with which we were conducted into the House on the present occasion. I must say, there is not a heart that beats with more gratification, or feels more elevation, than my own, at the countenance given to our venerable Church at present by the high and honorable of the land ; but ours will be the fault, if, untrue to ourselves, if untrue to our privileges, we shall allow our Church to become a sounding brass and a tinkling cymbal—a hissing and an astonishment to all passers-by."

Mr. Dunlop's motion was carried by a large majority. The interdict served upon the recognized representatives from Strathbogie, as well as other interdicts, by which the Court of Sessions attempted to interrupt or embarrass the proceedings of the Assembly, were treated with silent and dignified disregard. The ministers of Cambusnethan and Stranraer were deposed from the sacred office, Mr. Clark was deprived of his license. The settlement of Mr. Middleton, as minister of Culsalmond was rescinded, and those ministers, who held communion with the deposed clergymen of Strathbogie were suspended from the exercise of their judicial functions as members of the church courts till the March commission of the following year. At the same time, the reports of progress made within the past year in the various fields of christian enterprise were most encouraging. The gross revenue of the church's schemes for ten months in 1841, exceeded by £8,000 that for the whole preceding year ; and looking back to the time when the evangelical interest became predominant, not only had three additional schemes of christian usefulness been added to the two then existing, but the whole sum raised for religious purposes in 1842 was six times greater than that raised in 1834, each intervening year witnessing a growing increase. Coupling this with the greater frequency of meetings for prayer over the country, and the remarkable revivals in Kilsyth, Blairgowrie and Dundee, we perceive the sources of that activity in reformation which had ruled in the late Assemblies, to have been the spirit of piety reacting from the heart of the people.

The principal discussions of this Assembly, "and the only ones in which Dr. Chalmers took a part, were those relative to patronage, and to the Church's claim of Right. On Monday the 23d May, Dr. Cunningham moved a resolution to the effect that as both in itself a grievance, and as the main cause of the difficulties, in which the church had been involved, patronage ought to be abolished. This motion, which was supported by Dr. Chalmers, was carried by a majority of 216 to 147. For more than half a century after the restoration of patronage by the Act 1712, the General Assembly had annually renewed her protest against this grievance, and had given it as an instruction to the Commission, to take all suitable opportunities for effecting its removal ; and now once more, after the lapse of another half century, and on the last opportunity given for doing so, the ancient testimony against the yoke of patronage was renewed. On Tuesday the 24th Dr. Chalmers moved the adoption of the Claim of Right." This document presented a comprehensive, but condensed " statement of the great principles which the Church asserted—of the scriptural, constitutional, and legal grounds, on which these principles rested—of the violence done them by the Civil Court—of the wrongs which the church had consequently sustained, and the claim for protection which she put forth. It closed with the solemn declaration that, subject to such civil coercion as was now attempted the church would not and could not carry on its government; and that, at the hazard of losing all the secular benefits conferred by the State, and all the public benefits of an establishment, it would resist that coercion, and maintain to the last the inalienable liberties of a church of Christ." This motion was also carried by a large majority; and the Lord High Commissioner was requested to transmit the document " to Her Majesty, as the head of the State.—Her principles thus faithfully declared, her final purpose thus solemnly announced —the Church committed her ways to God, and waited the evolutions of His will."

On the 11th of June following, when Mr. Campbell of Monzie was prepared to move the second reading of his bill, which was expected to effect the desired harmony, it was found that, as many livings in the Scottish Church were in the gift of the Crown, no change could be made in the state of patronage without the royal consent. This obstacle it was understood, the Premier possessed the privilege of removing; but he refused to exercise it, and the Bill was accordingly withdrawn. "A few days afterward, Sir Robert Peel informed the House ' that after a full consideration of the subject, Her Majesty's government had abandoned all hope of settling the question in a satisfactory manner, or of effecting any good by introducing a measure relative to it.' " The government by thus relinquishing all attempts at legislation, left the encroachments of the civil courts to take their course. " Lord Kinnoul and Mr. Young had raised a second action against the Presbytery of Auchterarder, to recover damages, laid at £16,000, by way of compensation for the injury sustained by patron and presentee in consequence of Mr. Young's rejection. The Court of Session found this action relevant, and on the 9th August, 1842, the House of Lords, sitting as a Court of Appeal, confirmed this judgment, and declared that damages were recoverable by the pursuers. The former decision of the Supreme Civil Court in the Auchterarder case had gone no further than to declare that in setting the presentee aside on the ground of the popular dissent, the Presbytery had acted illegally. Believing that the only legitimate effect of this decision would be to bring into operation the remedy specially provided by Statute for such a case, namely the withholding the fruits of the benefice, the church had relinquished all claim to them. By this second decision, however, of the House of Lords, it was distinctly declared that the obligation to 'receive and admit,' which still lay upon the Presbytery, was a *civil* obligation, the violation of which was to be regarded and punished as a civil offense, as a crime committed against the common law of the country. The four English Judges, Lord Lyndhurst, Lord Cottenham, Lord Brougham, and Lord Campbell, were quite unanimous. It is true that in the opinions which they delivered, not one of them ever alluded to one of the Statutes referred to by the Church of Scotland as ratifying her exclusive spiritual jurisdiction, and shielding it from invasion. They regarded the case as exhibiting no peculiarity, presenting no difficulty, and finding its perfect parallel in that of any common civil corporation violating one of the statutes upon which it was founded. In such an instance, if any individual could plead that by the act of the corporation, his patrimonial interests had been injured, an action for damages was a fair and legal mode of obtaining redress. It was the same, in the judgment of these noble Lords, with the Church of Scotland. By putting the church in such a category, and by subjecting her to such legal treatment, her title to any peculiar exclusive spiritual authority and jurisdiction was ignored, was absolutely and entirely repudiated. It had been clear enough from the whole current of their recent judgments, that the Court of Session conceived itself to be entitled to review, and if it saw reason, to reverse any proceedings of the Ecclesiastical Courts, by which a civil injury of any kind had been inflicted. Now, however, and for the first time, the determination of the Supreme Civil Court was given forth, that the judgments of the Court of Session imposed on the church an obligation to obedience, which she could not disregard without subjecting herself to civil pains and penalties. This amounted not simply to a change, but to the entire overthrow and reversal of the constitution of the Scottish Establishment, so far as that constitution had guaranteed to the church a sphere of action within which no secular power could control or coerce. The first Auchterarder decision put a new interpretation on the Law of Patronage, from the injurious results of which the church might have been protected by a change effected by the Legislature in that single law. This second decision gave a new interpretation of the nature and conditions of that relationship in which the church stood to the Civil Courts, and through them to the State itself, whose organs these Courts were. These conditions were such that the church could not fulfill them consistently with her principles. A mere Non-intrusion measure would no longer meet the difficulties of her position. Yet in that position, without some relief, it seemed impossible for her any longer to remain."

Dr. Chalmers spent the months of July and August in Ireland, at Rosstrevor, a lovely village a few miles from Newry, employed in the work of completing his lectures on Romans. Upon hearing of these events, he seems to have felt that separation from the Establishment was inevitable; and that the only remaining question was how that step could most effectively be taken. At the suggestion of Dr. Hanna, he proposed the calling of a general convocation of the evangelical clergy to take that matter into consideration, and having written to several of the oldest and most influential ministers in the church, and received their approbation of the method, a circular was drawn up, signed by thirty-two of them from various quarters, and sent to all the evangelical clergy throughout the land, inviting them to meet at Edinburgh on the 17th of November. And in view of that meeting, a proposal of united prayer drawn up by the Rev. Mr. M'Cheyne of Dundee, was extensively published.

The convocation was opened in St. George's Church on the forenoon of Thursday the 17th November, by devotional services conducted by the Rev. Dr. Macdonald of Ferintosh, and a discourse by Dr. Chalmers; and " assembled for business at seven o'clock in the evening in a small chapel in an obscure part of the old town. About 450 ministers were present—a larger number than had ever met in council in Scotland, many of them from the remotest parts of the country. Dr. Chalmers was invited to take the chair. In doing so, he briefly stated that the Convocation was met not for debate, but for deliberation. Its great object was to ascertain the mind and purpose of the church in the present perilous emergency, and he noticed this at the outset to encourage all to come forward with their sentiments. To secure this object, the public were carefully excluded from this and all the other after conferences. The proposal that two eminent lawyers, elders of the church, whose advice, it was imagined, might occasionally be serviceable, should be admitted, was met with an immediate and general negative. It was arranged that the ordinary formalities of debate should be dispensed with—that the discussion of each topic should be conducted, as much as possible in a colloquial form—that after the more aged and eminent ministers had stated their opinions, the members should be invited, Synod by Synod, to express their views; and that no conclusion should be come to, no practical measure resolved upon, till as full an expression and interchange of opinion as possible had been elicited. It was arranged, also, that three times, at least, each day, the Convocation should engage in devotional exercises, accompanied by reading of the Scriptures and praise, and that through all the ordinary business prayer should be interspersed. After some preliminary consultation, the attention of the Convocation was concentrated upon the two following topics:—
1*st.* The exact bearing and effect of the late decisions of the Civil Courts, and especially of the recent Auchterarder judgment, involving a consideration of what would be required in order to effect any right adjustment of the questions now at issue between the church and the civil authorities; 2*d.* The

duty and prospects of the church in the event of no adequate remedy being provided."

In course of discussion, a series of resolutions were offered by Dr. Candlish, in which, after reciting and characterizing some of the late decisions, it was declared—" That as the principle involved in these decisions, and particularly in the recent Auchterarder judgment, is that of the supremacy of the Civil Courts over those of the Established Church in the exercise of their spiritual functions, so the members of the Convocation declare, that no measure can in conscience be submitted to, which does not effectually protect the church against the exercise of such jurisdiction of the Civil Courts in time to come, and, in particular, fully prevent all future encroachments of the nature specified in the preceding resolutions." Only seven in the convocation refused to entirely concur in these resolutions. The next subject of consultation was what their duty should be in the event of no adequate relief being granted. On this head Dr. Chalmers was already prepared to submit a plan for the support of all the outgoing ministers. He asked and received permission to lay this plan before the Convocation. It was no rude outline, but the complete and finished system which was afterward adopted without alteration, and carried out with such success by the Free Church. By the Convocation, however, it was listened to with evident incredulity, as the Utopian scheme of a sanguine man.

A second series of resolutions were proposed by Dr. Patrick Macfarlan, concluding with the solemn declaration, that " 'in dependence upon the grace of God, it was the determination of the brethren now assembled, if no measure such as they have declared to be indispensable be granted, to tender the resignation of their civil advantages, which they can no longer hold in consistency with the free and full exercise of their spiritual functions, and to cast themselves on such provision as God in his providence may afford ; maintaining still uncompromised the principle of a right scriptural connection between the church and the State, and solemnly entering their protest against the judgments of which they complain, as in their decided opinion altogether contrary to what has ever hitherto been understood to be the law and constitution of this country.' On Tuesday night, after prayer by Dr. McDonald, the roll was called, and 270 voted that these resolutions should be adopted. It was felt by all to be a vote not lightly to be given, and for a day or two many held back their names.

"On Wednesday forenoon, Dr. Chalmers asked how many names were now appended to the resolutions of the preceding evening. When told that already there were above 300 he broke forth with the exclamation—'Then we are more than Gideon's army—a most hopeful omen.' As he proceeded to picture forth all the oppositions which this little army might encounter—all the victories it might win, the inward fire kindled into a perfect ecstasy of excitement. He stepped into the center of the group, his whole frame quivering with emotion, and looking round upon that band of faithful men, upon whose constancy in the hour of trial he felt now that he could count, he exclaimed—'For throwing up our livings—for casting ourselves with such unequal odds into so great a conflict, men may call us enthusiasts; but enthusiasm is a noble virtue rarely to be found in calm and unruffled times of prosperity: it flourishes in adversity—it kindles in the hour of danger. Persecution but serves to quicken the energy of its purposes. It swells in proud integrity, and, great in the purity of its cause, it can scatter defiance amid a host of enemies.' It was the spirit of chivalry baptized with the fire from Heaven."

"The two sets of resolutions which had been adopted having been embodied in a memorial addressed to Sir Robert Peel and the other members of Her Majesty's government, the Convocation," whose sittings had been eminently marked by the spirit of prayer and brotherly love, broke up on Thursday, the 24th November.

The appeal to government resulted, as all its predecessors had, in nothing save a further attempt to encourage, as far as a full declaration of non-interference could encourage, the Court of Session in its course of domination. And that court seems to have fully understood and availed itself of that

encouragement. The church had lately received into her bosom
"a body of dissenters bearing the name of the Associate
Synod. The clergymen of this Synod were admitted as members of the respective Presbyteries within whose bounds their
charges were situated, and these Presbyteries were proceeding
to attach a territorial district to their churches. The Presbytery of Irvine had in this way received the Rev. Dr. Clelland,
minister at Stewarton, into their court, and were engaged in
allocating to him a special district for the purpose of pastoral
superintendence and spiritual discipline, when an interdict was
served upon them prohibiting them from receiving Mr. Clelland
as a member of Presbytery, and from establishing an additional
pastoral charge in the parish. The church, for a hundred years
and more, had been admitting additional ministers into her
courts, and creating new parishes *quoad spiritualia*, and the validity of her acts had been recognized by decisions of the Civil
Court. Her title was now for the first time challenged, upon the
ground that, as a State-created institution, she could have no authority and exercise no privilege which had not been expressly
granted to her by statute. This case was so novel and important
that it was brought before all the judges of the Court of Session.
Their decision, delivered on the 20th January, 1843, was to the
effect, that the church had acted illegally in receiving such
ministers as Mr. Clelland, and in placing any part of an original parish under their spiritual care. This judgment was one
of wide compass, applying, as it did, not only to the members
of the Associate Synod, but to all the unendowed clergymen
recently admitted into the church. Its effect, if submitted to,
would have been to extinguish about two hundred pastoral
charges, and to annihilate as many kirk-sessions, by whose
vigorous agency a considerable inroad had been already
made upon the ignorance and irreligion of many of the most
overgrown parishes. It is one of the simplest and most harmless privileges which any society can enjoy, that of adding to
to the number of its office-bearers, and of originating methods
by which their labors on behalf of the great objects of the institution may be most effectively prosecuted. This privilege

was now denied to the Scottish Establishment. Taken in conjunction with a previous decision of the Court of Session, that all the Sabbath collections at the doors of the churches belonged to the heritors for the behoof of the poor, this judgment of that court overturned the whole work of church extension as an attempt to break down the unmanageable masses which had accumulated in so many parishes, and threw them back upon the exclusive pastoral superintendence of a single clergyman. In other circumstances, the church might have attempted, by appeal to the House of Lords, to obtain a reversal of a sentence so fatal to her progress, so pregnant with injury to the highest interests of the country. As it was, she received it as a last token of the hopelessness of any recognition of her spiritual independence by the Court of Session, and she engrossed it as the last specimen of the injustice which had been done her in that petition which, at a meeting of Commission held on the 31st January, it was resolved should be presented to the British Legislature." This petition was brought before the House of Commons on the 7th March, 1843, by Mr. Fox Maule—" founding upon it a motion that the House should resolve itself into a committee to take into consideration the grievances of which the Church of Scotland complained. Mr. Maule, Mr. Campbell of Monzie, Sir George Grey, Mr. Rutherford, and Mr. P. M. Stewart stated the case for the church so temperately, so judiciously, and so comprehensively, as left the church nothing either to desire or regret," while more than two-thirds of all the Scottish members voted in favor of the motion. It was, notwithstanding, lost, from the persistence of the English members in those views of the case drawn from their own theory of what the relations of church and State ought to be. This action of the Legislature rendered the course to be pursued by the church perfectly plain. Turning now from the distressing and profitless negotiations of five years, the evangelical party devoted their efforts to preparation for the new state of existence which they saw awaiting them. "The clergymen who had signed the resolutions of the Convocation lost no time in explaining to their congregations the important step which had been taken, and inviting their adherence. Acting under direction of a Committee appointed by the Convention, the ablest of their number were deputed to itinerate over the country, holding meetings in every parish to which they could find access, announcing to the people their principles and final purposes, and obtaining a large and hopeful amount of popular concurrence. All this however, did not satisfy Dr. Chalmers, whose grand device for meeting the coming crisis was the organization of local associations, upon the plan and for the purposes indicated in his address to the Convocation. Unable to persuade others to unite with him, he instituted of his own accord, immediately after the Convocation broke up, an association of this kind in the parish of Morningside, where he resided. Districts were laid down, collectors were appointed, donations for erecting the churches, and termly subscriptions for the support of the ministers of the Free Church were obtained, six months before that Church had a substantive existence in the country." The late act of the government had "opened the eyes of many to the necessity of more instant and practical measures of preparation, and at last the Committee appointed by the Convocation, united itself with another Committee, instituted at an influential meeting of the eldership, held at Edinburgh, on the 1st February. This most effective body, organized under the title of the Provisional Committee, held its first meeting on the following day, and to its labors the Free Church mainly owes that state of orderly preparation and absence of all division and confusion by which the days of the Disruption were so signally characterized. The Provisional Committee divided itself into three sections, the Financial the Architectural, and the Statistical. Dr. Chalmers took his position at the head of the first of these sections. The task for which he had been so long reserving himself was now put into his hands; and with an energy scarcely paralleled in the busiest periods of his past history he set himself to its execution. A circular inviting subscriptions and donations, was instantly drawn up by him, and sent in thousands over Scotland, bearing the mottoes—' Surely I will not come into the tabernacle of my house, nor go up into my bed : I will not give sleep to mine eyes, nor slumber to mine eyelids, until I find out a place for the Lord, an habitation for the mighty God of Jacob '—' The God of heaven He will prosper us ; therefore we his servants will arise and build.' The acts which followed were in good correspondence with these mottoes. As preliminary to those local and detailed operations, to which he attached such primary importance, Dr. Chalmers addressed a large and influential meeting, held at Edinburgh, on the evening of the 16th February. 'This meeting,' he said, ' is not for argument, but for action. I think that the reasoners upon this question have done their work. The time for argument is now over, and the time for action has come on. We have entered upon a new era, the era of deeds, which has followed the era of speeches, and arguments, and memorials and manifestoes." He had already to report some progress made in the work. "This brief circular," he added, "was only sent forth a few days ago, and the amount of subscription, though we have yet merely broken ground, is £18,550. It has come in upon us like a set rain, at the rate of £1,000 a day." He, however, attached much less importance to these large subscriptions than to the smaller but more numerous and regularly sustained contributions, on which the support of the ministry must ultimately depend ; and urgently pressed the necessity of organization for that purpose. " Having addressed a meeting in Glasgow, held for a like object, Dr. Chalmers devoted himself to the forming and fostering into vigorous operation of local associations all over the country. Every hour he could spare from the duties of the Theological class was now consecrated to this work—every day he was to be found presiding at the meeting of committee, and directing and stimulating his willing fellow-laborers. Writing to Mr. Lennox, of New York, on the 19th April, 1843, he thus speaks of their state of preparedness for the contemplated disruption.—' Our crisis is rapidly approaching. We are making every effort for the erection and sustentation of a Free Church, in the event of our disruption from the State, which will take place we expect in four weeks. I am glad to say that the great bulk and body of the common people, with a goodly proportion of the middle classes, are upon our side, though it bodes ill for the country that the higher classes are almost universally against us. Notwithstanding this, however, we are forming associations for weekly payments in rapid progression all over the country, and I am glad to say, that by this day's post they amount to four hundred and five. We expect that by the meeting of our General Assembly, the country will be half organized, and are looking for a great additional impulse from the Disruption, when it actually takes place. I am hopeful that ere the summer is ended, we may number about a thousand associations, or as many as there are parishes in Scotland, so that unless there be an attempt to crush us by persecution, I have no fear of our getting on. But the Lord reigneth, and He alone knoweth the end from the beginning. Let us look to His providence and grace, without which there can be no security from without, nor vital prosperity within.

'THOMAS CHALMERS.'

"The faith in one another, and the fervid activity in prospect of the Disruption, displayed by Dr. Chalmers and his associates, found a singular contrast in the apathy of the Government, and the infatuated incredulity of the public generally." It had been repeatedly asserted that very few would forsake their comfortable houses under the establishment. Men incapable of appreciating their principles could have no idea of the sacrifice they were willing to make for it, and many even of their own brethren misapprehended the force of their convictions of duty. Such was the public declaration of Dr. Cumming of London. "If government is firm, I venture, from pretty accurate information, to assert that less than one hundred will cover the whole secession * * * * * *But I am not satisfied that any will secede.*" "Mark my words," wrote one of the best informed and most sagacious citizens of Edinburgh, a day or two before the disruption, "Mark my words—not forty of them will go out."

"The day of trial at last arrived. For some days previously, an unprecedented influx of strangers into Edinburgh foreshadowed the approach of some exciting event. Thursday, the 18th of May, the day named for the meeting of the General Assembly, rose upon the city with a dull and heavy dawn. So early in the morning as between four and five o'clock, the doors of the church in which the Assembly was to convene opened to those who hastened to take up the most favorable positions, in which they were content to remain for nine weary hours. As the day wore on, it became evident that the ordinary business of the city had to a great extent been suspended, yet the crowds that gathered in the streets wore no gay or holiday appearance. As groups of acquaintances met and commingled, their conversation was obviously of a grave and earnest cast. Toward mid-day, the throne-room at Holyrood, in which the Marquis of Bute, as Lord High Commissioner, held his first levee, was filled with a numerous assemblage of noblemen, clergymen, military and naval officers, the city magistrates, and country gentlemen from all quarters of Scotland. A portrait of King William III, hung upon the wall of the room, opposite to the spot on which Her Majesty's Representative was standing. The throng of the levee was at its height, when, loosened somehow from its holdings, this portrait fell heavily upon the floor; and, as it fell, a voice was heard exclaiming, 'There goes the Revolution Settlement.' When the levee closed, the customary procession formed itself. In his state-carriage, accompanied by a splendid *cortège*, and escorted by a troop of cavalry, the Commissioner proceeded to the High Church. The service was conducted by the Rev. Dr. Welsh, the Moderator of the preceding Assembly, whose discourse was made all the more impressive by the frequent allusions to the event by which it was so instantly to be followed. Elsewhere, within the Assembly-Hall, as hour after hour passed by, the strained feeling of the multitude, by whom every inch of sitting and standing ground had for so long a time been occupied, was beginning occasionally to relax. At last, however, the rapid entrance of a large body of ministers into the space railed off below for members, told that the service at St. Giles was over. Every symptom of languor at once gave way, and expectation was at its utmost stretch. Dr. Welsh, the Moderator, entered and took the chair. Soon afterward, His Grace the Lord High Commissioner was announced, and the whole assemblage rose and received him standing. Solemn prayer was then offered up. The members having resumed their seats, Dr. Welsh rose. By the eager pressure forward—the hush! hush! that burst from so many lips — the anxiety to hear threatened to defeat itself. The disturbance lasted but a moment. 'Fathers and brethren,' said Dr. Welsh, and now every syllable fell upon the ear amid the breathless stillness which prevailed, ' according to the usual form of procedure, this is the time for making up the roll. But, in consequence of certain proceedings affecting our rights and privileges, proceedings which have been sanctioned by Her Majesty's Government, and by the Legislature of the country ; and more especially, in respect that there has been an infringement on the liberties of our Constitution, so that we could not now constitute this Court without a violation of the terms of the union between Church and State in this land, as now authoritatively declared, I must protest against our proceeding further. The reasons that have led me to come to this conclusion, are fully set forth in the document which I hold in my hand, and which, with permission of the House, I will now proceed to read.' In this document, after the wrongs of the church had been succinctly recited, the parties who signed it proceed at its close to say—'We protest, that in the circumstances in which we are placed, it is and shall be lawful for us, and such other Commissioners chosen to the Assembly, appointed to have been this day holden, as may concur with us, to withdraw to a separate place of meeting, for the purpose of taking steps, along with all who adhere to us, maintaining with us the Confession of Faith and Standards of the Church of Scotland, for separating in an orderly way from the Establishment, and thereupon adopting such measures as may be competent to us, in humble dependence on God's grace, and the aid of the Holy Spirit for the advancement of his glory, the extension of the Gospel of our Lord and Saviour, and the administration of the affairs of Christ's house, according to his holy word : and we now withdraw accordingly, humbly and solemnly acknowledging the hand of the Lord in the things which have come upon us because of our manifold sins, and the sins of the church and nation ; but, at the same time, with assured conviction, that we are not responsible for any consequences that may follow from this our enforced separation from an Establishment which we loved and prized, through interference with conscience, the dishonor done to Christ's crown, and the rejection of His sole and supreme authority as King in his Church.' Having finished the reading of this protest, Dr. Welsh laid it upon the table, turned and bowed respectfully to the Commissioner, left the chair, and proceeded along the aisle to the door of the church. Dr. Chalmers had been standing immediately on his left. He looked vacant and abstracted while the protest was being read ; but Dr. Welsh's movement awakened him from the reverie. Seizing eagerly upon his hat, he hurried after him with all the air of one impatient to be gone. Mr. Campbell of Monzie, Dr. Gordon, Dr. Macdonald, Dr. Macfarlan, followed him. The effect upon the audience was overwhelming. At first a cheer burst from the galleries, but it was almost instantly and spontaneously restrained. It was felt by all to be an expression of feeling unsuited to the occasion ; it was checked in many cases by an emotion too deep for any other utterance than the fall of sad and silent tears. The whole audience was now standing gazing in stillness upon the scene. Man after man, row after row, moved on along the aisle, till the benches on the left lately so crowded showed scarce an occupant. More than 400 ministers, and a still larger number of elders, had withdrawn.

"A vast multitude of people stood congregated in George's street, crowding in upon the church doors. When the deed was done within, the intimation of it passed like lightning through the mass without, and when the forms of their most venerated clergymen were seen emerging from the church, a loud and irrepressible cheer burst from their lips, and echoed through the now half empty Assembly Hall. There was no design on the part of the clergymen to form into a procession; but they were forced to it by the narrowness of the lane opened for their egress through the heart of the crowd. Falling into line, and walking three abreast, they formed into a column which extended for a quarter of a mile and more. As they moved along to the new hall prepared for their reception, very different feelings prevailed among the numberless spectators who lined the streets, and thronged each window and door, and balcony, on either side. Some gazed in stupid wonder; the majority looked on in silent admiration. A few were seen to smile, as if in mockery : while here and there, as the child or wife of some outgoing minister caught sight of a husband's or a father's form accomplishing an act which was to leave his family homeless and unprovided, warm tear-drops formed, which, as if half ashamed of them, the hand of faith was in haste to wipe away. There were judges of the Court of Session there who had placed themselves where they could be unseen observers of what took place, who must have felt perplexed, it may be saddened, when they saw realized before their eyes the fruits of their decisions. Elsewhere in the city, Lord Jeffrey was sitting reading in his quiet room, when one burst in upon him saying, 'Well, what do you think of it?— more than four hundred of them are actually out.' The book was flung aside, and springing to his feet, Lord Jeffrey exclaimed, 'I'm proud of my country; there's not another country upon earth where such a deed could have been done.'

"The large hall at Cannonmills prepared for the new Assembly, and fitted up so as to receive 3000 auditors, had been filled in the part allotted to the public from an early hour in the morning. When the procession from St. Andrew's Church arrived, and the space marked off for ministers and elders was fully occupied, Dr. Welsh opened the proceedings with prayer, after which he rose and said (we quote now from a cotemporary account) : 'Reverend fathers and brethren, I presume our first duty in the circumstances in which we are placed unquestionably is to constitute ourselves by the choice of a Moderator; and I feel assured that the eyes of every individual in this Assembly—the eyes of the whole church and country—the eyes of all Christendom are directed to one individual whom to name is to pronounce his panegyric. In the exhausted state in which my duties have left me, it is scarce in my power to say more, but indeed I feel that more would be superfluous. The extent of his labors in connection with our present position would justly entitle Dr. Chalmers—(the mention of Dr. Chalmers's name here, was received with extraordinary enthusiasm, the whole of the vast audience rising, cheering for some minutes with the utmost enthusiasm, and the house presenting a perfect forest of hats and handkerchiefs)—would justly entitle that great man to hold the first place in this our meeting. But surely it is a good omen, or I should say a token for good from the Great Disposer of all events, and the alone Head of the Church, that I can propose, to hold this office, an individual who, by the efforts of his genius and his virtues, is destined to hold so conspicuous a place in the eyes of all posterity. But this I feel is taking but a low view of the subject. His genius has been devoted to the service of his Heavenly Master, and his is the high honor promised to those who, having labored successfully in their Master's cause, and turned many to righteousness, are to 'shine as the stars forever and ever.' In taking the chair, Dr. Chalmers proposed that the proceedings should be commenced by another act of prayer and praise. The psalm selected to be sung commenced with the verse—

> 'O send thy light forth and thy truth;
> Let them be guides to me,
> And bring me to thine holy hill,
> Ev'n where thy dwellings be.'

As the vast multitude stood up to sing these words, and as the swell of 3000 voices rose up in melody to heaven, a sudden burst of sunlight filled the building, and there were some who thought of Dr. Chalmers's text, but six months before—'Unto the upright there ariseth light in the darkness.' The Assembly being constituted proceeded to business; and on the following Tuesday, the act of the Disruption day was formally and legally completed by the subscription of the 'Act of Separation and Deed of Demission,' by which 470 ministers did 'separate from and abandon the present subsisting ecclesiastical Establishment in Scotland, and renounce all rights and emoluments pertaining to them in virtue thereof.' A revenue of more than one hundred thousand pounds a year was thus voluntarily relinquished for the keeping of a good conscience and on behalf of the liberties of the church. Five years had passed since the first decision of the Auchterarder case, and the fruit of the conflict which then commenced was this rending in twain of the Scottish Establishment. When that conflict began there were none on any side who contemplated the possibility of such an issue, and perhaps none who, had it been pre-announced to them, would not willingly have labored to prevent it. It was an event not only beyond all human foresight, but done without human concert, in great measure against human will. Step by step the church was involuntarily led on from the lower and less essential to the larger and vital question upon which her very existence as an Establishment came finally to be staked. Guided by a way that she knew not, her path was hedged up on the right hand and on the left till no opening but one seemed left for preserving her principles and keeping her honor pure and clean. It lightened amazingly the sacrifice which so many of her ministers were called at last to make, that not a shadow of uncertainty hung over the closing act, and that amid all the bitterness of regret felt by them in separating from an Establishment which they had so loved and venerated, there mingled no feeling of hesitation as to the propriety of their final step. It was an act forced on them by the moral necessities of their position, from the weighty responsibilities of which they felt as if providentially relieved. Those statesmen who constrained them to this alternative might with more show of reason have denied the spiritual independence which they craved to a church which shuts out the laity from all part and influence in her affairs, and holds high notions of the priestly office and the spiritual powers which accompany it; but can they be forgiven for denying this liberty, and that on the ground of an alarm about clerical domination, to a church which opened every court to an equal, in some instances to a predominating lay influence, and which utterly repudiated the whole doctrine of priestly authority and power? Can the British Government be forgiven for breaking up the venerable fabric of the Scotch Church upon a plea so groundless, and for putting so mournful a close to that career of Christian usefulness upon which that church had so vigorously and so hopefully embarked? That an Establishment manned principally by such devoted ministers as were now driven beyond its pale, and guided in its advancing movements by such men as Dr. Chalmers and his associates, would have proved an instrument of greater power for penetrating and evangelizing the masses than any which we now see existing, we cannot doubt; and as the picture of what might have been rises before our eye—the picture of the Church of Scotland, aided by the countenance and liberality of the aristocracy—strong in the growing attachment of the great bulk of the middle classes—numbering among her adherents more than two-thirds of the whole population of the land—advancing year by year in numbers and in strength—reclaiming larger and larger portions of the waste places of the wilderness, and turning them into the garden of the Lord—we sigh in heart-felt sorrow over an event which has put the fulfillment of such a prospect forever out of sight. We cannot doubt that for a calamity so great, Divine Providence has some compensating benefits in store, which as yet we do not see; and with a hopeful faith we look for it, that in some great and beneficent issue, as unlike to any which our sagacity or foresight can now foreshadow as was the Disruption of 1843 to the anticipations of 1834, when the future shall have unfolded and illustrated them, the purposes of that wise and gracious Providence which watches over the Church of Christ will receive their ample vindication.

CHAPTER XVIII.

After the withdrawal of those who now constituted the clergy of the Free Church of Scotland, the ministers who remained in the Establishment left to their own course, quietly bowed their shoulders to the burden and the scourge of those whose bread they ate. The seven of Strathbogie were treated by them as though no censure had been incurred. "The veto law —the proceedings of previous Assemblies relative to the settlements at Marnoch, Culsalmond, and Lethendy—the Acts of 1833, 1834, and 1839, by which the ministers of the Associate Synod, Parliamentary and Extension churches had been admitted were all subjected to the same simple and summary treatment." "Mr. Clark had his license restored to him, and the settlements of Mr. Edwards at Marnoch, and of Mr. Middleton at Culsalmond were recognized and confirmed." All measures that had been taken for increasing the extent and activity of the establishment were canceled, and all things thrown back into the condition in which they had been before the evangelical movement took place with the condition now expressly admitted that the church supported by the State is the creature and engine of the State. If Scotchmen can look with pride upon the noble act of independence and self-sacrifice of the founders of their Free Church, they have also cause of shame in that so many of their countrymen were capable of sustaining the domination complained of, and still more in that so many consented to retain their places in an establishment under such humiliating conditions. Something is, however, to be ascribed to previous habits of thinking; and the strongly retained notion that State support is indispensable to the efficiency of a church.

The tenacity with which Dr. Chalmers clung to this idea of dependence upon the funds of the State, even in the act of relinquishing them, from the most painful experience of the evils therewith connected, is proved by his declaration made on that very occasion while defining the attitude of the Free Church toward the government. "The voluntaries mistake us, if they conceive us to be voluntaries. We hold by the duty of government to give of their resources and their means for the maintenance of a gospel ministry in the land; and we pray that their eyes may be opened, so that they may learn how to acquit themselves as the protectors of the church, and not as its corruptors or its tyrants"..... "Again, if we thus openly proclaim our difference with men, who under the guise of principle— and of this principle we question not the honesty—refuse in the affairs of the church, to have any participation with the government, still more resolutely do we disclaim all fellowship with men who, under the guise of direct and declared opposition, lift a menacing front against the powers that be; or, disdaining government, and impatient of restraint, manifest a spirit of contention and defiance."

Dr. Chalmers's sustentation scheme was the temporal stronghold of the Free-Church, without which all her efforts would have been feeble and disconnected, and more than two hundred of her churches must have been abandoned. "His report as to the progress made in its establishment, was in the highest degree encouraging. Six hundred and eighty-seven associations had been organized. Two hundred and thirty-nine of them were in full operation, and had already transmitted to the general treasury upward of £17,000. The average yielded by each of these associations was £73, per annum."

"The report relative to the Building Fund, also given in by Dr. Chalmers, was not less encouraging. In one week by means of the local associations £16,578 had been collected in smaller sums, which, added to the more magnificent donations made during the few months preceding the disruption, presented no less a sum than £104,776 already available for the erection of churches. And the day of the Disruption sprang a new mine of charity in the hearts of thousands. Their ministers having led the way, and given to the world a clear and convincing testimony to the reality and power of religious principle, in the pecuniary sacrifices which they made many a noble-hearted layman was in haste to follow and to rival their example. First among those Christians and generous men who have furnished a new standard of individual liberality, stood Mr. William Campbell of Glasgow, whose benefactions to the Church of Scotland during the progress of her extensions had already amounted to about £15,000, began a new career of a still wider liberality, by a donation £2000 to the Building Fund of the Free Church. The Marchioness of Breadalbane, Mr. Ewing of Levenside, Mr. Nisbet of London, and Mr. Brown Douglas of Edinburgh, were mentioned also by Dr. Chalmers as the donors of sums equally munificent; and we regret only that the delicacy of a genuine humility forbids our naming one, the overflowings of whose altogether princely generosity crossed the Atlantic, and of which Dr. Chalmers felt himself to be be honored in being chosen as the channel. These were the offerings of the rich, but greater and more precious in the eyes of Him who still sits over against the Church's Treasury, were the offerings—approaching far more to the character of pecuniary sacrifices—made at this time by thousands in the humblest walks of life."

The remarkable harmony of the first Assembly of the Free Church, which was such that all its business was conducted without debate, and not once had a vote to be taken, was due, in a great degree, to the care with which Dr. Chalmers and others had prosecuted the work of previous preparation. Its proceedings awakened an intense interest in the public mind and were daily listened to by thousands. On the Sabbaths such multitudes assembled to worship, that, the hall of Assembly being unable to contain them, five separate congregations were formed without the walls.

Yet, amid their many encouragements, the members of this Assembly had also grave and affecting cares resting upon them personally, which nothing but an imperative sense of duty could have warranted them in incurring. It was in the rural parishes that the severest privations were borne by the families of the out-going clergy. This was foreseen and alluded to by

Dr. Chalmers before they separated. "'Just conceive,' he said, 'these clergymen returning to their homes, finding their houses in process of being dismantled and their parishioners saddened by the prospect of an approaching separation.' We stay here in our hilarity, in the presence of each other, but these gentlemen go to what were once their welcome and comfortable homes, and what is the spectacle that meets them on their return? I can not venture on the description. Going, they and their families, they know not whither—resigning all those places to which they are attached by so many fond and intense local affections—their garden walks where they freely enjoyed the hours of their relaxation—the peaceful study where the man of learning enjoyed many a raptured hour of converse with his books, or which the man of piety converted into a sanctuary, aud held intercourse there with his God—all these to be resigned and given up.' 'One venerable minister had to send his wife and children away to a distance of seventy miles —not a house or a hut nearer being open for their accomodation—and he had himself to take a room in the only inn which the district supplied. Another was asked by his widowed daughter to share a cottage, within his parish, in which she lived, but the noble proprietor interfered. She was warned that if she harbored her own parent in her house she would forfeit her right to her dwelling, as it was not desired that any house on this estate should be a 'lodging place for dissenters.' A third, driven from one of the loveliest homes, compelled to study in a wretched garret, and to sleep often with nothing between him and the open heavens but the cold slate, covered with hoar frost—his very breath frozen upon the bed clothes —sunk into the grave.'

"But toil came as well as trouble. To meet the wants of the adhereing population upward of 600 congregations had to be regularly supplied with all the means of grace, and as many churches had to be erected. Never in the history of the Christian Church were so many sermons delivered, so many prayer meetings held, so many addresses delivered, by the same number of clergymen, within the same period of time as by the outgoing ministers during the twelve months which elapsed from the day of the Disruption till the General Assembly of 1844; and never over the same surface of country, or within so short a time, were so many churches built. In towns the kindness of their dissenting brethren afforded many facilities for ministers meeting with their people on the Sabbath days. In the country it was different. Here and there the hand of tyranny was stretched out, and from the church and church-yard—from the bare hill-side and from the public highways, on all of which they sought to assemble and to worship God—ministers and people, were driven, till they took their station within high water-mark on the lone sea-beach their feet upon the damp and tangled sea-weed—the roll of those breakers whose spray the breeze drove over them keeping time to their solemn psalmody. It was a summer in which there was scarcely a rainy or inclement Sabbath, and very generally in the rural districts, even where no opposition of any kind was encountered, there was preaching in the open air. When this was impracticable or inexpedient, strange shifts and expedients were frequently employed. At Morningside, Dr. Chalmers opened his own dwelling-house, and converted it into a church; and perhaps he never occupied a more picturesque position than when, planted midway up the staircase, he preached to a disjointed congregation scattered into different rooms, all of whom could hear, but not half of whom could see the clergyman. In addition to the increased amount of purely pastoral labor which devolved upon them, the leading ministers of the Free Church had large draughts made upon their time and strength for public services. The lively interest which the Disruption had created in other countries, suggested the idea of dispatching numerous deputations to explain the principles and to plead the cause of the Free Church. Familiar as the Presbyterians of Ulster were with the great principles involved in the controversy, and looking with the strong attachment of children to the parent Church in Scotland, they needed less either to be informed or to be stimulated, and, as became them, they were the foremost, both by word and deed, in expressions of attachment. In England, the deputations from the North were received everywhere with extraordinary demonstrations of affection and good-will. Public meetings were held in the metropolis and most of the principal towns. In Manchester, thirty-five pulpits were opened upon one Sunday, that sermons might be preached, and collections taken. In Birmingham fifteen pulpits were placed, in like manner, upon the same Sabbath, at the disposal of the friends of the Free Church. London was not so well organized, but it exhibited a no less generous spirit. Over all wide England, fervent and substantial expressions of desire were given to aid the men who, after making so great a personal sacrifice, were attempting the task of building up a national institute in a year. The event which had occurred in Scotland had power also to stir profoundly and extensively the sympathies of the American churches, and a deputation, headed by Dr. Cunningham, crossed the Atlantic. In one or other of these public services Dr. Chalmers was again and again solicited to engage. It was pressed upon him in particular and in the strongest terms, that he should deliver a few lectures in London, explanatory of the principles involved in the Disruption ; but he steadily resisted all the urgency by which he was beset. He had the profoundest conviction that all which Ireland, England, or America would or could do for her, was utterly insignificant as compared with what Scotland could and ought to do for herself. Those bursts of generous feeling, which it was so pleasant to witness or excite, would in a year or two subside, and the contributions begotten by them would die away in like manner. To meet all the temporary necessities of her position, it was proper and needful that the Free Church should avail herself of them to the uttermost. They served, besides, a higher and more enduring object—that of binding together the churches in the bonds of a brotherly unity, and upon that ground especially were they to be cherished. But ere very long the church would be thrown back upon her own internal resources—the foreign springs would fail, and it would be upon the home fountain that all would finally depend. It was to the striking out of that fountain, to the rendering it as deep and productive as possible, that Dr. Chalmers's whole and undivided strength was given. In August and September he made a sustentation tour, taking in Perth, Dunkeld, Aberdeen, Arbroath, Dundee and St. Andrews." In one or two instances he addressed large audiences; but what he specially sought was a private conference with some "ten, twenty or thirty of those, who in each place were ready to undertake the work of making the regular rounds of the families of their district, that he might impress them with the magnitude of their office, and animate them to punctuality and zeal in the discharge of its duties."

Returning from this tour, he attended the "meeting of the General Assembly held at Glasgow in October, which he opened by a sermon on the 'outward business of the house of God,' from the text, Nehemiah xi, 16. The object of this meeting was, to revive in the west of Scotland that impulse which the presence of the outgoing ministers had created in Edinburgh. Interim reports of the various operations of the church were read, all bright with promise, but covering too brief a period to give accurate augury of the future. Reanimated by their intercourse, the ministers returned to prosecute their labors amid greater outward difficulties, but with undiminished ardor, during the succeeding winter. The results, as announced at the meeting of the General Assembly in May, 1844, were in the highest degree encouraging.

"Without exception, all the Missionaries in foreign stations had declared their adhesion to the Free Church. This testimony was doubly valuable, as coming from men who had been quiet spectators of the conflict, the purity and devotedness of whose character was above all suspicion, and who must have had many fears as to the probabilities of an infant church, struggling for life at home, being able to continue their services abroad. Their fears were disappointed; for, notwithstanding all that she otherwise had to do, the Free Church, in the first year of her existence, raised no less than £32,000 for her various schemes of Christian philanthropy—a sum greater by

£12,000 than had been raised by the whole church in the year 1842.

"It had been looked upon as a marvel, that in the course of seven years previous to the Disruption, two hundred churches should have been built, in connection with a church the whole number of whose ministers numbered about a thousand. But that marvel was lost in this—that by a church, whose ministers numbered at the commencement only 470, nearly 500 churches were built in a single year. And yet the work of church-building was far from finished ; for, contrary to all anticipations, the people had forsaken the Establishment in a much higher ratio, as to numbers, than the ministers ; and it would have required more than 700 churches to accommodate the congregations who were ready to attach themselves to the Free Church. To meet the spiritual wants of more than 200 unprovided congregations, the church had only 130 licentiates at command, some of whom, it might be presumed, were unlikely to be elected as ministers. Of these, so many as 114 were ordained in the course of a year, which saw the original church of the Disruption, making an addition of about one-fourth to the number of her ministers.

"Setting aside the generous aid rendered by strangers, upward of £300,000 had been contributed by a community, which at this period could not embrace so much as one-third of the population of Scotland. That particular branch of the general revenue which was devoted to the maintenance and extension of the ministry appeared also to be in a prosperous condition. Adopting the suggestions embodied in a pamphlet by Dr. Chalmers, printed and privately circulated in 1843, two sources of ministerial income had been opened. The produce of all the local associations constituted a general fund, out of which each minister received an equal dividend ; while from the collections at the church doors, each congregation was permitted and encouraged to supplement the salary of its clergyman. With the Central Sustentation Fund, established by the Free Church, the name of Dr. Chalmers is imperishably connected. It stands and will long abide as the best monument of his genius in ecclesiastical finance. Compared with the system under which each separate congregation sustains its own ministry, it presented many and peculiar recommendations. By drawing from the abundance of the rich a fixed supply for the necessities of the poor, it preserved a Christian ministry in many districts where otherwise it must have expired. By binding the strong and the weak together, it created a new species of unity in the church, and breathed throughout it a fresh and healthful spirit of brotherhood. By erecting orderly channels through which the overflowing liberality of the wealthier congregations was spread equally within the whole area of the church, it established a security against the fitful and capricious distributions of individual benevolence. By inviting every member of the church to unite, not simply in supporting that clergyman whose services he personally enjoyed, but in sustaining and extending a gospel ministry throughout the land, wherever it was needed, it gave a new, if not a purer motive to his liberality, supplying it 'with a wider aim, and a nobler arena.' The actual income, it is true, which in the first year of its existence it supplied, was comparatively small and insufficient. The whole sum yielded by the Associations throughout that year amounted to £68,700, which, divided among 600 clergymen, afforded to each a salary of £100. Many, however, of the Associations had but recently been organized—many had been in full working order, under the eye of an ordained clergyman, during a portion only of the past year; and when the large and exhausting efforts expended upon church-building were over, it was confidently and generally expected that the Sustentation Fund would be largely replenished. To some extent Dr. Chalmers participated in this expectation. He rejoiced that one of the primary objects of the fund—the maintenance of the Church of the Disruption in all its original magnitude, had been more than realized." But still perceived a defect in the scheme, which he thought might be remedied by the introduction of some principle, which making the " gettings out" bear some regular proportion to the "givings in," should be self-acting, self-regulating, needing not the constant interference or agency of any central authority. With this view, he proposed to the General Assembly of 1844, "that the equal dividend should be abolished; that no congregation should be put upon the Fund till its annual contributions should amount to £50; and that each congregation should receive from the Fund one-half more than it transmitted, till the ministerial income should amount to £150." The Assembly, however, did not yet perceive the necessity of the improvement, and almost unanimously rejected it. Later results have gone to prove the actuality of the evil which Dr. Chalmers foresaw, and the Free Church may yet feel herself under the necessity of adopting the remedy which he suggested.

The Free Church movement had a most salutary effect upon the interests of true religion throughout the whole region of its influence, among all denominations of protestants, on the continent as well as in the British Isles. The delegations from so many different churches which met in her Assembly suggested the idea of a general evangelical union, which met with the most zealous support of Dr. Chalmers. Though his failing health prevented him from being present in any of its meetings, yet with his pen he ably contributed to direct the course which the union should pursue.

Though Dr. Chalmers could no longer sustain the fatigue of great public efforts, and had withdrawn from the principal management of the financial concerns of the church, yet he still wished to devote his remaining strength to the cause which for thirty years had been the nearest to his heart—the religious instruction and elevation of the neglected poor. "I have determined" he says, writing to Mr. Lennox on the 26th July, 1844, "to assume a poor district of 2000 people and superintend it myself, though it be a work greatly too much for my declining strength and means, yet such do I hold to be the efficiency of the method, with the Divine blessing, that, perhaps, as the concluding act of my public life, I shall make the effort to exemplify what, as yet I have only expounded." Preparatory to the execution of this purpose he " delivered four public lectures in the months of June and July, directed mainly to the illustration of the superior efficacy of local schools and local churches, so related to the limited districts in which they are planted as to bear with special and concentrated effect upon the surrounding families.

"The locality selected by Dr. Chalmers as the scene of his projected enterprise was the West Port; a part of Edinburgh to which a few years previously an infamous notoriety had been attached by those secret murders, the discovery of which sent a thrill of horror through the land. By an accurate survey, it was found that the main street and its adjoining wynds contained 411 families, of which 45 were attached to some Christian communion; 70 were Roman Catholics; and 296 had no connection with any church whatever. Out of a gross population of 2000, three-fourths of the whole, or about 1500 of the inhabitants were living—within sound of many a Sabbath-bell, and with abundance of contiguous church accommodation—lost to all the habits and all the decencies of the Christian life. In these families the number of children capable of attending school was only 411, and of these, 290 were growing up altogether untaught. The physical and moral condition of this community was deplorable; one-fourth were paupers on the poor-roll, and one-fourth were street-beggars, thieves, or prostitutes. When Mr. Tasker, the minister of the West Port made his first visits to some of the filthiest closes, it was no uncommon thing for him to find from twenty to thirty men, women and children, huddled together in one putrid dwelling, lying indiscriminately on the floor, waiting the return of the bearer of some well-concocted begging-letter, or the coming on of that darkness under which they might sally out, to earn by fair means or by foul, the purchase-money of renewed debauchery." Formidable as the undertaking seemed, to reform and christianize such a population, Dr. Chalmers, aided by that band of zealous associates, which his lectures had called around him, went hopefully forward. He divided the West Port into twenty districts, containing each about twenty families, "Over each of these districts a visitor was appointed, whose duty it was to visit, once each week, all the families committed to his care ; by all such attention and services as he could offer to win their good will—by reading the Scriptures, by distributing tracts, by entering into conversation, and by engaging in prayer—to promote, as fit openings were given him, their spiritual welfare. A printed slip, drawn up by Dr. Chalmers, was to be left in every house by each visitor, explaining the object of his present and future calls." A school was established in the very neighborhood where Burke and his accomplices had perpetrated their horrible murders, and under an excellent and prudent teacher, was opened on the 11th November, 1844, with sixty-four day scholars and fifty-seven evening scholars. The school house was the upper loft of a deserted tannery, " low roofed and roughly floored, its raw, unplastered walls pierced at irregular intervals with windows of unshapely form, it had little of either the scholastic or ecclesiastical in its aspect ; but never was the true work of school and church done better than in that old tannery-loft of the West Port." Dr. Chalmers had told the people in an address delivered to them, a few days previously, what it was his purpose to do for them, that they should be furnished with one of the best teachers of the country, but that they must make the school their own by paying for it, at the rate of two-pence a week for each child's education ; that, however, as the article they were to be supplied with was worth a great deal more, he had no doubt they would gladly pay it. The people were quite delighted both with the speech and the proposition, and evidently won by the kindness evinced thereby.

" The educational part of the process having been fairly set a going, the higher and more difficult operation was commenced, of bringing the adult population under regular spiritual instruction. On the forenoon of Sabbath the 22d December, Dr. Chalmers opened the tan-loft for public worship.'" Dr. Hanna, who was present on the evening of that day when the city missionary officiated, says that when he looked round and saw that the whole fruit of the advices and requests, and entreaties which for many previous weeks had been brought to bear upon all the families by the visitors, was the presence of about a dozen adults, and those mostly old women, he confessed to strong misgivings as to the result. But the services were regularly continued three times every sabbath, and the system of visiting faithfully carried out; and in April, 1845, Dr. Chalmers was peculiarly happy in securing the services of the Rev. Mr. Tasker, under whom the congregation steadily increased. The enterprise was one which occupied much of the labor of Dr. Chalmers, and a still more prominent place in his petitions before the Throne of Grace. In the course of the year 1846, the liberality of several christian friends, whom he had interested in it, enabled him to hasten its progress considerably, by furnishing the means " not only to build a church and school-room, but also to purchase and fit up a tenement of houses, as model houses for working men, in which, at a low rent, additional means of cleanliness and comfort were enjoyed.

" On Friday the 19th February, 1847, the West Port church was opened for public worship by Dr. Chalmers, and on the 25th April, he presided at the first sacrament administered within its walls. On the following Monday he said to Mr. Tasker—' I have got now the desire of my heart—the church is finished, the schools are flourishing, our ecclesiastical machinery is about complete, and all in good working order. God has indeed heard my prayer, and I could now lay down my head in peace and die.'" That consummation was not long delayed.

As to the after progress of the church and school thus founded, it is remarked by Dr. Hanna, five years after Dr. Chalmers's death, that " under the admirable management of Mr. Tasker, each year has witnessed an advancing progress. In its educational department the work is complete. In the different schools, male and female, day and evening, between 400 and 500 children are in attendance; nor is it known that there is a single child of a family resident within the West Port who is not at school. The habit of church attendance has become as general and regular in the West Port as it is in the best conditioned districts of Edinburgh. The church is filled to overflowing, and, while these pages are passing through the press, the people of the West Port, who among themselves contributed no less than £100 to the building of their church at first, are contributing, at an equal rate of liberality, for the erection of a gallery. It was Dr. Chalmers's conviction that in the worst localities the means existed, and could be evoked, by which an effective gospel ministry, if once created, could afterward be sustained ; and the history of the West Port confirms that conviction. The ecclesiastical machinery is now complete, and were it separated from the rest it could be maintained in all its present efficiency by the freewill offerings of the people themselves. During the last year, beside meeting all the expenses necessary for the due support of Christian ordinances, amounting to nearly £250, the West Port congregation has contributed £70 to missionary and educational objects. Nor has the cost been great at which all this has been effected. A site has been purchased, a church, seated for 520, has been erected, commodious schoolrooms have been built and furnished, a large adjoining tenement has been bought and fitted up, the minister's and the schoolmaster's, and the schoolmistress's salaries have been paid, and all incidental expenses discharged, during seven years and a half, for less than £5500."

The efforts made by Dr. Chalmers to obtain an improvement in the course of college and theological instruction, have already been mentioned, together with the apathy with which they were regarded by the University authorities of his native land. It was in the new collegiate arrangements of the Free Church that he had the satisfaction of seeing his scheme for Theological education adopted ; both in the number of instructors and the distribution of subjects among them. With five theological professors instead of three, the highest number in the Scottish Universities, formerly, a more complete course of instruction is now furnished in the institution established under his auspices than in any other in the British dominions.

Dr. Chalmers in the earlier part of his professorial career in Edinburgh went through a wide course of lectures, publishing portion after portion, as delivered, thereby entailing upon himself the continual task of new composition for the succeding session. Subjects, besides, were constantly occurring to him "of a character somewhat extraneous to the proper topics of his course, upon which a brief set of lectures were drawn up and delivered to his students. The result of the whole, while impairing the orderly treatment of the common heads of Divinity, was eminently favorable to that freshness and force of impulse which it was his great distinction as a teacher to communicate. He who studies attentively the first four volumes of the one, and the last three volumes of the other series of his Works, will not readily believe, that even in respect of the amount and variety of information communicated to them, the students of Dr. Chalmers fared worse than others; but it was not here that his power and glory lay, as the greatest teacher of Theology our country has ever seen. Others have amassed larger stores of learning, and conveyed them to their students in more comprehensive and compendious forms. But who ever lit up the evidences and truths of Christianity with a light so attractive; and who ever filled the youthful breasts of those who were afterward to occupy the pulpits of the land, with the fire of so generous and so devoted an enthusiasm! His professorial career had lasted for twenty years when the Disruption occurred. Even at that time he could travel, he said, from one end of Scotland to the other, and spend each night in the manse of one of his former pupils; and if the growing majorities in the General Assembly by which that event was preceded were analyzed, it would appear that nine-tenths at least of those who had listened to his fervid prelections in the University, counted it honor to stand by the side of their venerated instructor when the hour of trial came. Immediately after the Disruption, Dr. Chalmers resigned his Chair at the University, and accepted the appointment of Principal and Primarius Professor of Divinity in whatever collegiate institution the Free Church might be able to erect. Strongly convinced that with the slender attractions which its unendowed and under-paid offices held out, the future ministry of the Free Church could alone maintain its position in the country by the superior scholarship and deeper piety of its ministers, he gave an increased measure both of time and care to the duties of his professorship; and after the experience of three sessions he had this hopeful testimony to bear : 'The convener of your Committee has the satisfaction of bearing witness, and this after the experieuce of eighteen winters as a Professor of Theology, and five more as the occupier of a previous chair, that his class of last session stands the highest in his estimation of all which have preceded it; if not in its superior number of eminent and distinguished students who stand above the level of their fellows, in what is far better—a more elevated table-land of general proficiency and good scholarship. But it is of greatly surpassing moment that we should have to report an obvious increase, from year to year, in their sense of things sacred, and devotedness of heart and spirit to the great objects of the Christian ministry.' In the hope of contributing to this increase, during his last collegiate sessions Dr. Chalmers was in the habit of inviting his students to private interviews, devoted wholly to conversation relative to their own spiritual condition and prayer."

After his transference to the Free Church College, Dr. Chalmers's "undivided labor was bestowed upon systematic theology. It had for many years been the highest object of his literary and professorial ambition to leave behind him a complete body of Divinity, containing the fruits of his maturest reflections, both on the credentials and contents of the Christian Revelation. Had his Lectures on Natural Theology and the Evidences not been already given to the public, they would have been subjected to the same process of condensation through which his other lectures were made to pass, and his 'Institutes of Theology,' when given to the world, would have presented a more uniform and homogeneous aspect than they now wear. As for many years he had, however, to go over the same ground with his students which the first four volumns of his works embraced, he adopted the plan of employing these volumes as text books, accompanying his examinations with that summary and review of their contents which form Book II. and Book III. of his 'Institutes of Theology.' With the obvious disadvantage of subjecting the reader of this last work to a reiteration of familiar topics, those two books of the 'Institutes' exhibit a compactness of diction, which amply proves that he could when he pleased transfer the brevity and force of his spoken into his written language, and what will be of no ordinary importance to any one who undertakes the hitherto unattempted task of estimating the direct and original contributions which Dr. Chalmers had made to theological science, they give us his own estimate of what he conceived to be most valuable in his earlier writings. It is, however, to that portion of the 'Institutes' which treats of the subject-matter of Christianity that we would especially solicit attention. Upon no part of his published writings was so large a share of their author's care and thought bestowed. There are to be found here his latest and ripest thoughts upon some of the profoundest questions with which the human intellect has engaged; if not set forth in the gorgeous amplifications in which he loved previously to indulge, yet in the simpler purer, weightier diction which became one who was leaving his last intellectual legacy to the world.

The 'Institutes of Theology' and the 'Daily Scripture Readings' were commenced about the same time, and were carried on simultaneously, a portion of each being written daily, and the transition being frequently instantaneous from the one composition to the other. Engaged with the one, he brought to the Divine oracles a mind singularly free of theological prejudice; he sat as a little child at the feet of Divine wisdom, and received into a meek and loving heart, according to its plain and natural meaning, each utterance she gave forth. Engaged with the other, he brought to the sacred oracles a mind full-fraught with the true spirit of the Inductive Philosophy, and collecting the varied testimonies of the Divine record as they lay scattered over the sacred page, he combined them into one complete and harmonious system. The two engagements were most unlike. Very rarely has the same simplicity in the one, and the same science in the other, been exhibited; but where shall we find another instance in which the two, brought into such daily and close proximity, went on so harmoniously together? The many prayers, however, which Dr. Chalmers offered that he might be preserved from the fetters of an artificial orthodoxy, may be taken as an evidence that even in his instance it was not without an effort that simplicity sat embosomed in system, while system did nothing to hurt simplicity.

Besides the composition of his 'Institutes of Theology,' the only other literary occupation of Dr. Chalmers's later years was an occasional contribution to the 'North British Review.' This publication, which under its present accomplished Editor, ranks with the best conducted and most influential of our literary journals, was established in 1844 by Dr. Welsh, Mr. Edward F. Maitland, and a few friends in Edinburgh, to whom it appeared that there was both room and need for a Review of the highest class, the organ of no party, political or ecclesiastical, and which instead of ignoring or affecting to disown Christianity, was imbued with its spirit." It was designed to embrace, in the language of Dr. Arnold respecting another periodical, "not so much articles on religious subjects as articles on common subjects written in a decidedly Christian tone." The contributions of Dr. Chalmers to this review are now published in the volume of his miscellaneous writings.

The publication of Morell's History of Modern Philosophy awakened in his mind a lively interest in the German Philosophy. Valuable truth he discovered in it, and yet the wholesale adoption of any of its systems he thought very much to be deprecated, and to be best guarded against by a strong and faithful discussion of its truths and errors. Such a work he greatly desired to undertake, and actually delivered a short course of lectures, as an entry upon the subject, which were afterwards embodied in an article for the North British Review. The amount of his information on that head was not adequate to the completion of his plan; but, notwithstanding his advanced age, which seemed to forbid the labor of so large a new attainment, he laid out his design for lectures on Kant, Fichte, and Cousin, which to execute in his usual manner would have involved years of intense study. While still engaged in this pursuit he was gratified by the appearance in Edinburgh of Prof. Tholuck of Halle. The attachment, which sprung up in a few days between those two illustrious men was in the highest degree beautiful. Their first meeting is thus mentioned by Dr. Russell, at whose house Prof. Tholuck was residing. "Dr. Chalmers seated himself on a low chair, close to the learned German, and listened with an air of genuine docility to all he said, throwing in a stray characteristic observation now and then, always, however in the way of encouragement, never in the way of contradiction. Dr. Tholuck had published some verses of a religious character, which had given umbrage to some sect or other. He showed the lines to Dr. Chalmers, who admiring them, observed that he had often been taken to task himself for a similar latitudinarianism; 'for, my dear Sir,' he added, 'some people have a very fine nose for heresy.' While Dr. Chalmers was sitting in this posture, drinking in all that was said to him, Tholuck turned to his host, and said in German, that he had never seen so beautiful an old man. The words coming out so suddenly in an unknown tongue, instantly changed the expression of Dr. Chalmers's face from that of happy acquiescence, to one of puzzled amazement, which was in the highest degree comic, and this effect was not lessened by his eager putting of the question, 'What is it, Sir, that he says?'—a question impossible to answer, and yet not easy to evade. The result of this interview was an amount of mutual confidence and esteem, as deep and sincere as it was sudden. Dr. Tholuck took an early opportunity of returning the visit, and spent some hours with Dr. Chalmers, urging upon him in the most direct and homely way, the necessity of directing his mind to the study of the German Theology, for, as it was from that quarter the bane had come which was poisoning the simple faith, so it was there alone that the antidote could be found. The day before Tholuck's departure, Dr. Chalmers called upon him and found him at his mid-day repast. He sat with him only for a minutes, and said little, but looked at him constantly with an expression of earnest interest and affection. He rose to take leave; and, instead of taking him by the hand, he threw his arms around his neck and kissed him, while 'God bless you, my dear friend,' broke with apparent difficulty from his overcharged heart. After he was gone, it was noticed that a tear had gathered in the eye of him who had received the apostolic benediction and seal of brotherhood from one he loved and venerated so much. His only observation was a half-muttered half-spoken, *eben ein Kuss*—even a kiss."

His speculations in German philosophy were interrupted by a more imperative call, kindling all the sympathies of his nature. The fearful famine of 1846 and 1847 arising from the failure of the potato crop, "left 300,000 of the population in the Highlands and Islands of Scotland, and many millions in Ireland, to face the coming year with food in hand sufficient to sustain them only for a few weeks. The extent of the failure of the crop was no sooner announced than the awfulness of the impending catastrophe filled Dr. Chalmers with alarm and anxiety. He foresaw that nothing but an act of prompt and unparalleled generosity could ward off the fearful calamity of hundreds and thousands in a Christian land miserably perishing from want of food. To wait till the cry of actual hunger was heard, the sight of the dying kindled sympathy, was to ring the death-knell over multitudes to whom the relief would come too late. Fastening his first thoughts upon the Highlands, he not only hastened to gather up all the information conveyed through public channels, but by private circulars of his own, widely distributed, he obtained the most minute and trustworthy accounts of the state of the suffering population. As a great proportion of them were members of the Free Church, it became that Church to step prominently forward in this emergency, and to do what she could to save them from the horrors of famine. Nor did she fail in her duty at this time; being the first public body that moved organizing an effective Committee of Relief, and ordering a public collection to be made in all her churches on Sabbath, the 6th December, 1846." The amount of that collection was uncommonly large, "the Committee of Relief being put into possession of no less a sum than £15,000. This denominational effort was soon merged into those larger measures of relief which Scotland so promptly and successfully adopted, so that while thousands died in Ireland—whole households perishing together, and many lying unburied till the dogs came and devoured their bodies—it was not known that in Scotland a single individual died solely and directly from want of food. It required, however, incessant vigilance, and no small amount of generosity, to be sustained all through the winter. In addition to the public tide of charity flowing in upon the Highlands, innumerable lesser streams were kept constantly flowing. Very large sums were committed to Dr. Chalmers for private distribution. There was scarcely, indeed, a daily post which did not bring him some donation; and he never watched for letters more eagerly, and he never read any with greater delight. He had many methods of communicating directly or indirectly with the Highlands, and of dispensing the money intrusted thus to his care. To one lady alone, the late Mrs. Mackay, we are aware of his having committed £500. Nor was Ireland forgotten. Her greater sorrows claimed a large share of his sympathy; and, through Miss Pringle of Edinburgh, and Dr. Edgar of Belfast, he had pleasure in conveying his own and other gifts of charity. The extraordinary spectacle of upward of 300,000 men employed on the relief works—of upward of three millions of people fed daily by the hand of public charity, and yet many perishing notwithstanding—afforded matter of most interesting speculation. When the spring months came, there was a fear that large breadths of country would be left uncultivated. The crofters had neither seed-corn of their own, nor money to buy it; and even after it was furnished to them, they knew little or nothing of the new modes of agriculture which it would be necessary for them to adopt. The state of a country thrown suddenly into circumstances so new, appeared to Dr. Chalmers so worthy of investigation that he resolved to devote himself to the task. Having presented his general views in a paper entitled, 'The Political Economy of a Famine,' he proposed to prosecute a minute and searching inquiry into the past condition and future prospects both of the

Highlands and of Ireland, with a view to determine what were the likeliest means of permanently improving the economic condition of their inhabitants. It is ever to be regretted that he did not live to execute a work for which much preparation had been made, and many materials collected. We can but indicate, that from the singular history of the Relief Works in Ireland he meant to draw a fresh illustration of the evils by which all public charity is accompanied, and of the inseparable connection which obtains between the moral and economic well-being of a community. He meant to test the various expedients for promoting the future prosperity of Ireland, by applying to them the general axioms, that it was out of her own soil, and by the industry of her own inhabitants, that she must be taught to draw her support, and that the best and most effective aid which could be given her, was that which promised the soonest to set her free from all foreign help."

CHAPTER XVIII.

It must have been with a keen but saddening delight that Dr. Chalmers, in the spring of 1845 paid a visit to his native village and renewed his acquaintance with the scenes and now few surviving companions of his early days. In the spring and summer of the next year a tour in the south of Scotland, amid the haunts of border romance, to the charms of which he had a poetical sensibility, and the vale of the classic Yarrow, brought him round upon the footsteps of his incipient ministry at Cavers, where he was attended by the grandson of the clergyman whose assistant he had been. And his last summer afforded him a ramble among the retreats of his busy life in Glasgow.

"It may gratify a natural curiosity should we follow Dr. Chalmers through the different engagements of a day at Morningside, and furnish some details of his personal habits and mode of domestic life. Whatever variety the day exhibited, it had one fixed essential feature. The motto, '*Nulla dies sine linea*' never met with a more rigorous fulfillment. The period allotted to what he called ' severe composition ' had never (if we except his first winter at St. Andrew's) exceeded two or three hours at a time, and in ordinary circumstances there was seldom more than one sitting daily at such work. The tension of the mind during the effort was extreme, but it was never so long continued as to induce fatigue or exhaustion. During the last six or seven years of his life, his daily modicum of original composition was completed before breakfast, written in short hand, and all done in bed. The preparatory ruminating or excogitating process was slow, but it was complete. He often gave it as a reason why he did not and could not take part in the ordinary debates of the General Assembly, that he had not the faculty which some men seemed to him to possess, of thinking extempore; nor could he be so sure of any judgment as to have comfort in bringing it before the public till he had leisurely weighed and measured it. He was vehement often in his mode of expression; but no hasty judgment was ever penned or publicly spoken by him. 'I have often fancied,' he once said to me, 'that in one respect I resemble Rousseau, who says of himself that his processes of thought were *slow but ardent*'—a curious and rare combination. In proportion, however, to the slowness with which his conclusions were reached, was the firmness with which they were riveted. He has been charged with inconsistencies, but (putting aside the alteration in his religious sentiments) I am not aware of any one opinion formerly expressed or published by him, which he ever changed or retracted. This slow and deliberate habit of thinking gave him a great advantage when the act of composition came to be performed. He never had the double task to do, at once of thinking what he should say, and how he should say it. The one was over before the other commenced. He never began to write till, in its subjects, and the order and proportion of its parts, the map or outline of the future composition was laid down; and this was done so distinctly, and as it were, authoritatively, that it was seldom violated. When engaged, therefore, in writing, his whole undivided strength was given to the best and most powerful expression of pre-established ideas. So far before him did he see, and so methodically did he proceed, that he could calculate for weeks and months beforehand, the rate of his progress, and the day when each separate composition would be finished.

"The same taste for numerical arrangement was exhibited in the most insignificant actions and habits of his life. It regulated every part of his toilet—down even to the daily stropping of his razor. Beginning with his minimum, which was two strokes, he added one stroke more each day successively, till he got up to the number fixed on as his maximum, on reaching which he reversed the process, diminishing the number of his strokes by one each day, till the lowest point was touched; and so, by what he would have called a series of oscillations between his maximum and his minimum, this matter of the stropping undeviatingly progressed. It would be tedious, perhaps trifling, to tell how a like order was punctually observed in other parts of his toilet. He did almost everything by numbers. His staff was put down to the ground regularly at each fourth foot-fall; and the number of its descents gave him a pretty accurate measure of the space over which he walked. Habit had rendered the counting of these descents an easy, indeed almost a mechanical operation; so that, though meeting friends, and sustaining an animated conversation, it still went on. This mode of measuring distances was variously applied. When he lived at No. 7 Inverleith Row, a complication of streets lay between him and the University, and he imposed upon himself the problem of discovering a new route each day, and keeping a register of their relative lengths. Next to the pleasure of being introduced to an altogether new locality, was that of thoroughly exploring one already known. 'I like,' he said to one of his favorite students, ' to find out new spots in places I am familiar with. The other day I had some time to spare, so I tried if I could extemporize a new route between Comely Bank and Inverleith Row. I sauntered, rather dubious, I must confess, up a sort of cart-lane, and, before I was aware, I got involved in the accessories of a farmhouse, where I was set upon by a mastiff, and so obliged to turn back.' When, in the spring of 1843, he removed to a dwelling-house which he had built for himself at Morningside, as the distance was too great for him to walk from College, he generally drove to the outskirts of the town. While walking from Wright's Houses, the point at which he was set down, to his house at Churchhill, he, one winter, kept an accurate reckoning of the number of persons he met upon the road each day—curious to know whether a fixed average would be observed, or whether it would vary as the days shortened or lengthened. Many more like instances might be quoted, but we must return to our details of his daily life.

"'I find,' he says, 'that successful exertion is a powerful means of exhilaration, which discharges itself in good-humor upon others?' His own morning compositions seldom failed in this effect, as he came forth from them beaming and buoyant, with a step springing as that of childhood, and a spirit overflowing with benignity. If his grandson, or any of the younger members of his family were alone in the breakfast-room, a broad and hearty 'Hurro! hurro!' ringing through the hall, announced his coming, and carried to them his morning greeting. As his invariable mode of dealing with introductions was to invite the introduced to breakfast, very interesting groups often gathered round his breakfast table. In the general conversation of promiscuous society, Dr. Chalmers did not excel. There are minor acts of governing, such as those needed for the management of a House of Commons, or the conduct of a General Assembly, in which he was utterly defective; and there are minor graces of conversation required for its easy guidance through varied and fluctuating channels, which his absorption with his own topics, and the massive abruptness of his movements, made it difficult, perhaps impossible, for him to practice. But at his breakfast table, with half a dozen strangers or foreigners around him, his conversation was in the highest degree rich and attractive. Opportunities naturally occurred, or were willingly made, for him to 'expatiate' upon some passing public topic, or upon some of his own favorite themes, and he was never seen nor heard to greater advantage. His power of pithy expression (remarkably exhibited in his occasional employment of vernacular Scotch), and of pictorial narrative, his concentrated and intense moral earnestness, his sense of humor, his boundless benignity, the pure, transparent, and guileless simplicity of his character—received many of their happiest illustrations at such times. He had one morning in the week reserved especially for his students." In the art of making youth at ease in his company, he was remarkably happy. His extensive knowledge of the topography of Britain contributed to that end; the young man must have come from a very out-of-the-way region if Dr. Chalmers was not able to enter into familiar conversation with him about the localities of his native place. He " was much gratified by the reception given to his works in America, and had great pleasure in making the personal acquaintance of Dr. Elton, Dr. Sprague, Dr. Smyth, Dr. Cox, Dr. Beecher, and other eminent American clergymen. In the summer and autumn of 1845, many transatlantic visitors were his guests at Morningside.

"The interval between breakfast and dinner was devoted to the 'Biblical Readings,' and to extending the shorthand of the 'Institutes.' He dined latterly at one o'clock, and as he had to be at his class at two, the meal was necessarily a hurried one. He was indifferent about food, and remarkably abstemious; but there was no habit of life about which he was so scrupulous," or more frequently condemned himself of excess. His "evenings were given to general reading, and to the society of his family and friends. He kept steadily by one book at a time, and however small a portion of it might be overtaken each evening, the perusal was regularly prosecuted to a close. And here too, as well as in his summer visits, he sought out the friends of his youth." Within the last two or three years of his life, he completed an entire perusal of Gibbon, Shakspeare, and Milton. 'I don't wonder now,' he said, 'at Milton's own preference for Paradise Regained over Paradise Lost.' The single passage of Shakspeare which he most frequently recited, was that one in Henry IV., which commences

'I saw young Harry—with his beaver on,
His cuisses on his thighs, gallantly armed,' &c.;

and the single play in which he took most pleasure was Midsummer Night's Dream, among the fairy pictures of which he delighted to revel. 'I look,' he would say, after laying down the book, 'I look on Shakspeare as an intellectual miracle; I would put him before Milton from his exhaustless variety.' One of his students once told him of the enthusiasm of the Germans about Shakspeare, and related the anecdote of Goëthe's comparison between Tieck, Shakspeare, and himself, in which, with a singular mixture both of pride and humility, he said, 'That relation which Tieck holds to me, I hold to Shakspeare. . I regard Shakspeare as a being of a superior nature.' 'Well, sir, do you know,' said Dr. Chalmers, after hearing the anecdote, 'I like that very much. I dare say Shakspeare was the greatest man that ever lived — greater perhaps even than Sir Isaac Newton.' In February, 1845, two years after the Disruption, we find the following entry in Dr. Chalmers's journal : ' A few days ago finished the complete perusal of Shakspeare. Began Paradise Lost, and am reading with great interest, Edwards on the end of God in Creation. Let me henceforth betake myself to serious reading.'

"In his domestic intercourse with his daughters, there was much playful familiarity. Finding one of them sitting alone in a room, he said to her—'.Well, my dear little howlet—

> Hail, mildly pleasing solitude,
> Companion of the wise and good ;

but I'm no for us growing perfectly uncognizant of one another, sitting in corners like sae mony cats.' A spirit of chivalry ran through all his intercourse with his daughters : they not only ministered to his comfort in the hours of relaxation, he made them companions, as it were, of his public life, and sought their intellectual sympathy with even his highest exercises of thought."

"About the beginning of 1834" writes the Rev. Mr. Couper of Burntisland, "Dr. Chalmers became the proprietor of a house in this locality, and here for seven or eight years following, nearly one-half of his time was spent. His mode of life, while here, was tolerably uniform and exceedingly simple. The earlier portion of the day he generally devoted to study and correspondence, reserving the afternoon and evening for the society of his family and friends, and for the exercise of walking, in which he took great delight. He had many visitors, not a few of them from other countries ; and he scarcely ever failed, when time and weather permitted, to conduct them to his favorite points of view, where he expatiated with wonderful enthusiasm on the varied beauty of the surrounding scenery. It was scarcely possible to take even one short walk with him without perceiving that his capacity of enjoyment was singularly large. He could find beauty everywhere ; at least he could single out from the most ordinary scene, some feature or other on which his mind could dwell with interest and pleasure.

"His youthful freshness of feeling imparted a singular charm to his manners and conversation. Even when verging on old age, he was very strikingly characterized by the simplicity of vivacious and unsuspecting boyhood. Of this peculiarity he was himself quite conscious, and I have heard him more than once allude to it. Having equipped himself one evening to go to Edinburgh, he appeared to have outgrown his ordinary dimensions—the pockets of his great-coat being well stuffed, I think, with books and pamphlets. This occasioned some merriment, in which he heartily joined. Placing his hands on his sides, he went on to say, 'I have now somewhat of the solidity and gravity, and somewhat also of the breadth of middle age; but I can scarcely shake off the feeling of boyhood. I remember, Mr. Couper, when I was a student at St. Andrew's, with what profound veneration I regarded the Professors; when I came to be a Professor there myself, I used to wonder if these gilpies could have the same feeling toward me.' I may give another instance equally characteristic. A steep wooded bank overhanging the sea, commences about a mile and a half to the west of Burntisland, and terminates near the village of Aberdour. Here Dr. Chalmers delighted to ramble, and great was his satisfaction when he had one or two friends along with him to explore the Hews—for such is the name of the locality. One day on reaching the west end of the Hews, we found the gate locked, and, as we intended to proceed to Aberdour, we had to scale the wall. Dr. Chalmers declined the offer of assistance, feeling assured that he was quite competent to the task himself. He soon succeeded in planting himself on the top of the wall, but felt it expedient to rest for a little before attempting to come down. Perched on this rustic eminence, he felt as if carried back into the scenes of his boyhood; and, looking blandly down upon the companions of his walk, gave vent to his feelings in a very curious and racy strain of observation: the purport of it was that he felt it very difficult to realize his progress in life, and that there was often a great contrast between his feelings and his years. 'When I meet,' he said, 'a respectable matron, who is perhaps a dozen years younger than myself, I feel quite disposed to look up to her with the same sort of veneration that I felt when I was a boy.'

"While engaged in conversation, Dr. Chalmers would occasionally fall into a reverie, which, by those not acquainted with him, was felt to be embarrassing. The reverie, when not broken in upon by others, was generally terminated by the abrupt utterance of some important sentiment which he had been revolving in his mind. Thus, he one day remarked, after we had walked for a while in silence, 'What a blessed thing it is, Sir, that it is confidence that is required of us.' At another time, a pretty long pause was broken by his saying with much emphasis, 'I know no point of orthodoxy that is not susceptible of a practical treatment. Take an extreme case—the doctrine that man can do nothing of himself; I would just say, Pray all the harder.' I may record another of the sayings which fell from him in this abrupt but impressive manner; it is one which young ministers especially would do well to ponder. 'It is of great importance to keep up a tone of pulpit preparation; the efficacy of your private ministrations will depend very much upon it.'

"He often became extremely animated—sometimes even vehement—though conversing with only a single individual. This was especially the case when his mind was occupied with any great question in which he had been led to take a prominent part. He might begin calmly, but as he spoke, 'the fire burned,' and a torrent of glowing eloquence soon came rushing from his lips. I have heard him at a fireside, in the recess of a window, and even while sitting up in bed, break forth in a style of stormy grandeur sufficient to electrify a whole assembly."

"He had a wonderful store of anecdotes of which he could avail himself with a happy promptitude, for the illustration of any subject that turned up in conversation, and on such occasions his keen sense of the ludicrous was often evinced with irresistible effect." Yet, "with all his social cheerfulness and beaming joy, there were tokens not a few of an internal conflict—glimpses of an inward desolation which told unmistakably that, like David, he felt himself to be a stranger upon this earth. 'I would not live alway,' was a sentence often uttered. 'What a wilderness the world is to the heart with all it has to inspire happiness! I have a great and growing sense of desolation. What a marvelous solitude every man bears about with him; and then that other and mysterious seclusion—the intercepting vail between us and the Deity. You would think [speaking in a hesitating tone] that He would delight to manifest himself to his creatures. No doubt the obstacle must be in the subjective — the clearer the reflecting medium, the brighter the manifestations. That is strikingly put in Matthew, 'the pure in heart they shall see God.' * * * I look on it as a strong proof of our alienation from God, how short a time we can sustain a direct contemplation of Him; what a mighty transformation when the vail of outer things shall be withdrawn, and we stand naked and alone before Him with whom we have to do!'

"Into the peace and rest of the Sabbath Dr. Chalmers entered with a peculiar joy. Beside his usual evening interviews with his children in his study, there was one duty of a peculiar kind thrown always upon the afternoon of this day. He never received the notification of a death without writing to some member of the afflicted family, and these letters of sympathy were always written on the Sabbath evenings."

Though holding very distinctly and firmly his own views of scriptural truth, the extent of his liberality in judging of others was often manifested in conversation: as once beautifully in connection with a remark on the piety of the monks in the Middle ages. "We would need" he said, "to penetrate the counsels of God, and the secrets of another bosom, before we could pronounce through how much distorting error a man may grope his way to a blissful immortality."

Dr. Chalmers had now lived to behold the entire success of that great evangelical movement in the church, in which he had been the most prominent agent. The voluntary action of the people had nobly sustained it. A body of 470 ministers had been increased 720. The community upon whom they had thrown themselves, though far from the wealthiest, had erected churches for all its congregations, at a cost of more than £450,000, " and in addition to this, had subscribed £100,000 to build manses for all its ministers. It had instituted a College with nine Professorships, to each of which a salary of from £300 to £400 per annum was attached. It had 340 students under education for the holy office, among whom bursaries and scholarships to the amount of £700 had been distributed in a single year. By a single effort it had raised £50,000 for the building of 500 school-houses, and it had already connected with it about 600 schools, in which nearly as many children were instructed in the ordinary branches of education as were in attendance at all the endowed parochial schools of Scotland. For the teaching and training of schoolmasters it had two extensive normal establishments in Glasgow and Edinburgh. At home 110 licentiates and 116 catechists were engaged in the spiritual instruction of the people, while abroad it had agents laboring in every quarter of the habitable globe. At Pesth, at Jassy, at Berlin, at Constantinople, seventeen missionaries and assistants were endeavoring to promote the conversion of the Jews. At Calcutta, Madras, Bombay, Puna, and Nagpur, it supported fifteen European clergymen ordained as missionaries, nine converted natives engaged in the work of the Christian ministry, and a large band of teachers and assistants, both native and European, from whom 4000 Indian children were receiving a complete Christian education. In Nova Scotia, the Canadas, the West Indies, the Cape, Australia, Madeira, Malta, Leghorn, and Gibraltar, there were ministers supported in whole or in part by the bounty of the Free Church, while £1000 per annum had been intrusted to the Evangelical Societies of France and of Geneva, to aid in circulating the Gospel over the continent of Europe. In 1847, the Free Church raised for educational and missionary objects three times as much as the united Church of Scotland did in

1843. It had continued for four years to yield the princely revenue of £300,000, and in that short period had contributed about a million and a half to the Christian cause." Yet Dr. Chalmers still expressed himself unsatisfied as to the final success of the voluntary system, and considered it of great importance that the Free Church should never fall away from her testimony for the principle of a national establishment, when that could be obtained without a compromise of her spiritual independence.

On the subject of national education he entertained similar views. Conceiving that the Free Church, by its voluntary efforts, was as unable to supply the educational as the spiritual wants of the country, he thought it necessary for the government to undertake that work, though what method to pursue was a question of some difficulty. During the last few months of his life it occupied much of his attention. His final opinions were stated by him in conversation to Mr. Fox Maule and other members of the government, whom he met in London, in May, 1847, and afterward, at Mr. Maule's request embodied in a paper, written during a visit to his sister, Mrs. Morton, the purport of which is, that the State should furnish means fc erecting schools throughout the country, including religious instruction ; but leaving the introduction of the particular religious element to the parties who had to do with the erection and management of the respective schools.

On the occasion of that same visit to London, which, indeed, was undertaken for that express purpose, he gave before a parliamentary committee, his last testimony in relation to the Free Church. " At the Disruption a large body of the landed aristocracy of Scotland had refused upon any terms to grant sites on which churches or manses might be built. Such stable fabrics would give permanence to a movement which they intensely disliked, and might prevent that re-union with the Establishment which, when the flush of the first excitement was over, they hoped to see accomplished. When these anticipations were falsified, and it became evident that the Free Church was to rank among the permanent institutions of the country, many of these hostile proprietors gave way, but a goodly number still stood out. Having waited patiently, but in vain, for two years, in the hope that this spirit of intolerance would spontaneously subside, and having exhausted all means of private influence and remonstrance, the General Assembly of 1845 petitioned Parliament and the Legislature, stating the grievance, and praying for legislative redress. The Government having shown no disposition to move in the matter, Mr. Maule, in June, 1846, introduced a bill into the House of Commons, the object of which was to oblige the proprietors to concede. The leading members of the House concurred in condemning the conduct complained of, but as its conclusion was thought to be too stringent, and the hope was cherished that their own good sense and good feeling would induce the proprietors to yield without the necessity of legislative interference, the Bill was thrown out. No symptoms of concession appearing, Mr. Bouverie, in March, 1847, moved and carried the appointment of a Committee of the House ' to inquire whether, and in what parts of Scotland, and under what circumstances, large numbers of her Majesty's subjects have been deprived of the means of religious worship by the refusal of certain proprietors to grant them sites for the erection of churches.' It soon became evident that the examination of witnesses before the committee was to take a wide and important range, and that an attempt was to be made by representing the grounds of the Disruption as so untenable, and the opposition offered to the Establishment so violent, as to palliate if not excuse even the wrong step of refusing sites for churches. In these circumstances, it was deemed desirable that Dr. Chalmers should appear as a witness before the committee."

While in the metropolis, and enjoying the society of many old friends, he formed some new acquaintances whom he valued highly, among whom were Lord Morpeth and Mr. Morell. The following entry in his journal makes mention of several of them, as well as his last interview with Mr. Carlyle.

"*Friday, 14th.*—A most splendid party breakfast in our lodgings—Isaac Taylor, Mr. Morell, Rev. James Hamilton,

Mr. Baptist Noel, his son Wriothesly Noel, now a grown-up lad, and George Weakner. A deal of talk: the main subject was Mr. Irving. Mr. Taylor, whom I had not seen for ten years, looks a great deal more than ten years older. The most interesting appearance and manner of a man were those of Mr. Morell—modest and quiet, and very intelligent; but Taylor the person of the greatest vigor. Mr. Hamilton's recent tracts are truly beautiful, particularly the 'Vine,' from John xv. They left after ten, Taylor and Morell going off together. * * * We took a cab to Carlyle's at Chelsea. Nothing could be warmer than Mrs. Carlyle's reception of me (formerly Miss Welsh, who visited us at Ardincaple Inn). She is remarkably juvenile-looking still. He came to us in a minute or two. I had lost all recollection of him, though he told me of three interviews, and having breakfasted with me at Glasgow. A strong-featured man, and of strong sense. We were most cordial and coalescing, and he very complimentary and pleasant; but his talk was not at all Carlylish, much rather the plain and manly conversation of good ordinary common sense, with a deal of hearty laughing on both sides. The points on which I was most interested were his approval of my territorial system, and his eulogy on direct thinking, to the utter disparagement of those subjective philosophers who are constantly thinking upon thinking. We stopped more than an hour with him. * * * Mr. Carlyle professed his willingness to write for the 'North British,' I think Morell would do the same."

Visiting his sister, Mrs. Morton, at her residence in Gloucestershire, "Dr. Chalmers preached his last sermon in the Independent chapel of the Rev. Mr. Dove—his text being Isaiah xxvii, 4, 5." This occurred on Sabbath the 16th of May. After spending a few days in quiet domestic intercourse with Mrs. Morton and her family, he returned to Edinburgh on the night of Friday the 28th, " bearing no peculiar marks of fatigue or exhaustion. At breakfast the next morning his conversation was as lively and vigorous as ever. He inquired of the Rev. Mr. Gemmel of Fairlie, who was staying in his house, what business had been before the General Assembly on the preceding evening. When told that it was an overture relative to the renewal of an old testimony by the church, he was not satisfied as to the testimony required to be given—he hoped that they would let the matter alone—he expressed himself unfavorable to anything like a renewal of the National Covenants, and that he preferred the making the church's testimony known rather by what it did than what it declared. The forenoon of Saturday was occupied in preparing a report which he was to read before the General Assembly on the following Monday, part of which he now completed, leaving the remainder to be executed on Monday morning before he rose. On Sabbath morning he did not rise to breakfast. 'He sent a message to me,' says Mr. Gemmel, 'after breakfast, to go and see him in his bedroom. On entering the room, I found him in bed, reclining on his back, propped up with pillows, his head being very considerably elevated, which I believe was his usual way of resting in bed. His bland and benevolent countenance beamed upon me as I came up to his side, and he grasped me warmly by the hand. 'I am sorry that you are unwell, to-day, Doctor.'—'I do not by any means feel unwell; I only require a little rest.' He spoke with the greatest clearness and vigor; and I could not think that anything was wrong, but what might arise from the lassitude produced by his late journey and exertions in the South. 'I am rejoiced,' said he, 'that the Assembly have agreed to avail themselves of the grant for national education; and I trust that a sound Scriptural education will pervade the whole length and breadth of the land. Your resolutions are, I think, to that effect?' I replied, 'Yes; but one of our resolutions characterizes the national scheme as unsound and latitudinarian. I fear that the scheme is latitudinarian; but I am not quite so clear as to the use of the word unsound. Doddridge, for example, is latitudinarian; but I should be very unwilling to call him unsound. And Baxter is still more latitudinarian; but I should be very unwilling, in the full sense of the word, to call him unsound. There are what are called Baxterian errors, I am aware, and one of these is in relation to the extent of the sacrifice of Christ; Baxter, I think, holding that Christ died for all men.' Dr. Chalmers answered, ' Yes: Baxter holds that Christ died for all men; but I cannot say that I am quite at one with what some of our friends have written on the subject of the atonement. I do not, for example, entirely agree with what Mr. Haldane says on that subject. I think that the word *world* as applied in Scripture to the sacrifice of Christ, has been unnecessarily restricted; the common way of explaining it is, that it simply includes Gentiles as well as Jews. I do not like that explanation; and I think that there is one text that puts that interpretation entirely aside. The text to which I allude is, that 'God commandeth *all men, everywhere* to repent.' Here the Doctor spoke of the connection between the election of God, the sacrifice of Christ, and the freeness of the offer of the Gospel. He spoke with great eloquence, and I felt as if he were in the pulpit, as some of his finest bursts rolled from his lips. 'In the offer of the gospel,' said he, 'we must make no limitation whatever. I compare the world to a multitude of iron filings in a vessel, and the gospel to a magnet. The minister of the gospel must bring the magnet into contact with them all: the secret agency of God is to produce the attraction.'—' But,' said I, ' a common objection of the sinner, when awakened to a sense of his state, is, ' Perhaps I am not elected; and, therefore, I need not try.' 'That,' said he, ' is cutting before the point. I am a predestinarian: my theology is that of Jonathan Edwards.' 'You are a Necessitarian,' said I. 'Yes,' was the reply, ' a Necessitarian; but I would always wish to be borne in mind a saying of Bishop Butler—viz.; ' That we have not so much to inquire what God does, or should do to us, as what are the duties which we owe to Him.'

" 'Human beings,' continued Dr. Chalmers, ' have the most strange way of keeping their accounts: they have one way of keeping their accounts with the world, and another way of keeping their accounts with Heaven. In relation to the world, you will find men often open, and generous, and unsuspicious; but then they keep their accounts with Heaven in the most suspicious and niggardly manner—in a manner with which I can have no sympathy—continually striving against, and fighting with the goodness and sincerity of God, and will not take God at his word.'

"In the course of the forenoon, the Rev. Dr. Cunningham called, and went with Dr. Chalmers to the afternoon service in his usual place of worship—the Free Church at Morningside. In accompanying Dr. Cunningham a short distance on his way back to Newington, Dr. Chalmers expressed his great satisfaction at the opportunity he had in London of giving his evidence before the Sites Committee, dwelling with particular complacency on the representation he had given of the position in which the Free Church stood toward the Establishment. Returning by Bruntsfield Links, he made his last call on Mrs. Coutts, one of the oldest and most beloved of his Fifeshire friends. After tea he retired to his siesta, wrote a note to Mrs. Morton, and afterward went into the garden behind his house; sauntering round which he was overheard by one of his family, in low but very earnest tones, saying, ' O Father, my Heavenly Father!' On returning to the drawing-room, he threw himself into his usual reclining posture. His conversation at first was joyous and playful; a shadow passed over him as some disquieting thought arose—but a light spread over his face as he said, that disquietudes lay light upon a man who could fix his heart upon heaven. ' I'm fond,' he said, ' of the Sabbath. Hail sacred Sabbath morn! Do you like Grahame's Sabbath, Mr. Gemmel? Dr. Johnson was very wrong in saying that there can be no true poetry that is religious.' ' At supper,' says Mr. Gemmel, ' I sat near him, at his right hand. ' Are you much acquainted with the Puritan Divines, Mr. Gemmel?' said he. I answered that I was, in some measure. ' Which do you chiefly admire?' ' I think very much of Howe,' was my reply. ' And so do I,' said he; ' he is my favorite author. I think that he is the first of the Puritan divines. I cannot say that I take much to his image of a living temple; but I have been lately reading his ' Delighting in God,' and I admire it much.'

"After supper, addressing me, ' You gave us worship,' said

he, 'in the morning; I am sorry to ask you again to give worship in the evening.' 'Not at all,' said I, 'I will be happy to do so.' 'Well,' said he, 'you will give worship to-night; and *I expect to give worship to-morrow morning.*' Before worship commenced, and just as the servants were preparing to come up-stairs, he asked me whether I had read the sermons of Mr. Purves of Jedburgh. I answered that I had not. 'They are very excellent sermons,' said he; 'and there is one, in which he rids the marches between the election of God on the one hand, and the freeness of the Gospel on the other, which is admirable.'

"During the whole of the evening, as if he had kept his brightest smiles and fondest utterances to the last, and for his own, he was peculiarly bland and benignant. 'I had seen him frequently,' says Mr. Gemmel, 'at Fairlie, and in his most happy moods, but I never saw him happier. Christian benevolence beamed from his countenance, sparkled in his eye, and played upon his lips.' Immediately after prayers he withdrew, and bidding his family remember that they must be early to-morrow, he waved his hand, saying, 'A general good-night.'

"Next morning before eight o'clock, Professor MacDougall, who lived in the house adjoining, sent to inquire about a packet of papers which he had expected to receive at an earlier hour. The housekeeper who had been long in the family, knocked at the door of Dr. Chalmers's room, but received no answer. Concluding that he was asleep, and unwilling to disturb him, she waited till another party called with a second message; she then entered the room—it was in darkness; she spoke, but there was no response. At last she threw open the window-shutters, and drew aside the curtains of the bed. He sat there, half erect, his head reclining gently on the pillow; the expression of his countenance that of fixed and majestic repose. She took his hand—she touched his brow; he had been dead for hours: very shortly after that parting salute to his family he had entered the eternal world. It must have been wholly without pain or conflict. The expression of the face undisturbed by a single trace of suffering, the position of the body so easy that the least struggle would have disturbed it, the very posture of arms and hands and fingers, known to his family as that into which they fell naturally in the moments of entire repose—conspired to show, that, saved all strife with the last enemy, his spirit had passed to its place of blessedness and glory in the heavens."

The General Assembly of the Free Church then in session, upon learning the mournful event, immediately suspended all business, and remained convened only, to render the last offices to the illustrious departed.

The body of Thomas Chalmers was committed to the tomb on the 4th of June, with every mark of honor which his countrymen could bestow.

It was thus that a writer in the 'Witness' described the solemn procession which represented a nation mourning over her greatest fallen.

"The day was one of those gloomy days, not unfrequent in early summer, which steeps the landscape in a sombre neutral tint of gray—a sort of diluted gloom—and volumes of mist, unvariegated, blank, and diffuse of outline, flew low athwart the hills or lay folded on the distant horizon. A chill breeze from the east murmured drearily through the trees that line the cemetery on the south and west, and rustled amid the low ornamental shrubs that vary and adorn its surface. We felt as if the garish sunshine would have associated ill with the occasion. As the procession approached, the shops on both sides, with scarce any exceptions, were shut up, and business suspended. There was no part of the street or road through which it passed sufficiently open, or nearly so, to give a view of the whole. The spectator merely saw file after file pass by in what seemed endless succession. In the cemetery, which is of great extent, the whole was at once seen for the first time, and the appearance was that of an army. The figures dwindled in the distance, in receding toward the open grave along the long winding walk, as in those magnificent pictures of Martin, in which even the littleness of man is made to enhance the greatness of their works and the array of their aggregated numbers.

And still the open gateway continued to give ingress to the dingy, living tide, that seemed to flow unceasingly inward, like some perennial stream that disembogues its waters into a lake. The party-colored thousands on the eminence above, all in silence, and many of them in tears—the far-stretching lines of the mourners below—the effect, amid the general black, of the scarlet cloaks of the magistracy—for the Magistrates of Edinburgh, with much good taste and feeling, had come in their robes of office, and attended by its officials and insignia, to manifest their spontaneous respect for the memory of the greatest of their countrymen—the slow, measured tramp, that, with the rustle of the breeze, formed the only sounds audible in so vast an assemblage—all conspired to compose a scene solemn and impressive in the highest degree, and of which the recollection will long survive in the memory of the spectators. There was a moral sublimity in the spectacle. It spoke more emphatically than by words, of the dignity of intrinsic excellence, and of the height to which a true man may attain. It was the dust of a Presbyterian minister which the coffin contained; and yet they were burying him amid the tears of a nation, and with more than kingly honors."

THE END.

CPSIA information can be obtained
at www.ICGtesting.com
Printed in the USA
BVHW09*1738200818
525056BV00014B/1498/P